D1785276

STUDIES IN HONOUR
OF
ARTHUR DALE TRENDALL

ARTHUR DALE TRENDALL

STUDIES IN HONOUR
OF
ARTHUR DALE TRENDALL

Editor
ALEXANDER CAMBITOGLOU

SYDNEY UNIVERSITY PRESS

SYDNEY UNIVERSITY PRESS
Press Building, University of Sydney

UNITED KINGDOM, EUROPE, MIDDLE EAST, AFRICA
International Scholarly Book Services (Europe)
Letchworth, England

NORTH AND SOUTH AMERICA
International Scholarly Book Services, Inc.
Forest Grove, Oregon

National Library of Australia Cataloguing-in-Publication data

Studies in Honour of A.D. Trendall
    Index
    ISBN 0 424 00063 6

    1. Archaeology — Addresses, essays, lectures.
    I. Cambitoglou, Alexander, ed.

930.1

First published 1979
© **Sydney University Press 1979**
Typeset by Noela Whitton, Sydney
Printed in Australia by Macarthur Press (Books) Pty Limited, Parramatta

PREFACE

Arthur Dale Trendall is undoubtedly one of the most distinguished scholars of the twentieth century and his contributions to the study of classical archaeology are among the most significant ever made in the field by a single person. His research on Italiote pottery and vase painting, on which he is the greatest living authority, is characterised by an unparalleled thoroughness that has earned him his fame as a great specialist; but he is also an all-round scholar and cultivated man of a type becoming increasingly rare in our times. Few archaeologists have written as much as Trendall and his future place in the history of classical studies is guaranteed by his books on South Italian Greek pottery which, like Beazley's books on Attic vase painters, will remain the standard reference works for generations to come. However, Trendall's colleagues all over the world, admire in him, not only the writer of monographs and articles, but also the responsive and helpful correspondent; whilst those who studied under him have the most profound respect also for the dedicated teacher and the lively lecturer.

In addition however, Trendall made a name for himself as a great academic administrator, since he became a key figure in the shaping of tertiary education in Australia far beyond the boundaries of the two Universities which he served before his retirement. From the date of his appointment to the University of Sydney in the late thirties as Professor of Greek to the date of his departure for the Australian National University in Canberra in 1954, he held important administrative positions and became responsible for the establishment of its Department of Archaeology (in 1948). Concurrently, as Curator of the Nicholson Museum, he enriched its collections and made them accessible to a larger public. In Canberra between 1954 and 1969, he played an important part in the running of the newly established Australian National University, both as Master of University House (1954–1969) and as Deputy Vice-Chancellor (1958–1964). Finally he was able to use his exceptional administrative talents at a national level by serving as a member of the Australian Universities' Commission.

I felt that it was my duty to organize the publication of this volume because of my position as Professor of Archaeology (now Classical Archaeology) and Curator of the Nicholson Museum, which made me, in effect, Trendall's successor at the University of Sydney; what moved me even more, however, to undertake this pleasant task was my profound admiration for a great scholar, which is the result of a collaboration with him over many years.

There are many principles that one might adopt to guide one in the compilation of a list of contributors to a volume such as this one. In the present case I adopted the expedient of consulting Professor Trendall himself. I would like to apologise to the authors of articles in this volume for the long delay in its publication. It arose due to the difficult financial conditions which the University of Sydney faced at a critical moment. Further delays were necessitated because some articles had to be brought up to date or re-written. The articles appear in alphabetical order with the exception of that by the late Mrs. Noël Oakeshott (née Moon), which I decided to put at the top of the list for two reasons: firstly, because it makes an excellent introduction to the volume by outlining the history of studies of "Magna Graecia" and placing Trendall's work objectively in its proper context, and secondly because of the long association and friendship between the two scholars — Trendall and Noël Oakeshott had known each other for over forty years. It is worth mentioning here that her article "Some Early South Italian Vase Painters" in the *Papers of the British School at Rome* vol. XI (1929) constitutes the first serious attempt at a classification of Italiote vases according to painters. To it we all acknowledge a great debt.

PREFACE

I would like to take this opportunity to thank the Vice-Chancellor of the University of Sydney, Professor B.R. Williams, and the Deputy Vice-Chancellor, Professor M.G. Taylor, for making this project financially possible. My thanks are also due to the Australian Academy of the Humanities for a generous contribution and to the Director of the Sydney University Press and his colleagues for the careful presentation. I am also much beholden to Mrs. Aedeen Madden for her assistance to my work as editor: without her help my task would have been considerably harder. Finally, I wish to express my deep gratitude to Mrs. Noela Whitton for the fine type-setting and for her kind help in many other ways during the preparation of this volume.

Alexander Cambitoglou
University of Sydney
October, 1978

TABULA GRATULATORIA

Adamesteanu, Dinu — Museo Nazionale, Taranto

Amandry, Pierre — École française d'archéologie, Athènes

American Academy (The Library) — Rome

Amyx, D.A. — Department of Art, University of California, Berkeley

Andreassi, Giuseppe — Museo Archeologico della Provincia di Bari, Bari

Archeologisch Instituut, Rijksuniversiteit — Utrecht

Arias, Paolo Enrico — Istituto di Archeologia, Università degli Studi, Pisa

Ashmole, Bernard — University of Oxford

Åström, Paul — Classical Institute, University of Gothenburg

Australian Academy of the Humanities — Canberra

Balty, Jean Charles — Musées royaux d'art et d'histoire et Université libre de Bruxelles

Bastet, F.L. — Rÿksmuseum Van Oudheden, Leiden

Benson, J.L. — Department of Art, University of Massachusetts, Amherst

Bérard, Claude — Séminaire d'archéologie classique, Université de Lausanne

Berger, Ernst — Antikenmuseum, Basel

Bernabò-Brea, Luigi — Museo Eoliano, Lipari

Bernhard, Marie Louise — Uniwersytet Jagielloński, Kraków

Birchall, Ann — The British Museum, London

Bloesch, Hansjörg — Archäologisches Seminar, Universität, Zürich

Boardman, John — Ashmolean Museum, Oxford

Bothmer, Dietrich von — The Metropolitan Museum of Art; New York University, Institute of Fine Arts, New York

Brilliant, Richard — Department of Art History and Archaeology, Columbia University, New York

Brommer, Frank — Archäologisches Institut der Universität, Mainz

Cahn, Herbert A. — Münzen und Medaillen A.G., Basel

Cambitoglou, Alexander — Department of Archaeology and The Nicholson Museum, University of Sydney

Carter, Joseph Coleman — Department of Classics, The University of Texas at Austin

Catling, H.W. — British School at Athens

Centro di studi del Consiglio Nazionale delle Ricerche per l'archeologia etrusco-italica — Roma

Chamay, Jacques — Université de Genève

Chiaro, Mario del — University of California, Santa Barbara

Chiesa, Gemma Sena — Istituto di Archeologia, Università Statale di Milano

Clairmont, Christoph W. — Rutgers, The State University of New Jersey

Clarke, G.W.	Department of Classical Studies, University of Melbourne
Coldstream, J.N.	Bedford College, University of London
Connor, P.J.	Department of Classical Studies, University of Melbourne
Cook, B.F.	The British Museum, London
Cook, R.M.	Museum of Classical Archaeology, Cambridge
Coulton, J.J.	Department of Classical Archaeology, University of Edinburgh
Damevski, Valerija	Arheoloski muzej, Zagreb
Dareggi, Gianna	Istituto di Archeologia, Università degli Studi, Perugia
Degrassi, Nevio	Roma
Deutsches Archäologisches Institut	Athen
Deutsches Archäologisches Institut	Berlin
Deutsches Archäologisches Institut	Rom
Direzione Generale, Monumenti Musei e Gallerie Pontificie	Città del Vaticano
Dohrn, Tobias	Archäologisches Institut, Universität, Köln
Dörig, José	Université de Genève
Ede, Charles	London
Elliott, Ralph W.V.	University House, Australian National University, Canberra
Forti, Lidia	Istituto di Archeologia, Universita di Salerno
Franciscis, Alfonso de	Istituto di Archeologia, Università di Napoli
Frel, Jiri	The J. Paul Getty Museum, Malibu, California
Gehrig, Ulrich	Antikenmuseum, Staatliche Museen Preussischer Kulturbesitz, Berlin
Genière, Juliette de la	l'Université de Lille
George, Sir Arthur	The Association for Classical Archaeology, University of Sydney
Ginouvès, René	L'Université de Paris
Grace, Virginia R.	American School of Classical Studies, Athens
Green, J.R.	Department of Archaeology, University of Sydney
Greifenhagen, Adolf	Berlin
Hampe, Roland	Archäologisches Institut der Universität, Heidelberg
Handley, Eric W.	Institute of Classical Studies, London
Haspels, C.H.Emilie	Institute of Classical Archaeology, University of Amsterdam
Haynes, D.E.L.	The British Museum, London
Hemelrijk, J.M.	Archeologisch-Historisch Instituut der Universiteit v. Amsterdam
Higgins, Reynold	The British Museum, London

Hiller, Stefan	Institut für Klassische Archäologie, Universität, Salzburg
Himmelmann, Nikolaus	Archäologisches Institut der Universität, Bonn
Hoffmann, Herbert	Archäologisches Seminar der Universität, Hamburg
Hölscher, Tonio	Archäologisches Institut der Universität, Heidelberg
Hood, Ronald G.	John Elliott Classics Museum, University of Tasmania, Hobart
Iakovidis, Spyros	University of Pennsylvania, Philadelphia
Institute of Classical Studies	London
Istituto di Etruscologia e Antichità Italiche dell'Universita di Roma	Roma
Istituto di Studi Etruschi ed Italici	Firenze
Joyner, Graham	School of History, Philosophy and Politics, Macquarie University, Sydney
Jucker, Hans	Archäologisches Seminar der Universität, Bern
Kahil, Lilly	Université de Fribourg
Karouzou, Semni	National Museum, Athens
Kenner, Hedwig	Institut für Alte Geschichte, Archäologie und Epigraphik der Universität, Wien
Keuls, Eva C.	Department of Classics, The University of Minnesota
Kron, Uta	Deutsches Archäologisches Institut, Athen
Lohmann, Hans	Rheinfelden
Lo Porto, Gino	Museo Nazionale, Taranto
McPhee, Ian	Department of Art History, La Trobe University, Bundoora, Victoria
Moret, Jean-Marc	Séminaire d'Archéologie, Université de Fribourg
Pallottino, Massimo	Istituto di Etruscologia e antichità italiche dell'Università di Roma
Parlasca, Klaus	Archäologisches Institut, Universität, Erlangen
Phillips, Jr., Kyle Meredith	Bryn Mawr College, Bryn Mawr, Pennsylvania
Ponti, Giovanna Delli	Museo Provinciale, Lecce
Ragusa, Alessandro	Taranto
Riccioni, Giuliana	Istituto di Archaeologia dell'Università, Bologna
Ritchie, William	Department of Greek, University of Sydney
Robertson, Martin	Ashmolean Museum, Oxford
Rohde, Elisabeth	Staatliche Museen zu Berlin
Santangelo, Maria	Roma
Schauenburg, Konrad	Kiel
Schefold, Karl	Archäologisches Seminar der Universität, Basel
Schmidt, Margot	Antikenmuseum, Basel
Schneider-Herrmann, Gisela	The Hague
Scuola Archeologica Italiana di Atene	Atene

Sear, Frank	Department of Classics, University of Adelaide
Sichtermann, Hellmut	Rom
Simon, Erika	Archäologisches Institut der Universität, Würzburg
Smith, Bernard W.	Melbourne
Society for the promotion of Hellenic Studies	London
Society for the promotion of Roman Studies	London
Sparkes, B.A.	Department of Classics, The University of Southhampton
Stenico, Arturo	Istituto di Archeologia, Università degli Studi, Pavia
Steven, M.K.	Department of Classics, University of Canterbury, New Zealand
Stewart, Andrew	Department of Classics, University of Otago, Dunedin
Strocka, Volker Michael	Deutsches Archäologisches Institut, Zentraldirektion, Berlin
Stucky, Rolf A.	Archäologisches Seminar der Universität, Basel
Szilágyi, J.G.	Museum of Fine Arts, Budapest
Thomson, Dorothy Burr	Institute for Advanced Study, Princeton
Thomson, Homer A.	Institute for Advanced Study, Princeton
Townsend Vermeule, Emily	Department of the Classics, Harvard University, Cambridge, Massachusetts
Toynbee, J.M.L.	University of Cambridge
Tusa, Vincenzo	Universita di Palermo
Wade, John P.	Museum of Applied Arts and Sciences, Sydney
Ward-Perkins, John	British School at Rome
Whitehouse, David	British School at Rome
Yalouris, Nikolaos	National Museum, Athens
Zevi, Fausto	Museo Nazionale, Napoli

BIOGRAPHICAL NOTE

Arthur Dale Trendall was born in Auckland, New Zealand, in 1909 and received his earlier education there. He attended the Universities of Otago and Cambridge and became a Fellow of Trinity College from 1936 to 1940. He became Professor of Greek at the University of Sydney in 1939 and the first Professor of Archaeology at that University in 1948, holding both chairs until 1954. During his stay in Sydney he was also Curator of the Nicholson Museum.

From 1954 to 1969 he was Master of University House at the Australian National University in Canberra and was also Deputy Vice-Chancellor of the University from 1958 to 1964. On his retirement he moved to Melbourne where he is now resident Fellow at La Trobe University.

Decorations: A.C. (Companion of the Order of Australia), 1976

C.M.G. (Companion of the Order of St. Michael and St. George), 1961

K.C.S.G. (Commendatore dell' Ordine di S. Gregorio Magno), 1956

Commendatore dell' Ordine al Merito della Repubblica Italiana (1965; Cav. Uff. 1961)

Awards: 'Galileo Galilei' Prize (gold statuette by Emilio Greco), Pisa, 1971

Cassano Gold Medal for Magna Graecia Studies, Taranto, 1971

Britannica (Australia) Award for the Humanities, 1973

Honorary Degrees: Hon.Litt.D. (Melbourne, 1956; A.N.U., 1970)

Hon.D.Litt. (Adelaide, 1960; Sydney, 1972)

Fellowships, etc.: Fellow of the Society of Antiquaries (F.S.A.) 1939

Fellow of the British Academy (F.B.A.) 1968

Foundation Fellow of the Australian Academy of the Humanities (F.A.H.A.) 1969

Corresponding Member of the German Archaeological Institute

Foreign Member of the Accademia dei Lincei, Rome 1973

Corresponding Member of the Pontifical Academy of Archaeology, Rome 1973

Member of the Academy of Athens 1973

Honorary Fellow of the Athens Archaeological Society 1975

Foreign Member of the Royal Netherlands Academy of Arts and Sciences 1977

PRINCIPAL PUBLICATIONS OF
ARTHUR DALE TRENDALL

Books

Paestan Pottery (British School at Rome, 1936)

Frühitaliotische Vasen (Bilder griechischer Vasen, vol. 13, 1938)

Vasi antichi dipinti del Vaticano —Vasi italioti ed etruschi a figure rosse (3 vols., 1953, 1955, 1976)

Phlyax Vases (Institute of Classical Studies, London, *Bulletin Supplement* 8, 1959)

Phlyax Vases 2nd edition (*Bull. Supp.* 19, 1967)

South Italian Vase Painting (British Museum, 1966, second edition, 1976)

The Red-figured Vases of Lucania, Campania and Sicily (Clarendon Press, Oxford, 2 volumes, 1967)

First Supplement to the above (Institute of Classical Studies, London, *Bull. Supp.* 26, 1970)

Second Supplement (Institute of Classical Studies, London, *Bull. Supp.* 31, 1973)

Greek Vases in the Logie Collection, University of Canterbury, N.Z. (Christchurch, 1971)

Early South Italian Vases (Mainz, 1974)

> *In collaboration with others*
>
> with J.R. Stewart:
> > Handbook to the Nicholson Museum, University of Sydney (2nd edn., Sydney, 1948)
>
> with Alexander Cambitoglou:
> > Apulian Red-figured Vase-Painters of the Plain Style (Arch. Inst. of America, 1961)
>
> with T.B.L. Webster:
> > Illustrations of Greek Drama (Phaidon, 1971)
>
> with Margot Schmidt and Alexander Cambitoglou:
> > Eine Gruppe Apulischer Grabvasen in Basel (Mainz, 1975)
>
> with Alexander Cambitoglou:
> > The Red-figured Vases of Apulia, vol. 1 (Oxford, 1978)

Small Books

The Shellal Mosaic (Australian War Memorial, Canberra, 4th edn., 1973)

The Felton Greek Vases (Australian Humanities Research Council, 1958)

Greek Vases in the Felton Collection (National Gallery of Victoria, 1968)

Gli Indigeni nella pittura italiota (Taranto, 1971)

Notes on Greek and Roman Art (Melbourne University, 1972)

Notes on South Italian Red-figure Vase-Painting (La Trobe University, 1975)

Greek Vases in the National Gallery of Victoria (Melbourne, 1978)

Articles

In the *Journal of Hellenic Studies:*
> "A Volute-krater in Taranto", 54, 1934, pp. 175–9
> "Early Paestan Pottery", 55, 1935, pp. 35–55
> "Attic Vases in Australia and New Zealand", 71, 1951, pp. 178–193

In *Archaeological Reports:*
> "Archaeology in South Italy and Sicily", 1955, pp. 47–62; 1958, pp. 26–42; 1961, pp. 36–53; 1964, pp. 33–50; 1967, pp. 29–46; 1970, pp. 32–51; 1973, pp. 33–49.

In *Papers of the British School at Rome:*
   "Paestan Pottery — a revision and a supplement", 20, 1952, pp. 1–53
   "Paestan Post-script", 21, 1953, pp. 160–167
   "Paestan Addenda", 27, 1959, pp. 1–37

In *Annual Bulletin of the National Gallery of Victoria:*
   "Recent Additions to the Greek Vase Collection", 3, 1961, pp. 1–8
   "A Sicilian Neck-amphora", 7, 1965, pp. 1–6
   "Two new South Italian Vases", 8, 1966, pp. 1–8

In *Art Bulletin of Victoria:*
   "Additions to the Greek Vase-collection in 1969", 1970–71, pp. 1–10
   "Additions to the Greek Vase-collection in 1971–2", 1973, pp. 6–12
   "A Campanian Phlyax Vase", 1975, pp. 11–15
   "Three Recently Acquired Greek Vases", 1978, forthcoming

In *American Journal of Archaeology:*
   "A South Italian Fragment in New York", 66, 1962, pp. 349–351
   "Addenda to *Apulian Red-figure Vase-painters*" (with A. Cambitoglou), 73, 1969, pp. 423–433

In *Jahrbuch der Berliner Museen:*
   "The Cassandra Painter and his Circle", 2, 1960, pp. 7–33
   "Three Apulian Kraters in Berlin", 12, 1970, pp. 153–190

In *Apollo:*
   "The Painter of B.M. F 63", 1, 1961, pp. 29–52
   "Head-Vases in Padula", 2, 1962, pp. 11–34
   "The Fratte Painter", 3–4, 1963–4, pp. 15–32

In *Antike Kunst:*
   "The Slaying of the Suitors" (with A. Cambitoglou), 13, 1970, pp. 101–2
   "Callisto in Apulian Vase-painting", 20, 1977, pp. 99–101

   In other publications

"Medicine and the Classics", *Proc. Aust Coll. of Physicians,* IV, 2, July 1949, pp. 69–76
"The Medicine Man and the Medical Man", *Medical Journal of Australia,* 24 July 1954, pp. 117 ff.
"Three Vases in Sydney", in *Charites* (Festschrift Langlotz), 1957, pp. 165–9
"Il Pittore del Ciclope", in *Atti Società Magna Grecia,* n.s.3, 1960, pp. 85–92
"South Italian Red-figured Pottery" in *Atti del VII Congresso di Archeologia classica,* 1961, pp. 117–141
"Lukánské a Kampánské vázy v Československu", in *Jednoty klasických filologů* IV, 2, 1962, pp. 82–92
"Early Lucanian Vases in the Museum of Reggio Calabria", in *Klearchos,* 15–16, 1962, pp. 51–65
"The Felton Painter", in *In Honour of Daryl Lindsay,* 1964, pp. 45–52
"The Lipari Vases and their Place in the History of Sicilian Red-figure", in *Meligunis-Lipara* 2, 1965, pp. 271–289
"The Painter of the Birth of Dionysos" (with A. Cambitoglou), in *Mélanges Michalowski,* 1966, pp. 675–699
"The Nicholson Museum", in *Art and Australia* 1967, pp. 528–537
"The Stevenson Collection from Lipari — Greek Vases", in *Scottish Art Review,* 12, 1969, pp. 1–5

"The Mourning Niobe", in *Revue Archéologique,* 1972, pp. 309–316

"Il Museo Provinciale di Lecce", in *Ricerche e Studi* 6, 1972, pp. 5–8

"La Ceramica di Taranto", in *Atti del X° Convegno di Studi sulla Magna Grecia* (Taranto, 1970), 1973, pp. 249–65

"T.B.L. Webster Memorial Lecture", in *Bull. Inst. Class. Studies,* London, 21, 1974, pp. 1 ff.

"Eros with a Whipping-top on an Apulian Pelike" (with Mrs G. Schneider-Hermann), in *BABesch* 50, 1975, pp. 57–60

"Poseidon and Amymone on an Apulian Pelike", in *Festschrift für Frank Brommer* (1977), pp. 281–287

"South Italian and Etruscan Red-figured Vases in the National Museum, Athens", in *Archaeologikon Deltion* 29, 1974 (1977), pp. 165–186

"Some Vases connected with the Workshop of the Creusa and Dolon Painters", in *Quaderni Ticinesi* 6, 1978, pp. 53–74

Various

In *Enciclopedia dell' Arte Antica, Fasti Archaeologici,* etc.

Reviews

In the *Journal of Hellenic Studies, The American Journal of Archaeology, The Antiquaries Journal,* etc.

CONTENTS

Preface   v

Tabula Gratulatoria   vii

Biographical Note   xi

Principal Publications of Arthur Dale Trendall   xiii

List of Plates   xx

List of Figures in the Text   xxvi

Abbreviations   xxvii

Noël Oakeshott †
FROM LENORMANT TO TRENDALL   1

Dinu Adamesteanu
HYDRIA APULA DI HERACLEA   9

D.A. Amyx
TWO ETRUSCO-CORINTHIAN VASES   13

Giuseppe Andreassi
UNA IDRIA INEDITA CON RILIEVI E LA FABBRICA DELLE 'PLAKETTENVASEN'   21

J.L. Benson
THE BOROWSKI PAINTER   31

John Boardman
A SYMPOSIUM IN ABERDEEN   35

Frank Brommer
EIN OSTGRIECHISCHER SKYPHOS   39

Alexander Cambitoglou
THREE APULIAN RED-FIGURE FRAGMENTS IN THE NICHOLSON MUSEUM, SYDNEY   47

Mario del Chiaro
AN ETRUSCAN (CAERETAN) FISH PLATE   57

P.J. Connor
A GEOMETRIC BRONZE HORSE IN THE UNIVERSITY OF MELBOURNE   61

R.M. Cook
AN ITALOCORINTHIAN CONTEXT   69

CONTENTS

Jiri Frel
A LUCANIAN CHOUS IN MALIBU
71

Juliette de la Genière
UN FAUX AUTHENTIQUE DU MUSÉE DU LOUVRE
75

J.R. Green
EARS OF CORN AND OTHER OFFERINGS
81

Adolf Greifenhagen
ZWEI GRIECHISCHE SCHMUCKSTÜCKE
91

Herbert Hoffmann
ATTIC AND TARENTINE RHYTA: ADDENDUM
93

Lilly Kahil
UNE 'RONDE' SUR UN COL D'AMPHORE EUBEEN
97

Ernst Langlotz †
ZWEI UNGEWÖHNLICHE GRIECHISCHE BILDWERKE
103

Felice Gino Lo Porto
UN VASO APULO CON SCENA FLIACICA
107

Paolino Mingazzini †
UN' ANFORETTA NELLO STILE DI KAIRUAN
111

Giuliana Riccioni
KYLIX INEDITA DA SPINA DEL PITTORE DI ANTIPHON CON *DOKIMASIA*
125

Martin Robertson
A MUFFLED DANCER AND OTHERS
129

Elisabeth Rohde
DREI SIANASCHALEN DER BERLINER ANTIKEN-SAMMLUNG
135

K. Schauenburg
DAS MOTIV DER *CHIMAIROPHONOS* IN DER KUNST UNTERITALIENS
149

Karl Schefold
DIE ANDROMEDA DES NIKIAS
155

Margot Schmidt
EIN DANAIDENDRAMA (?) UND DER EURIPIDEISCHE ION AUF
UNTERITALISCHEN VASENBILDERN
159

G. Schneider-Herrmann
THE DANCE OF THE AMAZONS   171

Arturo Stenico
UN' ANFORA PANATENAICA DEL PITTORE DI EUPHILETOS   177

T.B.L. Webster †
SOME TERRACOTTA DEDICATIONS   181

Nikolaos Yalouris
STESICHOROS' FABLE   185

The Plates   189

LIST OF PLATES

1   Figs. 1—3   Apulian red-figure hydria from Herakleia.
                   Policoro 38462.
                   Photos: courtesy author.

2   Figs. 1—4   Etrusco-Corinthian olpe.
                   Los. Angeles. Collection of Mrs. Aaron Dechter.
                   Photos: Dietrich Widmer; courtesy Dr. Herbert Cahn.

3   Figs. 5—7   Etrusco-Corinthian olpe.
                   Munich, Staatliche Antikensammlungen S.H.641.
                   Photos: Staatliche Antikensammlungen; courtesy Dr. F.W. Hamdorf.

4   Figs. 8—10   Etrusco-Corinthian alabastron.
                   Cambridge, Museum of Classical Archaeology No. 137.
                   Photos: Museum of Classical Archaeology; courtesy Professor R.M. Cook.

5   Figs. 1—4   Hydria decorated with relief panels.
                   Bassano del Grappa. Chini Collection R.7.29-1-72.
                   Photos: Sopr. alle antichità Taranto; courtesy Professor F.G. Lo Porto.

6   Figs. 5—10   Details of vase illustrated on Pl. 5.
                   Photos: author.

7   Figs. 1—3   Corinthian aryballos.
                   Basel, Antikenmuseum Kh.97 (Borowski Loan).
                   Photos: Antikenmuseum; courtesy owner and Dr. Margot Schmidt.

     Fig.   4   Corinthian aryballos.
                   Laon, Musée 37.727.
                   Photos: courtesy Musée de Laon.

     Figs. 5—6   Corinthian aryballos.
                   Princeton Art Museum 40—151.
                   Photos: author; courtesy Museum.

8   Figs. 1—3   Attic red-figure cup.
                   Aberdeen, Marischal College No. 748.
                   Photos: author; courtesy of the College.

9   Figs. 4—7   Details of the cup illustrated on Pl. 8.
                   Photos: author; courtesy of the College.

10   Figs. 1—2   East Greek skyphos.
                   Private Collection.
                   Photos: courtesy of the owner.

11   Fig.   1   Fragment of an Apulian red-figure calyx-krater.
                   Sydney, Nicholson Museum No. 51.47.
                   Photo: Mr. R.K. Harding.

12   Figs.   2—3   Two fragments of an Apulian red-figure amphora.
                      Sydney, Nicholson Museum No. 51.48 (Fig. 2) and 53.12 (Fig. 3).
                      Photos: Mr. R.K. Harding.

13   Figs.   4—5   Apulian red-figure amphora.
                      Naples, Museo Nazionale 2147 (inv. 82138).
                      Photos: Museo Nazionale, courtesy Museo Nazionale.

14   Figs.   1—2   Etruscan fish plate.
                      Cerveteri, Museo Nazionale Cerite.
                      Photo: courtesy Dr. Mario Moretti.

15   Figs. 1, 3—4   Geometric bronze horse.
                      Melbourne, University of Melbourne Inv. Mus.15.

      Fig.   2   Geometric group of two horses back-to-back on long stand.
                      Copenhagen, Ny Carlsberg Glyptotek.
                      Photo: courtesy Ny Carlsberg Glyptotek.

16   Fig.   1   Corinthian cup (reverse).
                      Cambridge, Museum of Classical Archaeology CE1.
                      Photo: courtesy Mus. of Class. Arch.

      Fig.   2   Italo-Corinthian amphora.
                      Cambridge, Museum of Classical Archaeology CE2.
                      Photo: courtesy Mus. of Class. Arch.

      Fig.   3   Details of vase illustrated in Fig. 2.
                      Drawing by Mr. B.D. Thompson.

17   Fig.   4   Bucchero jug.
                      Cambridge, Museum of Classical Archaeology CE3.
                      Photo: courtesy Mus. of Class. Arch.

      Fig.   5   Bucchero cup.
                      Cambridge, Museum of Classical Archaeology CE4.
                      Photo: courtesy Mus. of Class. Arch.

      Fig.   6   Bucchero kantharos.
                      Cambridge, Museum of Classical Archaeology CE5.
                      Photo: courtesy Mus. of Class. Arch.

18   Figs.   1—2   Lucanian red-figure chous.
                      Malibu, J. Paul Getty Museum inv. 71.AA.445.
                      Photos: J. Paul Getty Museum.

19   Figs.   1—2   Mouth of Attic red-figure lekythos on modern stem stuck on to ancient foot.
                      Paris, Louvre inv. G.614 (Campana 3218).
                      Photos: author, courtesy Musée du Louvre.

20   Figs.   1—2   Gnathia epichysis (parts missing).
                      Corinth Museum C-32-64.
                      Photos: Corinth Museum; courtesy Professor Charles K. Williams.

Fig. 3   Gnathia round-bodied epichysis.
           Corinth Museum C-69-138.
           Photo: Corinth Museum; courtesy Professor Charles K. Williams.

Fig. 4   Gnathia deep bowl (fragment).
           Athens, Agora Museum P12748.
           Photo: Agora Museum; courtesy Professor H.A. Thompson.

21   Fig. 5   Gnathia handle of oinochoe.
               Athens, Agora Museum P18336.
               Photo: Agora Museum; courtesy Professor H.A. Thompson.

Fig. 6   Gnathia pelike.
           Athens, National Museum 2162.
           Photo: author; courtesy National Museum.

Figs. 7–8   Gnathia oinochoe.
             Athens market.
             Photo: author.

22   Fig. 9   Gnathia amphora, West Slope type.
               Vienna, Kunsthistorisches Museum IV 450.
               Photo: author; courtesy Kunsthistorisches Museum.

Fig. 10   Gnathia amphora, West Slope type.
           Detail of vase illustrated in Fig. 9.
           Photo: author; courtesy Kunsthistorisches Museum.

Fig. 11   Bowl fragment, Gnathia technique.
           Syracuse, Museo Archaeologico Nazionale.
           Photo: author; courtesy Professor L. Bernabò Brea and Dr. G. Voza.

Fig. 12   Round mouthed jug, Gnathia technique.
           Zurich, Archäologisches Institut der Universität inv. 3330.
           Photo: Professor H. Bloesch; courtesy Professor H. Bloesch.

23   Fig. 1   Attic head-vase (oinochoe).
               New York, Metropolitan Museum 30.11.10.
               Photo: archives of the the late R. Zahn.

Fig. 2   Fragment of bell-krater.
           Once Erbach.
           After *Élite céramographique* I, pl. 29.

Fig. 3   Gold head-vase (detail).
           Plovdiv.
           Photo: I. Luckert.

Fig. 4   Gold head-vase (same as Fig. 3) (detail).
           Plovdiv.
           Photo: I. Luckert.

Fig. 5   Necklace.
           Once Constantinople market.
           Photo: archives of the late R. Zahn.

24   Fig.   1   Attic rhyton.
                 New York market (Mathias Komor).
                 Photo: courtesy of the owner.

     Figs. 2—4 Attic red-figure kantharos-rhyton (ram-head).
                 Hamburg, Museum für Kunst und Gewerbe.
                 Photo: Dietrich Widmer; courtesy Mus. für Kunst und Gewerbe.

25   Figs. 5—6 Attic red-figure rhyton: ram-head and donkey-head (dimidiated).
                 Swiss private collection.
                 Photos: courtesy of the owner.

     Figs. 7—8 Apulian red-figure rhyton (head of Laconian hound).
                 Ascona market (Casa Serodine).
                 Photos: courtesy Casa Serodine.

26   Figs. 9—11 Details of the red-figure rhyton illustrated on Pl. 25, Figs. 5—6 (satyr with drinking
                    horn, ithyphallic donkey, satyr).
                 Photos: courtesy of the owner.

27   Figs. 1—2 Neck of Euboean geometric amphora.
                 Eretria Museum inv. 3275, FK 2786.
                 Photos: courtesy Eretria Museum.

     Fig.   3   Five of the dancers decorating the neck of the Euboean geometric amphora illustrated
                    in Figs. 1—2.
                 Drawing by A. Brenk.

28   Fig.   1   Handle of a terracotta lamp (top).
                 Private collection.
                 Photo: author; courtesy of the owner.

     Fig.   2   Underside of the object illustrated in Fig. 1.
                 Photo: author; courtesy of the owner.

     Fig.   3   Tondo of fragmentary red-figure cup.
                 Lost.
                 Photo: I.G. 37193; courtesy of the German Archaeological Institute, Rome.

29   Figs. 1—3 Apulian calyx-krater (details of the obverse).
                 Bari, Malaguzzi-Valeri Collection No. 52.
                 Photo: Museo Archeologico; courtesy of the owner.

     Fig.   4   Reverse of vase illustrated in Figs. 1—3.
                 Photo: Museo Archeologico; courtesy of the owner.

30   Figs. 1—3 Small amphora in the Kairuan style.
                 Private collection.
                 Photos: courtesy of the owner.

31   Figs. 4—5 Two other views of the vase illustrated on Pl. 30.
                 Photos: courtesy of the owner.

32   Fig.   1   Attic red-figure eye-cup (B).
               Ferrara 41D-V.P.
               Photo: Laboratorio Manlio Agodi; courtesy Museo Archeologico Nazionale di Ferrara.

      Fig.   2   Attic red-figure eye-cup (I); same as Fig. 1.
               Ferrara 41D-V.P.
               Photo: Laboratorio Manlio Agodi; courtesy Museo Archeologico Nazionale di Ferrara.

33   Fig.   3   Attic red-figure eye-cup (A); same as Figs. 1—2.
               Ferrara 41D-V.P.
               Photo: Laboratorio Manlio Agodi; courtesy Museo Archeologico Nazionale di Ferrara.

      Fig.   4   Attic red-figure eye-cup (B); same as Figs. 1—3.
               Ferrara 41D-V.P.
               Photo: Laboratorio Manlio Agodi; courtesy Museo Archeologico Nazionale di Ferrara.

34   Figs.   1—2 Attic red-figure oinochoe (side and front views).
               Oxford 1971.866.
               Photos: Ashmolean Museum; courtesy Mr. Michael Vickers.

      Figs.   3—4 Attic red-figure kotyle (A and B).
               Munich, Antikensammlungen inv. 8934.
               Photo: C.H. Krüger-Moessner; courtesy Antikensammlungen.

35   Figs.   5—6 Attic red-figure Nolan amphora (A and B).
               London E 307.
               Photos: British Museum; courtesy Trustees of the British Museum.

36   Figs.   1—3 Siana cup.
               Berlin, Staatliche Museen, Antikensammlungen Vas. Inv. 4516.
               Photos: Staatliche Museen zu Berlin.

37   Figs.   4—5 Siana cup.
               Berlin Staatliche Museen, Antikensammlungen F.1755.
               Photos: Staatliche Museen zu Berlin.

      Fig.   6   Siana cup (I).
               Berlin Staatliche Museen, Antikensammlungen Vas. Inv. 3402.
               Photo: Staatliche Museen zu Berlin.

38   Figs.   7—9 Siana cup (A and B); same as Fig. 6.
               Berlin, Staatliche Museen, Antikensammlungen Vas. Inv. 3402.
               Photos: Staatliche Museen zu Berlin.

39   Figs. 10—12 Siana cup (A and B); same as Figs. 6—9;
               Berlin Staatliche Museen, Antikensammlungen Vas. Inv. 3402.
               Photos: Staatliche Museen zu Berlin.

40   Figs.   1—2 Apulian oinoche (shape 3: chous).
               Kiel, Kunsthalle B509.
               Photos: Dietrich Widmer; courtesy Kunsthalle.

Figs. 3—4   Apulian oinochoe (shape 3: chous).
Private collection, formerly Zurich market.
Photos: courtesy Mr. H. Humbel.

41   Fig. 5   Lucanian oinochoe (shape 3: chous).
Metaponto inv. 20146.
Photo: courtesy Professor D. Adamesteanu.

Fig. 6   Apulian lekanis-lid.
Naples, Museo Nazionale 2302 (inv. 82198).
Photo: Museo Nazionale; courtesy Professor A. de Franciscis.

42   Apulian volute-krater.
Ruvo, Museo Jatta 1097.
Photo: courtesy German Archaeòlogical Institute, Rome.

43   Figs. 1—2   Apulian alabastron.
Oxford 1945.55.
Photos: Ashmolean Museum; courtesy Department of Antiquities, Ashmolean Museum.

Figs. 3—4   Apulian dish.
Kiel, private collection.
Photos: courtesy of the owner.

44   Figs. 1—2   Panathenaic amphora.
Once, Milan market.
Photos: courtesy Galleria d'Arte Geri.

Fig. 3   Panathenaic amphora (A) (before removal of modern restorations).
Bologna, Museo Civico PU198.
Photo: Museo Civico; courtesy Dr. R. Pincelli.

45   Fig. 4   Panathenaic amphora (B) (before removal of modern restorations).
Bologna, Museo Civico PU198.
Photo: Museo Civico; courtesy Dr. R. Pincelli.

Figs. 5—6.   The panathenaic amphora illustrated in Figs. 3 and 4: authentic parts after removal
of modern restorations (A and B).
Photos: Museo Civico, Bologna; photo-montage: Dr. Morigi Govi.

46   Figs. 1—2   Attic Geometric neck-amphora (A and B of neck).
Munich, Staatliche Antikensammlungen Inv. No. 8748.
Photos: Staatliche Antikensammlungen.

Fig. 3   Fragment of bichrome painted larnax.
Oxford Inv. No. 19291.
Photo: Department of Antiquities, Ashmolean Museum.

47   Figs. 4—5   Attic black-figure neck-amphora.
Vatican 310.
Photos: Museo Vaticano.

LIST OF FIGURES IN THE TEXT

Page 48   Fig. 1   Fragment of Apulian red-figure calyx-krater.
Sydney, Nicholson Museum No. 51.47.
Profile drawing: Mr. Geoffrey Neil.

            Fig. 2   Fragment of Apulian red-figure amphora.
Sydney, Nicholson Museum, No. 51. 48.
Profile drawing: Mr. Geoffrey Neil.

            Fig. 3   Fragment of Apulian red-figure amphora.
Sydney, Nicholson Museum, No. 53.12.
Profile drawing: Mr. Geoffrey Neil.

            Fig. 4   The Apulian red-figure fragments Sydney, Nicholson Museum 51.48
and 53.12 reconstructed as parts of an amphora.
Drawing: Mr. Geoffrey Neil.

Page 70   Corinthian cup (obverse).
Cambridge, Museum of Classical Archaeology CE 1.
Drawing: Mr. B.D. Thompson.

Page 73   Lucanian red-figure oinochoe (shape 3: chous).
Malibu, J. Paul Getty Museum inv. 71.AA.445.
Drawing of dipinto on the undersurface.

Page 100   Neck of Euboean geometric amphora.
Eretria Museum (inv. 3275 FK 2786).
Drawing of profile by A. Brenk.

Page 126   Fig. 1   Attic red-figure eye-cup. Profile drawing.
Ferrara 41.D-V.P.
Drawing by Adriana Cavicchi.

             Fig. 2   Attic red-figure eye-cup. Profile drawing.
Houston, Texas; formerly Basel market.

ABBREVIATIONS

Periodicals and Serial Publications

AA	Archäologischer Anzeiger
AAA	Athens Annals of Archaeology
AC	L'Antiquité Classique
ADelt	Archaiologikon Deltion
AdI	Annali dell'Istituto di Corrispondenza Archeologica
AJA	American Journal of Archaeology
AM	Mitteilungen des Deutschen Archäologischen Instituts. Athenische Abteilung.
AntK	Antike Kunst
ArchCl	Archeologia Classica
ArchEph	Archaiologike Ephemeris
ArchReps	Archaeological Reports
ASMG	Atti e memorie della Società Magna Grecia
Atti . . CSMG	Atti del . . Convegno Studi sulla Magna Grecia
AuA	Antike und Abendland
AZ	Archäologische Zeitung
BABesch	Bulletin van der Vereeniging tot Bevordering der Kennis van de Antieke Beschaving te's-Gravenhage
BASOR	Bulletin of the American School of Oriental Research
BCH	Bulletin de Correspondance Hellénique
BdA	Bollettino d'Arte
BICS	Bulletin of the Institute of Classical Studies
BJb	Bonner Jahrbücher
BMMA	Bulletin of the Metropolitan Museum of Art
BSA	Annual of the British School at Athens
BSR	Papers of the British School at Rome
ClRh	Clara Rhodos
CSDIR	Centro Studi e Documentazione sull'Italia Romana. Atti
CVA	Corpus Vasorum Antiquorum
Délos	Exploration archeologique de Délos, École Française d'Athènes
ÉT	Études Thasiennes. École Française d'Athènes
IstMitt	Istanbuler Mitteilungen (Mitteilungen des deutschen archäologischen Instituts. Abteilung Istanbul)
JdI	Jahrbuch des Deutschen Archäologischen Instituts
JHS	The Journal of Hellenic Studies
JNES	Journal of Near Eastern Studies
MEFR	Mélanges d'Archéologie et d'Histoire de l'École Française de Rome
MemLinc	Atti dell'Accademia Nazionale dei Lincei. Memorie
MetrSt	Metropolitan Museum Studies
MonAnt	Monumenti Antichi
MonPiot	Fondation Eugène Piot. Monuments et Mémoires
MusHelv	Museum Helveticum
NSc	Notizie degli Scavi di Antichità

ÖJh	Jahreshefte des Österreichischen Archäologischen Instituts
OMLeiden	Oudheidkundige Mededelingen uit het Rijksmuseum van Oudheiden te Leiden
RA	Revue Archéologique
RBPh	Revue Belge de Philologie et d'Histoire
RendLinc	Rendiconti dell'Accademia Nazionale dei Lincei
RendNapoli	Rendiconti della R. Accademia di Archeologia, Lettere e Belle Arti di Napoli
RM	Mitteilungen des Deutschen Archäologischen Instituts. Römische Abteilung
StEtr	Studi Etruschi

Books and special publications

ABV	J.D. Beazley, *Attic Black-Figure Vase-Painters,* Oxford 1956
APS	Alexander Cambitoglou and A.D. Trendall, *Apulian Red-Figure Vase-Painters of the Plain Style,* (Archaeological Institute of America) 1961
Arias-Hirmer	P.E. Arias and Max Hirmer, *Tausend Jahre griechische Vasenkunst,* Munich 1960
Arias-Hirmer-Shefton	P.E. Arias and Max Hirmer (trans. B.B. Shefton), *A History of Greek Vase Painting,* London 1962
ARV, ARV²	J.D. Beazley, *Attic Red-Figure Vase-Painters,* Oxford 1942, and 2nd ed., Oxford 1963
Beazley, *EVP*	J.D. Beazley, *Etruscan Vase-Painting,* Oxford 1947
Beazley, *VPol*	J.D. Beazley, *Greek Vases in Poland,* Oxford 1928
Beazley-Magi, *RG*	J.D. Beazley e Filippo Magi, *La Raccolta Benedetto Guglielmi nel Museo Gregoriano Etrusco,* (Città del Vaticano 1939 and 1941)
Bieber, *Hist²*	Margarete Bieber, *The History of the Greek and Roman Theatre,* Princeton 1961
Borda	Maurizio Borda, *Ceramiche apule,* Bergamo 1966
Buschor, *GV*	Ernst Buschor, *Griechische Vasen,* Munich 1940 and 1969
Caskey-Beazley	L.D. Caskey and J.D. Beazley, *Attic Vase Paintings in the Museum of Fine Arts, Boston,* Oxford 1931–63
Coldstream, *GGP*	J.N. Coldstream, *Greek Geometric Pottery,* London 1968
Cook, *GPP*	R.M. Cook, *Greek Painted Pottery,* 2nd ed. London 1972
Daremberg-Saglio	*Dictionnaire des Antiquités Grecques et Romaines,* Ch.Daremberg and E. Saglio (eds.), Paris 1877–1919
EAA	*Enciclopedia dell'Arte Antica Classica e Orientale*
ESI	A.D. Trendall, *Early South Italian Vase-Painting,* Mainz 1974
FR	Adolf Furtwängler and Karl Reichhold, *Griechische Vasenmalerei,* Munich 1900–1932
Graef-Langlotz	Botho Graef und Ernst Langlotz, *Die Antike Vasen von der Akropolis zu Athen,* Berlin 1925–33
Helbig, *Helbig⁴*	Wolfgang Helbig, *Führer durch die öffentlichen Sammlungen klassischer Altertümer in Rom,* Leipzig 1891, and 4th ed., Tübingen 1963–1972
Ill.Gr.Dr.	A.D. Trendall and T.B.L. Webster, *Illustrations of Greek Drama,* London 1971
Kleine Pauly	*Der Kleine Pauly. Lexikon der Antike,* Stuttfart 1964. . .
LCS	A.D. Trendall, *The Red-Figured Vases of Lucania, Campania and Sicily,* Oxford 1967

Moon	Noël Moon, "Some Early South Italian Vase-Painters", *BSR* 11, 1929, pp. 30–49
Moret, *Ilioupersis*	J.-M. Moret, *L'Ilioupersis dans des céramique italiote* (Institut Suisse de Rome, 1975)
Neugebauer, *Führer*	K.A. Neugebauer, *Staatliche Museen zu Berlin. Führer durch das Antiquarium. II. Vasen,* Berlin 1932
Nilsson, *GGR*	M.P. Nilsson, *Geschichte der griechische Religion,* Munich 1940, and later editions
Paralipomena	J.D. Beazley, *Paralipomena. Additions to Attic Black-Figure Vase-Painters and to Attic Red-Figure Vase-Painters,* Oxford 1971
Payne, *NC*	Humfry Payne, *Necrocorinthia,* Oxford 1931
PBD	A.D. Trendall and Alexander Cambitoglou, "The Painter of the Birth of Dionysos" *Mélanges offerts à K. Michalowski,* Warsaw 1966
Pfuhl, *MuZ*	Ernst Pfuhl, *Malerei und Zeichnung der Griechen,* Munich 1923
Photo(s): R.I	Rome, German Institute photograph(s)
Picard, *Manuel*	Charles Picard, *Manuel d'Archéologie Grecque. La Sculpture,* Paris 1935. . .
RE, RE²	Georg Wissowa and others, *Paulys Realencyclopädie der classischen Altertumswissenschaft. Neue Bearbeitung,* Stuttgart 1894. . . , 1st series, A–R, 2nd series, R–Z
Richter-Milne	Gisela M.A. Richter and Majorie J. Milne, *Shapes and Names of Athenian Vases,* New York 1935
Roscher, *ML*	W.H. Roscher, *Ausführliches Lexikon der griechischen und römischen Mythologie,* Leipzig 1884–1937
RVAp I	A.D. Trendall and Alexander Cambitoglou, *The Red-Figured Vases of Apulia,* vol I, Oxford 1978
Schmidt	Margot Schmidt, *Der Dareiosmaler und sein Umkreis,* Münster 1960
Schneider-Herrmann	G. Schneider-Herrmann, *Apulian Red-Figured Paterae with Flat or Knobbed Handles,* London 1977, (*BICS* No. 34)
Sichtermann, *GVU*	Hellmut Sichtermann, *Griechische Vasen in Unteritalien,* Tübingen 1966
Sieveking-Hackl	Johannes Sieveking und Rudolf Hackl, *Die königliche Vasensammlung zu München,* Munich 1912
SIVP²	A.D. Trendall, *South Italian Vase-Painting,* London, British Museum, second edition 1976
Tocra II	John Boardman and John Hayes, *Excavations at Tocra* II, London 1973
VIE	A.D. Trendall, *Vasi antichi dipinti del Vaticano – Vasi Italioti ed Etruschi a Figure Rosse, Città del Vaticano* 1953 and 1955
Webster, *MMC²*	T.B.L. Webster, *Monuments Illustrating Old and Middle Comedy,* Second Edition, 1969 (*BICS* No. 23)

FROM LENORMANT TO TRENDALL

Noël Oakeshott

There can be no one alive today who has seen, studied and evaluated — often many times over — as many painted vases from South Italy as has Professor Trendall. To assess appropriately the magnitude of this unparalleled achievement would not be easy. Nor, as I had at first intended, would it be possible in a short article to mention more than a fraction of the eminent scholars of many nationalities who have made fundamental contributions to this vast field of study, as his predecessors, contemporaries and followers. The only short cut to some sort of assessment of his life's work to date — for he and Professor Cambitoglou have another major book in press — has seemed to me to take a long backward glance at some of his early predecessors and among them, pre-eminently at François Lenormant.

Although this outstanding scholar, traveller and man of letters was not really an expert on Italiote vases, Wuilleumier is surely right in saying that he initiated the scientific exploration of 'Magna Graecia'.[1] As a result of Lenormant's four journeys to Southern Italy, between 1879 and 1883 (preceded by several shorter visits), the serious attention of professional archaeologists was for the first time drawn to this almost unknown region.[2] The reasons for this neglect could have been partly the prevalence of malaria,[3] but also the dangers of brigandage, which, as Lenormant asserts, had been vigorously tackled by the Government after the unification of Italy, and, above all, the paucity of ancient remains to be seen above ground.

Talfourd Ely, as late as 1896, wrote that the extremity of Italy was 'Nobody's Way No-where',[4] and that he·had never met a single Englishman, travelling west from Taranto. All turned off eastwards to Brindisi for Greece and Asia Minor. He quotes Lenormant in describing Metapontum as a desert: apart from the temple of Apollo Lykeios, the 'Tavole Paladine' near Metapontum, and the single column of the temple of Hera Lacinia near Croton,[5] there were virtually no monuments to attract visitors.

While Lenormant may have thought of himself in some degree as emulating Chateaubriand in literary style, his two great historical travel books, *La Grande Grèce* and *À travers l'Apulie et la Lucanie,*[6] although discursive and leisurely, were not the work of a dilettante explorer. As a scholar he must be reckoned something of a prodigy, since his first publication appeared when he was fourteen,[7] others following when he was seventeen and twenty, and since he was awarded the numismatic prize of the Académie des Belles Lettres in 1857, when he was twenty. A year after his father's death at Epidauros in 1859, he returned to Greece and took part in excavations at Eleusis and along the Sacred Way, publishing his results in 1862.[8] In 1863 he visited Santorini and 'witnessed important volcanic phenomena' which perhaps helped him to describe in such masterly style the appalling Calabrian earthquake of 1783;[9] indeed he attributed the dearth of material remains above ground in 'Magna Graecia' in part to the prevalence of earthquakes. In 1869 he got himself to Egypt as a member of a deputation to attend the opening of the Suez Canal and made there a study of the Egyptian domestication of animals. He became Professor of Archaeology at the Bibliothèque Nationale in 1874, a position he held until his death in 1883, and founded the *Gazette Archéologique* in 1875.

In his journeys in Southern Italy Lenormant set out to find and study principally the sites with remains, if any, of the former great cities of 'Magna Graecia' and to give a detailed outline of their mythological background and history.[10] Let us see first what he found in Taranto, now recognised as the prime centre of manufacture of early red-figured Italiote vases, as he had indeed believed it to be. He had been there fourteen years earlier, when important remains of Roman buildings could be seen along the sea shore, mostly shops, but also some private houses with traces of luxurious decoration, marble revetments and fragments of mosaic. All these, he found, had been completely demolished by 1880 to furnish material for the Borgo Nuovo, built over the ancient Agora. This demolition and re-building was totally unsupervised by any government inspector. Naturally, many antiquities came to light, but all, according to Lenormant, were either purloined, destroyed, or sent to Naples for sale to dealers, with no notes of provenance.

Since the epoch-making discoveries in 1828 of Attic vases in Etruscan graves at Vulci,[11] vases from South Italy were no longer fashionable. They had been prized in the days of Sir William Hamilton and Tischbein, but now Greek dealers calling in at Naples on their way to Paris and London bought vases and small antiquities there which they sold as coming from Athens or Corinth. In 1880 Lenormant found no museum in Taranto, or even any private collections worthy of mention, except for coins. Earlier, one of the Cathedral canons had had a small collection of some note, which no visitor failed to inspect, but this had now been sold by his heirs. Drago, in his guide to the Taranto museum[12] makes short work of this poor little collection, which he says consisted mainly of *murex* shells, laboriously collected by the old man along the shores of the Mar Piccolo, bric-à-brac in the worst taste, and small bits and pieces from the Cathedral. Lenormant nevertheless bought in Taranto a few good terracottas for the Louvre.

The immense piles of *murex* shells from the ancient dyeworks were still conspicuous in Lenormant's time, as well as a few remains of the buildings used for the industry, with traces of purple dye still visible on the plaster. Lenormant speaks at some length of this important Tarentine industry. He had visited the huge shell heaps at Tyre and at Gythion, in Laconia, and was therefore in a position to assert that the Tyrians and Laconians used only the *Murex Trunculus,* whereas the Tarentines made equal use of *Murex Brandaris,* producing the especially red tint of the Tarentine purple mentioned by Pliny.[13] Talfourd Ely, too, saw these shell heaps, which were perhaps removed when the Naval Base was constructed.

Lenormant was of course aware that with so much new building in process, vases, bronzes and terracottas were coming to light all the time and, believing that Taranto had been in antiquity a great centre for these industries, he would have liked to have had these finds housed locally in a museum; but although a supervisor of Tarentine Antiquities, Viola, a capable and industrious young archaeologist who had trained at Pompeii, was appointed in 1881, the fine museum we now know was not to be built until 1907. In Lenormant's time the museum at Lecce, founded in 1868, was the foremost Italian provincial museum south of Naples. He speaks highly of its bronzes, vases and terracottas, though he notes the inclusion of some fakes.[14] The museum at Bari was not opened until 1883, the year of his death. Both these foundations owed much to the enthusiasm and support of local residents. Following the death in 1895 of Lecce's aristocratic patron,[15] Taranto gradually replaced Lecce as the principal centre of Apulian antiquities and received of right the first-fruits of any excavations.

When the new museum at Taranto was built, on the site of the crumbling remains of an old monastery where the antiquities had till then been housed, it was put under the direction of Quagliati, who is said to have been overwhelmed by the quantity of material he was expected to sort and display, in addition to taking a leading part in excavations.[16] Both Quagliati and his successor Drago published short, illustrated guides to their museum.[17] It is therefore somewhat surprising that neither of the two splendid volute-kraters, one by the Painter of the Birth of

Dionysos, the other the famous Karneia vase, both excavated at Ceglie in 1898, should be illustrated in these guides. The presumption is that Quagliati always hoped to have time to get this done.[18] Wuilleumier, who would have liked the opportunity to study them more closely,[19] is not quite accurate in saying that Beazley had only given them a glance: he showed me full notes in 1925, but regretted that he had no photographs.

Wuilleumier succeeded by inscrutable ingenuities in publishing the Karneia vase in 1933.[20] It was then bandied around between several painters of the last quarter of the fifth century, for some thirty-five years, until a few years ago it came to rest in the *P K P* Group, assigned to the Karneia Painter, along with Bari 7694 (also a volute-krater) and closely associated with two new pelikai from Policoro.[21] Tillyard, whose introductory remarks on the South Italian vases from the Hope Collection[22] were fundamental to the early stages of their classification, was another who had deplored that these two great volute-kraters remained unpublished.

To follow Lenormant's itinerary from Taranto to Reggio and subsequently to all the important inland towns with a classical and a modern atlas is a rewarding exercise, but cannot be attempted here. Mention of a few of his stopping places will perhaps highlight the enormous changes that have taken place since his time. Metapontum, was an obvious port of call: not only were the remains of the temple of Apollo Lykeios and the Tavole Paladine to be seen, but, as I have mentioned elsewhere,[23] there were also a few fragments of sculpture housed in the station.[24] On his final visit to Metapontum, in 1883, Lenormant found the little station museum enlarged and improved. Some at least of these antiquities, including pieces of painted architectural carving which had disappeared by the time George Gissing went there in 1897,[25] were eventually transferred to the museum at Potenza, which in its present state dates from 1957, though there had been a small museum since much earlier. Their preservation over more than half a century appears to have owed much to the devotion of local antiquarians.[26]

Only at Heraclea and at Thurii did Lenormant find unmistakable traces of ancient occupation.[27] At Heraclea, to scratch only just below the surface of the ground was to reveal stone foundations. Coins and small objects were there for the picking up, but as yet there was no attempt at any scientific exploration. According to Wuilleumier there was none in Magna Graecia before 1880, except at Rudiae.[28] Lenormant naturally devoted a long chapter to Sybaris. He was convinced that he knew the exact location of the site, and wished keenly that his country could institute excavations, preceded by the necessary pumping. He was fully aware of the colossal expense that would be involved, but felt that France, once so pre-eminent archaeologically in Egypt and the Peloponnese, had now fallen behind England and Germany. He was writing only a decade after the Franco-Prussian war and it was hardly likely that the French government would have had funds to spare for so vast an undertaking, but one can sympathise with his hints of jealousy at the outstanding successes of 'our colleagues over the border' at Olympia and Pergamon, and at the large sums voted by the British government for excavations at Ephesus and Halicarnassus.

Though Lenormant found few museums in the course of his travels, he was of course acquainted with the two 'marvellous' private collections of vases at Ruvo, where he affirms that remains of a potter's kiln and implements had been found;[29] while reckoning that Taranto was the main centre of the vase industry, he thinks there may have been others, as is now indeed believed likely.

No account of Professor Trendall's predecessors can omit a tribute to the Jatta and Caputi families, who founded their splendid collections at Ruvo in the face of considerable obstacles. Prior to about 1810, the rich local cemeteries were being haphazardly plundered. Then some systematic digging was started by a few of the leading local inhabitants, directed by a priest from the Cathedral. Italiote vases being at this date still in high favour with collectors, the result was a 'furore' of illicit excavation by intruders and the disappearance of a great many vases to foreign markets. At this point the Jatta brothers, Giovanni and Giulio, intervened, bought up all that they could and spared no pains or cost to keep at least the best pieces and assemble them as a collection. Special credit is owed to Giovanni's sister-in-law, herself coming from a keen collector's family. It was she who built the Palazzo Jatta in 1842 to house the collection (her husband Giulio had been killed in battle) and it was she who successfully petitioned the King of Naples, on her brother-in-law's death in 1845, to allow the collection to remain in the family's possession, for Giovanni had stipulated in his will that the collection be sold to the kingdom of Naples on condition it be not dispersed.

The son of Signora Giulio Jatta, a second Giovanni, carried on his mother's work, adding to the Palazzo, procuring cases, and finally producing a comprehensive catalogue in 1869.[30] Later, his son, Michele, produced important, more up-to-date articles in *Japigia*.[31] Sichterman's excellent publication of 1966 gives this collection the crowning tribute it deserves.[32] Giovanni Jatta II also published the Caputi collection, sold in 1921 to the Marchese De Luca Resta in Rome and recently transferred to Milan.[33] The original owner, Giuseppe Caputi, a priest, in 1868 gave Giovanni permission to publish, but died before the work appeared in 1877.[34]

A number of eminent scholars included some of the products of the South Italian potteries in their works on Greek ceramics and published articles on individual vases or groups, which led over many years to much controversy and differences of opinion.[35] Professor Trendall, however, was the first to decide to make his life work the complete classification of the entire output of Italiote red-figured vases, a task that might well have daunted a scholar of less devoted tenacity. The final result to date, as we all know, is his great comprehensive catalogue of the vases of Lucania, Campania and Sicily, now with two supplements, and the classification of Apulian red-figure vase-painters by him and Professor Cambitoglou, which in now in press.

His first step on the road was a study of the red-figured vases of Paestum.[36] This was a very intelligent début, since Paestan vases are mostly quite distinctive and numerically, at the time, less unmanageable and controversial than those of the other fabrics. As he says in his preface to *Paestan Pottery,* 'The problem of South Italian pottery is still rather a confused one, and this work is an attempt to put in order one of its more clearly defined fabrics'.[37]

Paestan vases had been known since the late eighteenth century. Trendall lists some fifty (excluding fragments) that were excavated at Paestum in 1805 and placed in the Naples museum.[38] The famous calyx-krater signed by Asteas and depicting the madness of Herakles (Madrid 11094) was discovered and published by Hirtzel in 1864.[39] Hirtzel grouped with it and described the four other signed vases then known. The 'Style of Asteas' was first officially so designated by H. Winnefeld,[40] but it is to Patroni that Trendall attributes its first analytical study.[41] Tillyard, in his invaluable catalogue of the Hope Vases, next identified as Paestan a few pieces anterior in date to Asteas and without the most salient characteristics of Asteas and Python.[42] From this point Trendall forged ahead, first with an article on Early Paestan in the *Journal of Hellenic Studies,* 1935, and then with his comprehensive study of this fabric in 1936. From this time on, except for the interruption of the war years, he travelled tirelessly and repeatedly round all the vase collections of Europe, on both sides of the Iron Curtain, and of America and, as the years went by, assiduously visited the innumerable new sites and the many new museums of Magna Graecia.

The astonishing increase in the material excavated since the war, the books and periodicals published, the new museums founded, the old ones enlarged or reconstructed, all these developments are described in Trendall's triennial reports in the *Journal of Hellenic Studies* and in the bibliographies in *The Red-Figured Vases of Lucania, Campania and Sicily* and its supplements. More detailed accounts are of course to be found in the *Notizie degli Scavi* and in other periodicals, Italian and German par excellence. The *Cassa per il Mezzogiorno e la Regione Siciliana* has provided important financial support for these activities. The *Società Magna Grecia* was inaugurated in 1925 and has contributed considerably to South Italian studies. Since the war years there has been a steady increase in the number of formal excavations. The splendid results are well known. The *Convegno di Taranto,* an annual congress devoted to South Italian studies was started in 1961 and publishes its proceedings with admirable promptitude.

To enumerate all the new books, articles and museum-guides that have recently appeared, to list the new museums, to mention the old ones that have been reconstructed or enlarged, would not be possible here. Let us attempt an evaluation of the work done by means of two examples already mentioned. The Karneia vase, though known to leading experts since its discovery in 1898, was not published with illustrations until 1933.[43] Its bibliography is now impressively extensive.[44] The Potenza museum, in its present organised state, dates only from 1957, although antiquities from the neighbourhood, including Metapontum, had been carefully cherished by local enthusiasts since the end of the last century. In 1883, when Lenormant visited Potenza, there was no museum and he does not mention seeing any private collections.[45]

What of Potenza itself, as a city? That, said Lenormant, depended on the direction from which one reached it. To the traveller from Naples it appeared 'un trou de province, arrière, vulgaire et mort', but the traveller arriving after a tour round the neighbouring towns of the Basilicata, found at Potenza both life and civilisation — gas-lighting, a theatre, shops brilliantly lit, some with modern plate-glass windows, one French dressmaker, a good clean inn, and, above all, a restaurant with a Milanese chef. The streets, alas, were still thronged by people maimed in the terrible earthquake of 1857.

Although there were no collectors there was not a total dearth of educated and cultured persons, among whom Lenormant evidently had friends. One family offered him some 'gracious hospitality' during his stay, culminating in presenting a celebration cake in his honour, all iced in white, with his initials and the flags of France and Italy in colour. He had become understandably antagonistic to the local cuisine, which he describes in some detail: he reckoned it to be the same as that of the ancients, and that if Apicius' recipes were followed, the same results would be achieved. But the cake looked very promising to the eye. His horror, however, at the interior ingredients could only be concealed by summoning every vestige of politeness at his command — ham pâté, hard boiled eggs, almonds, gherkins in vinegar, 'fruits glacés', all seasoned with sugar and a strong cheese. *Perhaps,* he reflected, a German would have stood up to it better, but for a *Frenchman!*

If Trendall's travels have not involved him in precisely similar gastronomic ordeals, I can myself recall a dish of 'verdura' shared with him and another companion in 1937. 'Obviously', our fellow traveller commented, 'the lawn mowings.' But in his case the chef had not attempted to follow the Mrs Beeton of Antiquity.

FOOTNOTES

1. P. Wuilleumier, 'Questions de céramique italiote', *RA* 5e série 30, 1929, 185–210.

2. Not of course *entirely* unknown as the Abbé de Saint-Non had already published the five-volume *Voyage pittoresque, ou Description des royaumes de Naples et de Sicile,* Paris 1781–6.

3 Malaria was also endemic in Greece, where Lenormant's illustrious father, Charles, 'l'un des chefs de cette brillante pléiade d'érudits qui renouvelle en France l'étude de l'antiquité', had died in 1859, while conducting his son around the principal sites.

4 'The Vases of Magna Graecia', *Archaeologia* 55, 1896, 114.

5 At that time only approachable on horseback or by sea.

6 *La Grande Grèce, paysages et histoire,* 3 vols, Paris 1881–4; *À travers l'Apulie et la Lucanie, notes de voyage,* 2 vols, Paris 1883. The latter was published shortly before his premature death at the age of forty-seven.

7 A letter to M. Hase translating some Greek inscriptions on a mummy from Memphis, *RA* 1851, 461 ff.

8 'Recherches archéologiques à Eleusis exécutées dans le cours de l'année 1860', *Recueil des Inscriptions,* Paris, 1862.

9 *Apulie* (*supra* n. 6), chap. VI. This is of course based on the description by the great French geologist Déodat de Dolomieu (1750–1801), *Mémoire sur le tremblement de terre de la Calabre,* Rome 1783.

10 The author purposely dispensed with references and footnotes. He hoped his books would appeal as travel guides to a wider public as well as to specialists. To the latter, he reckoned, he was known as impeccably conscientious about his facts. For them therefore references were unnecessary.

11 E. Gerhard, 'Rapporto Volcente', *AdI* 1831, 5–270.

12 *Il Museo Nazionale di Taranto,* Rome 1957.

13 *Nat. Hist,* IX, 137. Some of Lenormant's further remarks on this passage do not seem to interpret Pliny's meaning quite accurately. I owe the reference to Pliny to Professor M.L. Clarke. Lenormant also speaks of a silky muslin material made from the filaments with which certain types of mussels, which he calls 'pinnes marines', attach themselves to rocks, the Tarentine product rivalling that of Cos, but gives no reference. He reckons that the transparent garments worn by dancers on Herculaneum paintings were made of this material, and equally, one might think, the fine transparent garments depicted on so many late Attic and Italiote vases. This delicate material was golden-brown in colour. Whereas the dyeing industry was long extinct, the fish-filament tissue still continued to be made in Taranto, Naples and Malta, for small articles such as gloves and bonnets: *La Grande Grèce,* 14. See also Daremberg-Saglio under Byssus, and *Purnell's Encyclopedia of Animal Life* under Mussel. The *byssos* or anchor which holds the Fan-Mussel (*Pinna Fragilis*) to its rock consisted of a tuft of very fine gold threads: 'the *byssos* threads are so strong that they can be woven into cloth...The cloth woven from the large bivalves was once used to make garments with a golden sheen and was worn by the aristocracy, especially that of Southern Europe. The Field of the Cloth of Gold was so called because so many of the nobles there wore tunics made from the beard of bivalves. It had nothing to do with gold thread...' I owe this reference to Mr Humfrey Wakefield.

14 *Gazette Archéologique* 1881, pt 2, 7.

15 Sigismondo Castromediano (1811–95), Duke of Moriano. He was a well-known patriot who took part in the Rising of 1848 and was subsequently condemned to 30 years' hard labour, of which he served 9 years before escaping in 1859. He was deputy for his region during the years 1860–65.

16 The *on dit* in Oxford archaeological circles in the early 1920s was that under this régime, if the director had cause to be absent, he had his glass showcases pasted over with newspaper; and who shall say that he had not his good reasons ?

17 Quintino Quagliati, *Il Museo Nazionale di Taranto,* Rome 1932; Ciro Drago, *Museo Nazionale di Taranto,* Rome 1940 and 1957.

18 Professor J.D. Beazley made a tactful reference to this in 1929, *VPol,* 72, n. 4.

19 (*supra* n. 1), 189.

20 'Cratère inédit de Ceglie', *RA* 6e série 2, 1933, 3–30.

21 *LCS* I, 55.

22 E.M.W. Tillyard, *The Hope Vases,* Cambridge 1923.

23 N. Moon, 'Some Early Italian Vase-Painters', *BSR* 11, 1929, 48. See also Lenormant, *Apulie (supra* n. 6) I, 360.

24 In addition, from the practical angle, Metapontum, being a junction, boasted a station buffet, where at least bread, wine and cheese were on offer, with the almost unknown luxury of crockery and cutlery. Lenormant could recommend with confidence three bedrooms above the station to anyone prepared to be philosophical about fleas. In 1883, however, he was less philosophical about the fleas, advising archaeological visitors to inspect the antiquities in between trains.

25 *By the Ionian Sea. Notes of a Ramble in Southern Italy,* London 1901, 65.

26 Maria Sestieri-Bertarelli, *Il Musio Archeologico Provinciale di Potenza,* Rome 1957, 4. The remains of sculpture from the metopes of the temple mentioned by Lenormant (aside from the remains of painted terracotta decorations) are not shown in the Guide.

27 *La Grande Grèce,* 164, 324.

28 *(supra* n. 1), 185. The Italians had in fact organised important excavations near Thurii in 1879 when the first Orphic gold tablets were found. Three others were found in a tumulus in 1880, in the course of official excavation.

29 *La Grande Grèce,* 93.

30 *Catalogo del Museo Jatta,* 1869.

31 'La Collezione Jatta e l'ellenizzamento della Peucezia', *Japigia* 3, 1932, 3–33 and 241–282; see also his Introduction to the reprint in 1929 of Giovanni Jatta's 'Cenno storico sull' antichissima città di Ruvo (1884).

32 Hellmut Sichtermann, *Griechische Vasen in Unteritalien,* Tübingen 1966. I owe the knowledge of the history of this collection to Sichterman's introduction.

33 Philippart, Collections de la céramique grecque en Italie' ii, pp. 28–33; *CVA,* Milano – Collezione 'H.A.', I and II.

34 G. Jatta, *I Vasi Italo-greci del Signor Caputi di Ruvo,* Naples 1877. The heir to the collection, an 'egregio giovane', ransacked the house and discovered a great many more vases, neglected and mouldering in uninhabited apartments. To our regret, he had these thoroughly cleaned up; but highly undesirable as such proceedings seem nowadays, it should be remembered that in over a century ideals have changed. Mid-nineteenth century collectors would not have wanted their prized pieces to appear tatty. If portions of a vase were badly defaced or missing, an artist was called to restore them.

35 See *supra,* notes 1, 4, 18, 20 and 22.

36 *Paestan Pottery,* London 1936.

37 *Ibid.,* vii.

38 The Naples Museum as an entity only came into being after the return of the Bourbons following Napoleon's downfall. It was not catalogued by Heydemann until 1872 (*Die Vasensammlung des Museo Nazionale zu Neapel*).

39 *AdI* 1864, 323 ff. (It is incidentally of considerable interest to read some of these early publications, written so much more subjectively than is usual nowadays, and with a literary rather than a stylistic bias.

40 See his article 'Asteas' in *Bonner Studien* 1890, pp. 166–175.

41 'Early Paestan Pottery, *JHS* 55, 1935, 35; G. Patroni, 'La ceramica antica nell'Italia meridionale', *Atti della R. Accademia di Archeologia, Lettere e Belle Arti di Napoli* 1897, 37–79.

42 *(supra* n. 22), 16.

43 Wuilleumier *(supra* n. 20).

44 Arias-Hirmer-Shefton, 388.

45 There was a 'Commission des monuments et antiquitiés'.

HYDRIA APULA DI HERACLEA

Dinu Adamesteanu

Tavola 1

Già dall'inizio degli scavi nell'area abitata dell'antica Heraclea,[1] ci siamo imbattuti in un vero 'quartiere industriale' situato sul lato meridionale della grande *plateia* che attraversa l'intero abitato.[2] Il quartiere industriale e caratterizzato da numerose fornaci, di ogni tipo, destinate alla cottura di vasi e statuette ed anche alla lavorazione del ferro.[3] Anche sotto lo strato classico e quello ellenistico, non una sola volta, sono state rinvenute fornaci databili, per la loro produzione di coppe del tipo B2[4] e di numerose coppe ioniche nel periodo arcaico.[5] Nessuna fornace è stata incontrata a N della *plateia;* tutte, come si è detto, si trovano sul lato meridionale di essa, ai margini degli isolati formati da questa e dagli *stenopoi.*[6]

Altre fornaci, destinate alla produzione di anfore grezze ed ai vasi di tipo Gnathia, sono state individuate e parzialmente scavate nella parte orientale della città bassa. In qualche caso, come in quello delle fornace per anfore, queste ultime sono state rinvenute sistemate in un vero deposito.

Non meno sorprendente è la presenza di fornaci arcaiche e di qualcuna di età ellenistica ancor più ad O del quartiere industriale, in un quartiere in cui si lavorava nell'anno 1975. Questa volta, diversamente da quanto si è constatato nel primo quartiere, le fornaci si trovano disseminate in tutti e due i quartieri situati ai lati della stessa grande *plateia.* Ed è da questo nuovo quartiere che sono apparsi i primi documenti di una produzione di vasi decorati risalente al VII secolo a.C.[7]

In poche parole, e come aveva già sostenuto da molto tempo lo Hauser,[8] la colonia di Heraclea, come anche quella di Siris, ha avuto la sua non minore importanza, in rapporto a colonie come quella di Metaponto, nella produzione vascolare.[9] Come aveva già dimostrato la serie dei vasi rinvenuti nella grande tomba di Policoro,[10] la colonia aveva seguito le grandi trasformazioni vascolari locali di età arcaica già a qualche decennio dalla sua fondazione, nel 434–433 a.C.[11]

Ma la sua grande attività, a quanto risulta finora, cade nella seconda metà del IV secolo a.C: a questo periodo spettano i maggiori frammenti di ceramica dipinta od acroma, tipologi-camente databile in quell'epoca. Quest' attività non cessa con i diversi disturbi che la battaglia di Heraclea[12] avrebbe potuto arrecarle; questa continua anche nell'ultima parte del III quarto del II secolo a.C., quando viene constatata, sempre nel quartiere industriale, la produzione dei c.d. vasi megaresi. Se non erriamo, in base ai documenti di cui disponiamo fino ad oggi, la produzione vascolare locale finirebbe intorno agli inizi del I secolo a.C. Una produzione vascolare quindi che si prolunga dal VII fino al I secolo a.C.

Queste scoperte avvenute a Heraclea, assieme a quelle recentemente fatte a Metaponto,[13] stanno ora a dimostrare non soltanto le capacità dei *plastai* locali in generale ma anche, com'è stato evidenziato ultimamente,[14] anche l'aspetto economico-sociale delle colonie della Magna Grecia. Quando si vorrà dare una più grande attenzione anche a queste scoperte, per qualcuno ancora di minore importanza, si avrà un quadro ancora più chiaro del mondo della Magna Grecia e delle sue possibilità artistiche in uno tra i più difficili momenti delle città greche dell'Italia meridionale.

Una prova di queste possibilità ci è offerta da una scoperta avvenuta nell'autunno del 1972 nella necropoli meridionale di Heraclea,[15] necropoli ben nota già dai primi interventi nell'area della zona archeologica di Heraclea-Policoro.[16]

Ad una profondità di circa m.1, in mezzo ad altre tombe con pareti in blocchi di carparo, è stata messa in luce una hydria che fungeva da recipiente per una cremazione di uomo adulto.[17] La parte superiore del collo era spezzata, come anche il piede. Il coperchio era formato da una kylix a vernice nera, ben databile nella seconda metà del IV secolo a.C. L'hydria era ricoperta da un grosso strato di incrostazione sabbiosa talchè, appena fuori terra, soltanto in qualche tratto si potevano scorgere tracce di pittura. A ripulitura e restauro ultimati risultava una hydria alta cm.61, con una larghezza massima di cm.39, con la decorazione divisa in due riquadri (Tav. 1, Figg. 1–3).[18] La vernice nera e pittura in bianco e giallo hanno certamente perso molto a causa dell'incrostazione ma è altrettanto certo che la vernice nera almeno è stata maldestramente stesa sulla superficie del vaso; si possono osservare benissimo le irregolari pennellate, specialmente sulla parte inferiore del vaso e sulla spalla. Si tratta di una vernice irregolarmente stesa su tutto il corpo del vaso.

Un altro difetto è la posizione sbilenca del vaso, simile a quella di molti altri esemplari rinvenuti tanto nelle necropoli[19] quanto nell'ambito della città, nel quartiere industriale di Heraclea, o in quell'altro, recentemente messo in luce, nel *kerameikos* di Metaponto.[20] Per quanto concerne la forma stessa del vaso, più che altrove, questa, quasi nelle stesse dimensioni, si ritrova spessissimo, e quasi nello stesso periodo, a Heraclea; quelle del santuario di Demetra, anche se acrome,[21] presentano anch'esse diversi piccoli difetti.

Sulla parte principale, le scene si sviluppano in due riquadri mentre l'altra facciata raffigura un motivo floreale in cui i girali e le palmette si presentano in un fantasioso disegno soltanto apparentemente complicato ma, in realtà, molto simmetrico (Tav. 1, Fig. 3).

Il riquadro superiore (Tav. 1, Figg. 1–2) è dominato dalla solita raffigurazione di un'edicola così ben nota specialmente ai pittori apuli. In mezzo all'edicola è raffigurata un'hydria mentre ai lati, volte verso l'edicola, tre figure, una maschile seminuda, le altre due femminili con un Erote alato che si avvicina, recante un ramo, probabilmente di olivo, alla fanciulla che sta sulla destra. A sinistra, la figura maschile, con la gamba sinistra poggiata su uno sgabello. Mentre quest'ultima figura maschile, con il braccio destro teso, sta per indicare l'hydria che domina l'edicola, la figura femminile, seduta su una invisibile sedia, regge con la destra un lembo del vestito. La donna porta una collana resa in bianco, armille al braccio e scarpette decorate con cuciture anch'esse in bianco. Le stesse armille si notano anche sulla gamba sinistra dell'Erote. Più sontuosamente vestita, anch'essa con la faccia tesa verso l'edicola, v'è un'altra figura femminile poggiata su un invisibile rialzo.

Nel riquadro inferiore (Tav. 1, Figg. 1–2) l'azione si svolge intorno ad un pithos, per tre quarti infilato nella terra ed intorno al quale v'è tutto un campo di erba. Il pithos è protetto dall'alto da una forma di tendaggio.

Da un lato e dall'altro v'è un gruppo di fanciulle, tre per parte, di altezze decrescenti, dai lati verso il centro, dove domina il pithos, quasi ognuna in movimento e tutte e sei recanti una hydria sulla testa, appoggiate al corpo o, come nel caso dell'ultima a destra, con l'hydria poggiata a terra. Le tre donne sulla parte sinistra del pithos sono separate da due alberelli, anche questi discendenti, come altezza, dalla parte esterna verso il centro. Sul lato destro, le tre fanciulle sono separate da un alberello ancora e da una hydria posta tra la seconda e l'ultima fanciulla, che regge in mano una coroncina.

La presenza del riquadro inferiore, meglio di quello superiore, ci aiuta ad intuire il soggetto, facilmente riferibile, grazie al pithos mezzo interrato ed alle fanciulle che versano e portano l'acqua con le hydriai. Si tratta evidentemente della leggenda delle Danaidi condannate a riempire un pithos senza fondo.[22]

Per quanto riguarda la scena del riquadro superiore, il Trendall ha già proposto l'identificazione con Poseidon ed Amymone,[23] personaggi ben noti dalla letteratura antica riguardante le cinquanta figlie di Danaos.[24] Il tema, variamente interpretato e variamente realizzato nell' arte greco-romana,[25] non crediamo abbia bisogno di una nuova trattazione: i confronti offerti dal Trendall sono tra i più completi.

A questo punto a noi interessa insistere su un piccolo particolare e precisamente sul fatto che un cratere a calice di Napoli presenta anch'esso la scena con Poseidon ed Amymone.[26] Le indicazioni sulla provenienza di questo cratere lo riferiscono ad Armento e, a nostro avviso, certamente a quella zona oramai ben nota attraverso la ripresa dello scavo, ch'è Serra Lustrante, località, questa, in cui, come affermavamo altrove, il mondo ellenistico della costa greca era così profondamente presente e diversamente di come lo stesso mondo si presenta in altri centri lucani ellenizzati.[27] Attraverso la vallata della fiumara di Armento e di altri affluenti minori, l'intera vasta zona archeologica di Serra Lustrante è strettamente legata alla grande vallata dell'Agri, una delle piu importanti vie commerciali di Siris e poi di Heraclea nella loro *chora* e nella *proschoros*.

Non è improbabile quindi che anche quest'ultimo vaso, come tanti tra i seguaci del Pittore di Licurgo provengano dalle officine di Heraclea o da qualcuna operante nell'area di dominio o d'influenza di Heraclea. Ma è certo che tanto Siris quanto Heraclea hanno avuto una grande importanza nello sviluppo delle officine vascolari tra il settimo ed il primo secolo a.C.

NOTE

1 I primi scavi risalgono al 1958−1959 ma si tratta di piccoli interventi: F.G. Lo Porto, *BdA* 46, 1961, pp. 133 sgg.; B. Neutsch, *Archäol. Forschungen in Lukanien* II, *Herakleiastudien*, Heidelberg 1967, 100−108. Dal 1967 sono stati iniziati gli scavi, su più ampia scala, tanto nell'abitato quanto nelle necropoli: D. Adamesteanu, 'Siris-Heraclea', in *Policoro,* Matino 1969, 3−38 (dall'estratto), e *Atti IX CSMG,* Taranto 1969, 236−237.

2 D. Adamesteanu, "Origine e sviluppo di centri abitati in Basilicata", *CSDIR* 3, 1970−71, 146. Idem, *Basilicata antica: storia e monumenti,* Cava dei Tirreni 1974, 98−111. Cfr. anche *Atti IX CSMG,* 485. Sulla *plateia,* cfr. D. Adamesteanu, *Herakleiastudien (supra* n. 1), 96−99.

3 D. Adamesteanu, *Basilicata antica,* ibidem.

4 G. Vallet e F. Villard, 'Mégara Hyblaea V', *MEFR* 68, 1955, 14−31; D. Adamesteanu, *Siris-Heraclea (supra* n.), 18 sgg.

5 Adamesteanu, *Siris-Heraclea (supra* n. 1), 33.

6 Quattro finora messi in luce.

7 Per questi dati cfr. *Atti XII CSMG.* Oltre al grande dinos del VII secolo a.C., alle stesse fabbriche arcaiche appartengono numerosi altri frammenti di stile orientalizzante ma più strettamente legati al mondo micrasiatico.

8 F. Hauser in FR II, 1909, 264. Cfr. anche N. Degrassi, *BdA* 1965, 20−21.

9 È oramai accertato che anche a Metaponto v'era un vero *kermaeikos* situato a ridosso della fortificazione settentrionale Alle officine che operavano in questo nuovo quartiere metapontino appartengono le coppe ioniche, qualche frammento del Pittore di Pisticci (*LCS,* 699) nonchè i vasi del periodo di attività dei Pittori del Gruppo Creusa e Dolon: D. Adamesteanu, *Metaponto,* Napoli 1973, 26−28.

10 Per la bibliografia cfr. N. Degrassi, *BdA* 1965, 5−37; *LCS,* 50 sgg.; N. Degrassi, *Herakleiastudien (supra* n. 1), 193−231.

11 Per il problema della fondazione di Heraclea cfr. F. Sartori, in *Herakleiastudien* (*supra* n. 1), 20–23.

12 Sartori, *ibidem,* 78–83.

13 Cfr. nota 9.

14 Su questo tema verteva il *XII CSMG* 1972.

15 Per quanto risulta finora, le necropoli di Heraclea si estendono sul lato orientale (Propr. Cospito), su tutto il lato meridionale ed ai piedi della collina sul lato occidentale, ai lati della strada che continuava la *plateia* della collina attraverso i campi di Madonelle.

16 Cfr. Neutsch (*supra* n. 1), 151–158.

17 Policoro 38462. *RVAp* 407, no. 15/59. Una delle poche di questo tipo rinvenuta in questa parte della necropoli.

18 La prima notizia del rinvenimento e della sua importanza è stata data da A.D. Trendall, *ArchReps* 1972–73, 37, Fig. 8. Il vaso è trattato da Trendall anche in *Festschrift Brommer* (p. 284, no. 9, pl. 75, 3) e in questo volume da Margot Schmidt (p. 159 ff.). Ne fa menzione anche Eva Keuls nel suo libro *The Water Carriers in Hades* (Amsterdam 1974), p. 8.

19 Così sono, per esempio, le pelikai e le hydriai della grande tomba di Policoro (N. Degrassi, *BdA* 1965, 5, 7, 10, 14).

20 La stessa forma sbilenca presenta anche la grande hydria recentemente rinvenuta nelle officine del Pittore di Creusa a Metaponto (Adamesteanu, *Metaponto, supra* n. 9, 26–28 e Fig. 8) e molto probabilmente considerata di scarto.

21 Cfr. qualcuna, con dedica a Demetra, in B. Neutsch, *Siris ed Heraclea,* 39, Fig. 27.

22 Il tema del pithos senza fondo in Roscher, *ML,* s.v. (Bernhard).

23 Trendall (*supra* n. 18). La raffigurazione è un tema spesso incontrato nella decorazione dei vasi di questo periodo: K. Schauenburg, *AuA* 10, 1961, 84–86. Cfr. anche *LCS* pp. 43, 67, 82, 123. Per le acconciature cfr. Pelike 22 di Aja (di cui possiedo la fotografia grazie alla Signora Schneider-Herrmann).

24 La letteratura in RE^2, IV, 2094–2098, (s.v. Weser).

25 Bibliografia in *EAA* III, 1960 (s.v. Brommer).

26 Cratere 690, studiato da V. Macchioro, *JdI* 27, 1912, 285, Fig. 12b. Trendall, *Festschrift Brommer,* p. 284, no. 10, pl. 75, 4.

27 Cfr. D. Adamesteanu, 'Una tomba arcaica di Armento', *ASMG* 11–12, 1970–71, 83–92; Idem, *Popoli anellenici,* Napoli 1973, 66–68, e *Atti X CSMG,* 481.

TWO ETRUSCO-CORINTHIAN VASES

D.A. Amyx

Plates 2, 3, 4.

Several years ago, there appeared in the market in Switzerland an Etrusco-Corinthian olpe of very remarkable style. This vase, now in the collection of Mrs. Aaron Dechter of Los Angeles, is one of the two pieces providing foci for the present essay. The other vase, a previously unpublished alabastron in Cambridge University, is also of highly distinctive character. A brief discussion of these vases is offered as a tribute to Professor Trendall, whose lifelong love of Italy and his keen interest in things Italic, as well as those Italiote, will insure his friendly acceptance of such a greeting.[1]

The Dechter Olpe

This vase[2] is published here (Pl. 2, Figs. 1–4) with the kind permission of its present owner. It is an olpe of normal shape and syntax of decoration, but it has some unusual features of style and subject matter which set it apart from the common run of Etrusco-Corinthian examples. The main decoration consists of three animal friezes:

> In the top frieze: floral scroll between crouching lions, between crouching sphinxes.
>
> In the middle frieze: small bird perched on a large rosette, between crouching sphinxes; between panthers, a small bird in front of each panther; small bird facing crouching lion, and (below handle) bird with spread wings.
>
> In the lowest frieze: crouching lion to right, between hen and cock, between sphinxes, a small bird to left above cock's back another to left facing lion; small owl to right, griffin walking to right, lion crouching to right, small bird to right. Thick filling ornament, consisting mainly of incised rosettes of different sizes.

With its elaborate incision and its highly decorative use of added color, this vase makes a vivid impression on the viewer. The style is wholly characteristic of a known artist, the Feoli Painter [once "Mingor Painter", i.e., painter of the MIN(otaurish) GOR(gon) on an olpe in the British Museum], to whose hand the Dechter olpe has already been attributed. It differs from the other olpai by this artist mainly in its greater tendency toward symmetry in the composition of its friezes (on the Painter's earliest vase, all of the creatures move to right), as if in closer imitation of Corinthian practice, but even in this respect the artist's own prolific fancy has led him to introduce many odd variations.

The constantly accelerating pace of Etrusco-Corinthian research has brought the Feoli Painter, wholly unknown until just a few years ago, into prominence as one of the leading artists in that ware. The first published notice of his style appears in my article of 1965,[3] wherein two vases were attributed to one (unnamed) Painter. This nucleus was expanded in 1967,[4] to consist of seven pieces, and the name "Mingor Painter" (see above) was given to the artist. Starting from the two pieces cited in my earlier article (1965), and naming the artist the "Feoli Painter" after the previous owner of the alabastron in Würzburg (below, no. 11), Szilágyi[5] independently attributed the olpe in Vulci (below, no. 5) and added an alabastron in Grosseto (below, no. 12). In this article, Szilágyi deals with much the same classes of materials as I do in my two articles, with comfortingly similar conclusions. He has carried his studies still further in his book on Etrusco-Corinthian vase-painting,[6] and places the Painter in context in two summarizing articles.[7] But, for the most important recent advances in our specific knowledge of the Feoli Painter's works we are indebted to Marina Martelli, whose painstaking and perceptive article of 1977[8] introduces four new attributions (below, nos. 1, 2, 8, 9), and, making full use of this expanded repertoire with its extended chronological range, gives an exhaustive study of the Painter's stylistic development and his place among Etrusco-Corinthian vase-painters. Her list includes all of the following except the alabastron in Milan (below, no. 13).

Here, then, is a list of the Feoli Painter's works, so far as they are known to me:

Oinochoai (with trefoil mouth)

1 Turin, Private. Height: 0.270. Martelli (1977), 11, no. 1 and figs. 1–3. (Martelli)

2 Florence 97645, from Poggio Buco (sequestro). Height: 0.190. Martelli (1977), 11, no. 2 and figs. 4–10. (Martelli)

Olpai

3 London, B.M. 1924.4–15.1, "from Viterbo." Height: 0.392. Amyx (1967), 95, no. 1 and pls. 35–37; Martelli (1977), 11, no. 4.

4 Munich 641. Pl. 3, Figs. 5–7. Original height: 0.395. Sieveking and Hackl, 76f and pl. 8; Amyx (1965), 6; Amyx (1967), 95f, no. 2; Szilágyi (1975), pl. 23, fig. 32; Szilágyi (1976), pl. 9, fig. 9; Szilágyi (1977), pl. 19a; Martelli (1977), 11, no. 3.

5 Vulci, Antiquarium 64230, from Vulci (Tomba della Panatenaica). Height: 0.390. *Kunst und Kultur der Etrusker* (Exhibition Catalogue, Vienna, 24 May – 4 September 1966), 61 no. 222 and pl. 223a, top row, third from left (wrongly captioned); *Arte e Civiltà degli Etruschi* (Exhibition Catalogue, Turin 1967), no. 257, illustrated; Amyx (1967), 96, no. 3; Szilágyi (1968), 19 and note 50; G. Riccioni and M.T. Flaconi Amorelli, *La Tomba della Panatenaica di Vulci: Quaderni di Villa Giulia,* 3, Rome 1968, 47 and fig. 30, no. 30; Martelli (1977), 11 no. 6. (Banti; also Szilágyi)

6 Los Angeles, Mrs. Aaron Dechter. Pl. 2, Figs. 1–4; Height: 0.358. Amyx (1967), 96, no. 4 ("Basel Market"); *The Art of Ancient Italy,* André Emmerich Gallery, New York, 4–29 April 1970, 6, no. 7; *Sotheby Sale Catalogue,* 6 December 1971, no. 172; Szilágyi (1975), pl. 23, fig. 31; Martelli (1977), 11, no. 7.

7 Basel, Private. Amyx (1967), 96, no. 5; Martelli (1977), 11, no. 8. (Same hand as no. 6, Cahn)

8 Turin, Private. Height: 0.370. Martelli (1977), 11, no. 9 and figs. 11–15. (Martelli)

9 Florence 3729. Height: 0.349. Martelli (1977), 11, no. 9 and figs. 16–24. (Martelli)

Alabastra

10 Berkeley, UCLMA 8–67–6683. Height: 0.176. Amyx (1967), 96, no. 7 and pl. 38, a–d; Martelli (1977), 11, no. 5. Sphinxes, birds.

11 Würzburg L 768. Height: 0.168. Ernst Langlotz, *Griechische Vasen in Würzburg,* Munich 1932, pl. 225; Amyx (1965), 6; Amyx (1967), 96, no. 6; Szilágyi, "Az etruszko-korinthosi vázafestészet osztályozásának kérdési," in *Különlenyomat az antik tanulmányok 1967: Évi 1. Számából,* Budapest 1967, 56, figs. 26, a–b; Szilágyi (1968), pl. 13:1–2; Erika Simon und Mitarbeiter, *Führer durch die Antikenabteilung des Martin von Wagner Museums der Universität Würzburg,* Mainz 1975, 265, no. L 768; Martelli (1977), 11, no. 10. Sphinxes, birds. (Also Szilagyi)

12 Grosseto, Museo Archeologico 2052c, from Ischia di Castro. Height: ca. 0.175. Szilágyi (1968), 19 note 50; Martelli (1977), 11, no. 11. (A "near-replica" of no. 11, Szilagyi)

13 Milan, Coll. "H.A." Height: 0.105. *CVA* 2, Italia 51, III C, 6 and pl. 9:5. Swan between winged lion and sphinx. (E. Paribeni)

The following possible additions to the foregoing list should be noted: A round aryballos, seen by me in the Swiss market in 1973, seemed also to belong, but I am not sure of this attribution:

> On top of mouth, rays pointing inward; edge of lip glazed; on shoulder, tongues; on body, between bands, animal frieze; underneath, concentric circles. In animal frieze, owl between lions (fancy incised details).

An olpe which was once in the Swiss market (1974), and later in the London market (Samia, 1976), is by the Feoli Painter, but I do not know whether it is the same vase as no. 7 above ("Swiss, Private"). Szilágyi (1977), 55 f., gives a summary of the Painter's main stylistic traits, then adds, obscurely, "Le sue opere note, un terzo delle quali sono visibili nel museo di Grosseto, . . . " To my knowledge, in his own publications Szilágyi has specified only one piece as being in Grosseto, the alabastron listed above (no. 12). The oinochoe, now Florence 97645 (above, no. 2), was, according to Martelli (1977), 4, col. 2, provisionally housed in Grosseto before being transferred to Florence. I have not visited Grosseto, but Szilágyi's language makes one wonder whether there may be in Grosseto further pieces attributable to the Painter.

The olpai and the oinochoai are to be regarded as the Feoli Painter's major works. As Martelli has noted, the two oinochoai are his earliest pieces, and the olpe, Florence 3729 (no. 9), is evidently his latest. The Dechter olpe is described above, and the vase in London (no. 3) was described in sufficient detail in the article already cited. The olpe in Munich (no. 4), however, deserves some fresh notes. It is published by Sieveking and Hackl (pl. 8, no. 641) in a view which clearly enough reveals the hand of the artist, but does not do full justice to the vase.[9] This olpe suffered severe damage in World War II, but the surviving fragments have been carefully gathered and reassembled, with the results that appear in Pl. 3, Figs. 5–7. Very little of the frieze decoration has been lost:

> In the top frieze, a lion bites into the rump of a goat; between them is a small bird; after these, a large gap.[10]
>
> In the second frieze: lion to left, small bird to left, ram to right, bird to right, griffin to right, panther to right, small seated panther with forepaw raised, confronted sphinxes, between them a small bird, under sphinx at right a small owl.
>
> In the lowest frieze are a lion, panther, boar, griffin, confronted bulls, between these last a bird standing on a branch-like ornament; in the field a small owl, a lizard (seen from above) and a snake, each of these last two biting the tail of a quadruped.

All of these vases bear the characteristic traits of an artist with strangely hypnotic powers. Partly, this effect is derived from conventional subjects treated in unconventional ways. But there is also weird subject matter, like the gorgon[11] on the olpe in London (no. 3); the centaurs of unusual form and activity on that vase and on the olpe in Vulci (no. 5); the lizard and the snake stretched out horizontally above the animals in the lowest frieze of the Munich olpe (no. 4); and in the human figures ("Theseus and Ariadne") in the top frieze of the olpe in Turin (no. 8). In his densely packed friezes, the artist has created his own world of fantasy and imagination, a bizarre wonderland of creatures about which, one could suppose, strange stories exist or could easily spring into being. In this atmosphere, the Dechter olpe seems very much at home.

The Cambridge alabastron

The second vase to be presented is an alabastron in Cambridge (Pl. 4, Figs. 8–10)[12] which seems very near the work of the Feoli Painter. Also, it is very close to that Painter's close companion, the American Academy Painter (formerly called the "Warrior Painter"), who is introduced and discussed in my two articles.[13] On this vase there is an elaborate quasi-floral pattern of highly schematized, vertically opposed lotuses, between a seated sphinx and a seated lion; in the field there are several large rosettes with simple criss-cross incision. There is much added color, including rows of white dots, as on the American Academy Painter's "warrior" alabastron in London.[14] The lion may be compared especially with those on an alabastron once in the Philadelphia market.[15] Indeed, I was at one time tempted to believe that the Cambridge vase was decorated by the American Academy Painter, but Szilágyi (*per litteras*) has convinced me that this cannot be so. Another of its most noteworthy features is, as has been said, its close likeness to the style of the Feoli Painter,[16] reinforcing our previously formed impression that these two artists are very close to each other.

The list of attributions to the American Academy Painter continues to grow rapidly. The original nucleus, published in 1965, consisted only of two alabastra and, provisionally, a plate; by 1967 there were seven alabastra, an aryballos and, still provisionally, a plate.[17] Szilágyi, in the article already cited, and in a still more recent study,[18] has added many new attributions. I do not know all of the pieces listed by him, but his decisions concerning the attribution to Etrusco-Corinthian vase-painters of pieces known to me agree so closely with mine that, *pro tempore,* I feel much inclined to accept the others on faith.[19] If this premise is allowed, we then had, as of 1972, a grand total of thirty vases attributed to the American Academy Painter. Furthemore, Szilágyi and I have independently agreed on the attribution of three more examples, plates from the Bryn Mawr excavations at Murlo which will eventually be housed in La Sala Marcolina, Palazzo Comunale, Siena (nos. 71–726/727, 71–777, and 71–778).[20]

Thus, from a small beginning made scarcely more than a decade ago, the American Academy Painter's known oeuvre has grown to a substantial body of works which clearly define the nature of his activity and, at the same time, provide important interlocking contextual associations with a much wider range of Etrusco-Corinthian art. The same can be said of the works attributed to the Feoli Painter. In this setting, the Cambridge alabastron (to the decorator of which attributions of other vases should be forthcoming) fittingly finds its place as a strong link between these two leading artists of the Vulcian school of Etrusco-Corinthian vase-painting.

The pace of scholarship in Etrusco-Corinthian studies has quickened, and the body of materials brought to notice has expanded, to such an extent that only by the most intensive specialization could one keep abreast of all new developments. The present contribution is only a modest footnote to the massive investigations that are being carried out by Szilágy and our Italian colleagues. Yet it does add something of value, I hope, to our knowledge of the particular ambience of the two Painters whose works are considered here. The relationships among the various artists in the region of the Feoli Painter and the American Academy Painter are still somewhat obscure, but they are gradually becoming clearer. Some observations of mine,[21] so far as they go, seem to be in reasonably close agreement with those of Szilágyi,[22] who has, however, treated the questions more broadly and more searchingly, with some refinement of the criteria for attributions to individual hands, and has firmly fixed the home of this school of vase-painting at Vulci.

To recapitulate briefly, and within the narrow scope of the present article: the Feoli Painter and the American Academy Painter are companion artists, closely related to each other, and to another remarkable artist, the Carnage Painter ("Pittore dei Caduti").[23] From this tight cluster of leaders we can look sidewise toward the Pescia Romana Painter[24] as an allied figure working in the black-polychrome technique, and downward (in quality) toward the

Bobuda Painter[25] as a routine decorator of alabastra who weakly initates the style of the American Academy Painter. The more talented practicioners in this school of Etrusco-Corinthian vase-painting, as they become better known, produce increasingly the impression of a lively and at times richly inventive company of artists.

NOTES

1 The photographs reproduced here in Pl. 2, Figs. 1–4 were made by Dietrich Widmer; they are published through the kindness of Dr. Herbert Cahn, who brought the vase to my attention. My thanks are due also to Dr. F.W. Hamdorf (Munich, Antikensammlungen und Glyptothek) for permission to publish the olpe illustrated in Pl. 3, Figs. 5–7, and to Professor R.M. Cook for information and permission to publish the alabastron shown in Pl. 4, Figs. 8–10. It is a pleasure also to aknowledge my indebtedness, for favours applying to the present study, to the late Professor Luisa Banti, to Dr. Klaus Vierneisel, to Dr. Janos Szilágyi, and to Dr. Marina Martelli. In this article, the following abbreviations are used: Amyx (1965) = Darrell A. Amyx, "Some Etrusco-Corinthian Vase-Painters," in *Studi in Onore di Luisa Banti,* Rome 1965, 1–14 and pls. 1–5; Amyx (1967) = *idem,* "The Mingor Painter and Others: Etrusco-Corinthian Addenda," *StEtr* 35, 1967, 89–111 and pls. 35–40; Martelli (1977) = Marina Martelli, "Per il pittore di Feoli," *Prospettiva: Rivista di Storia dell'arte antica e moderna,* Florence, no. 11, Oct. 1977, 2–12 and Figs. 1–26; Szilágyi (1968) = Janos György Szilágyi, "Remarques sur les vases etrusco-conrinthiens de l'exposition etrusque a Vienne," *ArchCl* 20, 1968, 1–23 and pls. 1–14; Szilágyi (1975) = *idem, Etruszko-Korinthosi Vázafestészet,* Budapest 1975; Szilágyi (1976) = *idem,* "Entwurf der Geschichte der etrusko-korinthischen figürlichen Vasenmalerei", in Andreas Alföldi (ed.), *Römische Frühgeschichte: Kritik und Forschung seit 1964,* Heidelberg 1966, Chapter 10, 183–193 and pls. 5–16; Szilágyi (1977) = *idem,* "Considerazioni sulla ceramica etrusco-corinzia di Vulci: risultati e problemi," in *La civiltà arcaica di Vulci e la sua espansione: Atti del X. Convegno di Studi Etruschi ed Italici,* Florence 1977, 51–63 and pls. 15–21.

2 Height to lip: 0.354–358; height to top of rotelles: 0.378–383; max. diameter: 0.205; mouth diameter: 0.182; base diameter: 0.128. Mended and skilfully repaired; restored areas in plaster tinted to color of ground. Irregularly applied black glaze, added red and white, incision for details. Ovoid body, flaring neck, rolled-out mouth, triple-rolled handle flanked above rim by disk-like rotelles. Reserved band on edge of lip, red band inside mouth. On body, three animal friezes, with black-polychrome bands between; white dot-cluster rosettes on neck. At base of body, rays.

3 Listed, Amyx (1965), p. 6, under no. 4. Further bibliography in new list, herein, no. 6.

4 Amyx (1967), 95 f.

5 Szilágyi (1968), 19 note 50.

6 Szilágyi (1975), in Hungarian. For help in translating certain passages in this book, I am much indebted to Ili Lattimore. A fuller work, with complete lists of attributions, to be published in a western European language, is promised. I am glad to yield to Szilágyi's insistence on the name, "Feoli Painter" instead of "Mingor Painter", not so much for the reason given by him (1975, 252 note 16), that the word "Mingor" sounds grotesque and outlandish (for are not the Painter's style and choice of subject matter strange enough?), but rather because Szilágyi, as the fully established "custodian" of Etrusco-Corinthian studies, should be the one to settle on the names for the various Painters.

7 Szilágyi (1976) and (1977).

8 Martelli (1977).

9 A back view of the vase (in its present condition) is illustrated in three of Szilágyi's recent publications: see bibliography in list.

10 Damage to this part of the vase antedates World War II. According to Sieveking and Hackl, two animals

in this frieze were already missing in 1912. In Otto Jahn's Catalogue (*Beschreibung der Vasensammlung*, Berlin 1854), the frieze is described as complete, with a deer and a panther in addition to the now surviving animals.

11 On horned Gorgons (Amyx 1967, 90 f. and note 12), I should have noticed the article by Werner Herrmann, 'Gorgo und Acheloos.' *RM* 70, 1963, 1–3.

12 Cambridge University, Museum of Classical Archaeology, no. 137. Height: 0.173; diameter 0.096; diameter of mouth 0.047. "Buff clay, darker than Corinthian" (R.M. Cook).

13 Amyx (1965), 10; *idem* (1967), 98 f. (with list of attributions); Szilágyi, "Le fabbriche di ceramica etrusco-corinzia a Tarquinia", *StEtr* 40, 1972 (hereafter cited as Szilágyi 1972), Appendice, 71–73 (with a much longer list of attributions). Brief notes also appear in Szilágyi (1975), 93–97; *idem* (1976), 185; and *idem* (1977), 56 f. Again, I gladly yield to Szilágyi on the choice of a name for the Painter, since, as he rightly remarks (1972, p. 32 note 16) confusion with the Corinthian "Warrior Group" might result from the use of the name "Warrior Painter".

14 Amyx (1967), 98, no. 1 and pl. 39, a–d.

15 *Ibid.*, no. 3; *Hesperia Art Bulletin* No. 36, No. A–4 (illustrated).

16 Compare the sphinx with those on the Feoli Painter's alabastra in Berkeley and Würzburg (above, nos. 10 and 11). The lion is also similar to that Painter's lions: for example, compare it with those on the Dechter olpe, Pl. , Figs. 1–4. See also Szilágyi (1975), 104, where the Cambridge alabastron is said to be closely related to the work of the Feoli Painter.

17 Amyx (1965), 10; *idem* (1967), 98 f.

18 Szilágyi (1968), 19, note 49; *idem* (1972: *supra*, note 13), 71–73.

19 I am still hesitant to accept his (1972) nos. 1, 19 and 27 (kylix, Cambridge, Fitzwilliam GR 1.1971; alabastra, Oxford, Ashmolean, Queens College loan, no. 8, and (lost?) Photo: R.I., Neg. 32–1216) which Szilágyi himself had at first (1968) set apart as works of a different but closely related artist. However, it may be that some of the newly attributed vases, unknown to me, serve to bring these pieces more surely within the Painter's canon.

20 K.M. Phillips Jr., "Bryn Mawr College Excavations in Tuscany, 1972", *AJA* 77, 1973, 323 f. and pl. 57, figs. 10–11; E. Nielsen and K.M. Phillips Jr., "Bryn Mawr College Excavations in Tuscany, 1973", *AJA* 78, 1974, 271 and pl. 56, figs. 8–9.

21 Amyx (1967), 99 f.

22 Szilágyi (1968), 18–20. See also his basic study of Etrusco-Corinthian black-polychrome vases in "Die Griechische Vase", *Wissenschaftliche Zeitschrift der Universität Rostock,* 16, 1967, 543–553, especially 549, on the Pescia Romana Painter, and his further observations in his more recent article (1972: *supra* note 13), 28–34. In his new book (1975), Chapter II (pp. 25–30) is devoted to black-polychrome vases.

23 Amyx (1965), 6 f.; *idem* (1967), 106; Szilágyi (1972: *supra* note 13), 91–93 (list); brief notice, *idem* (1977), 56 f. Another vase-painter who was active at Vulci, the Bearded Sphinx Painter, has gained many new attributions through the researches of F. Zevi, "Nuovi vasi del Pittore della Sfinge Barbuta", *StEtr* 37, 1969, 39–58 and pls. 14–26, and fig. 1. The olpe in Melbourne, no. 15 in Zevi's list, is also published in A.D. Trendall, *Greek Vases in the Felton Collection*, Melbourne 1968, 30 f., note 1 and pl. 10. For still more new discoveries concerning this Painter's work and his orbit, see G. Colonna, "Vulci: Tomba del Pittore della Sfinge Barbuta", in Mario Moretti (ed.), *Nuovi tesori dell' antica Tuscia*, Exhibition Catalogue, *Associazione Tuscia*. Viterbo 1970, 34–41, especially nos. 20–21. In the same tomb were found, incidentally, a kylix and a plate (nos. 26–27, not illustrated), which Colonna associates, respectively, with the American Academy Painter (Szilágyi 1972: *supra* note 13, p. 72 no. 2) and the Feoli Painter. On the Bearded Sphinx Painter and his surroundings, see further Szilágyi (1975), 31–56 and (briefly) *idem* (1976), 186.

24 On the Pescia Romana Painter: Amyx (1965), 9 f.; *idem* (1967), 107; Szilágyi, *opp. citt.* (*supra,* note 22); *idem* (1975), 28 f.; *idem* (1976), 185; and *idem* (1977), 55 f.

25 On the Bobuda Painter (and Boduda Group): Amyx (1965), 11 f.; *idem* (1967), 107.; Szilágyi (1975), 202–205; *idem* (1976), 171.

UNA IDRIA INEDITA CON RILIEVI E LA FABBRICA DELLE 'PLAKETTENVASEN'*

Giuseppe Andreassi

Tavole 5, 6.

Diversamente da altri gruppi, anche ristretti, di ceramiche antiche, che sono correntemente intesi nella letteratura archeologica come 'classi', grazie soprattutto ai cataloghi ed agli studi specifici ad essi dedicati, alle cosiddette Plakettenvasen[1] è sempre stato riservato un interesse piuttosto labile, sicché tuttora siamo in una condizione di notevole incertezza conoscitiva.[2] Non essendo possibile in questa sede elencarne tutti gli esemplari noti, né affrontare l'articolata problematica che vi si lega, cercheremo almeno di portare un contributo chiarificatore al controverso problema del luogo di produzione di tale ceramica, muovendo dalla conoscenza di una idria inedita, di eccezionali caratteristiche, che si trova attualmente a Bassano del Grappa nella collezione Chini,[3] e di cui pertanto si dà subito la scheda analitica (Figg. 1—4).

Altezza restaurata m.0,525; alt. conservata 0,465 circa; diametro del labbro 0,200.

Argilla ben depurata compatta, bruno-grigiastra. Vernice opaca a superficie scabra, di un grigio scuro metallico, ma tendenzialmente olivastra sul ventre; molto diluita e a tratti assente sotto il labbro e all'interno.

Il fondo del vaso è in parte rotto, con la rottura visibile dall'interno, mentre il piede è completamente rifatto in gesso. La vernice è variamente screpolata, specie sulle parti plastiche. Sono caduti in gran parte il rosa e il bianco sovrapposto al viola.

Corpo ovoidale rigonfio in alto; una risega sulla spalla segna lo stacco del collo, che ha profilo concavo con due coppie di scanalature alle estremità e due borchie coniche ai lati dell'attacco superiore dell'ansa verticale; labbro sporgente e revoluto, con la faccia superiore leggermente obliqua e incavata che sporge su quella discendente, su cui è una leggera scanalatura al margine inferiore. Anse laterali a sezione circolare e ripiegate verso l'alto, quella di destra impostata alquanto più in basso dell'altra; la superficie, liscia nel tratto rivolto verso la spalla, è per il resto irregolarmente scanalata, mentre al centro si avvolge ad anello un nastro con due scanalature, assenti sulla parte più bassa; gli attacchi sono segnati, ai lati e in basso, da cinque lamelle a margine arrotondato e incavate al centro. L'ansa sul retro è costituita da un triplice cordone ritorto, sulla cui estremità inferiore è applicata una testa femminile di prospetto (altezza circa 0,040 x 0,030) a rilievo piuttosto alto: porta un elmo, da cui ciocche di capelli sfuggono sulle tempie verso l'alto, mentre capelli più lunghi sembra che fluiscano ai lati del volto; probabilmente si tratta di un'Atena (Fig. 8).

Sulla parte superiore del corpo sono applicate cinque placchette a basso rilievo, tre più grandi sulla fronte e due sul retro, tutte completamente verniciate.

Giovane cacciatore (alt. ca. 0,165 x 0,100) (Fig. 5): di tre quarti a destra, sembra poggiato ad un rialzo del terreno, visibile a sinistra delle gambe, che s'incrociano in posizione di riposo; il corpo è robusto, con gli arti, specie le braccia, molto allungati; sulle spalle ricade la clamide, fissata con una borchia sotto il collo: nella destra abbassata tiene un piccolo oggetto di ardua identificazione; con la sinistra tocca il muso di un cane che, volto nella sua stessa direzione, gli è accovacciato davanti sulle zampe posteriori, con quella anteriore sinistra e la testa sollevate.

Leone di profilo a destra (alt. ca. 0,075 x 0,135) (Fig. 7): ha la testa volta di tre quarti all'indietro, la coda ripiegata verso l'alto, la zampa posteriore sinistra avanzata e sollevata quella anteriore dello stesso lato, che in origine doveva afferrare qualcosa, stando anche alla piccola zona liscia e depressa che vi rimane in corrispondenza.

Figura femminile seduta su roccia (alt. ca. 0,155 x 0,085) (Fig. 6): di tre quarti a sinistra, indossa un chitone trasparente che scivola lungo il braccio destro lasciando scoperto un seno, mentre l'himation, che ella trattiene con la mano sinistra poggiata sulla roccia e solleva con la destra, le doveva coprire le spalle e forse il capo, dove un ciuffo di capelli sfugge sulla tempia destra.

Figura maschile in atteggiamento di danza (alt. ca. 0,140 x 0,070) (Fig. 9): nuda, di tre quarti a sinistra, con la gamba destra arretrata; sulle spalle ricade il mantello, che si avvolge intorno al braccio sinistro abbassato a reggere un bastone, mentre il destro è sollevato con la mano semiaperta; dalla massa dei capelli sfuggono lunghi riccioli ai lati del collo (ma almeno in parte saranno difetti d'impressione).

Coppia di figure (alt. ca. 0,130 x 0, 080) (Fig. 10): entrambe in vivace movimento verso destra e retrospicienti; precede la donna, a capo scoperto e vestita del chitone, che regge con la sinistra un grande scudo, di cui si vede parte del profilo ricurvo, e protende il braccio destro, come a indicare qualcosa, dietro la testa dell'uomo. Questi, che in parte copre la figura femminile, è barbato e reca sul capo il pileo, da cui fuoriescono lateralmente ciocche di capelli; indossa l'*exomis*, che gli lascia scoperta la metà destra del petto, ed un mantello che è poggiato sul braccio sinistro e gli svolazza dietro le spalle (il panneggio più in basso, invece, si riferirà all'abito della donna); il braccio sinistro è flesso, con in mano il fodero della spada, che doveva essere impugnata con la mano destra rivolta in basso e verso l'esterno, e alla quale si riferirebbero i resti di rilievo al margine della placchetta. Da intendere probabilmente come Atena e Odisseo.

Il corpo del vaso è percorso da fitte solcature verticali, ad eccezione della parte superiore della spalla e di quella inferiore del ventre. Tale 'baccellatura' è stata eseguita a stecca senza eccessiva regolarità (specie sulla parte inferiore) dall'alto verso il basso, dopo l'applicazione delle anse e delle placchette; essa non presenta alcun segno di delimitazione in alto, sicché le estremità dei solchi non vengono ad esservi rigorosamente allineate, mentre al margine inferiore una radicale lisciatura a stecca determina una netta risega di confine; essa è inoltre interrotta da fasce piane sia in senso verticale in corrispondenza delle anse, dove sono sovrapposti due gruppi di tre solcature divergenti, con le due esterne curve nei gruppi più in alto, sia in senso orizzontale, circa a metà del corpo, dove due leggere solcature tracciate preliminarmente avevano anche la funzione di linee-guida per quelle più profonde verticali.

Sulla fascia orizzontale, nell'ultima fase di esecuzione del vaso è stata aggiunta, così come sul collo, una decorazione in parte graffita e in parte dipinta, prevalentemente in un colore bianco tenace e compatto, con molte intrusioni che appaiono a rilievo nella stesura, ma pure con elementi in viola sul collo e in rosa-lilla, a quanto sembra, sulla fascia ventrale.

Su questa, variamente interrotta dalle placchette e bordata di punti bianchi, vi è un ramo di edera destrorso, con stelo graffito ondulato nei cui seni sono grandi foglie cuoriformi bianche collegate da piccioli graffiti leggermente ricurvi; alla base di ciascuna si trova, in posizione variabile e spesso sovrapposto alle parti graffite, un corimbo staccato bianco, costituito da un circolo esterno di punti ravvicinati o addirittura fusi tra loro che ne racchiudono un altro o altri pochi. Su alcuni corimbi e su alcuni tratti delle serie di punti ai margini sono i resti di dischetti (?) e di linee in rosa-lilla, forse destinati a ravvivare la decorazione senza particolare riferimento al disegno di base.

Alle due estremità del collo, fra due linee graffite al fondo delle scanalature, è ripetuto in bianco una specie di astragalo, formato da segmenti allungati che si alternano a coppie di punti e interrotto in alto dall'attacco superiore dell'ansa e dalle due borchie, in basso in corrispondenza dell'ansa. Sull'astragalo inferiore poggia un motivo costituito da una specie di fiori di loto stilizzati, in viola, alternati a triangoli, questi ultimi determinati da quattro angoli a lati paralleli, quello più esterno costituito da punti bianchi, i tre interni da linee graffite, con il triangolo di risulta bianco e lo spazio compreso tra le due linee graffite esterne dipinto in bianco su fondo viola.

Secondo una testimonianza piuttosto attendibile, l'idria si sarebbe trovata in una tomba rinvenuta nei dintorni di Oria,[4] città a metà strada fra Brindisi e Taranto.[5] Di tutte le Plakettenvasen finora conosciute,[6] quindi, l'esemplare Chini verrebbe ad essere il primo la cui provenienza da un centro dell'Italia meridionale poggi su informazioni non troppo remote, sì da apparire come un ulteriore elemento a favore dell'ultima ipotesi che sia stata avanzata riguardo al luogo di origine di questa ceramica: ipotesi rivolta appunto verso la Magna Grecia, anzi verso una fabbrica tarantina attiva da circa la metà del IV secolo fino agli inizi del III, e che avrebbe esportato i suoi prodotti anche in centri come Creta e Alessandria, dove pure diversi ne sono stati rinvenuti.

A queste conclusioni giungeva, agli inizi degli anni cinquanta, lo Züchner,[7] ripreso più o meno incidentalmente da altri autori: Mingazzini, Hausmann, Lullies, Greifenhagen.[8] Ma sono conclusioni fondate su basi che appaiono piuttosto fragili: da un lato il fatto che alcuni frammenti (Heidelberg 25.09, 27.05)[9] e un'idria (Berlino F 3838)[10] risultano acquistati rispettivamente a Taranto e a Napoli, dall'altro i caratteri stilistici o iconografici tarantini che sarebbero riscontrabili nell'Eros e nella monomachia di Heidelberg così come nell'Eracle stante del vaso di Berlino, e infine la forma delle anse laterali di tale ultimo pezzo. A questo punto, poiché gli stessi soggetti ritornano su altri vasi, lo Züchner prende l'avvio per combinare il materiale a lui noto in una specie di reticolo fondato sulla presenza anche incrociata di placchette desunte dalle stesse matrici. In tale reticolo confluiscono quindi vasi di provenienza sconosciuta o anche dichiaratamente diversa da quella magnogreca; ma i tre pezzi assunti come caposaldi topografici consentono all'autore di chiudere il cerchio — sono sue parole — con un'anfora di Bruxelles (A 1489),[11] su cui una placchetta con Atena presenterebbe ancora una volta caratteri stilistici puramente italioti.[12]

Se tutto ciò prova senz'altro l'omogeneità della produzione o almeno della maggior parte di essa, e l'appartenenza di questa ad un'unica fabbrica attiva in un arco di tempo limitato, non credo invece che l'indagine dello Züchner, con i suoi ridotti punti di partenza e con i suoi discutibili collegamenti sulla base delle placchette, possa garantire della sua localizzazione a Taranto.

Certo sono innegabili le affinità che legano l'idria Chini a quella di Berlino, così come ad una della Bibliothèque Nationale (381 A = Y 4861),[13] formando quasi un sottogruppo omogeneo di vasi contraddistinti, oltre tutto, da una stessa ricercatezza decorativa e morfologica. La placchetta col leone, infatti, è applicata nella stessa posizione al centro della fronte sull'idria berlinese, mentre il giovane danzante[14] si ripete due volte su quella di Parigi, e su entrambe ritorna il rilievo con Atena e Odisseo.[15] Non solo, ma nessuna di queste tre placchette, per quanto ne so, ricorre mai altrove, mentre del tutto isolato resta il cacciatore, e riappare solo su un'anfora di Atene (2144) la figura femminile seduta.[16]

Le tre idrie, inoltre, sono accomunate dalla particolarissima forma delle anse laterali, che costituirebbero per lo Züchner un'ulteriore prova dell'origine tarantina delle Plakettenvasen.[17] In realtà, se è vero che anse non molto dissimili ricorrono su vasi apuli, e specialmente su idrie,[18] ciò non implica necessariamente un rapporto di dipendenza da quelli, mentre mi sembra più credibile una comune derivazione, con una più marcata libertà interpretativa nel caso delle Plakettenvasen, da un gruppo omogeneo di idrie in bronzo della seconda metà del IV secolo, caratterizzate altresì dall'aggiunta di un rilievo figurato nella parte posteriore.[19]

Quanto al manico tortile, ha tutta l'aria di essere stato mutuato dall'anfora, il più comune fra i vasi con placchette, su cui infatti le anse sono senza eccezioni di questa forma, ripresa evidentemente da un tipo di anfora attica a figure rosse;[20] ma tale imprestito non deve aver riscosso particolare successo, se è vero che ricorre soltanto sul vaso Chini e su quello di Berlino,[21] nonché su poche altre idrie, tutte o in massima parte di origine alessandrina.[22]

Gli esemplari di Berlino e di Bassano si staccano dalla massa delle Plakettenvasen anche per una particolarità della decorazione dipinta; sul collo, infatti, non è ripetuto il solito ramo di edera[23] ed anzi, mentre sul primo vi è pur sempre un tralcio orizzontale, su quello Chini[24] è attestato l'unico disegno di non immediata ispirazione vegetale. Se per tale motivo a triangoli non mi è stato possibile trovare confronti puntuali, pure è innegabile una certa consonanza con quelli dipinti su alcune idrie di Hadra[25] e in genere su vasi alessandrini,[26] tanto da farlo supporre derivato dalla commistione di particolari forme dei motivi ad ovoli e a triangoli piuttosto bene attestati per quelle ceramiche.[27]

Il vaso Chini, infine, si distingue per l'aggiunta, accanto al bianco, del rosa e del viola, un'associazione di colori che non trova finora riscontro nelle Plakettenvasen, ma che potrebbe essere assimilata a quella che si nota, e in abbinamento al rilievo, su di un ristretto numero di coppe con medaglione riferite a fabbrica prima alessandrina ed ora cretese.[28] Questi due colori sono anche sconosciuti alle ceramiche verniciate apule del primo ellenismo,[29] su cui anzi è completamente diverso, per tono e per consistenza, lo stesso frequentissimo colore bianco, o bianco-giallo; una divergenza che si aggiunge a quelle verificabili per la qualità ed il colore della vernice.

Tali caratteristiche tecniche non sono contraddette da quelle risultanti per le altre Plakettenvasen, e semmai trovano conferma in quanto altre volte osservato a proposito della ceramica alessandrina,[30] sicché non credo che su di esse possa prevalere, per una attribuzione a fabbrica apula, l'asserita provenienza da Oria dell'idria di Bassano. A questo proposito, invece, sembra essenziale rivedere le pur lacunose notizie disponibili sulla provenienza degli altri vasi con placchette. Se infatti una grossa percentuale ne è stata dispersa dal commercio antiquario, sicché nei cataloghi e negli inventari non si trovano mai, almeno esplicitamente, le indicazioni degli scopritori, è pur vero che per un certo numero di esemplari disponiamo di qualche sommario dato di scavo, o almeno possiamo essere certi del loro rinvenimento in un'area circoscritta; e sono proprio questi esemplari e queste notizie che lo Züchner non tiene in nessun conto.

Così per un'anfora dalla necropoli di Ialiso nell'isola di Rodi,[31] e per un'altra anfora e sei o sette frammenti recuperati o visti dal Savignoni nelle campagne della parte occidentale di Creta;[32] così soprattutto per almeno una diecina di pezzi provenienti dalle necropoli alessandrine.[33] Di fronte a questa documentazione, anche a voler trascurare i rimandi che altre volte si trovano agli stessi o ad altri luoghi, come Milo o la Cirenaica, la provenienza apula anche di quattro pezzi diventa percentualmente assai piccola cosa; ma insieme diventa meno strana l'assenza finora, nei pur numerosi scavi documentati della regione, di vasi del genere.[34]

Né mi pare che la carenza di documentazione locale possa spiegarsi pensando che la supposta fabbrica tarantina riservasse la produzione di Plakettenvasen a mercati più lontani. È nota infatti la forza penetrativa del commercio e della cultura apula nella seconda metà del IV secolo, testimoniata, per quanto ci riguarda, dal rinvenimento in diversi centri dell'Egeo e del vicino oriente di ceramica a figure rosse e soprattutto del tipo di Gnathia.[35] Ma per quello che finora se ne conosce, si tratta appunto sempre di vasi che rientrano in quelle vaste produzioni di serie che sono ben più largamente diffuse nella stessa regione apula.

Nel caso dell'idria Chini, invece, e in generale delle Plakettenvasen, sembra che tutta una serie di indizi, nella morfologia e nell'apparato decorativo così come nelle caratteristiche tecniche, riportino ad Alessandria; ed essi, sommati alla documentata provenienza alessandrina di un numero percentualmente alto di esemplari, inducono a localizzare in quel centro la fabbrica, senza con ciò negare gli stimoli e le suggestioni derivate da altri ambienti, e in particolare dall'Attica e dall'Apulia. Disporremmo così, per quanto riguarda l'inizio della produzione, di un riferimento cronologico meno vago di quello proposto dallo Züchner su basi essenzialmente stilistiche, trattandosi del 'terminus a quo' costituito dalla data di fondazione di Alessandria (inverno 332/331), cui sarà soltanto da aggiungere il lasso di tempo, non lungo, necessario per l'avvio di una normale attività produttiva.

Tale soluzione, del resto, non fa che riprendere, anticipando conclusioni che potranno essere meglio fondate in altra sede, quella che era stata l'opinione dei primi autori interessatisi all'argomento, dal Merriam al Furtwängler al Pagenstecher,[36] accolta spesso anche in seguito, ma senza ulteriori approfondimenti.[37] Le due proposte alternative, quella del Courby[38] favorevole a Creta e quella tarantina dello Züchner, sebbene, o forse proprio perché risultate da due fra gli studi più ampi sulla ceramica di derivazione metallica, sembrano viziate entrambe da un equivoco di fondo, in quanto in ambedue i casi viene sopravvalutata l'importanza dei rilievi al fine dell'individuazione della fabbrica dei vasi.

Se è vero infatti che alcuni soggetti ben s'inseriscono per iconografia o stile nell'ambiente cretese, ed altri altrettanto bene in quello magnogreco, già solo questa duplicità di caratteri dovrebbe indurre alla prudenza, così come, per esempio, la stessa meraviglia dello Züchner di fronte alla placchetta con la donna stante e a quella con Atena e Odisseo sull'idria di Berlino, in base al cui stile appunto, egli riconosce che non avrebbe osato arguire l'origine tarantina del pezzo.[39]

Dove che collochino la fabbrica delle Plakettenvasen, su un punto ovviamente tutti gli autori sono d'accordo, che i rilievi non erano originariamente creati per i vasi, ma ottenuti calcando più pregiate creazioni della toreutica. Per cui, anche avendo individuato su basi stilistiche o iconografiche l'ambiente di origine dei rilievi, si sarà al massimo accertato il luogo dove erano stati attivi i toreuti, e non quello dove operavano i figuli.[40] Per risolvere quest'ultimo problema saranno molto più utili, come rapidamente si è cercato di mostrare, le indicazioni ricavate dai dati di scavo e dalle caratteristiche tecniche, così come quelle risultate dall'esame della forma o della decorazione dipinta, che non essendo soggette alla riproduzione meccanica attraverso matrici, tradiranno più facilmente la genuina posizione del fabbricante.

NOTE

* Per le opere piu frequentemente citate si fa uso delle seguenti abbreviazioni: Breccia = E. Breccia, *La Necropoli di Sciatbi (Catalogue général des Antiquités Égyptiennes – Musée d'Alexandrie)*, Le Caire 1912; Diehl = E. Diehl, *Die Hydria. Formgeschichte und Verwendung im Kult des Altertums*, Mainz 1964; Pagenstecher = R. Pagenstecher, *Die griechisch-ägyptische Sammlung Ernst von Sieglin (Expedition Ernst von Sieglin. Ausgrabungen in Alexandria, II:3)*, Leipzig 1913; Züchner = W. Züchner, 'Von Toreuten und Töpfern', *JdI* 65/66, 1950/51, 175–205.

1 Tale denominazione sembra ricorrere per la prima volta in R. Pagenstecher, *Die Calenische Reliefkeramik (JdI 8. Ergänzungsheft)*, Berlin 1909, 10, accanto ai termini 'Plakettenhydrien' (p. 173) e 'Plakettenreliefs' (p. 143), ed è adoperata correntemente a distanza di pochi anni dallo stesso Pagenstecher (1913, 53–57) in quella che è la prima trattazione di un certo respiro, e tuttora forse la più equilibrata, su questa ceramica.

2 Ai vasi con placchette era dedicata la mia tesi di perfezionamento presso la Scuola Nazionale di Archeologia dell'Universita di Roma (1975, in corso di pubblicazione).

3 La collezione, di cui è in corso ora il transferimento nel Museo Civico di Bassano, si trovava fino alla primavera del 1972 a Bari, dove ero stato incaricato dalla Soprintendenza alle Antichità della Puglia di redigerne l'elenco ai fini della sua notifica da parte del Ministero della Pubblica Istruzione (avvenuta poi con Decreto Ministeriale del 19.11.1971). Al prof. Virgilio Chini va la mia più profonda gratitudine per avermi sempre consentito con la massima liberalità di accedere alla sua raccolta e per avermene concesso i diritti di pubblicazione; un ringraziamento devo anche alla dr. R. Stazio Pulinas per avermi affidato la stesura dell'elenco di notifica, ed al prof. F.G. Lo Porto per avermi ceduto le fotografie della Soprintendenza, eseguite dal sig. G. Carrano (mie sono invece le foto dei particolari).

4 Ebbi modo di parlare a suo tempo con il sig. A. Calabrese (deceduto nel 1974), che aveva segnalato il pezzo all'attuale proprietario: egli avrebbe visto il vaso, ancora incrostato, in un casolare della campagna oritana, a quanto ricordasse con pochi altri vasi più piccoli, almeno in parte a vernice nera, tutti facenti parte di un medesimo corredo. Egli stesso aveva poi ricostruito il piede dell'idria, prendendo evidentemente a modello i vasi apuli che gli erano più familiari, mentre la forma originaria sarà stata quella propria di tutte le Plakettenvasen (per esempio Diehl, tav. 43, 2).

5   Cfr. N. Degrassi, 'Oria', in *EAA* V, Roma 1963, 748–749; A. Franco, *La raccolta archeologica Pasanisi,* Oria 1964.

6   So finora di almeno quarantuno anfore, diciannove idrie e quattro crateri, cui vanno aggiunti non meno di diciannove frammenti. Da questi totali sono esclusi vari pezzi noti solo da rapide descrizioni, nonché alcuni frammenti già riferiti a vasi con placchette, che mancano però di caratteristiche tali da garantirne la natura, come un rilievo già a Monaco (7642) con Dioniso e Arianna [W. Züchner, *Griechische Klapp-spiegel (JdI, 14. Ergänzungsheft),* Berlin 1942, 48, 203, fig. 92], uno a Bonn (190) con testa fra girali (Züchner 1950/51, 184–5, fig. 10) ed uno ora a Berlino Est (F 3876) col ratto di Ganimede [F. Courby, *Les vases grecs à reliefs* (Bibliothèque des Écoles Françaises d'Athènes et de Rome 125), Paris 1922, 212, fig. 34, 5]. Vi sono invece compresi quegli esemplari che, pur forniti solo di una ridotta decorazione plastica e dipinta, non possono tuttavia essere separati tipologicamente dalle vere e proprie Plaketten-vasen (cfr. nota 31).

7   Züchner, 182–192, e sopratutto 186, 188, 192. Ad una probabile importazione dall'Italia meridionale accennava già E. Breccia, 'Fouilles de Hadra', in *Rapport sur la marche du service du Musée en 1912,* 16–17; *idem, Alexandrea ad Aegyptum. Guide de la ville ancienne et moderne et du Musée Gréco-Romain,* Bergamo 1914, 237 (ed. inglese, Bergamo 1922, 224), che in seguito, però, avrebbe aderito alla tesi della fabbrica alessandrina (*idem, Le Musée Gréco-Romain* 1925–1931, 35).

8   P. Mingazzini, 'Tre brevi note di ceramica ellenistica', *ArchCl* 10, 1958, 219–220; U. Hausmann, *Hellenistische Reliefbecher aus attischen und böotischen Werkstätten. Untersuchungen zur Zeitstellung und Bildüberlieferung,* Stuttgart 1959, 26–27; R. Lullies, *Vergoldete Terrakotta-Appliken aus Tarent (RM, 7. Ergänzungsheft,* Heidelberg 1962), 41; A. Greifenhagen, *Beiträge zur antiken Reliefkeramik (JdI, 21. Ergänzungsheft,* Berlin 1963), 48.

9   Züchner 185–186, fig. 11; 186, fig. 13.

10 Dopo Züchner, 186–191, figg. 14–18, cfr. A. Greifenhagen (*supra* nota 8), 1, nota 3. È forse sfuggita allo Züchner una vecchia notizia, di cui in effetti si è persa traccia nella bibliografia successiva e che risale a Th. Panofka, in E. Gerhard, 'Allgemeines', *AZ* n.s. 2, 1848, n. 13, col. 203 (nota 20), per cui il vaso sarebbe stato scavato ad Egnazia; una provenienza che avrebbe ancor più fatto il gioco della sua tesi tarantina, ma che comunque riterrei sospetta, in quanto riferita ad un centro che è eponimo di un tipo di ceramica sovraddipinta con cui l'idria potrebbe essere stata facilmente confusa.

11 F. Mayence e V. Verhoogen, *CVA* Bruxelles 3, Bruxelles 1949, IB, IIIN, tav. 2, 19 a–d; Züchner, 191–192.

12 Invero a questo punto lo Züchner s'impone d'interrompere le sue riflessioni, che andrebbero continuate soltanto — egli afferma — sulla base del materiale che si trova in Grecia, e specialmente nel Museo Nazionale di Atene. Mentre però, almeno sulla base dei pezzi già noti a G. Nicole, *Catalogue des vases peints du Musée National d'Athènes. Supplément,* Paris 1911 (nn. 1273–1275, 1277, 1278, 1280–1283) e dei quali nuove fotografie mi ha inviato la Direzione del Museo, il quadro delle Plakettenvasen resta immutato nella sostanza, va detto che nella sua apertura finale sul materiale di Grecia lo Züchner è stato frainteso da K. Parlasca, 'Das Verhältnis der Megarischen Becher zum alexandrinischen Kunst-handwerk', *JdI* 70, 1955, 149, e da J. Schäfer, *Hellenistische Keramik aus Pergamon (Pergamenische Forschungen 2),* Berlin 1968, 7, 66, che ne fanno un sostenitore della produzione attica dei vasi con placchette.

13 Züchner, 189; Diehl, T415, pp. 45, 235, tav. 43, 2.

14 Originariamente un satiro: cfr. W. Züchner (*supra* nota 6), KS 45, pp. 37–38, tav. 11, e sopratutto il più tardo frammento di vaso pergameno J. Schäfer (*supra* nota 12), E 4, pp. 74, 95, tav. 22.

15 Se si fa eccezione da E. Gerhard, *Neuerworbene antike Denkmäler des Königlichen Museums zu Berlin* III, Berlin 1846, n. 1968, p. 102, che credeva di riconoscervi uno scita e un'amazzone, è questa l'inter-pretazione che, per quanto dubitativa, si trova già espressa da Th. Panofka (*supra* nota 10).

16 Cfr. G. Nicole (*supra* nota 12), n. 1273, p. 291, che però scambia la donna con un Eracle seduto. La protome sotto l'ansa tortile del vaso Chini sembra invece ricavata da una stessa matrice con una delle teste sull'anfora ateniese 2142 (cfr. *ibidem*, n. 1275, p. 292).

17 Egli si fonda per questo su K.A. Neugebauer, 'Reifarchaische Bronzevasen mit Zungenmuster', *RM* 38/39, 1923/24, 430.

18 E. Pernice, *Gefässe und Geräte aus Bronze* (*Die hellenistische Kunst in Pompeji* IV), Berlin-Leipzig 1925, 15–16, fig. 21; P. Jacobstahl, *Ornamente griechischer Vasen,* Berlin 1927, tav. 111. K.Schauenburg, 'Bendis in Unteritalien ? Zu einer Nestoris von ungewöhnlicher Form', *JdI* 89, 1974, figg. 1–4, Ma si veda pure un'idria alessandrina a Monaco (6024), con decorazione a rilievo e sovraddipinta: A.Di Vita 'Un nuovo vaso dalla necropoli alessandrina di Hadra', *BdA* 41, 1956, 99–100, 102–103, figg. 5–6; L. Guerrini, *Vasi di Hadra. Tentativo di sistemazione cronologica di una classe ceramica* (*Studi Miscellanei* 8), Roma 1964, F 22, pp. 19–20, tav. X.

19 Ch. Picard, 'Trois urnes cinéraires sculptées du Musée Condé à Chantilly', *MonPiot* 37, 1940, 73–103, tavv. VI–VIII; G.M.A. Richter, 'A Fourth-Century Bronze Hydria in New York', *AJA* 50, 1946, 361–367, tavv. XXII–XXVIII.

20 Richter-Milne, tipo IIb, p. 4, figg. 20, 22–23.

21 L'ansa posteriore è nastriforme, con ampie solcature, sull'idria della Bibliothèque Nationale. Non era pertinente l'ansa a tortiglione che risultava da una vecchia foto per la hydria ZV 2600 G1 della Skulpturensammlung di Dresda: già citata da Pagenstecher, 55, ne devo l'ulteriore conoscenza al Dr. H. Protzmann.

22 Idrie di Hadra a decorazione monocroma: Breccia, n. 65, tav. XL, 52; n. 66, p. 38, no. 67, tav. XLI, 54 (tortili anche le anse laterali); n. 69, tav. XLI, 56; n. 74, p. 41; A. Adriani, 'Alexandrie. Nécropole de Ezbet El Makhlouf', *Annales du Musée Gréco-Romain* 1935/39, 113, fig. 48, 1; B.F. Cook, *Inscribed Hadra Vases in the Metropolitan Museum of Art* (*The Metropolitan Museum of Art Papers* 12), New York 1966, n. 16, fig. a, p. 27; K.T. Luckner, *The Toledo Museum of Art, The Art of Egypt* 2, s.d.e., testo a, fig. 18. Inoltre l'insolito esemplare CA 3138 del Louvre: F. Villard, *Les vases grecs,* Paris 1956, 88, 110, tav. XXXII, 2.

23 Su un'idria da Alessandria, invece, anch'essa contraddistinta da alcune particolarità morfologiche, al ramo di edera sul collo è sovrapposta una fascia con spirali e piccoli rami penduli: Pagenstecher, pp. 54–55, 57, fig. 59.

24 Su entrambi le serie di punti sono sostituite dall'astragalo.

25 Vedi sopratutto L. Guerrini (*supra* nota 18), F12; nonché, per esempio, Breccia, n. 78, fig. 32 (anfora con anse tortili); L. Guerrini, (*supra* nota 18), B24, B29, C3, D26, F4; B.F. Cook (*supra* nota 22), n. 8, tav. II; n. 11, tav. III.

26 Si vedano almeno le due pissidi con decorazione geometrizzante bicroma Breccia, n. 87, pp. 45–47, tav. XLV, 64, e p. 47, fig. 34, e forse la bottiglia Pagenstecher, 26, fig. 33.

27 Una interessante e rara varietà di kyma ionico, in cui gli ovoli si alternano a piccoli elementi trifidi discendenti si trova anche su alcuni tardi vasi di Gnathia: L. Forti, *La ceramica di Gnathia* (*Monumenti antichi della Magna Grecia* II), Napoli 1965, tavv. XXIII, c, e XXVI, d.

28 I colori usati sono rosa, celeste, bianco e rosa salmone: V. Hadjimichali, 'Recherches à Latô, III', *BCH* 95, 1971, 204–208, figg. 40–42. Secondo C. Watzinger, 'Recensione a R. Pagentescher, *Die Calenische Reliefkeramik*', *Berliner Philologische Wochenschrift* 30, 1910, col. 725, i colori tenui (rosa, celeste, viola) possono ritenersi caratteristici di Alessandria, e per influsso alessandrino sarebbero passati in Apulia. Bianco e rosa sono savraddipinti anche su una pisside da Eretria: K.G. Vollmoeller, 'Über zwei euböische Kammergräber mit Totenbetten', *AM* 26, 1901, 356–357, fig. 5.

29 Fanno eccezione alcuni vasi a figure rosse da Canosa, su cui però i colori aggiunti oltre il bianco, e fra questi il rosa, sono evidentemente derivati dalla locale ceramica policroma; cfr. M. Jatta, 'Tombe canosine del Museo Provinciale di Bari', *RM* 29, 1914, 90–126, e soprattutto 117–126.

30 In generale, però, nelle peculiarità tecniche della ceramica di Alessandria vengono sottolineate le differenze da quella attica. Cfr. A. Furtwängler, *Die Sammlung Sabouroff. Kunstdenkmäler aus Griechenland* I, Berlin 1883–1887, testo a tav. LXXIV, 1 e 1a; Pagenstecher, 54, 56; A. Di Vita (*supra* nota 18), 100; Ch. Clairmont, 'Greek Pottery from the Near East, II. Black Vases', *Berytus* 12, 1956/58, 1–2; P.M. Fraser, *Ptolemaic Alexandria,* Oxford 1972, 138.

31 G. Jacopi, 'Scavi nella necropoli di Jalisso (1924–1928)', *Clara Rhodos* 3, 1929, 273, fig. 272. Essa rientra in quel gruppo non grande di vasi che sarei propenso a intendere come 'precursori' delle vere e proprie Plakettenvasen, ancora senza fascia ventrale e senza rilievi sulle spalle (cfr. nota 6).

32 L. Savignoni, 'Esplorazione archeologica delle province occidentali di Creta, I. Topografia e monumenti', *MonAnt* 11:2, 1902, rispettivamente col. 385, figg. 69, 69a, e coll. 341–344, figg. 37–40. Da Creta provengono alcune poche altre anfore di qualità scadente, con proprie esclusive caratteristiche, che fanno sospettare l'esistenza di una tarda officina locale: G. Nicole (*supra* nota 12), n 1280, pp. 292–293; A. Furtwängler (*supra* nota 30); Pagenstecher, 54–55, fig. 61.

33 G. Botti, *Catalogue des monuments exposés au Musée Gréco-Romain d'Alexandrie,* Alexandrie 1900, 538 (e Pagenstecher, 55, fig. 60). E. Breccia, 'La Necropole de l'Ibrahimieh', *Bulletin de la Société Archéologique d'Alexandrie* 9, 1907 (n.s. II:1), 51–52, 58–60, fig. 17 (e Pagenstecher, *supra* nota 23). Breccia, n. 47, p. 32. *Idem, 'Fouilles* de Hadra' (*supra* nota 7), n. 8, pp. 16–17. *Idem,* 'Nuovi scavi nelle Necropoli di Hadra', *Bulletin de la Société Archéologique d'Alexandrie* 25, 1930, (n.s. VII:2), 110, 119, tav. XVI, 1; pp. 112, 119. *Idem, Le Musée Gréco-Romain* 1925–1931, 34; 34–35, tav. XXIV, 89–90; A. Adriani (*supra* nota 22), 113, tav. XLVIII, 7. Alcuni altri esemplari di Alessandria mi sono noti da nuove fotografie del Deutsches Archäologisches Institut, Abteilung Kairo, ottenute grazie al Prof. G. Grimm.

34 A questo proposito va precisato come le stesse "Henkelmasken" del Museo di Bari, provenienti da Taranto, che a Pagenstecher, 54, sembravano parti di 'Plakettenhydrien', alessandrine per il tipo della vernice, ad un più attento controllo risultino frammenti di altra natura. Il Pagenstecher, infatti, doveva riferirsi ai nn. inv. 2533, 2844, 3295, 3295a, 3295b, 4138, 4139, 4140, 4142, 4143, che sono frammenti o di oinochoai con mascherone all'attacco superiore dell'ansa, oppure di coppe, vuoi con piedini configurati, vuoi con medaglione centrale a rilievo. Solo in un caso (4141) una protome femminile è posta alla base di un'ansa tortile, ma la sua pertinenza ad un vaso con placchette è esclusa sia dalle dimensioni a quanto pare ridotte del vaso, sia dall'ampio uso di colori aggiunti sulla testina e alla base dell'ansa, quale non risulta per nessun esemplare certo di Plakettenvase (vedi piuttosto il frammento ZV 2600 G3 della Skulpturensammlung di Dresda: Pagenstecher, fig. 65, a sinistra).

35 Vasi a figure rosse: Ch. Clairmont, 'Greek Pottery from the Near East', *Berytus* 11:2, 1955 nn. 364–371, pp. 135–136, tav. XXXI, 10, e XXXII, 1–3. Per vasi di Gnathia cfr. H. Walters, in *Excavations in Cyprus,* London 1900, 77, fig. 140; Ch. Picard, 'La fin de la céramique peinte en Grande-Grèce, d'après les documents des Musées d'Italie', *BCH* 35, 1911, 182–183, 198; C.C. Edgar, *Greek Vases (Catalogue général des Antiquités Égyptiennes du Musée du Caire),* Le Caire 1911, 33–34, tav. XIII; Breccia, 28–29, 188–190, nn. 617–624, tavv. LXXXI, 277–280, LXXXII, 281–292; A. Rowe, 'Painted Pottery Situla from "Pompey's Pillar" ', *Bulletin de la Société Archéologique d'Alexandrie* 35, 1942 (n.s. XI:2), 54–62, tavv. XVII–XVIII; L. Forti (*supra* nota 27), 25–26, 33 (nota 23), tavv. I c, II a, d, e, III c; e vedi ora sistematicamente l'articolo di J.R. Green in questo stesso volume.

36 A.C. Merriam, 'Inscribed Sepulchral Vases from Alexandria', *AJA* 1, 1885, 18–20; A. Furtwängler (*supra* nota 30); Pagenstecher, 53–57.

37 Per esempio I. Noshy, *The Arts in Ptolemaic Egypt. A study of Greek and Egyptian Influences in Ptolemaic Architecture and Sculpture,* Oxford 1937, 111–112, e di recente P.M. Fraser (*supra* nota 30), 138–139.

38 F. Courby (*supra* nota 6), 201–219.

39 Züchner, 188.

40 Per la facilità con cui si spostavano le creazioni della metallotecnica antica — offrendo perciò svariate possibilità di imitazioni ai figuli, cfr. G.M.A. Richter, 'Greek Bronzes recently acquired by the Metropolitan Museum of Art', *AJA* 43, 1939, 192–194; D.M. Robinson, 'New Greek Bronze Vases. A Commentary on Pindar', *AJA* 46, 1942, 188–189; M.J. Milne, 'A Greek Footbath in the Metropolitan Museum of Art', *AJA* 48, 1944, 40.

THE BOROWSKI PAINTER*

J.L. Benson

Plate 7.

In a recent study of the Otterlo Painter I classified that artist with the Chimaera Group.[1] In the discussion of his style I qualified that placement so severely[2] that it might have been equally appropriate to classify him as 'near the Chimaera Group', that is, explicitly touching (influenced by or influencing) it in a few instances — otherwise, however, *sui generis,* pursuing seemingly an independent course. The next logical step in this reasoning would be to reconsider the whole question of artists somewhat peripheral to the Chimaera Group to see whether the material now available — considerably increased since the last time this was done[3] — will permit sharper contours to be drawn. While I do not propose for myself so ambitious a task in this paper, I am grateful for the opportunity to make an indirect contribution to future efforts in this direction by presenting material which has been accumulating on an artist who happens to be closely connected with the Laurion Painter. The latter has already been discussed fully[4] as an artist in the context mentioned above, that is, peripheral to the Chimaera Group. The former, whom I shall call the Borowski Painter after the owner of the best preserved example of his work, has in fact already been referred to in a tentative way in my study of the Laurion Painter, at which time I had insufficient access to only two works which could appropriately be designated as 'School of the Laurion Painter'. Since then, I have had occasion to study and publish briefly one of these works, a flat-bottomed aryballos in Princeton (see No. 2 of list below); at this point a fuller publication of this work is desirable. More importantly, I have learned of the existence of the name piece and am also in a better position to speak of the Laon aryballos (No. 3, below) and of a related piece (No. 3a). In the descriptive list which follows, the shape is consistently the flat-bottomed aryballos.

1. Basel, Antikenmuseum Kh 97 (Borowski Loan). Pl. 7, Figs. 1, 2, 3. K. Schefold, *Führer durch das Antikenmuseum Basel,* 57 and 152 (Vit. 64.11); *Record of the Art Museum, Princeton University* 31, 1972, 12.

The piece is complete and intact except for rubbing on the disc and on the back. The top of the disc is decorated with a broad stripe, the side of the disc with dots; horizontal stripes appear on the handle. Below petals on the shoulder are three heavy lines and two more corresponding below the frieze. At the centre of the frieze — but slightly to the left of the axis of the handle — is a large lotos-palmette cross, carefully balanced and incised, with double rings as stems in all cases but the upper stem, which consists of a single incised ring. The centre of the cross is a reserved lozenge. A small, oblong, incised blob was placed vertically in each of the quadrants created by the cross. On each side of the floral is a standing panther and they are virtually duplicates, so that the entire composition has an extremely formal symmetry. However, the left panther is placed at a somewhat greater remove from the floral than the right and the right leaf of the lower lotos extends far beyong the curled leaf of the palmette, almost touching the foot of the panther nearest it. The curious discrepancy in the placement of the panthers was probably caused by the artist's desire to intertwine their tails in a loop with two freely balancing extremities which are first narrowed and then widened at the ends like tassels (Pl. 7, Fig. 3). Since this design occurs well to the left of the handle, the panther on the left side had either to be elongated unconscionably — which the artist rejected — or displaced to the left at the front. Purple touches were added to the panthers' necks and to alternate petals of the flowers.

2. Princeton Art Museum 40–151. Pl. 7, Figs. 5, 6. *Oudheidkundige Mededelingen uit het Rijksmuseum van Oudheiden te Leiden* 46, 1965 (hereafter referred to as *LP*), 84, 1b; *Record of the Art Museum, Princeton University* 31, 1972, 11 No. 16.

The piece is complete but very badly rubbed on the back and on the top right at the front, including the right figure. The surface is also flaked in places. The top of the disc is decorated with a broad stripe and several narrower stripes continuing into the aperture. The frieze is bordered above and below by two heavy lines; otherwise the subsidiary decoration is like that of No. 1. At the centre of the frieze, but considerably to the left of the handle area, is a double palmette, the connecting stem of which is concave and devoid of any incision. There are two small, round, rather carelessly incised rosettes above and at either side of the floral and an additional one slightly lower at the right. The floral is flanked by standing lions. They are closely similar but the line from the ear to the lower jaw is wavy on the left-hand animal and sharply contoured on the right-hand animal, which also lacks any inner line in the shoulder balloon. The forward foot of the left-hand lion is excessively large, extending to the middle of the palmette. A large incised rosette with double rings at the centre stands over the back of each lion and a smaller incised rosette under the belly of each. Their tails are not intertwined, for the rears of the two animals are widely separated and a large incised rosette was placed under the handle with a few smaller rosettes scattered in the adjoining field. Purple paint as on No. 1.

3. Laon, Musée 37.727. Pl. 7, Fig. 4. See *LP*, 85, 2b.

About half the disc is broken off; I do not know how the top surface is decorated but the rest of the subsidiary decoration is like that of No. 1 and, as on that piece, there is no filling ornament. At the centre of the frieze — and probably slightly to the left of the handle axis — there is a double palmette. It differs from that of No. 2 in that the leaves do not end as equal-sized volutes but, crossing one another, are continued with swinging streamers, the lower one of which passes behind its panther and emerges in a great volute above the animal's back. The upper leaf swings under and disappears behind the front leg of the corresponding feline. At the point of intersection of upper and lower streamer (on the outside) a small additional — one might say vestigial — palmette has been rather inorganically inserted, in each case touching the breast of the panther. The panthers, like those of No. 1, are carefully drawn, virtually duplicates and the forward paw of the left panther is considerably closer to the floral than that of its counterpart. I am not able to say how the tails are drawn. Purple paint used as on No. 1.

3a. Oslo, collection of Mr K. Wiig, who has kindly supplied me with transparencies for study purposes. I owe my knowledge of this piece to Dr Axel Seeberg.

The surface has suffered considerably. The top was painted solid except for a narrow reserved line near the edge. The floral is like that of No. 2 except that a lotos has been substituted for the lower palmette. It is flanked by panthers, the tails of which do not at all touch. There is a large incised rosette well below the handle separating the two animals. The stylization of the palmette and the placement and type of filling ornaments correspond closely — despite very slack execution — with that of the other pieces. The incisions on the animals, however, vary greatly from those of the Borowski Painter to permit of a very direct relationship; the Oslo aryballos is perhaps a school piece. The Princeton aryballos seems somewhat less carefully drawn than Nos. 1 and 3; the Oslo piece is by comparison with even No. 2 rather slack in execution.

When I first recognised this painter, it was as an imitator of certain aspects of the Laurion Painter. It is, at least, possible to point to a strong resemblance between the lion type of the former (*LP* Pl. VII, 4, 6 — note especially the rounded ears) and of the latter; for example, the looped tail formula is almost exactly the same in both cases. Even the subsidiary decoration of the Laurion Painter No. 4 (*LP* Pl. X, 8) and Borowski Painter No. 2, the formula being a little unusual, is exactly the same. The drawing of the shoulder of the right-hand lion on the Princeton aryballos is extremely similar to the usual stylization employed by the Laurion Painter. Despite this, the Borowski Painter obviously preferred another formula for feline shoulders and the source of this may be the same as the source of his panther heads (a motif rarely attempted, it might seem from known works, by the Laurion Painter). That source might well be the Otterlo Painter, whose rather original formulations must certainly have attracted some attention in the Potters' Quarter. At any rate, there is a rather strong resemblance between the head of the panther on an aryballos in Amsterdam (*OP*, No. 8A) and the heads of the Basel and Laon panthers of the Borowski Painter: notice especially the eye sockets, side whiskers and the enclosed hatched band across the top of the head. The latter painter's version of all this is, however, distinctly more wooden. Again, the shoulder balloon and leg markings of the Borowski Painter's felines are somewhat like those used by this colleague, but it is nonetheless exactly in this area that our painter shows the greatest independence, for he almost invariably brings the forward line of the balloon horizontally back across the top of the leg and then forward in a parallel line forming a fishhook curve; furthermore, he generally renders the inner parallel incision of the balloon as a double curve. In such ways the Borowski Painter stands apart from a rather more conventional companion of the Laurion Painter, *viz.* the Reggio Painter[5], despite a somewhat superficial, if striking, similarity between the *shapes* of their respective felines.[6]

It appears, then, from an analysis of animal features that the Borowski Painter can be placed somewhere between the Laurion Painter and the Otterlo Painter. A consideration of the florals employed by our painter seems to support this. Although there is only one comparandum as of now among the Laurion Painter's works (*LP*, No. 4), his palmette-cross is quite reminiscent in its structure of that on No. 1 above (notice especially the central reserved lozenge). A very similar type was also used by the Otterlo Painter (*OP*, no. 31). If one were inclined to discount such interconnections on the ground that florals of themselves consist of widely used, rather limited formulae, a small detail on the upper palmette of the Laon aryballos (No. 3) may reinforce my argument: the painter has introduced a subsidiary row of small incised leaves below the main leaves – a peculiarity which is most particularly associated with the Otterlo Painter (*cf. OP*, No. 31, lower lotos, and No. 28).

The Borowski Painter's works, in sum, throw some light on the working relationships among a group of artists who are not without some connection with the Chimaera Group. From the parallels cited, it appears that the work of this artist is dateable to the latter half of the Middle Corinthian period; the Oslo aryballos, belonging to the workshop, does not help with the dating but it may represent a phase of style dissolution comparable to that which has been established for the Laurion Painter himself.

NOTES

* I am greatly indebted to Dr Margot Schmidt for providing me with excellent photographs of No. 1 and for obtaining for me permission from its owner to use his name as a designation for the painter.

1 'A Floral Master of the Chimaera Group: the Otterlo Painter', *AntK* 14, 1971, 13–24 (hereafter referred to as *OP*). See also my remarks and a further reference in *AJA* 79, 1975, 163 and, with a bearing on the problem there discussed, a new and certain attribution by Dr S.P. Boriskovskaja in *Reports of the Hermitage Museum (Soobščenija gosudarstrennogo ermitaža)* XXXVII, 1973, 40–41.

2 *Ibid.*, especially p. 20.

3 P. Lawrence, 'The Corinthian Chimaera Painter', *AJA* 63, 1959, 349–63; and 'Notes on the Chimaera Group', *AJA* 66, 1962, 185–7. In the same periodical, Vol. 68, 1964, 172, I suggested the term 'Group

of Louvre E 574'. Obviously a re-thinking of terms might be helpful in this area.

4 J.L. Benson, 'The Laurion Painter', *OMLeiden* (see p. 42) 16, 1965, 76—86 (hereafter referred to as *LP*).

5 D.A. Amyx, *Klearchos* 9/10, 1961, 13:11.

6 Another certain work of the Borowski Painter which has recently come to my attention is a flat-bottomed aryballos in the Istanbul Archaeological Museum from Pitane with panther(s).

A SYMPOSIUM IN ABERDEEN

John Boardman

Plates 8, 9.

But tell me whisky's name in Greek,
I'll tell the reason.

The Scots bard's question went unanswered, but the language, manners and art of Greece are no strangers north of the Border. So for auld acquaintance' sake a festive cup from Scotland is offered, from Aberdeen, where Dale Trendall stayed as Geddes-Harrower Professor of Classical Art and Archaeology in 1966–7, and where I followed seven years later.

The cup is in the University of Aberdeen's Marischal College, with a choice small collection of other vases which are well-loved there, but elsewhere little known.[1] Beazley placed the painting in the manner of the Tarquinia Painter, as early Classical artist, and we might date the cup to the 460s B.C. It has been restored from many pieces and the black and some of the figure work repaired in many places, but not seriously to deceive. It is from the collection of Alexander Henderson, a physician, but a close friend of Gerhard and one whose 'largest and most important work' was a *History of Ancient and Modern Wines.* He died in 1863.

The subjects are devoted to wine and song. Inside the cup (Fig. 1), in a tondo with a simple maeander border, a youth hurries to the party, a light cloak over his shoulders, a fat dotted headband on his hair with a fillet tied loosely over it, its ends flying like a college scarf. In one hand (the left arm and hand are restored) are his pipes, in the other a wineskin, half-empty, so perhaps he has made one call already.

On the exterior eight men recline, wrapped in himatia, supported by striped cushions (one with dotted zigzags, for the piper) (Figs. 2–3). They are rather cramped for space and two of them thrust the ball of their left foot and toes realistically out towards us. We should think of them as reclining two to a *kline,* but, as often on such symposion cups, the furniture is not shown. Instead, we have an uncommon scheme with a plain band representing the height from floor to mattress, on which are disposed, like so many still-life silhouettes, some of the *impedimenta* of the feast. The scheme had been used before on a few Late Archaic cups.[2] Here, we are shown two pairs of soft boots (one with the tops rolled down, and of these, one is end-on), and two pairs of shoes, two skyphoi, a stemmed cup, a footstool with its top out-lined; the only other non-silhouette object is a pipes-case with its strap, side purse for the mouthpiece, whiskered ends, and the animal skin material rendered in wash with black patches. Other trappings appear in the more conventional position, hanging from the top border of the scene: two baskets and, at the left on B, a pair of sandals, one edge-on (Figs 3 and 5). The youth here has his stick propped beside him. It is on this side of the vase too, at the right, that we have the most original feature: on the floor, but overlapping the reserved bodies of the komasts beside him, stands a cup boy, all black save for the reserved white of his eye (Figs. 3 and 7). His jaw and curly hair show that he is a Negro and he holds a sieve for the wine, gesticulating out of the picture with his left hand, perhaps to the tondo figure, a fresh source of wine and music. The scheme was recommended partly by the silhouettes of the objects in the plain frieze, partly by a desire, or at least willingness, to depict a Black, but we cannot be sure that the former did not prompt the latter. We are used to silhouettes in red-figure for shield blazons, but it is rare to find a whole 'live' figure treated in this way. The best examples are the black archers silhouetted against the gates of Troy on the Foundry Painter's cup in Boston,[3] but their silhouettes are enhanced by black-figure incision. Whatever prompted the scheme, the choice of a Negro for cup boy is an unfamiliar one, not readily paralleled, although not in itself surprising.[4]

We turn now to the main figures on the cup. The general scheme is again familiar. Beazley indicated a model in the Tarquinia Painter's cup from the Käppeli Collection[5] where the necessary third is added to the wine and song by the replacement of four men by four naked girls. Our komasts have other preoccupations. On the side without the cup boy the second man is swinging his cup in the usual position for the kottabos game (Figs. 2 and 4). His young companion imitates his gesture, but cupless, and his left hand is open, receptive, but not of wine, for all eyes are on the man at the right, who also makes the kottabos gesture, cupless. He is presumably demonstrating finer points of technique in the throw. His companion rests his hand on his shoulder, his chin on his hand, in a relaxed pose which we meet in symposia and for many sleepy figures, from Hypnos, through various slaves on grave reliefs, to the funerary Eros with down-turned torch. But our komast is listening too, not so absorbed as to fail to clasp his skyphos firmly and level.

The other side is devoted to music and song (Figs. 3 and 6). The piper plays, before him a man throws back his head to sing. He holds his cup steady enough but supports his head with a hand in a gesture well familiar from other singers or those overcome by the rapture of music, in red-figure. It is seen, for instance, on the Käppeli cup, already mentioned. The singer's couch-mate is a youth adjusting his head scarf and holding a skyphos, less impressed, it may be, than the older man at the right who waves encouragement. He is holding a phiale and is perhaps the host who holds the cup of ritual welcome and directs the cup boy.

All we need ask now is what the man is singing. The fragment of a rhyton,[6] also in the manner of the Tarquinia Painter, but not by our artist, shows another singer in this pose, and tells us his song — ΣΟΙ ΚΑΙ ΕΜ[ΟΙ, 'for thee, for me', a wistful song maybe, and though a far cry from other songs for other pipers, not perhaps so different from that nostalgia for northern hospitality which might touch others —

> While we sit bousing at the nappy,
> An' getting fou an unco happy.

NOTES

1   No. 748. Height: 12.5 cm; diameter: 31.0 cm. The shape is a normal Type B, with a hoop painted just within the resting surface underfoot. On B we read ΚΑΛΟΣ, inside ΗΟ ΠΑΙΣ ΚΑΛΟΣ. There is red for the fillets of most of the men on the outside, and to tie the wineskin within. There is a free use of relief line contour; paint blobs for the outlines of tight curly hair and for the cup boy's hair. The eye of the youth on the left on B has been repainted. In the interior, the whole left arm of the boy, the dress at that side, a band across the chest and centre thigh, are modern. *ARV*[2] 871, No. 9 (and see 872, on No. 26); W.M. Ramsay, *Descriptive Notes on the Classical Vases in the Henderson Collection,* Aberdeen 1881, 20, Vase XIX. The memoir on Dr Henderson, *ibid.,* 5–8, is by W.D. Geddes; R.W. Reid, *Illustrated Catalogue of the Anthropological Museum, Marischal College,* Aberdeen 1912, 69, No. 748.

2   As Berlin 2298 (Triptolemos Painter; *ARV*[2] 241, No. 29), *CVA* 2, Pl. 64: 1, 2; Greifenhagen, *ibid.,* 21, refers to other examples on cups and a psykter; and see B.A. Sparkes and L. Talcott, *Athenian Agora* XII, Princeton 1970, 15, n. 28.

3   Boston 98.933; *ARV*[2] 402, No. 23; *Paralipomena,* 370; Caskey-Beazley, I, Pl. 14; M.R. Scherer, *The Legends of Troy,* N.Y. 1963, 85, Fig. 67.

4   A deformed Negroid with a jug, beside a symposiast's discarded stick and boot, is seen in the cup Paris G. 100 (E. Pottier, *Vases antiques du Louvre,* II, Paris 1901, Pl. 99). For negroes as slaves in fifth-century art, see G.M.H. Beardsley, *The Negro in Greek and Roman Civilisation,* Baltimore and London 1929, 62–6. For Negroes in the Greco-Roman world see also Frank M. Snowden, Jr, *Blacks in Antiquity,* Cambridge, Massachusetts 1970.

5   *ARV²* 868, No. 45 (see on 872, No. 26); *Paralipomena,* 426; K. Schefold, *Meisterwerke griechischer Kunst,* Basel 1960, No. 220. Another closely comparable cup is in the Bareiss collection (*ARV²* 1673, No. 47 *bis; Paralipomena,* 426; *Ars Antiqua A.G. Auktion III,* Luzern, Pl. 47, No. 108). Features of the Tarquinia Painter in the cup are the fondness for curly forelocks, the hand-on-shoulder pose for a symposiast (e.g. on his Nos. 47 *bis,* 48, 53, *bis* in *ARV²* and *Paralipomena*), the phialai, hanging sandals, treatment of chests. On the whole our artist is the more careful and competent.

6   Villa Giulia 50329; *ARV²* 872, No. 26. On the song see Beazley, *AJA* 58, 1954, 190, with Pl. 31, Fig. 5, and *ARV², loc. cit.*

EIN OSTGRIECHISCHER SKYPHOS

Frank Brommer

Tafel 10.

A.D. Trendalls Arbeit gilt vornehmlich der griechischen Vasenmalerei. So sollen diese ihm gewidmeten Zeilen sich auch mit einer griechischen Vase beschäftigen. Aber während er die späten Vasen des Westens erforscht, sei hier im Gegensatz dazu mit antipodischem Standpunkt, wie er sich geographisch für den Verfasser von selbst ergibt, eine frühe des Ostens vorgestellt.

Es handelt sich um einen Skyphos in Privatbesitz. (Taf. 10, Abb. 1 und 2) Er ist aus vielen Scherben zusammengesetzt, aber fast ganz erhalten. Seine Höhe beträgt 6,5 cm, der obere Durchmesser ohne Henkel 10,7 cm. Der Mündungsrand ist ringsum eingezogen. Der Ton ist graubraun. Der nicht mehr überall haften gebliebene Glanzton ist schwarz. Innen ist das Gefäss ganz schwarz. Aussen ist im schwarzen Grund auf beiden Seiten ein Bildfeld ausgespart. Auch zwischen den jeweils zwei Henkelansätzen ist ein Feld von Glanzton freigelassen worden, das fast bis zum unteren Rand des Bildfeldes unregelmässig herabreicht. Die Unterseite des Fusses ist ebenfalls unbemalt.

Der obere Teil des Bildfeldes ist durch drei oder vier senkrechte Striche in drei fast quadratische Felder geteilt. Links und rechts befindet sich je ein gegitterter Rhombus mit doppelter Umrahmung, in der Mitte ein nach rechts stehender Vogel mit langem Schnabel, langen Beinen und gegittertem Körper. Unter diesem Bildstreif folgt — oben und unten durch zwei waagrechte Striche abgetrennt — eine Reihe von Punkten, die jeweils durch einen schrägen Strich mit dem oberen Rand, aber nicht dem unteren, verbunden sind. Darunter folgt noch eine unbemalte Zone von etwa einem Zentimeter Höhe. Die andere Seite ist genauso bemalt.

Man sieht also, dass es sich um ein eher anspruchsloses Gefäss handelt. Was ihm ein gewisses Interesse verleiht, ist der Fundort. Nach Angaben des Besitzers, dem ich hierfür und für das Veröffentlichungsrecht dankbar bin, wurde es in Herakleia am Latmos erworben. Der Verkäufer versicherte, dass es dort in unmittelbarer Nähe gefunden worden sei. Das ist glaubwürdig, zumal auch alle Indizien auf eine Entstehung im Osten weisen. Attika ist jedenfalls als Heimat schon wegen der Tonfarbe ausgeschlossen. Am ehesten lassen sich im Dekorationssystem ostgriechische Vogelschalen vergleichen. Deren Hauptmenge stammt aus Rhodos. Im Anhang werden hier nicht weniger als einunddreissig dieser aus Rhodos stammenden Gefässe aufgeführt. Kaum ein anderer Ort, kaum eine andere Insel hat annähernd so viele aufzuweisen. Ausnahmen sind Tarsus und Megara Hyblaea, wo aber niemand die Heimat der Gattung suchen wird und wo es sich auch nur um Bruchstücke handelt. Wenn Tarsus, wie man vermutet hat[1] eine Kolonie von Rhodos war, dann kämen die dortigen Funde noch als Bestätigung für die Annahme der Heimat in Rhodos hinzu. Die Zusammenstellung[2] im Anhang erstrebt keine umfassende Vollständigkeit, vermittelt aber doch hoffentlich ein statistisch repräsentatives Bild über Vorkommen und Verteilung. Allerdings kann, wenn an einem Ort mehrere Scherben vorliegen, die Zahl der Gefässe, auf die sie sich ursprünglich verteilten, nur geschätzt werden. Für manche Orte sind daher die hier gegebenen Zahlen nur Schätzwerte.[3]

Bestätigend zu den Funden aus Rhodos kommt hinzu, dass die Funde in der Nachbarschaft dieser Insel ebenfalls reicher sind als in anderen Gegenden. Unter den Inseln sind besonders zu nennen Chios und Delos mit je neunzehn, Thasos mit acht und Samos mit sieben Stücken, die allerdings zum Teil nur durch Bruchstücke belegt sind. Auffallend ist das häufige Vorkommen

auf Aegina. Im Museum dort ist eine fragmentierte Schale ausgestellt, sowie 18 weitere Bruchstücke, dabei fünf mit Vögeln. Dazu kommen weitere 55 Scherben aus der Kolonna-Grabung.[4]
Die Türkei hat Bruchstücke von 93 Gefässen geliefert, auch Italien viele, sowie Syrien und
Nordafrika mehrere. Bemerkenswert ist das Vorkommen bis hin nach Rumänien, Malta und
Spanien. Demgegenüber fällt es besonders auf, dass unter den bisher bekannt gewordenen oder
aus Scherben zu entschliessenden über 350–400 Gefässen nur drei, also weniger als jedes hund-
erste, aus dem griechischen Festland stammen, somit weit weniger als aus Italien oder Rumänien.
Die weite Streuung zeigt die Beliebtheit der Gattung. Das entschiedene Schwergewicht der
Streuung bestätigt, wie man schon seit längerem annimmt, dass die Heimat in Rhodos liegt,
wobei nicht ausgeschlossen ist, dass es anderswo lokale Nachahmungen gibt.

Gegenüber der grossen Zahl von Vogelschalen sind Vogelskyphoi zwar nicht unbekannt,[5]
aber sie sind ungleich seltener. Fundorte solcher Skyphoi sind zunächst die Inseln Rhodos, Samos
und Thera, aber auch Milet und Didyma. Das Verbreitungsgebiet liegt also innerhalb dessen der
Vogelschalen, ist aber nicht so weit gestreut und nach keiner Himmelsgegend so weit gedehnt.
Unter den hier aufgezählten Skyphoi kommt keiner dem Typus der Vogelschalen so nahe, wie das
Stück aus Herakleia, wo sich dieser Typus bis ins Einzelne auf die andere Form übertragen findet.

Vergleicht man beispielsweise eine Oxforder Vogelschale unbekannter Herkunft (hier S. 44,
Nr. 6), so findet man eine weitgehende Übereinstimmung bis auf die Tatsache, dass der Vogel
des Skyphos sich in einem engeren Feld einrichten muss.

Die übrigen bekannten Vogelskyphoi weisen grössere Unterschiede zu den Vogelschalen
auf.

Die aus Samos stammenden Bruchstücke haben meist das den Schalen fremde Ornament
des Mäanderbaums. Das gilt auch für drei aus Rhodos stammende und für das Gefäss aus
Thera, für das Coldstream ebenfalls rhodische Entstehung annahm. Ähnlich ist das Ornament
auch auf dem Gefäss in rheinischem Privatbesitz (hier S. 44, Nr. 1) für das wohl aus diesem
Grund auch schon die gleiche Heimat angenommen wurde. Hingegen fehlt dieses Ornament
dem Gefäss aus Vroulia, auf dem in anderer Weise abweichend nicht ein Vogel im Metopenfeld,
sondern vier Vögel im Fries wiedergegeben sind.

Auf den Gefässen aus Delos, die Coldstream ebenfalls unter die rhodischen gerechnet hat,
kommt der Mäanderbaum zwar manchmal vor, aber keineswegs immer, so dass sich unter den
in Delos gefundenen Vogelskyphoi solche befinden, die dem aus Herakleia näherstehen als alle
sonst bisher aufgeführten. Nie steht auf den delischen Skyphoi jedoch der Vogel allein in seinem
Feld. Immer sind noch Füllornamente bei ihm untergebracht. Das scheint auch so bei den
Bruckstücken aus Milet zu sein. Völlig anders ist der Skyphos im Kasseler Privatbesitz aus
Karien und der aus dem Kunsthandel unbekannter Herkunft (hier S. 45, Nr. 16 und S. 45,
Nr. 1).

Es gibt also unter den bisher aufgezählten Vogelskyphoi keinen, der dem aus Herakleia in
dem Masse ähnlich wäre wie sich die Vogelschalen untereinander ähnlich sind.

Obwohl die Vogelskyphoi weniger an Zahl sind als die Vogelschalen und obwohl ihr
Verbreitungsgebiet weit geringer ist, sind doch die Unterschiede grösser. Es hat offenbar verschiedene lokale Untergruppen gegeben.

Man kann nicht daran zweifeln, dass der hier vorgestellte Skyphos nicht allzu weit von
seinem Fundort entfernt geschaffen worder sein muss, wohl im frühen 7. Jh. v. Chr. Diese
Vermutung wird auch dadurch bestätigt, dass es solche Vogelskyphoi auch aus den benachbarten Orten Milet[6] und Didyma[7] gibt.

Angesichts der Tatsache, dass wir aus diesem Zeitraum noch nicht viel Werkstätten und Fundorte von Gefässen in Kleinasien kennen, verdient der unscheinbare Skyphos Beachtung.

ANHANG*

*Ausser den Abkürzungen, die am Anfang des Buches genannt sind, werden auf den nächsten Seiten noch folgende Abkürzungen benützt:

Akurgal, *KA*   Ekrem Akurgal, *Die Kunst Anatoliens,* Berlin 1961.

AO   R.M. Dawkins and others, *The Sanctuary of Artemis Orthia at Sparta,* 1929.

Baur   Paul V.C. Baur, *Catalogue of the Rebecca Darlington Stoddard Collection of Greek and Italian Vases in Yale University* (New Haven 1922).

Blinkenberg, *Lindos* I   Christian Blinkenberg and K.-F. Kinch, *Lindos, Fouilles et Recherches,* 1902−1919, I (Berlin 1931).

Boardman, *Emporio*   John Boardman, *Excavations in Chios* 1952−1955, *Greek Emporio, BSA* Sup. vol. 6.

Boehlau-Schefold, *Larisa* III J. Boehlau und K. Schefold, *Larisa am Hermos* 3, 1942.

Burke-Pollitt   Susan Matheson Burke and Jerome J. Pollitt, *Greek Vases at Yale* (1975).

Dragendorf, *Thera* II   H. Dragendorf, *Theraeische Graeber,* Berlin 1903.

Edgar, *Cat.*   C.C. Edgar, *Catalogue général des antiquités égyptiennes du Musée du Caire. Greek Vases* (Cairo 1911).

Fairbanks   Arthur Fairbanks, *Museum of Fine Arts, Boston. Catalogue of Greek and Etruscan Vases,* Boston, Massachusetts, 1928.

Heraeum   Ch. Waldstein, *The Argive Heraeum* II, Boston and New York, 1905.

Kinch, *Vroulia*   K.F. Kinch, *Fouilles de Vroulia,* 1914.

Kraiker, *Aigina*   Wilhelm Kraiker, *Aigina, die Vasen des 10. bis. 7. Jahrhunderts v. Chr.,* Berlin 1951.

Tarsus III   G.M.A. Hanfmann in H. Goldman, *Excavations at Gözlü Kule,* Tarsus 3, 1963.

Tocra I   John Boardman and John Hayes, *Excavations at Tocra* 1963−1965, *The Archaic Deposits I. BSA* Suppl. vol. 4, 1966.

Pottier, *Catalogue*   Edmund Pottier, *Vases antiques du Louvre,* Paris 1897−1922.

Wenn nur Bruchstücke erhalten sind, dann ist es oft schwer zu schätzen, auf wieviel Gefässe sie sich ursprünglich verteilten. Für Tarsus haben die Ausgräber bei 130 Scherben etwa 70 Vasen vermutet (*Tarsus* II, 295 f.) und damit die zweitgrösste Gruppe unter den importierten griechischen Vasen festgestellt.

Diesem Beispiel zahlenmässig ungefähr folgend sind hier für die 74 Scherben aus Aegina etwa 40 Vasen vermutet worden und für die 14 Bruchstücke aus Klazomenä etwa 7, für die 5 Bruchstücke aus Tocra 3, für die 150 Scherben aus Megara Hyblaea 80 Vasen. In mehreren Fällen können demnach hier nur Schätzwerte gegeben werden.

A. RHODISCHE VOGELSCHALEN

AUS RHODOS

1 Rhodos 10675   *ClRh* III 47, Abb. 33, 37; *CVA* II De Tf 6, 2.
2 Rhodos 11435   *ClRh* III 64, Abb. 54 oben r.
3 Rhodos 11436   *ClRh* III 64, Abb. 54 Mitte.
4 Rhodos 12099   *ClRh* IV 55, 30; *CVA* II De Tf 6, 4.
5 Rhodos 12487   *ClRh* IV 271, Abb. 301; *CVA* II De Tf 6, 5.

6	Rhodos 13750	*ClRh* VI/VII 61, Abb. 61, 64.
7	Rhodos 13757	*ClRh* VI/VII 65, Abb. 66.
8	Rhodos 13764	*ClRh* VI/VII 67, Abb. 70.
9	Rhodos 13765	*ClRh* VI/VII 68, Abb. 72.
10	Rhodos 13845	*ClRh* VI/VII 102, Abb. 114.
11	Rhodos 11437	*ClRh* III 64, Abb. 54.
12	Rhodos 11438	*ClRh* III 64, Abb. 54, T. 344 Kukia.
13	Berlin F 293	a. Kamiros 1881; Neugebauer, *Führer,* Tf 6; *CVA* Tf 155, 2.
14	Berlin Inv. 3976	a. Rhodos; *CVA* Tf 155, 1.
15	London, Brit. Mus. A 433	a. Kamiros; Kinch, *Vroulia* Abb. 52; Akurgal, *KA,* Abb. 124; Buschor, *GV* (1969), Abb. 59.
16	Paris, Louvre A 291	von Salzmann
17	Paris, Louvre A 290	a. Kamiros; Pottier, *Catalogue,* Tf 11.
18		Kinch, *Vroulia,* 134 f., Tf 25, 11.
19		Kinch, *Vroulia,* Tf 36, 34 a.
20—27		Kinch, *Vroulia,* 136 huit exemplaires.
28		Kinch, *Vroulia,* 136, Tf 23, 1.
29		Kinch, *Vroulia,* 136, Tf 23, 3.
30		Kinch, *Vroulia,* 136, Grab 42.
31		Kinch, *Vroulia,* 50, Tf. 42, 18:2.
32	Oxford 1934.94	a. Kamiros; Mrs. Drogo Montague Gift.

ÖRTLICHE NACHAHMUNGEN

Örtliche Nachahmungen sind bekannt von Sparta und Eretria. Ausserdem zitiert Akurgal, *Bayrakli* (1950), 61, solche von Bogazköy, Alacahöyük und Malatya.

Sparta, fr.	*AO,* fig. 85 c; *BSA* 34, 115.
Sparta, fr.	*AO,* fig. 85 b, fig. 40, 1; *BSA* 34, 115, fig. 9, b, c.
Eretria	*AntK* 11, 1968, 102 Nr. 4, Tf 28, 5.

VON DEN ÜBRIGEN INSELN

1 — 40	Aegina	a. Aegina; Kraiker, *Aigina,* Tf 7, 103.
41 — 59		a. Delos; *Délos* XV, 100 ff., Nr. 17 — 35, Tf. 47, 48, 54.
60 — 78	Chios	Boardman, *Emporio,* 103, 132, Nr. 437—455; Coldstream, *GGP,* 294.
79 — 86	Thasos	L. Ghali-Kahil, La céramique grecque *ÉT* VII, 1960, 17, Nr. 1—8.
87 — 93	Samos	Walter, *Samos* V, Nr. 476—482, Tf 85.
94 — 99	Ithaka	*BSA* 43, 1948, 99, Nr. 576—581, Tf 44.
100	Boston 72.101	a. Zypern; Fairbanks, Nr. 284, Tf 24.
101	Zypern	a. Cellarka; *AA* 1966, 244, Abb. 56.
102	Thera	a. Thera; Dragendorf, *Thera* II, 74, 195.
103	Kreta	a. Aja Pelajia Malevisiu; *AAA* 5, 1972, 237, fig. 7.
104 — 105	Kreta, Iraklion	
106 — 107	Mykonos	*ADelt, Chron.* 26, 1971 (1975) Tf 470.

AUS DER TÜRKEI

1 — 3		a. Larisa; Boehlau-Schefold, *Larisa* III, 170, Tf 57, 7.
4	Ankara	a. Ankara; Akurgal, *PK,* 50, Tf H 3; Akurgal, *Bayrakli* (1950), Tf A 1.
5	Ankara	a. Gordion; Young, *Bull. Univ. Pennsylvania* 17, 1949, 33, Abb. 26.
6		a. Ephesos; Price, *EGP,* 1.
7		a. Ephesos; Keil, *ÖJh* 1926, Beibl. 253 f., Abb. 44.
8		a. Bayrakli; Akurgal, *Bayrakli* (1950), 60.

9 – 16 Athen, NM	a. Klazomenä; Akurgal, *Bayrakli* (1950), 60; Kallipolitis, *Mikrasiatika Chronika* 1972, 19.
17	a. Mersin; Akurgal, *Bayrakli* (1950), 60.
18 – 87 Einige Fragmente in Cambridge, Mass. Peabody Mus.	a. Tarsus; *Tarsus* III, 295 ff., Nr. 1448–1464, Tf 99; Boardman, *JHS* 85, 1965, 5–7; Coldstream, *GGP*, 300, Nr. 28–32.
88 – 93	a. Milet; *IstMitt* 9/10, 1959/60, 59, Tf 62, 1; *IstMitt* 23/4, 1973/4, 86, Tf 24, Nr. 59, 60, 62, 'hohen Zahl der Funde – nur ein kleiner Teil ist hier abgebildet',
94	a. Sardes P 65.161; *BASOR*, 192; Coldstream, *GGP,* 298 ff.
95 Christchurch, Univ. Canterbury 98/69	Trendall, *Greek Vases in the Logie Collection* (Christchurch 1971), Nr. 7, Tf 2 f. aus Alt-Smyrna.
96 Amasya	19. August 1975 gefunden in Grab zwischen Merzifon und Sulnova.

Zu den angeblichen Schalen aus Didyma siehe hier unter Skyphoi.

AUS SYRIEN

| 1 Paris, Louvre A 07514B, fr. | a. Sidon. |
| 2 Oxford und Cambridge etwa 80 frr. | a. Al Mina; Boardman, *Emporio,* 132, Anm. 4; Coldstream, *GGP,* 299, Nr. 13. |

AUS NORDAFRIKA

1 – 4 Kairo 26 153/6	a. Naukratis; Edgar, *Cat.*
5 Oxford G 116.2	a. Naukratis; *CVA* (2) II D, Tf 1, 8.
6 Oxford G 116.4	a. Naukratis; *CVA* (2) II D, Tf 1, 9.
7 Oxford 1912.34	a. Naukratis; *CVA* (2) II D, Tf 1, 13.
8 – 14	a. Tocra; *Tocra* 1, 55, Nr. 733, Tf 38; Dies. II, 21, Nr. 2009–2014.
15	? a. Kyrene; Stucchi, *Cirene* 1957–66 (1967), 152 f. (L. Pandolfi), fig. 161/2: numerosi sono i esempi.

AUS ITALIEN

1	a. Gela; Orsi, *MonAnt* 17, 247 f.
2 Kopenhagen, NM.7 (ABC 899)	a. Italien; Kinch, *Vroulia,* 134, Abb. 44; *CVA* II, Tf 79, 7.
3	a. Syrakus; 25, 1919, 490, fig. 82; Coldstream, *GGP,* 299, Nr. 15. Vgl. Langlotz, *Studien z. griech. Kunst* 184, Tf 64, 1.
4	a. Syrakus; *NSc* 1925, 202, fig. 37; Coldstream, *GGP,* 299, Nr. 16.
5 Paris, Louvre D 12 = C1295	a. Slg. Campana.
6 Rom, Vatikan 381	a. Regolini-Galassi Grab.
7 Rom, Villa Giulia T 18	a. Cerveteri (Via Manganello).
8 – 88	a. Megara Hyblaea; Georges Vallet et François Villard, *Mégara Hyblaea* II, *La céramique archaique,* École Française de Rome 1964, Tf 62, 3–8; 63, 12. Dort etwa 150 Bruchstücke erwähnt.

VOM FESTLAND

1 Athen, Agora P26491 fr.	*Hesperia* 30, 1961, 377.
2	a. Argos; *Heraeum* II, 135, fig. 66.
3 Korinth	*Hesperia* 17, 1948, 223, D 53, Tf 82.

AUS HISTRIA

| 1 – 2 | Lambrino, *Les vases archaiques d'Histria,* Bucharest 1938, 39, fig. 7 u. 8; Coldstream, *GGP*, 300, Nr. 34. |
| 3 – 9 frr. | *Histria* II, 1966, Tf 2, 15–21. |

AUS SPANIEN

    Zwei Bruchstücke   Niemeyer, *Archivo Español de Arqueologia* 44, 1971, 152–156.

AUS FRANKREICH

    Aus St. Blaise   Rolland, *Fouilles de St. Blaise*, Abb. 90 (kein Vogel erhalten).

Die übrigen bei Ernst Langlotz, *Studien zur nordostgriech. Kunst*, (Mainz 1975) 184, Anm. 36 aufgeführten angeblichen Vogelschalen aus Frankreich sind keine.

UNBERKANNTER HERKUNFT

1		*Hesperia Art Bulletin* XXXVIII Nr. 3.
2	Dunedin, Otago Mus. E.67.507	*Hesperia Art Bulletin* XXXVIII Nr. 4.
3		*Hesperia Art Bulletin* XXXIX Nr. A 2.
4		*Hesperia Art Bulletin* XLIV Nr. A 10.
5	Heidelberg 61/10	*CVA*, Tf 123, 1 a. Kunsthandel.
6	Oxford 1927.313	*CVA*, II D, Tf 1, 6 ohne Herkunftsangabe; Cook, *GPP*, 116 f., Tf 29 D.
7	Oxford G 116.2 fr.	*CVA*, II D, Tf 1, 8 ohne Herkunftsangabe.
8	Oxford 1912.24 fr.	*CVA*, II D, Tf 1, 13 ohne Herkunftsangabe.
9	Kh.Mailand 1970	*Finarte* 101 Dez. 1970, Nr. 1, Tf II, ohne Herkunftsangabe.
10	Kh.1963	Basel, *Münzen und Medaillen Auktion XXVI*, 5.X.63, Nr. 56, ohne Herkunftsangabe.
11	Pb. Basel	Hansjörg Bloesch, *Das Tier in der Antike*, Zürich 1974, Nr. 194 (ist nicht hier Nr. 10).
12	Cambridge, Fitzwilliam Mus. GR 15.1952	(früher Mus. for Archaeology and Ethnology) klein.
13	Cambridge, Mus. of Class. Arch.	gekauft am 13.9.71 Dm 14 cm, mit Henkeln 18,8 cm[8].
14	Würzburg H 5381	*Führer Antikenabt.* (1975), 75, Tf. 10; *CVA*, Tf 21.
15	Yale 1913.65	Baur, Nr. 65, fig. 16; Burke-Pollitt, Nr. 24.
16	Bochum	Kunisch, Slg. Funcke Nr. 51.

B. VOGELSKYPHOI

AUS SAMOS

    1 – 29   H. Walter, *Samos* V, 1968, 40, Nr. 240–268, Tf 42, 43, 44.

AUS RHODOS

1	Rhodos 11754	*ClRh* III, 99, Abb. 92, Grab 415 Tsampiku (57).
2	Rhodos 11856	*ClRh* III, 105, Abb. 99, Grab 444 Tsampiku (62).
3		Kinch, *Vroulia*, Tf 36,2,39 a.
4		Blinkenberg, *Lindos* I, Tf 38,873.

AUS THERA

    1 Thera   a. Thera, Dragendorf, *Thera* II, fig. 80; Coldstream, *GGP* 277, Tf 61 d.

AUS DELOS

    1 – 10   *Délos* XV, Tf 46–47, 6–15; Coldstream, *GGP* 277.

AUS KLEINASIEN

    1 Pb.   *Antiken aus rheinischem Privatbesitz*, Köln 1973, Nr. 36 Tf. 16, (nur Rs. abgebildet, auf der sich kein Vogel befindet). "Aus Kleinasien".

2		a. Milet; Hommel, *IstMitt.* 9/10, 1959/60, 59, Tf 62, 2.
3 – 13		a. Milet; v. Graeve, *IstMitt.* 23/4, 1973, 86 ff., Nr. 47, 49–58, Tf 23.
14		a. Didyma; *IstMitt.* 13/14, 1963/4, 56, Nr. 61, Tf 24, 1 dort fälschlich als Schale bezeichnet.
15		*IstMitt.* 23/24, 1973/4, 149, Tf 47, 1–4, dort fälschlich als Schale bezeichnet.
16	Kassel, Slg. Dierichs Nr. 8	a. Karien.
17	Baltimore, Walters Art Gallery 48.2283	Erworben 1967.
18	Pb. (norddeutsch)	W. Hornbostel, *Kunst d. Antike* Nr. 194.
19	Marburg, Univ.	Fr. aus Klazomenä. *BSA* 47, 152, fig. 8.
20	Milet 66 S 231	*IstMitt.* 25, 1975, 53 Nr. 50 Abb. 24 Tf 10.

UNBEKANNTER HERKUNFT

1	Kh 1966	*Hesperia Art Bulletin* XXXIX, Nr. A 1, ohne Herkunftsangabe als *East Greek* bezeichnet. Auf jeder Seite ein Vogel auf 'folding stool'. Keine Rhomben.
2	Philadelphia L–29–2	
3	Bonn, Akad. Kunstmuseum	

Zu vergleichen sind: Vogelbruchstück *Larisa* III, Tf 57,3. Dazu heisst es a.0.170, dass die Form des Gefässes sehr an die Larisäer Skyphosdratere erinnere. Bruchstücke, darunter eins mit Vogel, die bei Akurgal, *Bayrakli,* in der Unterschrift zu IX b auf Skyphoi bezogen, im Test S.61 allerdings als Schalen angesprochen werden.

ANMERKUNGEN

1. J. Bing, 'Tarsus a forgotten colony of Lindos.' *JNES* 30, 1971, 99 f.

2. D. Ohly und D. v. Bothmer verdanke ich die Auskünfte, dass sich in ihren Sammlungen in München und New York keine rhodischen Vogelschalen befinden. Im Athener Nationalmuseum befinden sich nur die hier S. 43, Nr. 9–16 aufgezählten Bruchstücke aus Klazomenä. Darüberhinaus gibt es, wie mir B. Philippaki bestätigt, keine. In Athen sind also überhaupt keine Vogelschalen aus Griechenland. Frau U. Höckmann verdanke ich den Hinweis auf die beiden Schalen in Kreta, J.R. Green den auf die beiden in Neuseeland, meiner Frau den auf die schale in Amasya. In der Zeit seit Ablieferung dieses Manuskriptes sind verwandte Skyphoi aus Karien veröffentlicht worden von C. Özgünel, *AA* 1977, 8 ff. mit Verweisen auf frühere Literatur.

3. S. dazu hier die Vorbemerkung zu dem Katalog auf S. 41.

4. Nach freundlicher Metteilung von Frau Walter, die dazu bemerkt "keine andere ostgriechische Gattung gibt er in so grosser Zahl".

5. Siehe Anhang. S. 41.

6. Wie mir P. Hommel mitteilt, gibt es in Milet vergleichbare Exemplare aus der Grabung an der südlichen Stadtmauer.

7. Auf meine Anfrage bestätigte K. Tuchelt, dass die in Didyma gefundenen Bruchstücke, die Vogelschalen zugeschrieben wurden, in Wahrheit von Vogelskyphoi stammen (s. hier S. 45, Nr. 14).

8. Die Vase ist sehr ähnlich der hier unter "Unbekannter Herkunft" Nr. 3 aufgeführten. Aber R.M. Cook, dem ich auch die übrigen angaben hierzu verdanke, teilt mir mit, dass er die beiden Schalen nicht für miteinander identisch hält.

THREE APULIAN RED-FIGURE FRAGMENTS
IN THE NICHOLSON MUSEUM, SYDNEY

Alexander Cambitoglou

Plates 11, 12, 13.

The fragments discussed below illustrate two important stages in the development of the Apulian "Ornate Style";[1] they were acquired during Professor Trendall's curatorship of the museum. No. 51.47 is connected with the Painter of the Birth of Dionysos, one of the major painters of "Early Apulian" (c.435–c.365 B.C.); nos. 51.48 and 53.12 are attributed to the Iliupersis Painter, the most significant artist of the "Middle Apulian" phase (c.365–c.340 B.C.).

1 *Fragment connected with the Painter of the Birth of Dionysos.*

No. 51.47. (Pl. 11, Fig. 1; Fig. 1 on p. 48). *RVAp* I, p. 41, 2/27. Provenance unknown. Acquired in the international market. Height: 9.6 cm; width: 7.2 cm; consistent thickness: 6 mm. Bright pinkish clay, dark lustrous paint. Details in yellow paint over a white undercoat.

Shape: Since the inside surface is painted black and the figure work suggests a rather large scene, the fragment must belong to an open vase, a bell-krater or a calyx-krater. In deciding between the two shapes we must consider that the profile of the fragment is slightly concave and that in the scene represented (see below) the foot preserved on the left of the armed youth, at the height of his head, suggests the existence of a second figure, seated or standing, at a higher level. Since in bell-kraters the only concave part of the vessel is the short part between handles and lip, which could not possibly accommodate the assumed figure to the left of the armed youth, I suggest that our fragment comes from a calyx-krater.

Calyx-kraters appear in Apulian red-figure from the start of the fabric with the Painter of the Berlin Dancing Girl.[2] These early calyx-kraters, which are fashioned on the basis of Attic prototypes, are stocky and usually decorated with scenes of figures standing, sitting, or moving, within the limits of one register only. More elongated calyx-kraters, decorated with scenes spread over more than one level, are introduced a little later and become popular in the course of the fourth century. One more or less early example of this type is Taranto I.G. 4600 by the Painter of the Birth of Dionysos.[3] Two later characteristic examples, with figures spread over two levels, are attributed to the Lycurgus Painter and date from around the middle of the fourth century: they are London F271, with a representation of the madness of Lycurgus on the front side and Milan ST.6873 showing a scene with Parthenopaios on the obverse.[4] In this context it is also worth mentioning two calyx-kraters by the Darius Painter, Basel Antikenmuseum S34[5] and Matera 12538,[6] dating from the third quarter of the century. Both are again decorated with scenes spread over more than one level. The examination of the style of drawing, which follows, will show that our fragment should belong to a comparatively early calyx-krater of this kind.

Decoration: The remains of the scene represented consist of an armed youth in front of a building and of the shod foot of a second figure which is otherwise entirely lost.[7] The building in front of which the youth stands suggests at first glance a façade with a column and a half-open front door. Figures standing or sitting in front of façades of buildings are not uncommon in Apulian "Ornate"; a good example is that of Apollo represented in front of his temple on the fragmentary calyx-krater by the Painter of the Birth of Dionysos, Amsterdam 2579.[8] On

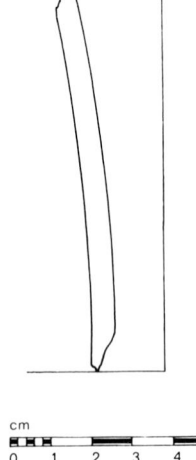

Fig. 1
Fragment of Apulian red-figure calyx-krater.
Sydney, Nicholson Museum No. 51.47.
Profile drawing: Mr. Geoffrey Neil.

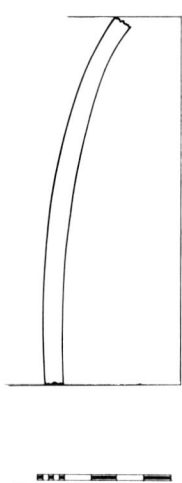

Fig. 2
Fragment of Apulian red-figure amphora.
Sydney, Nicholson Museum, No. 51. 48.
Profile drawing: Mr. Geoffrey Neil.

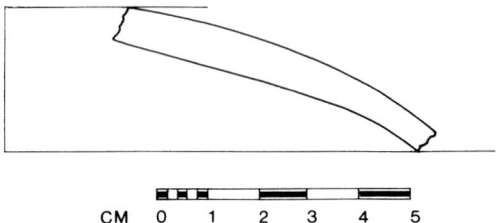

Fig. 3
Fragment of Apulian red-figure amphora.
Sydney, Nicholson Museum, No. 53.12.
Profile drawing: Mr. Geoffrey Neil.

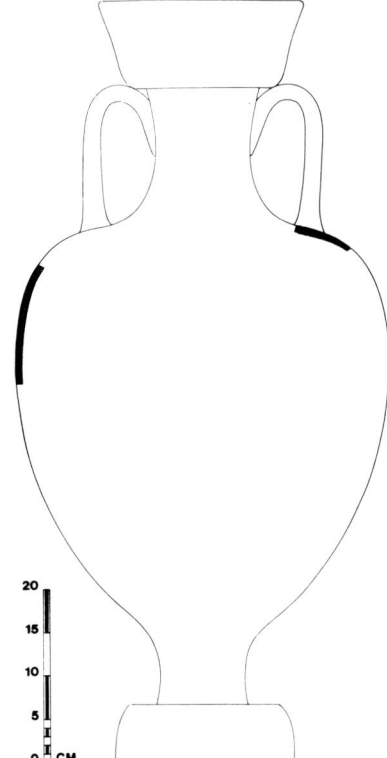

Fig. 4

The Apulian red-figure fragments Sydney, Nicholson
   Museum 51.48 and 53.12 reconstructed as parts of
   an amphora.
Drawing: Mr. Geoffrey Neil.

this vase the architectural features of the temple are clear, leaving no doubt about the relation-ship of the panels of the door, which are open inwards, to its jambs and to the corner columns of the porch. Similarly, on the fragment Heidelberg 2504,[9] we can easily identify behind the goddess Artemis the right panel and jamb of the entrance door of her temple and two columns of the peristyle to the right of the jamb. The door-panel is open inwards, allowing a view of the cult statue within the building.[10]

The architectural features on the Sydney fragment call for a careful examination. To the left of the youth's head is preserved the upper part of a column while to its right we can see the right panel of a door opened inwards, attached to a jamb. Both the column and the door-jamb are reserved. That the panel is meant to be half-open is suggested by the horizontal beam drawn in perspective.

Normally, in the representation on Apulian red-figure vases of buildings like this, one expects to see a front door with two half-open panels and columns on either side, belonging to the peristyle, as is the case on the Amsterdam calyx-krater mentioned above and on a number of other vases representing scenes with buildings as a background.[11] Since, however, on our fragment no left door-jamb and panel are visible, one has to assume either that the artist meant to draw a door with one jamb, one panel and one column only, more or less like the door on the reverse of the bell-krater by the Eton-Nika Painter London E 505[12] or that he meant to draw a normal two-panel door with the left panel hidden behind the armed youth. While the first reconstruction would make sense as a short-hand representation of a building in a simple scene like the one on the London bell-krater or on the phlyax skyphos London F 124,[13] it is not convincing in the picture of the high quality fragment in the Nicholson Museum. I am inclined therefore to reconstruct a façade with a two-panel door, comparable to that of Proitos' palace on the reverse of the stamnos Boston 00.349 by the Ariadne Painter[14] and to that of the stage building on the obverse of the calyx-krater New York 24.97.104, by the Tarporley Painter.[15] Such a reconstruction would imply that the vertical reserved band immediately to the right of the door panel is in fact not a jamb, but a column counterbalancing the one partly visible on the left of the youth's head.

The youth is nude except for a chlamys with a buckle on the chest. His right arm is stretched out while his left arm and side are covered by a round shield. The baldrick of his sword is slung over his right shoulder, but the scabbard is hidden behind the shield. It is likely that the youth held his sword in his right hand, since he is represented in an attacking position. His head is protected by a Corinthian helmet. The buckle of his chlamys, the helmet and the shield were covered by a coat of white-gold paint which has mostly flaked off. The helmet is decorated with what seems to be a bird painted in darker brownish colour. The tail of the crest of the helmet is painted white and is only partly preserved; the remains of the colour and its "ghost", which is not clearly visible in the illustration, show that it fell behind, across the door panel and along the curved edge of the shield, in the shape of a wavy band becoming thinner towards the end. The border of the shield was decorated with a wavy dark line which is only partly preserved. Along the inner black line of the border there is a band similar in colour to the wavy line, which is only partly preserved and not visible in the illustration.

Attribution: The drawing suggests that the fragment belongs to the "Ornate Style" and my first reaction was to seek parallels in the work of the Iliupersis Painter. More especially, I thought that the youth of our fragment recalled Ajax on the volute-krater London F 160, or Hermes on the volute-krater London F 277.[16] The style of drawing, however, of the Iliupersis Painter is considerably flatter than that of the youth on the Sydney fragment, and I finally placed it near the Painter of the Birth of Dionysos. More particularly, I think that the youth recalls Kyknos on the volute-krater Ruvo, Jatta 1088.[17] Apart from their obvious external similarities, the two figures are connected by the treatment of their profile heads and more particularly the eyes and hair. Noteworthy in the eye of our youth is the projecting line indicating the supra-orbital margin.

Date: The work of the Painter of the Birth of Dionysos, who was first identified by the late Mrs Noël Oakeshott ('The Dionysiac Painter', *JHS* 55, 1935, pp. 230 ff.), can be dated to the period between the close of the fifth century and about 385 B.C.[18] The Sydney fragment must be dated nearer to the 385 limit.

2 *Two fragments by the Iliupersis Painter.*

(a) No. 51.48 (Pl. 12, Fig. 2; Fig. 2 on p. 48) *RVAp* I, p. 200, 8/73. Acquired in the international market at the same time as no. 53.12 (see below). Height: 14.3 cm; width: 17.9 cm. Thickness: 6.7 mm increasing downwards. Pinkish-buff clay, lustrous dark glaze, traces of *miltos.*

Shape and decoration: The inner surface is unpainted, therefore the fragment must belong to a closed vase. Its size and the figures on it, which spread over at least two levels, as well as the remains of the floral ornament, suggest either a volute-krater or an amphora of panathenaic shape.[19] The rather sharp curvature of the profile, the fact the fragment must come from approximately the middle of the body of a vessel and the statement in the Museum records that it was acquired in the market at the same time as 53.12, which is by the same painter and could not possibly belong to a volute-krater (see below), point to a shape similar to Naples 2147 (inv. 82138) (Pl. 13, Figs. 4—5).[20]

Of the scene represented three figures are partly preserved: the left arm of a draped figure to left, the legs of a seated youth to right, as well as part of this cloak, left hand resting on a shield and lower part of his stick or spear, and the upper part of a woman, wearing earring and necklace, holding a wreath in her right hand.

To the right the floral ornament below the handle is also partly preserved suggesting a complex with horizontal as well as vertical palmettes like those on the amphora Vatican AA4.[21] In Apulian red-figure this kind of floral complex seems to occur mainly on the amphorae of panathenaic type[22] and volute-kraters.[23] On the former it is on the whole simpler and narrower, on the latter it is usually more complex and larger.[24]

If, as suggested, our fragment belongs to an amphora, this should be of the standard panathenaic type used by the Iliupersis Painter.[25] Although among the early Apulian vase-painters this shape, in general, is not very popular, it is nevertheless introduced very early, as four recently found examples by the Painter of the Berlin Dancing Girl and the Gravina Painter clearly show.[26] These amphorae resemble Attic prototypes[27] and amphorae of panathenaic type in early Lucanian.[28] By the Painter of the Berlin Dancing Girl we also have the only neck-amphora known to date in Early Apulian.[29]

Among the artists of the "Plain Style" in the first quarter of the fourth century, the amphora of panathenaic type is used more frequently than among artists of the "Ornate Style" especially in the school of the Tarporley Painter.[30] The proportions become gradually more elongated and on Milan "H.A." Collection 315, by the Painter of Karlsruhe B9, the mouth is decorated with a white laurel wreath.[31] On the whole, however, the Panathenaic Amphora of the "Plain Style" remains throughout a vase of moderate size and simple decoration.[32] In the "Ornate Style" the Iliupersis Painter, to whom our fragment is attributed, is the first artist to make extensive use of the shape.

His amphorae often have a mouth which curves slightly in toward the middle, flares out at the top and is decorated with a painted white wreath running around it. The Iliupersis Painter's amphorae can be big vases, as Madrid 11223 (L. 346) and Vatican AA4 (inv. 18256), with respective heights of 92 and 87 cm, clearly show,[33] as can be the Panathenaic amphorae used by his followers. Such large amphorae are Ruvo 423[34] and Ruvo 425[35] attributed to the Group of Ruvo 423, (with a height of about one metre) and Trieste S380 by the Lycurgus Painter.[36] The culmination of the trend toward an increased size is reached in the workshop of the Darius Painter, who favoured the shape.[37]

(b) No. 53.12 (Pl. 12, Fig. 3; Fig. 3 on p. 48). Acquired in the market from the same source as no. 51.48 (see above). Height: 6.9 cm; width: 16.5 cm. Thickness: 5 to 7 mm. increasing upwards. Pinkish buff clay, dark lustrous glaze.

Shape and decoration: The inside surface is unpainted therefore the fragment should belong to a closed vase. The downward curving wheel lines on the inside suggest that the fragment in its correct position should be only slightly tilted (see Text Fig. 3) and that it should belong to the shoulder of a vase, an area very close to the bottom of its neck. The spreading of the figure work, of the background decoration and of the floral ornament over the shoulder suggests an amphora rather than a volute-krater since the shoulder of Apulian volute-kraters is always covered with a tongue pattern and the figure work is confined to the body of the vessel. The thick line partly preserved above the half shield must be thought of as being contiguous to the bottom of the neck, as on the amphora Naples 2147 (inv. 82138) (Pl. 13, Figs. 4–5).[38] The diameter of the black line can be calculated to be approximately 15.20 cm long, a length which is in keeping with the dimensions of the large amphorae decorated by this artist. There is therefore no doubt that this fragment, like the fragment 51.48, belongs to an amphora of panathenaic shape.[39]

What is preserved of the decoration consists of the upper part of the body and the head of a youth turned to the left, of the hanging half shield mentioned above and of parts of a tendril belonging to a handle palmette complex. In view of what has been said about the shape of the fragment, a reconstruction of the palmette complex on the basis of those on other amphorae by the Iliupersis Painter seems convincing.[40] Even more convincing seems a reconstruction on the basis of the palmette complex on the amphora Amsterdam 3478, attributed to the Schlaepfer Painter but connected also with the Iliupersis Painter.[41]

Attribution: Both fragments can be safely attributed to the Iliupersis Painter.[42] The identification of his work is the result of research carried out by a number of scholars, but the credit for putting together for the first time three most important vases decorated by him must go to Miss Noël Moon (the late Mrs Oakeshott).[43] The subject on the obverse of the name vase, London F 160, has been carefully dealt with recently by Dr J.-M. Moret.[44] Although, generally speaking, the Iliupersis Painter follows the style of the Painter of the Birth of Dionysos and his school, he is most important in his own right for the development of Middle and Late Apulian "Ornate Style" and a great innovator, especially in the decoration of large vases. Although we are short of external evidence we can safely place the main part of his career on the grounds of style of drawing in the second quarter of the fourth century. His earlier vases may go back to about 380 B.C.[45]

The attribution of the fragment 51.48 to the painter is based on a comparison of the legs of the youth with those of male figures on a number of his other vases, but especially with those of the seated youth on the obverse of Naples 2147 (inv. 83138) *RVAp* p. 195, 8/26

(Pl. 13, Figs. 4—5). The similarity in both figures of the treatment of the *vasti* by means of two lines, one slightly, the other sharply curved, and of the *malleoli* by means of drop lines, is striking (see *RVAp* I, p. 192). One also notes the similarity in the indication of the line between the *tibiae* and the calf muscles, of the creases of the skin at the junctures between *tibiae* and metatarsal bones, and of the toes. The feet of both figures rest on the ground lines indicated by rows of white dots, another characteristic of the painter (see *RVAp* I, p. 191). The finely drawn profile face of the woman below the seated youth on the Sydney fragment finds a strikingly close parallel in the profile of the similarly seated youth on the Naples amphora (see *RVAp* I, p. 191).

The attribution of the fragment 53.12 is based on a comparison of the youth's head with those of the youths on the reverse of the volute-krater London F 283 and that of the standing right-hand youth on the reverse of the volute-krater Boston 1970.235.[46] His neck and thorax are very similar to those of the seated youth on the obverse of the Naples amphora (Pl. 13, Fig. 4). Note especially the indication of the sternomastoids, the sternum, and the vertical, slightly curving, line separating the clavicles from the shoulders. Hanging half-shields are fairly frequent on vases by the Iliupersis Painter, but the half-shield on this fragment is especially close to the shield on the reverse of Naples 2147 (Pl. 13, Fig. 5).

Reconstruction: I hope I have shown that the two Sydney fragments come from amphorae of panathenaic shape and that they are both works of the Iliupersis Painter. The similarity of the clay and glaze and their simultaneous acquisition by the Museum suggest that they should belong to the same vase, and that indeed fragment 51.48 must belong to the obverse and 53.12 to the reverse of a panathenaic amphora.[47] The drawing on p. 48, Fig. 4 gives the approximate respective positions of the two fragments in a reconstructed amphora, which turns out to be of the canonical dimensions used by the Iliupersis Painter, just over 0.80 m.

The subjects on the two fragments can also be plausibly reconstructed: the figures on 51.48 could have formed part of a scene at a naiskos or stele like those on the amphora Naples 2147 (Pl. 13, Fig. 4) and Vatican AA4 (see *supra* note 21);[48] the youth on 53.12 too could belong to a scene of funerary or conversational character (cf. the reverse of Naples 2147, Pl. 13, Fig. 5).

Date: Although the Iliupersis Painter begins his career in the later part of the Early Apulian phase, he is the most important artist of Middle Apulian. While it is easy to pinpoint his later vases, it is not always easy to differentiate between an early and a middle period. The two Sydney fragments are mature in style and should be dated between 375 and 360 B.C.

NOTES

1 For the distinction between Apulian red-figure vases of the "Plain" and "Ornate" styles, see *APS*, pp. 3—4; *ESI*, pp. 14 ff.; *RVAp* I, p. xlix.

2 *APS*, p. 6; *ESI*, p. 46; *RVAp* I, p. 7, 1/7—9.

3 *PBD*, p. 676, no. 6; *RVAp* I, p. 36, 2/11.

4 For London F 271, see Schmidt, p. 12, Pls. 2—3; *EAA* iv, p. 750, Fig. 909; Andrew Oliver Jr. 'The Lycurgus Painter', *BMMA* Summer 1962, p. 27, Fig. 2; Borda, Pl. VII; *Ill.Gr.Dr.* III, 1, 15; *RVAp* I, p. 415, 16/5. For Milan ST.6873, see *Finarte 5, Sale Catatogue,* Milan 14 March, 1963, No. 86, Pls. 44—45; *Ill.Gr.Dr.* III, 4, 1; *RVAp* I, p. 416, 16/6.

5 See Margot Schmidt, Arthur Dale Trendall and Alexander Cambitoglou, *Eine Gruppe apulischer Grabvasen in Basel,* Mainz 1976, Pls. 23—26.

6 See K.M. Phillips Jr, 'Perseus and Andromeda', *AJA* 72, 1968, Pls. 10—11, Figs. 27—29, and *Ill.Gr.Dr.* III, 3, 12.

7 There is, I think, no doubt that this is a shod foot. The sole of the shoe, indicated in a thick brown line, is clearly distinguished from the upper part. In the Apulian "Ornate" style, shoes, especially those worn by women, are often left reserved with details indicated by means of black lines only (see for example the shoes worn by Hypnos on the reverse of the bell-krater New York 16.140 attributed to the Sarpedon Painter, *ESI*, p. 53, No. 159; *RVAp* I, p. 164, 7/1; or those worn by Athena on the obverse of the volute-krater London F 160 by the Iliupersis Painter, Moret, *Ilioupersis*, Pls. 7–10; *RVAp* I, p. 193, 8/8). Very often details of shoes are indicated by means of white dots or lines, like those on the shoes worn by Athena on the volute-krater Adolphseck 178 by the Lycurgus Painter (*CVA* 2, Pls. 76–79; *RVAp* I, p. 416, 16/11). In many cases, however, shoes are almost entirely covered in white-yellow paint (see those of some of the figures on the pelike Zurich, Arch. Sammlung der Universität 2656, by the Painter of the Moscow Pelike, *CVA* Pls. 35–6 and 38; *RVAp* I, p. 170, 7/34, or those of the female figures on the amphora Naples 2272 (inv. 82380) by the Patera Painter. On the calyx-krater Amsterdam 2581 (*Gids* 1494) attributed to the Black Fury Group, (FR, Pl. 178; *Gids*, Pl. 77, 1; *RVAp* I, p. 168, 7/22) the boots of one of the Thracian women seem to be entirely covered in paint.

8 *PBD*, p. 676, no. 5 and Pl. V; *RVAp* I, p. 36, 2/10.

9 Related to the Painter of the Birth of Dionysos (*PBD*, p. 677, no. 13 and *RVAp* I, p. 41, 2/28).

10 The relation of the horizontal rafter near the top of the fragment to the features mentioned above is not clear. The exact position of the two partly preserved columns is not clear either: one of them may belong to the façade, while the other may belong to one of the sides.

11 See for example the building on the obverse of the volute-krater Naples 3223 (inv. 82113) (*FR* iii, Pl. 148; *Ill.Gr.Dr.*, 3, 28; *RVAp* I, p. 193, 8/3); the obverse of the volute-krater in Naples representing the theft of the Palladion (G. Patroni, 'La ceramica antica nell'Italia meridionale', 1897, p. 135, Fig. 92, and A.W. Pickard-Cambridge, *The Theatre of Dionysos in Athens*, Oxford 1946, p. 84, Fig. 12; *RVAp* I, p. 401, 15/29); the obverse and reverse of the volute-krater Bari 3648 (Margot Schmidt, 'Makaria', *AntK* 13, 1970 p. 71 ff., Pls. 33–34; *RVAp* I, p. 210, 8/144).

12 *APS*, 43, no. 6; *RVAp* I, p. 78, 4/88.

13 A.D. Trendall, *Phlyax Vases*, 2nd edition (*BICS* no. 19, 1967), 57, no. 94.

14 *ESI*, 50, no. 84, Pl. 23 b; Nikolas Yalouris, *Pegasus, The Art of the Legend*, (Mobil Oil Hellas) 1975, Fig. 44; *RVAp* I, p. 24, 1/104. For the reference to the vase in Boston, I am indebted to the kindness of Mr John Wade, who is making a special study of buildings in Italiote vase-painting.

15 *APS*, 34, no. 20; *ESI*, 51, no. B 122 and *RVAp* I, p. 46, 3/7.

16 For the Iliupersis Painter see Moon, 45 ff.; Carl Watzinger, *FR* iii, 349–350; Arturo Stenico, *EAA* iv, 107, *SIVP²*, 19 ff.; Gemma Sena-Chiesa, 'Vasi apuli di stile ornato', *Acme* 21, 1968, 327–379. For a discussion and a list of the painter's works see *RVAp* I, pp. 185 ff. For the volute-krater London F 160, see *RVAp* I, p. 193, 8/8; for the volute-krater London F 277 see *RVAp* I, p. 193, 8/5.

17 *PBD*, p. 676, no. 10, and pp. 694 ff.; *RVAp* I, p. 39, 2/23. The obverse of the Ruvo vase is beautifully illustrated in Sichtermann, *GVU*, Pls. 69–71.

18 *PBD*, p. 692; *RVAp* I, p. 35 and table Fig. 3.

19 The possibility of a column-krater should be excluded since, with few exceptions (see Vatican V 57 *VIE*, Pl. XXXVI, a–b) scenes on vases of this shape are framed by a reserved band on either side decorated with rows of blobs (*VIE*, Pl. XXXIV).

20 *RVAp* I, p. 195, 8/26.

21 *VIE* Pl. LV, a–e; *RVAp* I, p. 196, 8/30.

22 Cf. Trieste S 380, *CV* IVD Pls. 14–15 by the Lycurgus Painter, and my review in *AJA* 1972, p. 234; *RVAp* I, p. 418, 16/19.

23 Cf. Louvre CA227, Moon, Pls. XV–XVI; Eva Keuls, *The Water Carriers in Hades*, Amsterdam 1974,

Pls. IV–V, now attributed to the Painter of Athens 1714 (*RVAp* I, p. 211, 8/146). For a variant of this ornament see the situla by the Lycurgus Painter New York 56.171.64, Hôtel Drouot *Cat.* 18 March 1901, no. 57, illustrated on pp. 20–21; *BMMA* March 1957, p. 179 and Summer 1962, pp. 26 ff. figs. 1, 3 and 8; Dietrich v. Bothmer, "Greek Vase Painting", *BMMA* 31.1, Fall 1972, p. 4 (ill.); *RVAp* I, p. 417, 16/17.

24 Cf. the handle floral complex on Vatican AA4 (*VIE*, Pl. LV a–e) with those on the volute-krater London F 277 (Konrad Schauenburg, "Die Totengötter in der Unter-Italischen Vasenmalerei", *JdI* 73, 1958, 58, fig. 3) or Milan "H.A." Collection 285 (*CVA* 1, IVD, Pls. 3–4), all three by the Iliupersis Painter (*RVAp* I, p. 196, 8/30; p. 193, 8/5 and p. 194, 8/10).

25 Cf. Naples 2147 (inv. 82139) (Pl. 13, Figs. 4–5) and Naples 2417 (inv. 82309) (*RVAp* I, p. 195, 8/26 and p. 196, 8/28).

26 All four amphorae are in Taranto. The two by the Painter of the Berlin Dancing Girl come from Tomb 24 at Rutigliano: one represents a warrior on the obverse and a mounted Amazon on the reverse, the other Adrastos preparing for the expedition of The Seven Against Thebes, in a scene running right round the vase (*RVAp* I, p. 434, no. 9a and p. 435, no. 12b). Of the other two amphorae, by the Gravina Painter, one represents the death of Stheneboia on the obverse and two youths and two women on the reverse, the other three women and two youths beside the statue of a warrior on the obverse and two youths and two women on the reverse (*RVAp* I, pp. 32–33, 2/2–3).

27 Cf. Vienna 939 by the Naples Painter, ARV^2 1099, 50.

28 Cf. Taranto I.G. 8001 by the Pisticci Painter, *LCS* p. 22, no. 57 and Naples 2416 (inv. 82264) by the Amykos Painter, *LCS* p. 48, no. 246.

29 Lecce 571, *APS,* p. 7, no. 15; *ESI,* 46, no. B14; Borda, 31, Fig. 21 (*RVAp* I, p. 7, 1/13). After an interval of about seventy-five years the neck-amphora reappears in Apulian, no doubt under Campanian and Paestan influence [see the neck-amphorae by the Thyrsus Painter, Copenhagen 319, Geneva MF278, and Naples 1898 (inv. 81786), *APS,* p. 79, nos. 32–34; *RVAp* I, p. 280 10/168–171 and p. 281, 10/180].

30 See Philadelphia 31.36.17, *APS,* p. 34, no. 19; *ESI,* p. 52, no. B 134; *RVAp* I, p. 46, 3/8 and Matera 11999, *ESI,* p. 52, no. B 135; F.G. Lo Porto, 'Civiltà indigena e penetrazione greca nella Lucania orientale', *Monumenti Antichi, Accademia Nazionale dei Lincei,* serie miscellanea, vol. I, 3, Pl. XVI, 3–4, by the Tarporley Painter himself; *RVAp* I, p. 52, 3/51. See also Copenhagen 20 (218), *APS,* p. 38, no. 3; *CVA* Pl. 238, 2, by the Painter of Lecce 686 (*RVAp* I, p. 57, 3/68).

31 *CVA* 1, IVD Pl. 25; *RVAp* I, p. 138, 6/24.

32 See for example the amphora by the Truro Painter, Brussels, Errera Collection, *APS,* p. 70, no. 44; *RVAp* I, p. 122, 5/189.

33 For Madrid 11223 see *Ill.Gr.Dr.* IV 7b; Ricardo Olmos Romera, *Cerámica Griega,* Madrid 1973, Figs. 36–37; *RVAp* I, p. 196, 8/29; for Vatican AA4 see *VIE* pp. 207–9 and pl. 55 a–e; *RVAp* I, p. 196, 8/30. The height of the latter includes the modern foot and is therefore only approximately correct. Even larger must be a Panathenaic amphora in the Roman market: (a) Achilles and Troilos (?) at the fountain house with warriors and women around, (b) three youths and two women at a naiskos in which there is a large vase (*RVAp* I, p. 196, 8/31).

34 Ruvo 423 (much repainted). *Japigia* 3, 1932, 272, Fig. 53; Pickard-Cambridge, *op.cit.* (*supra* note 11) Fig. 13; Bieber, $Hist^2$, Fig. 117; Sichtermann, *GVU,* K 71, Pls. 114–116 and Pl. 117, 2; Photos: R.I. 62.1367–8, 64.1143–5; *RVAp* I, p. 403, 15/41.

35 Ruvo 425 (much repainted). *Japigia* 3, 1932, 273, Fig. 54; Sichtermann, *GVU,* K 70, Pls. 112–113, Pl. 117, 1, and Pl. 118. Photos: R.I. 62.1369–70, 64. 1140–1; *RVAp* I, p. 403, 15/42.

36 Trieste S 380, *CVA* IVD, Pls. 14–15; Moret, *Ilioupersis,* Pls. 71, 1, and 97, 2; *RVAp* I, p. 418, 16/19.

37 Cf. Naples 3221 (inv. 81945) (Anna Rocco, 'Il pittore del vaso dei Persiani', *ArchCl* 5, 1953, 170 ff., Pls. 87–88; Schmidt, 53 and Pls. 16–17; Borda, Pl. XVI; T.B.L. Webster, *Hellenistic Art,* Pl. 3) and Naples 3219 (inv. 81953) (Schmidt, 53; Konrad Schauenburg, 'Gestirnbilder in Athen und Unter-italien'; *AntK* 5, 1962, 59 and Pl. 19, 1; Lidia Forti, *Letteratura e arte figurata nella Magna Grecia,* Taranto, Museo Nazionale, Oct. 1966, No. 115, illustrated; Max Wegner, *Musikgeschichte,* Fig. 68, which Trendall and I now attribute to the painter himself). It is worth mentioning, however, that the painters of the developed "Ornate" style also use extensively a smaller version of this shape (cf. Bologna, Pellegrini PU '522–4', *CVA* III IVD, Pl. 4, 6, or London F 339, Alexander Cambitoglou, 'Groups of Apulian Red-Figured Vases Decorated with Head of Women or of Nike'; *JHS* 74, 1954, 119, no. 3, and 116, no. 3 (above), Pl. Va.

38 *Neapolis* 1, 1913, 35, Fig. 5; *RVAp* I, p. 195, 8/26.

39 The possibility that it could belong to a hydria should be excluded. Hydriai have narrower necks and the surface immediately above the shoulder, where the upper parts of the figures represented usually reach, tends to be concave rather than convex.

40 Cf. Vatican AA4, *VIE,* Pl. LV a–e (*RVAp* I, p. 196, 8/30).

41 (*Gids* 1506), *CVA* Scheurleer 2, IV Db, Pl. 5, 3–4; *RVAp* I, p. 246, 9/160.

42 See note 16.

43 The volute-kraters London F 283, London F 160, and Naples 3228 (Moon, pp. 45–47; *RVAp* I, pp. 193–4, 8/7–9.)

44 Moret, *Ilioupersis,* vol. II, p. 26.

45 *RVAp* I, Fig. 3 following p. 442.

46 *RVAp* I, p. 193, 8/7 and p. 194, 8/11.

47 The fact that on both fragments the remains of the floral handle-ornament are on the right of the figure-work precludes their belonging to the same side of one vase.

48 For the popularity of funerary scenes with naiskoi or stelai in the work of the Iliupersis Painter see *RVAp* I, p. 186.

AN ETRUSCAN (CAERETAN) FISH PLATE

Mario del Chiaro

Plate 14.

I welcome the opportunity provided by this volume – published in honour of Professor A.D. Trendall – to express my deep gratitude to a friend and scholar for the sage advice and constructive criticism he has offered me during occasional meetings in Rome and the United States, and through regular correspondence over the last two decades. His unchallengeable knowledge of South Italian vase-painting has in many instances helped me to understand better Etruscan red-figured pottery and deal more competently with perplexing problems encountered in my special studies of it. In view of this, and my long interest in Etruscan red-figured pottery produced at Caere (modern Cerveteri), I believe a rare example of Etruscan pottery – namely, a Caeretan fish plate – provides an especially appropriate theme for an article in his honour.

Cerveteri, Museo Nazionale Cerite[1] (Pl. 14, Figs. 1–2).
No inventory number.
Provenience, Caere.
Height: 6 cm.; diam. of plate: 18 cm.; diam. of foot: 7.5 cm.
Interior: four sea creatures – a squid, two sea-perch, and a torpedo or ray – swimming counterclockwise round a circular eight-wave motif. The center of the plate is without groove or channel, nor moulded ring.
A reserved band with dot decoration runs round the edge of the plate.
An overhanging rim or lip carries a continuous wave pattern. There is no use of relief-lines in the painted decoration. The heavy foot is high and elaborate.

Fish plates, adequately named for the marine life represented on their interior, which in all probability reflects their proper use, are known to Attic red-figure,[2] but are more commonly found in South Italian pottery – Campanian and Apulian in particular.[3] In Etruscan pottery, however, the type is rare (see above note 1). In its overall general character of shape, clay color (buff or yellowish-grey), and spontaneous style of drawing, the Cerveteri fish plate is unquestionably not the product of a South Italian workshop. More properly, on the basis of my prolonged studies in Caeretan red-figure, I am convinced that the plate is an Etruscan[4] – specifically a Caeretan – imitation of a South Italian fish plate.[5]

In sharp contrast to its South Italian counterparts,[6] the sloping interior of the Etruscan fish plate does not run into a central depression or cavity set off by a groove or moulded ring. Instead, this 'depression' – doubtless intended to gather the fish juices or hold a piquant sauce – is simply suggested by the Etruscan vase-painter who, within a reserved encircling band, has rendered a circular eight-wave motif with large central dot bordered by two concentric lines. Crude as this motif may be, it is undeniably based on the carefully executed wave pattern at the depression of South Italian fish plates. Around the upper edge of the Etruscan imitation, there runs a border composed of a narrow reserved band decorated with a series of painstakingly placed dots at each side. Such an enclosing band is also known in varying form on a number of South Italian examples.[7]

Although the vertical overhanging rim on the Cerveteri fish plate is not as broad as that found on South Italian plates, the choice of a continuous wave pattern as its decoration conforms to a motif normally employed by Campanian and Apulian vase-painters.[8] Whereas the South Italian fish plate presents a normally low, squat profile emphasized by the broad overhanging rim which obscures from view much of its underside, the Etruscan fish plate – by reason of its narrow overhanging rim and its high and clumsily proportioned foot which finds no parallel on South Italian specimens[9] — reveals considerably more of its underside. The underside of the Cerveteri plate is painted black well down over a portion of the convex join of foot and 'bowl'; the remaining horizontal portion is reserved, and below this the curved, convex area of the foot proper is painted black with the exception of the resting vertical edge. The high foot and relatively deep interior of the Cerveteri fish plate seems to follow the traditional fondness of the Etruscans for stemmed plates and bowls in their pottery forms.

As on South Italian fish plates, the major decoration on the Caeretan counterpart is executed in red-figure. The drawing is bold and fluid, and there is no use of relief-lines. The choice of four rather than of three sea creatures — the normal number found on South Italian fish plates[10] — results in a somewhat crowded composition. In sharp contrast to Attic fish plates on which the fish are represented with their bellies near the outer edge of the plate in an apparently 'upside-down' fashion,[11] the Etruscan and South Italian fish plates show the fish with their backs towards the rim. Although the sea-perch are rendered in profile — as, one might think, is the squid — the torpedo or ray fish is depicted as viewed from the top. As a rule, the general movement or direction of the sea creatures on South Italian fish plates and the Etruscan imitation is counterclockwise round the centre of the plate. Whereas the Caeretan vase-painter concentrated more on the outline or silhouette of his fish than on their internal details, the South Italian artist — primarily Campanian — delighted in details, frequently enhanced by rich use of added colour (yellow and white) and brownish washes in diluted glaze-paint.[12]

It is interesting to speculate as to whether or not the species of edible fish represented on the Caeretan fish plate reflect a variety of sea life abundant in Etruscan waters (i.e., the central Tyrrhenian Sea)[13] — as known to Etruscan fishermen and their clientele in the fish markets of Etruscan towns and villages — or whether, more simply, they are directly derived from the sea life depicted on South Italian fish plates.[14] It stands to reason that fish plates — Attic, South Italian, and now Etruscan — averaging but 20–25 cm. in diameter, were not intended to hold such large fish as represented on the plates themselves. More probably, such fish were cut up into bite size (as in the oriental, Japanese, custom) and dipped into an accompanying sauce in the central depression of the plate.

Although the Caeretan fish plate approximates to Apulian examples in its simplicity of drawing, the presence of the torpedo or ray fish and the general contours of the sea-perch point more closely to fish plates by the Torpedo Painter, a Campanian vase-painter active during the last quarter of the fourth century B.C., and so-named after the frequent appearance of the torpedo fish on plates by his hand.[15] As I have attempted to illustrate in past studies devoted to specific Caeretan vase shapes,[16] strong influences emanated from South Italian workshops on Etruscan potters and vase-painters throughout the second half of the fourth century B.C. Hence, the Etruscan (Caeretan) fish plate presented in this paper marks another instance of this important artistic and cultural influence from Southern Italy in Etruria.

NOTES

1 I wish to thank Dott. Mario Moretti, Soprintendente alle Antichità dell'Etruria Meridionale, Rome for his kind permission to photograph, study, and publish this unusual Etruscan fish plate in the Museo Nazionale Cerite at Cerveteri. The plate has been briefly discussed also in my *Etruscan Red-Figured Vase-Painting at Caere* (Berkeley 1974), p. 85 f. and pl. 90. For two additional fish plates by the same hand in Vienna (Kunsthistorisches Museum nos. IV.4040 and IV.4041) see *ÖJh* 51 (1976), pp. 11–15.

2 K. Schefold, *Untersuchungen zu den Kertscher Vasen,* Berlin 1934, 11 f. and Figs. 1–2; S. Aurigemma, *Il R. Museo di Spina in Ferrara,* Ferrara 1936, 148 f.; D.M. Robinson, *Excavations at Olynthus, V,* Baltimore 1933, Nos. 231–2 and Pl. 113; *XIII,* Baltimore 1950, Nos. 73–4, Pls. 80 and 92.

3 Of the sporadic appearance of Campanian and Apulian fish plates in the *Corpus Vasorum Antiquorum,* I call special attention to *CVA* Capua, Museo Campano 1, IV E r, Pls. 1–6 and *CVA* Lecce, Museo Provinciale Castromediano 2, IV D r, Pl. 59, figs. 3–6. For Apulian fish plates, L. Lacroix, *La Faune Marine dans la décoration des Plats à Poisson,* Verviers 1937, has excellent illustrations; *cf.* A.D. Trendall's review in *JHS* 57, 1937, 268 f. A seminar paper on South Italian fish plates by Michael Katzev, submitted to and called to my attention by Professor D.A. Amyx, has proved extremely serviceable.

4 My immediate impression, during a recent visit to Cerveteri, that the fish plate in the Museo Nazionale Cerite must be of local Caeretan manufacture is supported by Dr. J-G. Szilágyi who mentions the plate in 'Contributions à l'histoire de la peinture des vases à figures rouges campanienne', *Acta Antiqua Academiae Scientiarum Hungaricae* 18, 1970, 260 n. 60.

5 M. Del Chiaro, *Exhibition Catalogue, Greek Art in Private Collections of Southern California,* University of California, Santa Barbara, 1963, (rev. ed. 1966), No. 71; Campanian fish plate attributed to the Torpedo Painter.

6 For a sample of profiles of Campanian fish plates, see *CVA* Capua, Museo Campano 1, IV E r, Pl. 6.

7 See *CVA* London, British Museum 2, IV E a, Pl. 12, fig. 22; *CVA* Milano, Collezione H. A. 1, IV D, Pl. 41, fig. 3; and *CVA* Capua, Museo Campano 1, IV E r, Pl. 1, fig. 3.

8 The majority of published South Italian fish plates are not shown in profile, and their rim decoration is thereby generally described in the accompanying text rather than illustrated in the reproduction. Nonetheless, several specimens which utilise a vegetal motif in place of the usual wave pattern may be cited: laurel, *CVA* Capua, Museo Campano 1, IV E r, Pl. 6, fig. 6; ivy, *CVA* Baltimore, Robinson Collection 3, IV E, Pl. XXVI, fig. 3b. By comparison, Apulian decorators of fish plates prefer the laurel more than do their Campanian colleagues. In view of the marine decoration at the interior of fish plates, I believe the wave pattern at the rim and, at times, encircling the central depression, is far more appropriate and consistent than a vegetal or floral motif. Although the region of the central depression or cavity on South Italian fish plates is more commonly undecorated, when accented by a painted motif it is usually an encircling wave pattern. A variant is sometimes provided by a series of short, radiating lines.

9 See *supra* n. 6.

10 There are rare occurrences of only two fish or sea creatures on fish plates: e.g. *CVA* Capua, Museo Campano 1, IV E r, Pl. 5, fig. 5. However, on plates with only two fish, and frequently on the more usual examples with three much smaller fish, shrimp, shell fish, and other minute sea creatures may be used as 'fillers',

11 See *supra* n. 2.

12 *EAA* II, Rome 1959, coloured plate opposite p. 496.

13 See Lacroix (*supra* n. 3), and A. Palombi and M. Santarelli, *Gli animali commestibili dei mari d'Italia,* Milan 1969.

14 To the best of my knowledge, no South Italian fish plates have been recorded in an Etruscan context. On South Italian fish plates, the usual fish and sea creatures represented are: sea-perch, torpedo (ray), mullet, rock-fish, sargus, squid (cuttle-fish), octopus, shrimp, and an assortment of shell fish.

15 *Cf.* A.D. Trendall, *JHS* 57, 1937, 269.

16 See M. Del Chiaro, 'Caeretan Epichyseis', *ArchCl* 12, 1960, 51–6; 'A Caeretan Red-Figured Mug', *StEtr* 30, 1962, 317–19; 'A Faliscan Red-Figured Skyphos, Type B', *ArchCl* XXIV (1972), p. 107 f.

A GEOMETRIC BRONZE HORSE IN THE UNIVERSITY OF MELBOURNE

P.J. Connor

Plate 15.

Professor Trendall has long encouraged the formation of teaching collections and I feel sure that the study of a piece in such a collection will please him. It is a small bronze votive offering of the Late Geometric period, of unknown provenance, which has been in the collection of the Department of Classical Studies of the University of Melbourne since a little before 1930.[1]

Despite what might appear to be horns and a pig-like snout, and despite a double tail, the animal pictured in Pl. 15, Figs. 1, 3–4 is a horse, or, more accurately perhaps, a stallion: the sex of such bronze horses is sometimes indicated,[2] but its absence does not mean that the animal is a mare.[3] The object is 5.8 cm long, 5.4 cm high, and is in reasonably good condition; the surface is pitted with tiny holes (not so much on the neck) and has been rather harshly cleaned at some time.

In profile the animal looks substantial: a broad neck and broad haunches and legs. The base on which the horse stands is proportionate to the width of the legs, and these proportions are more or less sustained in the ears, snout and tail. A frontal view, by contrast, shows the thinness of the metal used, the thinness of a bronze sheet. This is true of the neck, the haunches and legs, and the upper tail; the lower tail has a section very much like a wedge. This thinness is also visible in the base which is not solid but rather resembles a raised platform, with triangular perforations pierced through its top cover. The triangular perforations in the base (almost the norm in votive offerings of this kind)[4] are formally placed in two rows in an interlocking fashion, the apex of any one triangle pointing to the space between the base angles of two contiguous triangles.[5] This means that the strip of metal remaining runs in a regular zigzag and is about as wide as the depth of the base, another instance where the proportions of the ensemble hang roughly together.

The short stalk-like body has more solidity about it, but it is not round. The top is pinched to form quite a distinct line which is continued to an extent along the rump. Certainly there is no roundness between the two rear-quarters. These start their formation from the top of the body; the front haunches take their rise at a lower point, somewhat nearer to the underbelly. There is a firm, though not indented, mark at the juncture of the neck and of the front haunches. The snout is approximately tubular, but it has flattened facets which give it the appearance of a whittled stick. It ends in a prominent flat disc. The ears jut forward, horn-like. As can be seen in Pl. 15, Fig. 4, they look rather like a horseshoe in top view, since the base of one ear merges uninterruptedly with the base of the other. The flat section of the neck and legs combine to give this horse a comical appearance when viewed head-on (Pl. 15, Fig. 3). The straddle of the legs produces a very awkward shape. There are particularly good parallels for many of these features in a horse in Copenhagen.[6] One strikingly similar feature is the slight turn of the head away from the axis of the body.

As decoration the horse has two dotted concentric circles punched on each side of the neck and one in the middle of each haunch. Although that of the fore-quarter is not visible in left profile (Pl. 15, Fig. 1), the dot which lies at the centre can be made out. There are incised striations around the base and on the legs, seemingly in two groups of four and five at the join of the leg and base and where the knee might roughly be located. Incised lines indicate the hair of the mane. The mane of another horse, published by Herrmann,[7] is very carefully and naturalistically treated, but on the Melbourne horse, the realistic effect of the incised hair is somewhat dimmed since the same marks appear on the front edge of the neck, so defining the middle space where the concentric circles are punched and giving this whole area a clear decorative quality.

Special attention must be drawn to the width of the legs and to the absence of a hoof. The legs simply merge with the base in the manner remarked on by Himmelmann-Wildschütz: 'Die Pferde stehen hier nicht mitten auf dem Gitterwerk der Standplatte, vielmehr verschmelzen die Umrisse ihrer Beine mit deren Aussenkanten. Standfläche und Figur bilden also materiell und dekorativ eine Einheit.'[8]

The muzzle with the disc-ending, the long forward-projecting ears, the flattened shapes joined with a stem-like body, are all characteristic of what has been described as the 'mannerist' style, which is seen at its most elegant in horses of a Peloponnesian origin attributed to a Corinthian school by Herrmann.[9] Particularly fine examples of these can be found in his Figs. 12–16, but if we are to locate the Melbourne horse as exactly as possible, we can find closer parallels: Firstly, a horse in the E. de Kolb collection (No. 19 in D.G. Mitten and S.F. Doeringer, *Master Bronzes from the Classical World,* Harvard 1967, attributed by Mitten to the Thessalian school); secondly, Volos Museum Inventory No. 410 (Y. Béquignon, *Recherches archéologiques à Phères de Thessalie,* Paris 1937, p. 67 No. 2 and Pl. xix, 2). Mitten refers for a parallel to his piece to L65, Pl. 51 in H. Biesantz, *Die thessalischen Grabreliefs,* Mainz 1965, but this is not so close to the Melbourne horse, on which the legs have no articulation. In this respect, closer parallels are Biesantz Pl. 52, L64 and L67 (front legs).

Biesantz (p. 159) records that the Thessalian bronzes can be distinguished into a silhouette-type, made from thin sheet-metal, or a solid cast type with a compact body, or even a third type which is a mixture of both techniques. This last type matches the technique of the Melbourne horse. In describing his No. 19 Mitten talks of 'combination solid-hollow cast', but to call these horses 'hollow-cast' is not to use the term as it is generally applied.[10] In a somewhat neglected paper, 'The Casting Techniques of Certain Greek Bronzes',[11] R. Raven-Hart, drawn by the obvious carved effect of many Greek bronzes (compare my comments on the snout of the Melbourne horse), claims that this effect 'is due rather to their having been cast from carved originals than to the extensive tooling of the metal cast as is frequently assumed' (p. 87). Extensive tooling, he points out, is laborious, expensive and dangerous — one slip could ruin the whole piece. Raven-Hart suggests that a more efficient way of achieving a carved effect would be to carve the original in *hard* wax 'which gives the finished cast a carved appearance and removes the difficulties inherent in multi-piece moulding.'

In his study of the regional workshops of Geometric bronzes, Herrmann attempted to identify the products of Corinth: a difficult task since no substantial finds come from Corinth itself. But he had already been at pains to show that early work in this field had stumbled through assuming that votive offerings were manufactured at the sanctuaries where they were found. So adopting his reasonable dictum that find-spot is no clue to stylistic origin, he proceeded to determine the dominant traits of a Corinthian school of bronze-workers, relying strongly on specimens from Ithaka and Aegina, both importers of much Corinthian pottery. This led Herrmann to attribute the finds from Thessaly to the Corinthian School (p. 30). Biesantz has since proposed a local Thessalian School, and this indeed seems more likely.

So far, I have concentrated on individual items of physiognomy, but a full perception and description of the Melbourne horse should include a characterisation of the piece as a whole. The mannerism of the Corinthian pieces (Herrmann, Figs. 12–15), with the abstract shapes creating curving forms as well as curving lines, have a litheness, a finesse, and a vitality that are often missing in the Thessalian pieces — certainly in the Melbourne example, and in Biesantz, pl. 52, L67.[12] Some Thessalian horses, such as Biesantz pl. 51, L65, and the de Kolb horse (Mitten No. 19), share this kind of springiness only in an imperfect way.

One important element of the more static, solid Thessalian types is the width of the legs. The Corinthian examples (and even a Laconian, Herrmann fig. 16) have slender legs: the horse stands more alertly. Although we have seen with Himmelmann-Wildschütz that the fusion of legs and base is an element of pattern, the pattern must be admitted to be a still shape, interesting enough in its surface, but flat and completely motionless. By contrast, the mannerism of the Corinthian horses (Herrmann, Figs. 14 and 15), whilst verging on the over-elegant, is varied and lively.

Herrmann (p. 32) has very neatly caught the differing mannerisms of Corinthian and Laconian. Between Corinthian and Thessalian there is a further difference. Thessaly received from Corinth an influence which it did not truly absorb in order to produce an identity of its own, and this more imitative quality of the Thessalian bronzes leaves them fairly lifeless. The date of manufacture of the Melbourne horse would seem close to the end of the eighth century, and could possibly go down a little past 700 B.C., as Boardman suggests for other comparable examples.[13]

The examination of the basic physical appearance of the Melbourne horse has so far passed lightly over one detail. At first this detail poses a problem, but on examination, it may lead to establishing the piece as an example of a relatively rare group of Geometric bronzes.

The horse, as was said earlier, has two tails (Pl. 15, Fig. 1), neither of which falls straight to the base as in numerous other examples of this type.[14] This curious feature can be explained by comparison with a bronze in the Ny Carlsberg Glyptotek (Pl. 15, Fig. 2),[15] a Geometric group of two horses back-to-back on a long stand. These horses are united at their tails which join together before dropping vertically to the stand, and are further united by an arc from rump to rump. The short double tail of the Melbourne horse, which shows signs of fracture at the ends, indicates that this horse was originally one of a pair, of which the former partner is now lost. It should be noted of course that the base of the Melbourne bronze is broken at the horse's rear: the narrow side is jagged, leaving in fact one of the perforated triangles incomplete, and is not closed off as is the front (Pl. 15, Figs. 3—4).

There are other similar pieces: one from Delphi, published by Rolley,[16] which is rather badly mutilated, though the central part is still preserved, and another from Ithaka, published by Sylvia Benton as horse-griffins.[17] Rolley has disputed this description, noting in particular that the animals' mouths are closed, not open as on the cauldron griffins; he mentions another such group from Pherai in Thessaly (Athens MN 15470). I have inspected this piece and can report that the tail proper is now broken, leaving two stumps similar to the 'lower' tail on the Melbourne horse. The base is a very thin strip of unperforated metal, but the legs merge with the base, as on the Melbourne horse, which it also resembles in frontal aspect, with similar bowed legs made of thin bronze.

In discussing double horses, scholars have turned for illustration of the motif to numerous bronzes from different parts of the ancient world where double animals have come to light. Vagn Poulsen illustrates a double horse from Luristan,[18] commenting that this motif strengthens our appreciation that Greek artists were not working, even in this period, in an isolated vacuum. Within the Greek world, we have a small double ram in Delphi.[19] Orlandini discusses a number of similar pieces, mostly from Italy, but with examples from Rhodes and Urartu.[20] Comstock and Vermeule illustrate a double ram in Boston, of the seventh century B.C., and provide further literature.[21]

Most of these examples are clearly later than the end of the eighth century, especially those from the West, and they are cited only to show the geographical spread of the motif (one scholar has pointed to its existence in China). Those from the East, however, are difficult to sort out chronologically. There is no certainty at the present time that 'Anatolian' bronze work (e.g. Urartan) gave an impetus to the rise of bronze figurines, both animal and human, in the Greece of the Geometric period. Such figures, after being popular with the Minoans, are hardly found in the Mycenaean world, of which H.W. Catling writes that 'Animal statuettes are as rare as human figures',[22] though he notes 'a miserable little quadruped from Mycenae'.[23] R.V. Nicholls argues for an indigenous impetus, contrasting the solid cast bronzes 'that flooded Greek scantuaries in the eighth century B.C.' with those found at Dreros, of the second half of the eighth century.[24] Sylvia Benton points out that the bases on which Greek horses invariably stand are not found in Eastern work and it must be remembered that although bronze figurines were not produced in Greece, the Greek world had not altogether lost an acquaintance with bronze-working; it concentrated on other objects (more practical ones, perhaps, as Catling suggests). There was also a constant tradition of modelling animals in clay and ivory (the horse on occasion has a rider). Hanfmann[25] summarises finds of terracotta horsemen in Mesopotamia, Syria, Palestine, Cyprus and Cilicia, whose ancestor is a helmeted terracotta horseman from Bronze Age Mycenae.[26] In other words, Eastern examples are always closely related to those from Greece so that a priority for one region or the other is difficult to ascertain.

E.L.B. Terrace establishes the already proposed dates of *circa* 1000–800 B.C. for animal bronzes of Talish-Amlash type.[27] The upper dates of these may be earlier than any bronze Geometric animal, but we have to reckon with the possibility of a Protogeometric horseman at Asine.[28] Furthemore, it is becoming clear that not enough is known about bronze-working centres in Luristan or Phrygia,[29] and also that the ideal picture of Urartan art passed on from Lehmann-Haupt and Herzfeld must be reappraised in the light of the findings from the Russian excavations at Karmir-Blur.[30]

It might, then, seem most proper at the moment to suspend judgement much in the way of Rolley: 'Les exemplaires occidentaux sont certainement postérieurs à ceux de Grèce; cela paraît moins certain pour ceux d'Ourartou et de la région de Bakou et de Koban.'[31] Rolley is speaking simply of the double-animal motif, but I think this view can be held to cover both the problems which we are presently discussing. Further finds from properly controlled excavations are needed before any definitive points of contact can be established.

Meanwhile there are two points I should like to make concerning double horses of the kind we are discussing here. Firstly the strong geometric style is characteristically Greek,[32] and it is of some interest to note, in view of the undoubted Eastern origin of the horse species, that the Geometric style applies more strongly to the rendition of horses than to that of any other animal.[33] Secondly the double-animal motif itself is most frequently found as a double protome, as described by Perdrizet: 'le motif de l'animal à double tête, formé de deux protomes pareilles.'[34] This is true of the mass of pieces to which reference is made in the studies already mentioned, where one naturally looks to study the motif of addorsed animals, and also in the long study by Anna Roes.[35] The Melbourne horse, on the other hand, and those cited above as its closest parallels are complete animals, not protomes, joined at the tail and again by an additional metal bar which curves from back to back.

The curved bar between the animals' backs is perhaps reminiscent of the arch of bronze which springs from the base of the necks of, for instance, the Luristan double horse already referred to.[36] Himmelmann-Wildschütz thinks it was used for suspending the piece.[37] Although Roes has argued for a devolution or simplification of motifs in their transmission, it is hard to see (and no one has claimed this; I am canvassing the possibilities) that it could be a survival of the arms of the goddess, as on a bronze from Van now in the British Museum,[38] even though this motif reached the sanctuary of Artemis Orthia more or less intact.[39] It should be noted that the curved bar on the Copenhagen example is proportionately much larger than that of the Luristan bronze. It plays an important part in the aesthetic composition of the group, since, if it were absent, there would be a long, flat, uninteresting space between the neck bases of the two horses.

In trying to sort out the tangled skein of influences, attention must also be drawn to some Iranian nails (or pins) whose heads are decorated with a pair of animals, horses or stags, back to back.[40] These are complete animals, not protomes, but do not appear to be joined at the tail, as far as can be judged from the illustrations, and there is certainly no instance of a double tail. Three examples are dated to approximately 1000 B.C. and one is stated to be ninth to eighth century B.C. They therefore represent the sort of object that could well have provided the inspiration behind the double-horse we are examining. The possibility of such contacts is increased when one considers the common occurrence of open-work bells surmounted by animals or birds in both Anatolia and Greece,[41] which suggests artistic exchanges, not at the beginning of the series of Geometric horses, but towards the close of the eight century and into the seventh.

There are other instances of multiple horses in the Geometric period. Some horses are side by side, as for example Biesantz, pl. 52, L64, and *Münzen und Medaillen,* cat. 34, 6 May 1967, No. 1 (with further references).[42] Biesantz also shows (pl. 52, L69a) two animals sharing one long base and facing in the same direction, but the Melbourne horse cannot be seen as belonging to this type. An interesting suggestion made by Vagn Poulsen, which would certainly account for the difference between double horses and double protomes, is that the horses are a chariot team,[43] an idea also found in *Münzen und Medaillen,* cat. 34, No. 1, 6 May 1967, with its reference to the Copenhagen piece as 'Zweigespann'. Given the difficulties of interpreting these pieces, the hypothesis that they are a chariot team should, I think, be given firm support.

A word on the decoration of concentric circles incised on the animal's body: Himmelmann-Wildschütz has claimed that these circles may represent the animal's coat (in his essay 'Ueber einige gegenständliche Bedeutungsmöglichkeiten des frühgriechischen Ornaments',[44] in which perhaps he follows Ch. Dugas[45]). I find this proposition very difficult to accept in view of the presence of concentric circles on the antlers of a stag in Boston,[46] and also on the crest and tail of two cocks.[47] The decoration is surely a traditional one, with its roots in Mycenaean times. Nicholls describes a bull which has a 'scale pattern on its flank, which may possibly reflect the net pattern occurring from time to time on Cretan rhyta',[48] and also mentions (p. 10) a bull of the late twelfth or early eleventh century which is decorated with dotted semi-circles. Geometric artists also used the dotted circle, with a fine sense of the appropriate, to represent the eyes of animals.[49] It is true that in some cases the decoration indicates the articulation of the horse or its trappings,[50] but, since in the horses we are considering the Geometric artist is fully aware of surface, the decoration (mainly concentric circles) is intended to enliven this surface.

The sense of tradition governing the decoration must also govern the choice of motif itself. Extravagant claims have been made for the horse as a chthonic[51] or as a solar symbol.[52]

J.M. Carter has expressed some objections to Kraiker's views,[53] though he says that 'the possible allusion to Poseidon Hippios remains'. A.D. Nock writes, 'I cannot see that it is established that either Poseidon or the horse was essentially chthonic';[54] the horse was not automatically and uncontrovertibly associated with death. Some archaeologists have seen the horse as votive-offering as indicative of the enthusiasms of a horse-loving and horse-breeding aristocracy.[55] This also seems an unsatisfactory interpretation, for we should then have to find a social answer for the dedication of all the other kinds of animals found in sanctuaries.

Anna Roes has noticed the relatively few motifs found in Greek Geometric art and asked what had happened to the supposed inventiveness of Greek artists. Her answer was that religious symbolism had imposed restraints, but Robert Cook, looking squarely at the types of figurines and the possible religious demands of the various sanctuaries, has argued for fashion: 'Fashion again had some part in the types of offerings made in Greek sanctuaries, and it is dangerous generally to argue from offering to belief. At Olympia, for instance, a principal sanctuary of Zeus and the site of the Olympic games, the normal offering of good quality around 700 B.C. was a bronze figurine of a horse or an ox. Yet there was no cult of a horse or ox deity or even of a deity specially connected with these animals.'[56] These are the principles to follow. They might seem cold and overly rational, but they restrain much ill-founded extravagance.

NOTES

1   Inv. MU 15. University of Melbourne, *Catalogue of Works of Art,* 1971, p. 115 and illustration opposite p. 49.

2   E.g. H-V. Herrmann, 'Werkstätten geometrischer Bronzeplastik', *JdI* 79, 1964, 17 ff. (hereafter cited as 'Herrmann'), Figs. 7, 12, 14 and 19 for one on a tripod-handle.

3   Paul Courbin, *La céramique géométrique de l'Argolide,* Paris 1966, 408; C. Rolley, *Fouilles de Delphes* V, Paris 1969, 61 (with a reference to Wiesner, 'Zur orientalisierenden Periode der Mittelmeerkulturen', *AA* 1942, col. 420 and No. 2); W.D. Heilmeyer, 'Frühe Olympische Tonfiguren', *Olympische Forschungen* 7, 1972, 20.

4   For examples of variations see *Bemerkungen zur geometrischen Plastik,* ed. Nikolaus Himmelmann-Wildschütz, Berlin 1964, Figs. 43, 45, 57. The Melbourne base, because the horizontal plate is raised in this fashion, is unlikely to have served as a seal. For bases as seals see Münzen und Medaillen, *Catalogue 51* (1975), No. 78, with references. A contrary opinion is expressed by John Boardman, *Island Seals,* London 1963, 155.

5   Himmelmann-Wildschütz (*supra* n. 4), Fig. 60.

6   *Meddelelser fra Ny Carlsberg Glyptotek* 18, 1961, 1–14, Figs. 3–7.

7   *Supra* n. 2, Fig. 20.

8   *Supra* n. 4, re Fig. 61.

9   *Supra* n. 2. Herrmann discusses Corinth on pp. 28 f. Some scholars have reservations about Herrmann's attributions; *cf.* Rolley (*supra* n. 3), 72.

10 *Cf.* Rhys Carpenter, *Greek Sculpture,* Chicago 1960, 67 f. Several Luristan bronzes in the Bomford Collection are described as 'open cast', a term much to be preferred to 'hollow cast' in reference to bronze horses such as we are discussing here; *cf.* Ashmolean Museum, *Antiquities from the Bomford Collection,* October 10–30 1966.

11 *JHS* 78, 1958, 87 f. Mitten mentions a wax model in D.G. Mitten and S.F. Doeringer, *Master Bronzes from the Classical World,* Harvard 1967, 35, n. 14.

12 It is the overall lithe pattern that makes me disagree with Himmelmann-Wildschütz (*supra* n. 4), 17, when he says that this Geometric style is not a mannerist reduction but 'ein inhaltliches Moment', that it is a hieroglyph for a 'strong-haunched horse'.

13 *BSA* 58, 1963, 6.

14 *Supra* n. 6, 7 and Figs. 5, 6; Herrmann (*supra* n. 2), Figs. 12-15, for example.

15 Vagn Poulsen, *Meddelelser fra Ny Carlsberg Glyptotek* 19, 1962, 10, Fig. 4.

16 *Supra* n. 3, Pl. xxi, No. 119, p. 81, Inv. 3909.

17 *BSA* 48, 1953, 340, Pl. 66, No. E198.

18 *Supra* n. 15, 11, Fig. 5.

19 *Fouilles de Delphes* V, Paris 1969, (Perdrizet), 56, No. 179, Inv. 4474, Fig. 176; (Rolley), Pl. xx, 117, 118; also C. Rolley, *Monumenta Graeca et Romana V,* 1, *The Bronzes* (English version 1961), 6, No. 18. In the same volume one might also note No. 191, horse's cheek bit from Delphi, Inv. 4394 (from the archaic period), called by Boardman, *BSA* 57, 1962, 30, No. 5, a 'rein-ring' (he is contrasting a forgery with this genuine piece), and Pl. 7, No. 30, a strange hollowed-out plaque in the Tegea Museum.

20 'Piccoli bronzi raffiguranti animali rinvenuti a Gela e Butera', *ArchCl* 8, 1956, 1–10. There is a piece in F. Weege, *AM* 36, 1911, 187 and Pl. 6, Fig. 8.

21 *Greek, Etruscan and Roman Bronzes in the Museum of Fine Arts, Boston,* Boston 1971, 180, No. 215.

22 *Cypriot Bronzework in the Mycenaean World,* Oxford 1964, 258.

23 Tsountas, *ArchEph* 1891, Pl. 2, 3. See also R.V. Nicholls, 'Greek Votive Statuettes and Religious Continuity, c. 1200–700 B.C.', *Auckland Classical Essays Presented to E.M. Blaiklock,* B.F. Harris ed., Auckland 1970, 19.

24 *Ibid.,* 20.

25 *Syria* 38, 1961, 248, n. 4.

26 M.S.F. Hood, 'A Mycenaean Cavalryman', *BSA* 48, 1954, 84 ff.

27 'Some recent finds from Northwest Persia', *Syria* 39, 1962, 212 f. See also the horseman from West Persia, Ashmolean Museum, *Antiquities from the Bomford Collection,* 1966, 47, No. 36, Pl. XXI, early first millenium B.C.

28 *Asine,* 310, Fig. 213, 4; Hood (*supra* n. 26), 92, n. 71, doubts that they are protogeometric.

29 *Cf.* H-V. Herrmann, *Olympische Forschungen,* 6, 1966, 59 f.

30 B.B. Piotrovskij, *Karmir-Blur* I–IV, (Akademija Armjanskoj S.S.R. 1, 2, 5, 6) 1950–55; see also A. Götze, *Kleinasien²*, Munich 1957, 187 ff.

31 *Supra* n. 3, 81, n. 1.

32 *Cf.* J. Boardman, *Pre-Classical,* (Harmondsworth) 1967, 108.

33 Heilmeyer (*supra* n. 3), 20.

34 Perdrizet (*supra* n. 19), 56.

35 Anna Roes, *Greek Geometric Art. Its Symbolism and its Origin,* Haarlem 1933. See for example p. 18, Fig. 9, p. 39, Fig. 31, and her discussion of double horses, p. 117 f.

36 Poulsen (*supra* n. 15), 11, Fig. 5. A two-protome animal is seen in Münzen und Medaillen, *Catalogue 51,* 1975, No. 75.

37 *Supra* n. 4, 28, n. 80.

38 M. Rostovtzeff, 'Dieux et chevaux', *Syria* 12, 1931, 48–57, Fig. 2; also in *Eurasia Septentrionalis Antiqua* IX, (Minns Volume) 1934, 90, Fig. 31.

39 Rostovtzeff (*supra* n. 38), Fig. 7.

40 *Cf. 7000 Jahre Kunst in Iran,* Catalogue of an exhibition held in the Villa Hügel, Essen, February 16 to April 24, 1962, 62, No. 74 (illustrated); *Bronzes antiques de la Perse,* catalogue of the sale of the Collection Jean-Paul Barbier, Hotel Drouot, Paris, 27 May 1970, Nos. 133 and 134.

41 P.R.S. Moorey, *Catalogue of the Ancient Persian Bronzes in the Ashmolean Museum,* Oxford 1971, 137; the Catalogues mentioned in n. 40, *supra,* have several examples. For material found in Greece, see D.M. Bailey, 'Some Grave Groups from Chauchitza in Macedonia', *Opuscula Atheniensia* 9, 1967, 34 f. See also D. Mitten (*supra* n. 11), Nos. 10, 20, 21.

42 See also D. von Bothmer, *Ancient Art from New York Private Collections,* N.Y. 1961, No. 125.

43 *Supra* n. 15, 14.

44 Akademie der Wissenschaften und der Literatur, Mainz, *Abhandlungen der Geistes- und Sozialwissen-schaftlichen Klasse,* Jahrgang 1968, Nr 7, p. 322.

45 *BCH* 45, 1921, 344.

46 B. Schweitzer, *Greek Geometric Art,* London 1971, Fig. 189.

47 Dugas (*supra* n. 45), 350, Nos. 24, 25; 'cercles incisés sur la crête et la queue.'

48 *Supra* n. 23, 9.

49 E.g. Herrmann (*supra* n. 2), Fig. 20.

50 Himmelmann-Wildschütz (*supra* n. 4), 231 and Fig. 25.

51 W. Kraiker, 'Die Anfänge der Bildkunst in der attischen Malerei des 8. Jhr. v. Chr.', *BJb* 161, 1961, 108–20.

52 Roes (*supra* n. 35).

53 J.M. Carter, 'The Beginning of Narrative Art in the Greek Geometric Period', *BSA* 67, 1972, 25 f., p. 27 n. 8.

54 *AJA* 56, 1952, 225.

55 N. Yalouris, 'Three Geometric Figurines', *AntK* 17, 1974, 21–23; G.M.A. Hanfmann, 'A Near Eastern Horseman', *Syria* 38, 1961, 250, seems to follow both opinions.

56 R.M. Cook, 'Archaeological Argument: Some Principles', *Antiquity* 34, 1960, 177 f., at p. 178.

AN ITALOCORINTHIAN CONTEXT

R.M. Cook

Plates 16, 17.

Professor Trendall, who as a young man frequented the Museum of Classical Archaeology in Cambridge, may remember this group of pots in its collection. They come, according to reliable information, from a chamber tomb on Monte Abbatone at Cerveteri and probably all from the right-hand bench of the outer chamber. The pots themselves are not of much interest, but few good contexts for Italocorinthian have been published and so this may be useful. I am grateful to Professor R.J. Hopper for his opinion of the date of CE 1, to Dr T.C.B. Rasmussen for advice on the dates and forms of CE 3–6, and to Mr B.D. Thompson for the drawings of the figures of CE 2. The inventory numbers are those of the Museum of Classical Archaeology.

1 CE 1 (Pl. 16, Fig.1; Fig. on p. 70). *Corinthian cup.* Missing parts of lip and foot. Profile of foot concave. Diameter at lip: 13.2 cm; height: 7.5 cm. Paint mostly perished, but generally leaving discoloration of surface. A: goose (under handle), panther, goat; B: panther, goat. Traces of purple on neck of goose (large spots); on rump and ribs and probably neck of panthers (at least of A); on neck, ribs, rump and belly of goats. Lip and lower part of the body banded. Interior covered with dark paint.

Middle Ripe Corinthian: *circa* 585–80 B.C. See Payne, *NC,* 311, type I B; R.J. Hopper, *BSA* 44, 1949, 226, II.

2 CE 2 (Pl. 16, Figs. 2–3). *Italocorinthian amphora.* Missing handles, much of the upper part of the body and all of the lower part. Height of preserved part (as made up): 57 cm; maximum diameter: 58.5 cm. Paint mostly perished; what remains is now green except in one small area where it is deep red (probably the original colour). There are some, rarely useful, traces of discoloration. No added colour has survived, but there are indications of spots on the scales and perhaps of filling of the outer links of the cables. Most contours are incised. Cables and scales are compass-drawn. Neck: no decoration. Shoulder: short tongues; scales. Body: cable; mixed animals; cable; animals (goats are commonest); cable; animals (horses most common); cable; reversed scales; cable. The drawing of Text Fig. 2 gives a representative sample of the animals and the palmette which links up the fourth row of cables.

This amphora, which belongs to the loose group of the Anforoni Squamati (W. Ll. Brown, *The Etruscan Lion,* Oxford 1960, p. 55 — short list; G. Colonna, *ArchCl* 1961, p. 11), is unusually elaborate, having three rows of animals. I have not been able to check many other amphorae of this group, but similarity of details shows that it is by the same painter and of the same stage of his development as Rome, Villa Giulia 22297, and another, of which I do not know the present location (C.M. Lerici, *Italia Sepolta,* Milan 1962, p. 11 — illustrated); both are from Cerveteri.

3 CE 3 (Pl. 17, Fig. 4). *Bucchero jug.* Missing most of handle and a few other pieces. Height: 13.6 cm. Three grooves on the neck.

This type begins towards the end of the last quarter of the seventh century and lasts well into the third quarter of the sixth.

4 CE 4 (Pl. 17, Fig. 5). *Bucchero cup.* Missing handles and part of the lip. Diameter at lip: 11.7 cm; height: 5 cm. On the outside, three grooves below the handles and three more above the foot.

This type begins in the last quarter of the seventh century and is rare after *circa* 575 B.C.

5 CE 5 (Pl. 17, Fig. 6). *Bucchero kantharos.* Missing handles and much of the lip and bowl. Original diameter: *circa* 11 cm; height: 6.3 cm. On the outside, two grooves below the rim; carination at the top of the bowl.

6 CE 6. *Bucchero kantharos.* Missing handles, most of the lip and much of the bowl. Original diameter: *circa* 11 cm; height: 5.9 cm. Decoration as on 5.

The type of these two kantharoi is very popular from the last quarter of the seventh century to the middle of the sixth.

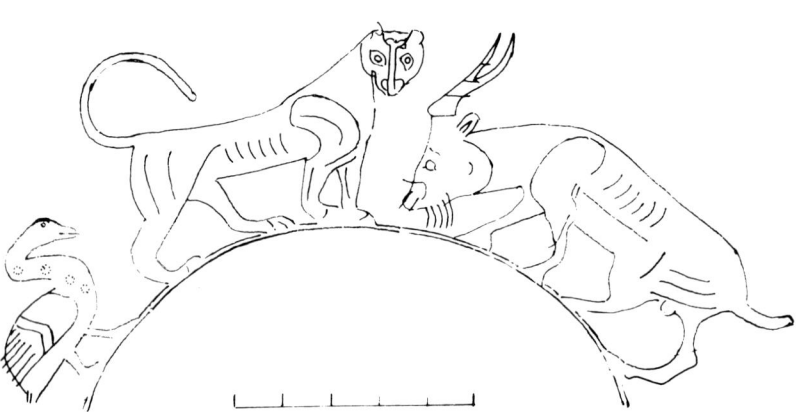

Corinthian cup (obverse).
Cambridge, Museum of Classical Archaeology CE 1.
Drawing: Mr. B.D. Thompson.

A LUCANIAN CHOUS IN MALIBU

Jiri Frel

Plate 18.

Among the Italiote vases in the J. Paul Getty Museum one Lucanian red-figured chous by its quality and by the uniqueness of its inscription deserves publication in a volume honouring the man who made the greatest contribution to the study of Italiote vases (Pl. 18, Figs. 1—2):

Inventory number 71.AA.445. Purchased on the art market in 1971. Intact. Height: 20.1 cm.

All reserved space was covered with a purple wash that has faded in most areas. Under the figures and around the vase runs a band with alternating meanders and St Andrew's crosses.

Under the handle is a double palmette with the usual flanking floral ornaments. At the top of the handle are two opposed palmettes. A panel with laurel branch decorates the neck above the scene.

In the middle of the scene Dionysos stands clad in a himation and crowned with a leafy garland. He holds a thyrsos in his left hand and a stemless kantharos in his right. Foliate ornament decorates the neck of the kantharos, while its body is ribbed. The god's eyes seem to seek out the gaze of the female wearing a chiton and a himation who sits before him. She sits absentmindedly, with her head bent, upon an ivy-entwined rock which assumes a curious bush form at its summit. Behind Dionysos, another woman, whose hair is tightly bound, stands holding aloft a blazing torch. It seems probable that the scene depicts the meeting of Dionysos, accompanied by a maenad, with Ariadne.

The drawing is precise if slightly sketchy. The painter seems to have paid special attention to the seated Ariadne. His lines have an indisputable delicacy, indeed a kind of relief contour is visible in the area of her left shoulder and arm as it extends over her lap. The application of glaze around the figures is somewhat clumsy, especially around the figure of Dionysos where an insufficient amount of it was applied, resulting in an unevenly black ground. On the other hand, the work of the potter is of very high quality.

At first glance, the drawing appears to be Lucanian with strong Apulian elements, and it must date from the early fourth century. Hence, a classification in the Intermediate Group is self-evident. A.D. Trendall has made this attribution even more precise, placing the pot in his Reggio Group.[1]

Thus far the chous presents nothing out of the ordinary with respect to the norm in Italiote vases. However, on the bottom of the vessel is a surprise. Here the purple wash is better preserved, and a dipinto inscription, NIKIΠΠΩ, designates in the genitive the name of the owner (Fig. on p. 73). Hence, the vase was given to Nikippos, and the gift was planned prior to the vase's firing. Inscriptions on Lucanian vases are rare,[2] and this is the first instance in which we have the name of an owner.

In addition to the vase discussed in this article the following is a list of the other Italiote vases in the J. Paul Getty Museum:[3]

1 Campanian amphora. 71.AE.298. Height: 69.8 cm. A: mourning woman seated before a heroon; on her left a nude warrior approaches while on her right two women approach. Neck: a youth in mantle. B: two youths adoring a grave stele. Neck: draped youth.
   Painter of Copenhagen 3757 (Szilagyi), see *LCS Suppl.* II, *BICS* 31 (1973), 217, no. 190 B.

2 Campanian chous. 71.AE.360. Height: 22.3 cm. Seated woman holding a mirror and a plate.
   Boston-Ready Painter, *LCS Suppl.* II, *BICS* 31 (1973), 244, no. 648 b.

3 Apulian bell-krater. 71.AE.248. Height: 34.2 cm. A: naked youth handing wreath to a woman. B: naked youth and a woman with a wreath.
   Thyrsus Painter, *RVAp* I, p. 275, no. 10/103.

4 Apulian bell-krater. 71.AA.301. Height: 23.3 cm. A: seated woman. B: female head.
   The Malibu Painter, *RVAp* II, no. 22/68.

5 Apulian bell-krater. 71.AE.302. Height: 23.9 cm. A: woman. B: female head. Companion piece to preceding.
   The Malibu Painter, *RVAp* II, no. 22/66.

6 Apulian plate. 71.AE.243. Diameter: 20.3 cm. Female head.
   Stoke-on-Trent Painter, *RVAp* II, no. 27/271.

7 Apulian dish with handles. 71.AE.236. Diameter: 33.3 cm. I: female head in medallion of vines. A: seated Eros. B: seated woman.
   G. Schneider-Herrmann, *Apulian Red-Figured Paterae, BICS* 34 (1977), p. 85, no. 112.

8 Apulian chous. 71.AE.361. Height: 22.3 cm. Standing woman.

9 Apulian pelike. 71.AE.253. Height: 36.1 cm. A: seated youth and standing woman holding a bunch of grapes. B: two youths in mantles.
   The Varrese Painter, *RVAp* I, p. 348, no. 13/105.

10 Apulian rhyton: hound's head. 71.AE.296. Young satyr.

11 Apulian rhyton: ram's head. 71.AE.195. Seated athlete with scraper.
    The Iliupersis Painter, *RVAp* I, p. 202, no. 8/93.

12 Apulian rhyton: bull-head. 71.AE.196. Dancing maenad.
    The Iliupersis Painter, *RVAp* I, p. 202, no. 8/90.

13 Campanian fish plate. 71.AE.218. Diameter: 17.3 cm. Two bass and one torpedo.

14 Gnathia pelike. 71.AE.211. Height: 23.7 cm. Nike holding plate and alabastron.

15 Apulian chous. 72.AE.128. Callisto being transformed into a bear, while Hermes to r. rescues the infant Arcas.
    Closely connected with the Black Fury Painter, *RVAp* I, p. 167, no. 7/12.

16 Apulian chous. 74.AE.50. Head of a bearded satyr.
    The Felton Painter, *RVAp* I, p. 178, no. 7/96b.

17 Apulian bell-krater. 76.AE.20. A: Eros and woman. B: two youths.
    The Como Group, *RVAp* II, no. 20/187.

18 Apulian volute-krater. 77.AE.13. (Recomposed from fragments; a good deal missing). A: Underworld scene with Orpheus; neck: female head. B: youth in Naiskos between two women.
    The Baltimore Painter, *RVAp* II, no. 27/17.

19 Apulian volute-krater. 77.AE.14. (Recomposed from fragments; much missing) A: Phoenix and Achilles; neck: rape of Chrysippos. B: youth and attendant in Naiskos; neck: Dionysos and maenads; Blinkers: Amazons on horseback.
    The Baltimore Painter, *RVAp* II, no. 27/26.

20 Apulian hydria. 77.AE.15. Fragments. Shoulder: woman, seated woman, woman wearing crown seated on *thronos,* woman leaning on it. Body: woman with situla and fan approaching Ionic building (most of the building and the woman in it missing).
    The Baltimore Painter, *RVAp* II, no. 27/60.

21 Fragment of Apulian loutrophoros. 77.AE.16.1. On shoulder of B: female head.

22 Apulian hydria. 77.AE.17. Offering at a stele.

23 Apulian pelike (small). 77.AE.18. A: female head. B: boy.

24 Apulian lekanis. 77.AE.19. Female heads.

25 Apulian skyphos. 77.AE.61. A and B: Female head.

26 Apulian calyx krater. 77.AE.93. (Fragmentary). A: Athena and other figures.

27 Apulian volute-krater. 77.AE.112. A: woman and youth with horse in building; on neck: Nike in biga preceded by Eros. B: Naiskos scene.
    The Baltimore Painter, *RVAp* II, no. 27/11.

28 Apulian volute-krater. 77.AE.113. A: youth and warrior with horse; neck: Nike in biga. B: Naiskos.
    The Baltimore Painter, *RVAp* II, no. 27/12.

29 Apulian volute-krater. 77.AE.114. A: woman and youth in building. B: stele.
    The Patera Painter, *RVAp* II, no. 23/14.

30 Apulian volute-krater. 77.AE.115. A: seated woman in building. B: stele.
    The Patera Painter, *RVAp* II, no. 23/33.

31 Apulian bell-krater. 77.AE.116. A: woman with two satyrs (or with youth and satyr). B: three youths.
    The Patera Painter, *RVAp* II, no. 23/154.

32 Apulian calyx-krater. 77.AE.93. Fragmentary. A: The three daughters of Kekrops with Athena.
    The Lycurgus Painter.

33 Campanian bell-krater. 78.AE.255. (Ex Deepdene, Hope 327). A: man in quadriga. B: three women.
    The Branicki Painter. *LCS,* p. 340, no. 775.

34 Lucanian bell-krater. 78.AE.256. A: satyr and Maenads. B: two youths.

35 Apulian lekanis. P.78.AE.15. A and B: female head.
    Stoke-on-Trent Painter (?).

36 Apulian plate. P.78.AE.16. Female head.
    Stoke-on-Trent Painter (?), *RVAp* II, no. 27/271 (?).

37 Black-figure lekythos. Pagenstecher class. P.78.AE.17. Seated female figure.

NOTES

1 *LCS, Suppl.* II, *BICS* 31 (1973), 161, no. 317b.

2 *LCS,* vol. II, 709.

3 The order in which the vases are listed is approximately the order in which they were acquired by the Museum.

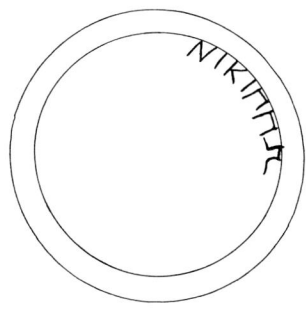

Lucanian red-figure oinochoe (shape 3: chous).
Malibu, J. Paul Getty Museum inv. 71.AA.445.
Drawing of dipinto on the undersurface.

UN FAUX AUTHENTIQUE DU MUSÉE DU LOUVRE

Juliette de la Genière

Planche 19.

Il a fallu l'aimable invitation de M. Cambitoglou, le désir d'honorer en la personne du Professeur A.D. Trendall un savant qui fut aussi l'un de mes maîtres, pour que je me résolve à compléter quelques notes rédigées en 1957. Au cours de rangements pratiqués alors dans les réserves du Musée du Louvre je remarquai un jour, au milieu de vases rangés parmi les faux, un objet étrange (Pl. 19, Fig. 1). Publié par Pottier dans son catalogue des vases grecs du Louvre, il était identifié comme un calice à pied haut attique.[1] Il m'apparut aussitôt que ni Pottier qui avait cru à l'authenticité de ce vase, ni les savants qui l'avaient ensuite classé parmi les faux, n'avaient eu raison, ni du reste tout à fait tort.

L'objet est en effet composé de deux parties authentiques appartenant à deux vases de formes différentes qu'un élément moderne relie l'une à l'autre. La partie supérieure est évidemment l'embouchure d'un lécythe d'assez grande taille;[2] le pied a appartenu à une coupe ou une cotylé du début du Ve siècle. Ces deux éléments ont été sciés et fixés sur une tige entièrement moderne dont le profil baroque choquait peut-être moins que nos contemporains les savants du début du siècle. Le caractère unique de l'embouchure explique à la fois le succès du faussaire au XIXe siecle et le scepticisme dont firent preuve par la suite les conservateurs du Musée à l'égard de l'objet: elle porte en effet un décor à figures rouges parfaitement authentique (Pl. 19, Fig. 2) qui était, lorsque je récupérai l'objet en 1957, encadré par de lourdes palmettes en peinture surajoutée moderne qui disparurent au nettoyage. A ma connaissance, il n'existe pas d'autre exemple de lécythe attique dont l'embouchure comporte un décor traité en figures rouges sur le fond noir.[3]

La scène peinte à cet emplacement exceptionnel est un enlèvement. Une femme ailée portant dans ses bras un enfant ou un très jeune homme court vers la droite en retournant la tête en arrière; elle est vêtue d'un péplos ourlé d'une bande noire dont le rabat retombe assez bas;[4] son visage et ses bras étaient peints en couleur surajoutée blanche (très effacée). L'éphèbe est nu et porte sur ses cheveux longs une guirlande de feuilles. L'aisance des attitudes, le modelé souple, la fluidité des plis du vêtement agité par la course, la facilité un peu négligente du pinceau orientent vers une datation du lécythe autour de 420.

Aucun doute ne paraît possible pour l'identification de la femme ailée; c'est Eos, déesse de l'Aurore. Peut-être l'utilisation exceptionelle du blanc surajouté sur les chairs, antique technique oubliée depuis l'abandon des figures noires, mais qui reparaît vers la fin du Ve siècle pour être largement utilisée au IVe siècle,[5] doit-elle être considerée comme une allusion à la luminosité du personnage, la $\varphi\alpha\iota\nu\acute{o}\lambda\iota\varsigma$ Ἡώς ainsi que l'hymme à Déméter la décrit,[6] ou Eos $\lambda\epsilon\upsilon\kappa\acute{o}\chi\rho\upsilon\varsigma$.[7] Et si l'on doit identifier l'éphèbe enlevé, on hésitera, parmi les amants de la déesse au coeur innombrable, entre Tithonos et Képhalos, l'absence des attributs propres à chacun d'eux ne permettant pas de certitude.[8]

C'est un lécythe, on l'a vu, qui reçoit l'image de cette aventure d'Eos. La technique de l'embouchure permet de penser que c'était un vase à figures rouges, mais, en présence d'un objet aussi atypique, on ne peut exclure qu'il ait pu s'agir d'un vase à technique mixte dont la panse aurait été à fond blanc. Au reste, si différentes que soient les deux séries de vases, on s'aperçoit que leur utilisation est sensiblement la même.

L'importance des lécythes à fond blanc dans les cultes funéraires est bien connue; ces vases sont posés sur les degrés d'une stèle au Céramique;[9] ils représentent une morte s'embarquant sur la barque de Charon,[10] des petites âmes voletant près du fleuve fatal,[11] Hermès psychopompe, des scènes de deuil, des adieux, bref toute une série de thèmes liés à l'idée de la mort et à la conception du culte funéraire dans la Grèce du Ve siècle. Les lécythes à fond blanc ont été trouvés dans des cimetières grecs, la grande majorité en Grèce propre, quelques-uns dans les nécropoles de Grande-Grèce,[12] mais il est tout a fait exceptionnel de les rencontrer dans les cultures non-grecques.[13] Quant aux lécythes à figures rouges, on constate, bien que leur imagerie soit rarement liée aux thèmes funéraires,[14] qu'ils ont une clientèle comparable à celle des lécythes à fond blanc. En effet ils proviennent surtout de nécropoles grecques, mais si 40% d'entre eux ont été trouvés dans des cimetières de Grèce propre, plus de 50% viennent des nécropoles grecques de Sicile.[15] Les cultures non-grecques, étrusques, italiques, en ont livré un très faible pourcentage.[16] Là encore on peut donc affirmer que, dans leur très grande majorité, ces vases étaient destinés aux morts, comme l'indiquent clairement les répliques acerbes du jeune homme soumis aux assiduités des trois vieilles de l'Assemblée des Femmes.[17] Nécessaires aux rites funéraires, ils contenaient l'huile parfumée que les vivants offraient à leurs défunts, avec plus ou moins de générosité du reste.[18]

Ainsi, que notre embouchure ait coiffé un lécythe à fond blanc ou un lécythe à figures rouges, elle était destinée en tout cas à un vase de cimetière grec, qui pouvait être déposé dans une tombe ou sur les degrés d'une stèle; à celui qui était enterré là un parent ou un ami a offert un lécythe portant dans sa partie supérieure l'image d'Eos enlevant un mortel.

Faut-il voir un simple hasard dans le choix du thème qui décore si curieusement notre embouchure ? Ne doit-on pas croire au contraire que, si le peintre du lécythe a pris une telle liberté par rapport aux traditions décoratives établies de longue date, c'est qu'il tenait à souligner l'importance particulière du mythe d'Éos et Tithonos ? Et dans ce das il convient de s'interroger sur la signification que pouvait avoir sur un vase funéraire de la fin du Ve siècle cette image d'enlèvement.

Charles Picard[19] et Jean Charbonneaux[20] ont souligné la fréquence des enlèvements dans l'imagerie de la fin du Ve siècle. Notre scène s'inscrit en effet dans une série abondante de thèmes analogues. On sait qu'outre Képhalos et Tithonos la déesse de l'Aurore avait poursuivi bien des jeunes gens; de nombreuses peintures de vases du Ve siècle illustrent ses aventures[21] et, à la même époque, les arts majeurs adoptent ces mythes qui prennent une place d'honneur sur des monuments d'importance. C'est l'enlèvement de Képhalos que les sculpteurs athéniens du temple de Délos ont choisi comme thème pour leur groupe d'acrotère, en même temps que le rapt d'Orithyie par Borée, le vent du Nord, qui fut aussi célébré par de nombreux peintres de vases de la deuxième moitié du Ve siècle.[22] Peu auparavant, au Théséion, un groupe d'acrotère a été sculpté, qui représente Déméter arrachant sa fille Perséphone au sombre Hadès pour la ramener à la lumière.[23] Dans un tel contexte les aventures amoureuses d'Eos ne sont plus seulement ces épisodes légers sur lesquels insistaient volontiers les artisans du Céramique: elles acquièrent une dimension en rapport avec le ciseau de la sculpture officielle. Et de fait la popularité des scènes d'enlèvement correspond, non pas à une vogue passagère chez les artistes, mais à un courant de pensée dont on tentera ici de préciser l'origine et de mesurer la diffusion.

L'enlèvement d'un mortel par une divinité est un mythe qui reparaît constamment dans la poésie comme dans l'imagerie grecque depuis les temps homériques. Ganymède, le plus beau des mortels, a été enlevé par Zeus dans l'Olympe, où il est l'échanson des dieux;[24] Homère connaissait l'histoire de Tithonos enlevé par la déesse de l'Aurore pour partager sa demeure au bord de l'Okeanos.[25] Ces destins exceptionnels tranchaient sur le sort lamentable des âmes communes qui, pour Homère, menaient après la mort une pâle vie d'ombre reléguée dans un au-delà ténébreux, sans espoir de retour. Erwin Rohde a montré combien l'esprit grec s'accommodait mal de cette sombre vision de l'au-delà,[26] et comment, très vite, les poètes introduisirent l'image nouvelle d'une terre fortunée où des dieux tout-puissants transportent Ménélas.[27] De même pour Hésiode la race des héros n'avait pas été engloutie dans les entrailles de la terre, mais beaucoup furent établis par la volonté de Zeus aux confins du monde, dans les Iles des Bienheureux, au bord de l'Océan.[28] Tandis que se perpétuent ces mythes d'enlèvement des privilégiés de Zeus vers une survie bienheureuse grâce à la seule faveur divine, d'autres croyances se développent, qui mettent à la portée d'un plus grand nombre un séjour d'éternelle félicité: les unes autour des déesses d'Eleusis placent sous la terre le séjour des initiés, où ils chantent et dansent au son de la flûte parmi les bosquets de myrte.[29] La religion orphique au contraire, bien enracinée en Italie méridionale, mais installée aussi à Athènes, présente une vision très différente des destinées de l'âme: élément divin, enchaîné à un corps nécessairement impur, elle doit parcourir le cercle de la nécessité par des réincarnations successives; une libération glorieuse lui est promise à travers les cérémonies de purification et grâce aux θεοὶ λύσιοι. Légère et immortelle elle se dirigera alors vers une lumière éternelle, vers le soleil, la lune et les étoiles.[30] C'est un sort analogue qui est promis par Pindare à Théron d'Agrigente vieillissant dans les célèbres vers de la deuxième Olympique:[31]

> ἔνθα μακάρων
> νᾶσον ὠκεανίδες
> αὖραι περιπνέοισιν

Et si Eschyle et Sophocle adoptent encore la conception homérique de la vie crépusculaire des âmes, les pièces d'Euripide répandent l'idée que l'âme, une fois separée du corps, s'élèvera dans l'éther luminuex au-dessus des nuages,[32] vision qui semble avoir eu à Athènes une large audience puisque l'épigramme dédié par l'Etat athénien aux morts de Potidée exprime clairement la croyance que l'éther a accueilli leurs âmes tandis que la terre a reçu leurs corps.[33]

Ainsi, d'un bout à l'autre du monde grec s'installe la croyance en un séjour des morts qui ne sera pas ce monde souterrain et lugubre que peignait Homère.[34] Les uns rappellent les enlèvements mythiques et y voient des raisons d'espérer. Les plus monbreux se tournent vers les sectes qui promettent un au-delà lumineux. Ces préoccupations trouvaient assurément un large écho chez les Athéniens à l'heure où la guerre et la peste avaient endeuillé tant de familles, et il est bien probable que les artisans du Céramique ne demeuraient pas étrangers à ce courant de pensée; on comprend alors mieux l'initiative curieuse du peintre qui plaça la scène d'enlèvement sur notre embouchure de lécythe. A-t-il voulu figurer, dans la tradition homérique, l'image d'un mortel choisi et enlevé par la divinité, c'est-à-dire soustrait aux lois de la mort et destiné à un séjour de bonheur ? A-t-il au contraire cherché à suggérer par la petitesse du mortel enlevé l'idée de l'âme entraînée, après la disparition du corps, vers des régions divines ? Si l'image qu'il a peinte peut se prêter à deux séries d'explications, c'est qu'aucune rigueur dogmatique n'a guidé son pinceau; c'est aussi qu'il observe, comme la plupart des artistes de cette période, une grande discrétion à l'égard des thèmes funéraires.[35] Il a voulu exprimer ici une aspiration commune à tous ses contemporains: au mort qui gisait dans la tombe il souhaitait d'être transporté tel Ménélas ou Rhadamante dans les Iles des Bienheureux ou bien d'accéder à un séjour céleste comme les Purs de l'Orphisme. Pour un tel voyage, qu'il s'achève au bord du monde dans les îles entourées par les bras de l'Okeanos, ou qu'il conduise au-dessus des nuages dans l'éther lumineux, quel meilleur guide choisir qu'Eos, la déesse ailée, porteuse de clarté, qui a sa demeure sur les bords

78 JULIETTE DE LA GENIÈRE

de l'Océan, qui parcourt chaque jour le ciel et qui est apparentée au Soleil et à la Lune ?

Lorsque Platon évoquera ensuite le sort des âmes assises au bord de l'air[36] ou parvenues aux hauteurs du pur séjour,[37] il répondra aux aspirations de ceux qui au Ve siècle croyaient à une âme aérienne et divine; une âme passionément désireuse d'échapper aux ombres du Tartare et de s'élever vers la lumière, comme les acrotères qui s'élancent au faîte des temples ou comme, au sommet du lécythe du Louvre, le mortel emporté par la divinité dans une ascension glorieuse.

NOTES

1 Inv. G.614, Campana 3218, acquis en 1863. E. Pottier, *Vases antiques du Louvre,* iii, Paris 1922, 294, Pl. 157.

2 Il mesurait 40 cm environ.

3 D. von Bothmer a bien voulu me signaler l'existence au Musée de Boston d'un lécythe aryballisque apulien du IVe siècle portant sur l'embouchure un décor à figures rouges (Satyres et ménades, *cf.* E.Robinson, *Museum of Fine Arts, Boston: Catalogue of Greek, Etruscan and Roman Vases,* Boston 1893, 184, n. 504); *APS,* p. 64, no. 23, Pl. 36, fig. 180; *RVAp* I, p. 125, no. 5/226.

4 L'embouchure a été sciée au-dessus de l'étoffe; les pieds visibles sur la photographie sont modernes. Lignes de contour en relief pour les ailes, les étoffes, le corps de l'éphèbe.

5 Ainsi le corps de Thétis sur la péliké à figures rouges du peintre de Marsyas au British Museum, *cf.* Arias-Hirmer-Shefton, Pl. XLVII.

6 *Hymne homérique* 5, 51.

7 *RE,* 2657–69; Roscher, *ML,* I, col. 1252-78.

8 On connaît assez peu d'images de la déesse jusqu'au début du Ve siècle. Elle apparaît souvent ensuite, et surtout en liaison avec les épisodes de Képhalos et de Tithonos. Beaucoup de variantes existent dans les représentations de ces deux mythes; pour l'un comme pour l'autre il s'agit le plus souvent d'une poursuite, Képhalos se défendant avec son lagobolon ou tenant des lances, Tithonos brandissant sa lyre contre les entreprises d'Eos. Parfois les deux personnages semblent discuter, Eos tendant ses bras ouverts dans un geste à la fois amical et persuasif (Amphore de Berlin, inv. 3759, *ARV*[2] 988, 12; Hydrie Londres E 214, *CVA* 6, III.Ic, Pl. 89, 6). Souvent le mythe est résumé dans la scène finale de l'enlèvement (Skyphos du Peintre de Lewis, Cambridge, Corpus Christi, *ARV*[2], 973, 15; Florence 4228, *CVA* Firenze, Pl. 70, 1 et 2), et lorsque l'éphèbe enlevé n'a pas les attributs traditionnels, il est très difficile en l'absence d'inscription d'identifier avec certitude le mortel enlevé par la déesse.

9 Par exemple Athènes 1935 (CC. 1692), *ARV*[2], 1227, 1.

10 Par exemple Palerme, coll. Mormino, lécythe n. 795, *CVA* III Y, Pl. 7, 3–4.

11 *Ibid.* lécythe n. 310, Pl. 6, 3.

12 Sur 1096 lécythes à fond blanc de forme classique pris en considération dans l'ouvrage de Beazley (*ARV*[2]), 430 ont une provenance connue; 90% viennent de sites grecs, dont 80% de l'Eubée et l'Attique, alors que 7% seulement ont été trouvés en Sicile et Grande-Grèce.

13 Les sites non-grecs ont fourni seulement 6 lécythes à fond blanc, soit 1,3% de l'ensemble. La présence de deux lécythes à fond blanc dans la nécropole de Spina (J.D. Beazley, 'Spina e la ceramica greca', in *Spina e l'Etruria padana, Supplemento a Studi Etruschi* XXV, 1959, 49) a été parfois considérée comme un indice de l'existence de Grecs dans le port étrusque; ces lécythes sont attribués au Peintre des Roseaux, *ARV*[2] 1382, 123–124 (de la tombe 136 C).

14 Cependant plusieurs lécythes à figures rouges du peintre d'Achille ou de ses imitateurs portent une scène figurée devant une stèle ou une tombe (*ARV*[2] 1003, 20, 22; 1007, 1–2; 1008, Laon 37952).

15 On pourra préciser les proportions indiquées ici lorsque seront connues les quelques 5000 tombes fouillées dans les dix dernières années à Sélinonte, dont une forte proportion appartient au Ve siècle. *Cf.* V. Tusa 'Le necropoli di Selinunte', *Odeon,* Palerme 1972, 177–229.

16 On sait qu'au Ve siècle l'Etrurie absorbait la grande majorité des beaux vases fabriqués à Athènes, notamment les amphores, péliqués, cratères, coupes et vases liés aux besoins du banquet. Et si l'on pense à cette immense moisson de vases attiques qui remplit les musées européens, on donnera toute sa signification au chiffre d'une douzaine de lécythes trouvés en Etrurie tyrrhénienne et autant en Etrurie padane: les lécythes ne sont pas demandés en Etrurie. Il est intéressant de noter que seule la région de Nola en Campanie a livrè un assez grand nombre de lécythes à figures rouges (une quarantaine) et aussi deux lécythes à fond blanc. Quelles peuvent être les causes de cette exception ? Doit-on imaginer qu'elle est due à l'intensité du commerce des régions grecques voisines ? L'histoire de la Campanie au Ve siècle ne plaide guère en faveur d'une telle interprétation. Faut-il penser à la présence d'éléments grecs sur le site de Nola, comme on croit pouvoir le suggérer pour le site indigène de Pisticci dans l'arrière-pays de Métaponte ? Une autre explication pourrait être également envisagée. La grosse majorité des amphores dites de Nola et produites à Athènes étaient livrées à la Campanie (65%), la région de Nola en absorbant à elle seule 46%. Or, parmi les centres non-campaniens qui recevaient aussi une quantité notable d'amphores de ce type, Gela figure en bonne place: 25 amphores de Nola y ont été trouvées, soit 15% de l'ensemble considéré ici (les chiffres cités sont fondés sur les listes d'*ARV²*). Or, on le sait, les artisans qui décoraient les amphores de Nola étaient souvent les mêmes que ceux qui peignaient les lécythes; ainsi les 160 amphores de Nola que nous prenons en considération ont été l'oeuvre de peintres qui étaient parallèlement les auteurs de nombreux lécythes dont 191 ont une provenance connue: or on constate que la seule ville de Gela a absorbé 45% environ de ces lécythes, c'est-à-dire près de la moitié. En résumé, si le site grec de Gela achète un très grand nombre de lécythes, quelques-uns parviennent toutefois à Nola en Campanie; si l'amphore de type Nola est destinée à la Campanie, un pourcentage notable est cependant acquis par les habitants de Gela. Puisque les mêmes peintres ont décoré les amphores et les lécythes, on peut se demander si ces deux séries de vases n'ont pas été chargés à Athènes sur un même bateau; certaines amphores auraient été acquises au passage à Gela où l'on déchargeait la quasi-totalité des lécythes demandés pour les cimetières; le reste de la cargaison aurait été ensuite acheminé vers la Campanie.

17 *Aristophane* 996, 1030–34, 1101.

18 L'existence des lécythes à double fond, c'est-à-dire à contenance très limitée, est bien connue; *cf.* J.V. Noble, *The Techniques of Painted Attic Pottery*, N.Y. 1965, fig. 150.

19 Charles Picard, *Manuel, La sculpture grecque classique au Ve siècle*, Paris 1938, 790–797.

20 Jean Charbonneaux, *L'Univers des Formes, L'art grec classique,* Sculpture, Paris 1969, 167.

21 *Cf.* index de *ARV²* 1724.

22 Charbonneaux (ci-dessus note 20), fig. 180. Pour les représentations sur les vases contemporains *cf.* index de *ARV²* 1722.

23 Charbonneaux (ci-dessus note 20), fig. 182.

24 *Il.* XX, 232.

25 *Il.* XI, 1; XIX, 1; *Od.* V, 1; XXIII, 244.

26 Erwin Rohde, *Psyché,* (trad. A. Raymond) Paris 1952, 56–91.

27 *Od.* IV, 560–8.

28 Hésiode, *Trav.* 170.

29 Aristophane, *Grenouilles* 315 *sq.*

30 Rohde (ci-dessus note 26), 370 et notes 4 and 5. G. Pugliese-Carratelli in *Atti del IV Convegno di Taranto,* 1964, 19–44, notamment pour les rapports entre orphisme et pythagorisme.

31 *Ol.* 2, 67–84. *Cf.* Platon, *Mén.* 81 b.

32 *El.* 59; *Suppl.* 531–6.

33 *Inscriptiones Graecae,* I, 2, 945. Stèle du British Museum. *Cf.* M.N. Tod (ed), *Greek Historical Inscriptions,* Oxford 1933, I, 127, n. 59.

34 A propos d'une tablette de Locres qu'elle interprète comme le retour marin de Perséphone, Mme
P. Zancani a suggéré que l'idée qui a inspiré le coroplathe serait celle d'un Hadès situé au bord de
l'Okeanos et non pas un monde des morts souterrain: 'Persefone e Afrodite sul mare' in *Essays in
memory of Karl Lehmann,* ed. L.F. Sandler, N.Y 1964, 386–395; *contra,* H. Prückner, *Die Lokrischen
Tonreliefs,* Mainz 1968, 82–83.

35 Mme. S. Karousou, publiant un cratère attique datable dans la première moitié du IVe siècle, l'interprète comme une scène des Champs Elysées, au bout du monde, dans une île de l'Ocean. Elle souligne
la discrétion observée par le peintre dans la représentation du séjour des Bienheureux, son refus de
préciser le lieu, d'individualiser les personnages; c'est une vision poétique, un rêve lointain où rien n'est
souligné mais où la récompense qui attend les héros ἀγνοί, ἄωροι est délicatement suggérée. (*ArchDelt*
19, 1964, 1–16).

36 *Phédon* 111a.

37 *Ibid.* 114b.

EARS OF CORN AND OTHER OFFERINGS

J.R. Green

Plates 20, 21, 22.

As Professor Trendall and I observed a sale of Greek pottery at Sotheby's not very long ago, we saw in the high prices paid for South Italian one result of his work — that this pottery is now well enough known and understood to attract the sort of attention that only Attic used to receive. I hope that he will accept as a token of appreciation of both his work for classical art and archaeology in Australia and New Zealand and the outstanding advances he has made in the daunting task of classifying the red-figure fabrics of South Italy, a few offerings that are intended to explore in a very minor and preliminary way some connections between South Italy and the Aegean, Egypt and the Eastern Mediterranean in the Early Hellenistic period.[1]

As is well known, with perhaps one exception (see note 5), no Apulian red-figure has yet been demonstrated to have been found in mainland Greece or the Aegean islands. It is therefore the more remarkable that there are some certain instances of Apulian Gnathia as well as some less certain. First, from the American excavations at Corinth come two fragments, one from a round-bodied epichysis of the workshop of the Rose Painter (Fig. 3).[2] It is to be dated ca. 340 B.C. or soon afterwards. This was a crucial period for Gnathia, the period in which the technique and manner of decoration were stabilised following the immediate introductory phase and yet a period in which there was some experiment and searching for a series of satisfactory shapes. One of the shapes that appeared occasionally at this stage was the bell-krater type B, to be distinguished from the standard Apulian red-figure version (type A) by the virtual absence of stem between body and foot.[3] The same shape is to be found at Corinth at the same period decorated with ivy, and it may not be too fanciful to suppose that Gnathia potters borrowed it from there.[4] The second fragment from Corinth is the body of a standard epichysis, a shape common also to Apulian red-figure (Figs. 1—2).[5] It is of a frequent enough type with laurel decoration on the shoulder. On the basis of the form of the body it is probably to be dated ca. 320 B.C. The presence of this piece does not solve the problem of the epichyseis from Olynthos, but it does make it look a little more possible that the potters of those vases, whether Athenian or Olynthian, were copying Apulian examples.[6]

The excavations of the Athenian Agora have also produced two fragments of Gnathia.[7] The first, P 12748, is a fragment of the upper wall of a deep bowl of the early third century B.C. (Fig. 4). It has a spray and a sash hanging from ivy that ran across the upper part of the vase. One may suppose that a mask was suspended in the centre of the scene. Such little as remains suggests that the piece may belong to the Alexandria Group, a large group in which two or three painters were active. The second fragment, P 18336, is less prepossessing: the top of the handle of an oinochoe with the end moulded into the form of a lion's head (Fig. 5). The date is difficult to determine but the way the mouth comes in under the knob and the apparent narrowness of the neck suggest that it too may be early third century rather than fourth. Compare the oinochoe (Figs. 7–8).

So much for material from controlled contexts on the mainland. Several other examples of Gnathia pottery are said with varying degrees of certainty to have been found in Greek lands. Most of them are fairly well known but I list them here for convenience. I am not sure that the list is complete.

Kephallenia

1   Skyphos. Kephallenia. Sprays with egg pattern above.
     ADelt 24B, 1969, pl. 267d. Laurel Spray Group. Ca. 325 B.C.

Siphnos

2   Ring-handled kantharos fr. (?). Siphnos (?). Fr. of upper wall with a line along the top of the ribbing.
     BSA 44, 1949, pl. 21, 29 (p. 62 no. 6). 300–275 B.C.

Melos

3   Oinochoe. Oxford, Ashmolean Museum, on loan from Queen's College, 1939 no. 6. Ribbed; around
     the neck, ivy.
     Ca. 280 B.C.

4   Kantharos. London F 553. A: priestess within ivy and sashes; B: ivy.
     CVA (1) pl. 1 (37), 6; Forti, pl. 2e. Ca. 290 B.C. ?

Kalymnos ?

5   Epichysis. Athens 2280. On the shoulder, laurel.
     Ca. 310 B.C.

Rhodes

6+   Many fragments.
     Cf. Fraser *Ptolemaic Alexandria* ii, 267 n. 178.[8]

Crete

7   Pelike. Athens 2162. A: female head between florals; B: pendant chain below a zone of egg and dart
     and a red band. Close to the late side of the Painter of the Louvre Bottle and perhaps by him.
     Ca. 310 B.C. (Fig. 6).

8   Oinochoe. Athens 2277. Mask within ivy, sashes and sprays.
     Buschor, *GV* (1940), 262, fig. 279; Forti pl. 1c; Webster, *MMC[2]* GV 26a. Later fourth century B.C.

9   Oinochoe. Athens 2158. Birds within sashes and ivy; ribbed.
     R. Pagenstecher, *Expedition E. von Sieglin* II, 3, 24, fig. 32. Alexandria Group. 290–280 B.C.

10   Oinochoe. Athens, Market. Mask suspended from ivy between sashes and sprays; ribbed.
     Alexandria Group ? Ca. 290–280 B. C. (Figs. 7–8).

11   Lekythos. Athens 2279 'from Crete or Italy?'[9] Eros and bird.
     Otto Benndorf, *Gr. und Sic. Vasenbilder*, (Berlin 1883) XXVI, fig. 10; Forti, pl. 2a. Ca. 330 B.C.

12   Kantharos. Athens 2161. On the neck, A and B, ivy; careful ribs.
     Ca. 310 B.C.

13   Ring-handled kantharos. Athens, Market. A: (?) between sprays (bird or female head ?); B: spray.
     Alexandria Group. 290–280 B.C.

14   Miniature situla. Heraklion, from Lyttos 9.7.70. Lion-head spout and relief female head at base of
     handle.
     Ca. 325 B.C. ? [As London F 583, *CVA* (1), pl. 6 (42), 13, but with double handle.]

Benghazi

15   Stemmed cup. Sèvres 4166. Ribbed with spray above.
     CVA, pl. 47, 15. About 300 B.C.[10]

Tocra

16   Deep bowl frr. Tocra. Female head, left, between sashes and ivy.
     Boardman and Hayes, *Tocra* ii, London 1973, pl. 42, 2364 (the upper fr. shown inverted). Later
     fourth century B.C.

Tocra (continued)

17   Epichysis frr. Tocra. On the shoulder, dot/ivy spray with red stem.
      Tocra ii, pl. 42, 2366 and fig. 42. The epichysis looks Apulian and from the description should be
      Ruvan or Canosan (note the acute observation p. 92, n. 4). Later fourth century B.C.

18.   Base of a ring-handled kantharos (?). Tocra. Dots around the foot.
      Tocra ii, 93, fig. 42, 2365. 300–275 B.C.

Cyrenaica

19   Bottle. London F 582. Bird within florals.
      CVA (1), pl. 4 (40), 5. Stockport Group (*BICS* 15, 1968, 23 no. 11). Ca. 330 B.C.

20   Pelike. London, old catalogue C 69. Female head between florals.
      CVA (1), pl. 5 (41), 22. Soon after 300 B.C.[11]

Alexandria

21+   Many fragments; see below and note 15.
      Mostly first quarter of the third century B.C.

Cyprus

22   Hydria. London 96.2–1.205, from Kourion. On the shoulder, satyr and women; on the belly, a
      garland; ribbed.
      CVA (1), pl. 5 (41), 8. Perhaps Alexandria Group. Ca 290 B.C.

23   Lekythos. Stanford 1205 (3841), ex Cesnola, Reticulate decoration.
      Ca. 320 B.C. ?

24   Lekythos. Stanford 1209 (3840), ex Cesnola. Reticulate decoration.
      Ca. 320 B.C. ?

25   Flat lekythos. Stanford 3282 (3842), ex Cesnola. Reticulate decoration.
      Ca. 320 B.C. ?

26   Skyphos. Stanford 66.540 (3836), ex Cesnola. Swan within vine.
      Ca. 330 B.C.

27   Skyphos. Stanford 1194 (3837), ex Cesnola. Vine.
      Ca. 310 B.C.

28   Cup-skyphos. Stanford 1200, ex Cesnola. Weak vine.
      Ca. 320–310 B.C.[12]

Antioch on the Orontes

29   Fragment of the lower wall of a kantharos (?).
      Antioch IV, 1, fig. 8, 12. 300–275 B.C.

Gezer

30   Ring-handled kantharos fr. (?). Gezer. On the rim, dot-spray.
      R.A.S. Macalister, *The Excavation of Gezer,* III, London 1912, pl. 177, 16. 300–275 B.C.[13]

Doura Europos

31   Fragments of bowl with painted handles. Laurel.
      The Excavations at Dura Europos. Final Report IV, 1, 2, pl. 1, 26. 300–275 B.C.

32   Fragments of bowl with painted handles. Floral.
      Dura IV, 1, 2, pl. II, 27. Alexandria Group. 300–275 B.C.

33   Fragment of base of a ring-handled kantharos. Egg and dart on the foot.
      Dura IV, 1, 2, pl. II, 28. 300–275 B.C.

Enez (Ainos)

    34+ Neck fragment of an oinochoe or a pelike. Mask between sprays.
          Türk Arkeoloji Dergisi 21, 1974, 30, fig. 7 (the illustration is inverted). Early third century B.C.
          Erzen (*ibid.*) mentions other fragments.

Olbia

    35   WS amphora. Berlin inv. 4956. Erotes.
          Pfuhl, *MuZ,* fig. 754; Buschor, *GV* (1940), fig. 280; Forti, pl. 28e. Ca. 280–270 B.C.

First, a caution. The proveniences of the vases in the National Museum in Athens (nos. 5, 7–9, 11–12 above) are far from certain. They are dealers' proveniences.[14] The same applies to nos. 10 and 13 although in this case I was inclined to believe the dealer in question and it was perhaps in his favour that he could not be persuaded that they were made in Italy. The example in Kephallenia is not specifically stated to have been found there.

The quantity of Gnathia pottery from Alexandria is impressive: a rough count of the pieces known to me provides fragments of some 130 vases, mostly ring-handled kantharoi with some oinochoai and a few pelikai.[15] Other Egyptian sites have yielded much smaller numbers. There are two ring-handled kantharos fragments from Naukratis in Bonn and another from Memphis in University College, London.[16] Doubtless more remain to be identified in museum collections. Almost all these pieces from Egypt are of the Alexandria Group, datable to the first quarter of the third century B.C. It may be that the expanding population of Greeks in Egypt, particularly in Alexandria, found the products of native clay too crude for their taste.[17] Certainly Apulian traders, and in particular one Apulian workshop, managed to capture a good share of the market. It is perhaps also worth noting that the Ptolemaic faience oinochoai, so admirably published recently by Mrs Thompson, seem to follow the shape of Apulian Gnathia oinochoai more closely than those of any other known fabric.[18]

The trade to Alexandria helps explain the trade to Crete as an obvious intermediate port, and thus perhaps to Melos. The Cretan situation, however, is somewhat difficult. The context of none of the pieces in the National Museum reported to have come from that island is known. An exploration of the storerooms of the Heraklion Museum revealed only the miniature situla no. 14 above.[19] There is no immediate evidence that any Gnathia was found in the recent British excavations of the Unexplored Mansion, but sorting of the Hellenistic pottery is not yet complete.[20] I have not had the opportunity to examine the possibilities of western Crete. Nevertheless the local overpainted pottery, which has a colourful and lively character not apparent in the wares of the Greek mainland, does show signs of Apulian and of Sicilian influence in a number of motifs.

The popularity of Gnathia in Rhodes must be connected with the trade to Alexandria, and this with the remarkable absence of Gnathia in Delos provides confirmation of Fraser's contention that Rhodes, through its merchant navy, took a more active part in Alexandrian trade than did Delos.[21] And with Rhodes a popular market, the possibility that no. 5 above was found in Kalymnos becomes less remote.

The material from the area of Cyrenaica (nos. 15–20) suggests another route to Alexandria, along the North African coast. But it has a wider range in date and one may suspect a trade that had built up over some years: certainly the early third century ring-handled kantharos from Tocra published by Boardman and Hayes[22] is a very competent imitation of Apulian Gnathia that argues for familiarity with the originals.

It is possible that more Gnathia pottery could be identified in Cyprus but at the moment the spread of dates would suggest a casual trade rather than any more specific marketing, whether or not through Rhodes. The pieces from Antioch, Gezer, and Doura (nos. 29–33) on the other hand, though few in number, are of the same character as the material from Alexandria and are probably carry-overs from there.[23]

The new evidence from Enez (no. 34) is important. The position of this site on the north Aegean coast near the Greek-Turkish border would indicate an additional pattern of trade to that outlined above. Although one would welcome other finds of Gnathia along the north Aegean littoral, it is probably a reasonable guess on the analogy of trade in other material that these pieces travelled from the Adriatic by the route of the Via Egnatia on the trade system that led eventually to the colonies of the Black Sea. And then one remembers the amphora of West Slope type in Berlin from Olbia (no. 35).

*   *   *   *   *

Amphorae of West Slope type lead us to a further problem. Reciprocal influences between Greek and Apulian material are not easy to determine but are perhaps clearer on shapes than decoration. One minor instance, the bell-krater type B soon after the middle of the fourth century has been mentioned above. At the other end of the scale, about 275 B.C., an even more minor instance is the tall stemmed kantharos with high curving cup handles known to me in only one example and at that clearly derived from metal such as the well-known silver vase from the Taranto treasure.[24] More important if more difficult is the question of the amphora of West Slope type. As a question it is probably insoluble at the moment and there will be no attempt here to do any more than state the South Italian viewpoint. The earliest example seems to be one from Taranto that can be dated by a red-figured squat lekythos found with it to ca. 325 B.C.[25] Indeed the ivy that decorates it, with three-dot fruit and incised stem, might suggest a somewhat earlier date. The vase is only 12 cm high but already has the relatively large neck, broadly set handles and depressed body that are typical of the type. The body, however, is still rounded rather than biconical; it is not ribbed. Our next earliest Apulian piece is a version from Lecce in Vienna that cannot be dated later than about 310 B.C. (Figs. 9–10).[26] Here we approach the canonical type much more closely. The body is ribbed and wider with a flatter shoulder; the lower wall has an in-curve but there is still no band at the greatest diameter. This is one of the few WS amphorae to have its lid. It is followed closely by another piece from Lecce in Vienna that is most likely from the same workshop, and by almost contemporary examples in Taranto and Brindisi both of which have the canonical shape.[27] Thereafter the changes in form are not so marked; there is simply a steady development towards a more pronounced biconical form with relatively large neck. As Dr Forti saw, the well-known amphora in Berlin from Olbia must be a late example.[28] One of the interesting features of the Apulian series is that while these amphorae are never numerous (fewer than twenty are known to me), they show a consistent development that seems self-sufficient within the series.[29] That is they do not have the appearance of copies. What inspired the original example in Taranto is less clear. One awaits the establishment of a more detailed chronology for their Greek counterparts with some interest.[30]

The Sicilians also had a version. It seems to derive from a model just slightly later in date than the Apulian prototype from Taranto, but theirs developed more slowly and seemingly in isolation from Apulian. Although they only lasted into the very early years of the third century, they preserved a relatively rounded body and were never ribbed.[31] Wherever the standard type was developed, Sicily was only marginally involved.

*   *   *   *   *

In another case, however, connections between Sicily and the Greek mainland were demonstrably close. Fig. 11 is a bowl fragment in the Museo Archeologico Nazionale, Syracuse; it is from Syracuse and fits well into the series of bowls from Syracuse and nearby sites.[32] It is decorated around the wall with ears of corn.[33] The ears are drawn as an oval of solid colour, in this case white, with dots of red over. The awn is incised on the glaze. Above is a white band that is presumably the stem from which the ears grow, and by analogy with other representations, one may assume that the ears alternated above and below the stem. The arrangement may be seen more clearly on the central band of another Sicilian vase, a round-mouthed jug in Zürich, (Fig. 12).[34] The drawing is similar if not quite as fine.

The motif of ears of corn occurs not uncommonly in Attica in the second half of the fourth century but in a different version that in fact seems to have virtually died out by the end of the century.[35] But in the later third century one finds versions that are almost identical with the Syracusan in form. A good example is found on a fragment from a cistern in the Piraeus published recently by Dr Ingrid Metzger.[36] Indeed it is so close that one could be forgiven for taking it as Sicilian. But other examples certainly belong to the mainland.[37]

To return to the Syracuse fragment, there are alternate red and white bands on the lower wall surrounding a relief tondo in the centre. The relief has the busts of two figures (the heads are to the right in the illustration) of which the face of the nearer is missing. To judge by the rays about the head it must have been Helios while the female figure to the rear is Selene with the moon crescent above her head. This piece seems to have been known both to Welcker and to Pagenstecher who listed the Helios and Selene type as no. 84 in his catalogue.[38] He took the whole group to be Syracusan, mentioning five examples in Syracuse and one each in Munich, Leipzig and the Louvre.[39]

Medallion bowls were not of course confined to Sicily but their painted decoration usually distinguishes them quite clearly from their Greek and Alexandrian counterparts.[40] The nearest parallel to the Sicilian version is the Apulian which is close in shape though usually without reliefs. The Apulian makes its appearance by about 280–270 B.C., shortly before the end of the main Gnathia sequence, both with and without painted decoration, and it seems likely that its appearance there is to be related to the appearance of the shape in Attica.[41] Not only do we have these in common but hemispherical bowls with plastic feet.[42] On the other hand no Sicilian bowls so far published have contexts demonstrably contemporary with the Apulian (or early Attic) examples, and their absence from the Lipari tombs of the first quarter of the third century may mean that the shape was not made there until later, until Apulian Gnathia was finished,[43] and therefore that it was derived from Attica, from Alexandria, or directly from metal prototypes. While direct derivation from metal is always possible, there is no positive reason to suppose it in this case. The ears of corn motif is not a good argument for derivation from Attic but it is certainly a concrete if small example of contact between Athens and Syracuse in the later part of the third century B.C.

Postscript

In the interval since these notes were written, there has inevitably been new material which should have been taken into account. Most noteworthy are G. Roger Edwards *Corinth* VII, 3. *Hellenistic Pottery* and the article by Klaus Parlasca "Ptolemäische Fayence-keramik ausserhalb Ägyptens" *JdI* 91, 1976, 135–156 which is now vital to any discussion of trade between Alexandria and South Italy. The bell-krater from Lamia mentioned above in n. 14 is now on secondary display in the National Museum, Athens. Peter Callaghan, who is publishing the Hellenistic material from the Unexplored Mansion at Knossos, tells me he has located no Gnathia there. Through the kindness of Professor D. Adamesteanu and Dr Antonio de Siena I have been able to examine important material from the potters' quarter at Metaponto which the latter is soon to publish. It includes a fine and elaborate kantharoid krater which is most probably Attic West Slope, found amongst kiln refuse that was mostly Gnathia of the third century. From these deposits also comes a clear series of bowls that begins in the early third century and continues to its end or even later. Finally, as this article goes to press, Mr P.M. Kenrick has kindly informed me that from recent excavations at Benghazi, there are "over 400 sherds of painted black-glazed wares, the majority of which belong to Italian Gnathia" and that many appear to belong to the Alexandria Group.

NOTES

1   On commercial relations in general at this period, see M. Rostovtzeff, *The Social and Economic History of the Hellenistic World,* Oxford 1941, esp. pp. 162, 396, 538, 1207, and 1415 n. 198. While it may seem captious to criticise details, it is perhaps worth pointing out that his identification of Gnathia at eastern sites was over-optimistic and has a persistent influence: e.g. L. Byvanck-Quarles van Ufford, *BABesch* 33, 1958, 46, on the Amsterdam grave group (if it really is such) Rostovtzeff pl. XX (and *Allard Pierson Museum. Algemeene Gids,* Amsterdam 1937, pl. XIX), which does not contain any South Italian although it does have Attic. For Egyptian trade, see the excellent chapter in P.M. Fraser, *Ptolemaic Alexandria,* Oxford 1972, 132 ff. and especially 154. For pottery contacts in the reverse direction, from Greece to Italy, there are useful comments by Johannowsky in *La circolazione delle monetà ateniese in Sicilia e in Magna Grecia. Atti del 1º Convegno del Centro Internazionale di Studi Numismatici, Napoli 5—8 Aprile 1967,* Rome 1969, 225 ff.

2   I am grateful to Mr Charles K. Williams both for showing me the pieces in Corinth and for permission to publish them here. The round-bellied epichysis is C—69—138 and was first published in *Hesperia* 39, 1970, pl. 1, 1. The identification of the shape is made certain by the handle-root at the lower right-hand edge of the fragment. For the Rose Painter see T.B.L. Webster, 'Towards a classification of Apulian Gnathia', *BICS* 15, 1968, 11—12; J.R. Green, 'Gnathian Addenda', *BICS* 18, 1971, 30—33, and *Gnathia Pottery in the Akademisches Kunstmuseum, Bonn,* Mainz 1976, 3—4. An example of the shape is *CVA* British Museum (1), pl. 7 (43), 16.

3   Some examples are Paris, Louvre N 2071 (with ivy), and (with vine) Bari 6685, Palermo 2254, Louvre N 2060 and Matera (L. Forti, *Ceramica di Gnathia,* Naples 1975, pl. 31a); also, without handles, Bari 6669 with the painted inscription ΣΩ (for Διὸς Σωτῆρος?), *La collezione Polese nel Museo di Bari,* Bari 1970, no. 237 but not illustrated.

4   See, for example, *Hesperia* 41, 1972, pl. 24, 20, and *Hesperia* 42, 1973, pl. 9, C—71—316 and C—72—25.

5   Corinth C—32—64, unpublished. Since these notes were written, Dr Ian McPhee has told me of two other pieces of Gnathia in Corinth: C—46—121, a fragment of a bottle with the head of an Amazon to the left, and C—75—222a—b, fragments of an epichysis. He tells me there are also two fragments of what appears to be an Apulian red-figured epichysis (Eros between palmettes on the shoulder) found in recent excavations on Acrocorinth (no. C—61—459, *RVAp,* p. xlviii).

6   The Olynthos vases, *Olynthus* V, pl. 57, 84, pl. 60, 92, and pl. 122, 270; the last, *ARV²* 1508, 11, Painter of Olynthos 5.156; see also my notes in *BICS* 19, 1972, 15—16. Dr. J—P. Descoeudres, who has kindly examined these vases in Thessalonike, informs me that the first has much mica, is unlike Attic in colour and is certainly local; the second, which also has plenty of mica, is less certain but is probably local; the third (which is closest to Attic in style of decoration) has browner clay than is normal for Attic and the glaze is of very poor quality, but it has virtually no mica and so is probably Attic. [On

this sort of question, see also E. Yiouri, *Kernos (Timetike Prosphora . . Bakalake),* Thessalonike 1972, 6–14]. There is a black-glazed epichysis with impressed palmette and lotus on the shoulder in the De Young Museum, San Francisco, no. 702. It has every appearance of being Attic and is certainly not South Italian. See also n. 5 above.

7   I am grateful to Professor H.A. Thompson for permission to publish them and to Professor G.R. Edwards for isolating them for me. Professor Edwards has also helped with a number of other aspects of this paper.

8   Mr Fraser has been kind enough to re-check his observation of the Gnathia in Rhodes on a recent visit.

9   Picard (*BCH* 1911, 198, n. 2) followed by Forti (*supra* n. 3) says the vase is from Melos. I follow the label on the vase and the inventory.

10   *CVA* British Museum (1), pl. 8 (44), 14, from Benghazi, is not Italian but most probably a local version. I am grateful to D.M. Bailey for discussing the vase with me.

11   *CVA* British Museum (1), pl. 7 (43), 13, from Cyrenaica, is not Apulian and most probably not Italian.

12   This looks very like the vase from Aradippo illustrated in Palma di Cesnola, *Descriptive Atlas of the Cesnola Collection of Cypriot Antiquities* II, 2, pl. CXLVIII no. 1092 (whence *Swedish Cyprus Expedition* IV, 3, fig. 21, 18) but Myres in the *Handbook of the Cesnola Collection,* New York 1914, 295–296, took the latter to be his no. 1758. One may also note the other vases mentioned by Myres. There is also Apulian red-figure in Stanford that seems to be from Cyprus. Mrs Isabelle Raubitschek kindly assisted my study of these vases.

13   I am grateful to Professor J.B. Hennessy for bringing this piece to my attention.

14   The most recent discussion of the material in the National Museum, Athens, is that by Forti (*supra* n. 3), 25 ff.; see also my own brief comments in *BICS* 18, 1971, 38, n. 2, and *Gnathia Bonn* (*supra* n. 2), 1. I am indebted to Dr Barbara Philippaki for assistance and permission to publish the material in the National Museum (even though my notes on this and so much else have fallen into the hands of Neapolitan car thieves). I do not know Athens 2160, from Crete, or the krater 2260 from Lamia mentioned by Picard (*supra* n. 9). The mug 2306 and the small hydria 2340 (Forti, pls. 2d and 3c) have no stated provenience. It should be noted that the plastic rhyton published in *AAA* 5, 1972, 427 (and *BCH* 97, 1973, 257, fig. 10), is not South Italian as suggested there.

15   The largest number is to be found in that part of the Benachi collection now housed in the National Museum, Athens. So far as I know only one of these fragments has been published, the deep bowl fragment B 1739, in *AntK* 3, 1960, pl. 9, 1 (Webster); it can now be shown to be somewhat later than Webster suggested. For other examples, see E. Breccia, *La necropoli di Sciatbi (Catalogue général des Antiquités Egyptiennes. Musée d'Alexandrie),* Cairo 1912, pls. 81–82; *Bulletin de la Société Archéologique d'Alexandrie* 35, 1942, frontispiece; for Egypt and Crete, R. Pagenstecher, *Expedition E. von Sieglin* II, Leipzig 1913, 3, 24. One should note that the Gnathia published in C.C. Edgar, *Greek Vases (Catalogue général . .),* Cairo 1911, pl. XIII, 26221–3, need not have been found in Egypt.

16   The Bonn fragments are illustrated in *Gnathia Bonn* (*supra* n. 2), pl. 21b; see also fig. 1, *ibidem,* for the shape.

17   But see the useful discussion of clays by Fraser, *Ptolemaic Alexandria,* 138–139. For connections between Alexandria, Crete and Taranto in the 'Plakettenvasen', see W. Züchner, 'Von Toreuten und Töpfern', *JdI* 65/66, 1950/51, 175–205, and the article by G. Andreassi in this volume; also K. Parlasca, 'Das Verhältnis der megarischen Becher zum alexandrinischen Kunsthandwerk', *JdI* 70, 1955, 129–154.

18   D.B. Thompson, *Ptolemaic Oinochoai and Portraits in Faience,* Oxford 1973, 13–14. Note that one of these oinochoai, Thompson 125 no. 1, seems to have been found at Canosa.

19   I am grateful to Miss A. Lembesis of the Heraklion Museum for her kindness in allowing me to examine the Hellenistic pottery there.

20 My thanks are due to Mr L.H. Sackett for this further instance of his hospitality.

21 *Ptolemaic Alexandria,* 162 ff. and especially 171.

22 *Tocra* ii, pl. 42, 2379 and p. 93, fig. 42.

23 C. Clairmont, 'Greek Pottery from the Near East', *Berytus* 11, 1955, 135–136, notes four examples of Apulian red-figure from Sidon, one from Tanturah, and three perhaps from Egypt.

24 The terracotta vase is Taranto 111429 from Taranto, Forti (*supra* n. 3), pl. 21a; *RendNapoli* 45, 1970, pl. 12, fig. 33. For the silver vase the basic publication is P. Wuilleumier, *Le Trésor de Tarente,* Paris 1930, pls. V–VI. Note the example in faience from Tanagra, A. Fürtwangler, *La Collection Sabouroff,* Paris 1883, I, pl. LXX, 3; *BABesch* 33, 1958, 51, fig. 12. Beazley, *EVP,* 234–5, listed black-glazed examples that may be Etruscan; perhaps add Munich 2912 (inv. 6497) and 2911 (inv. 6496) that has relief ivy on the neck in imitation of metalwork.

25 *NSc* 1940, 451, fig. 24.

26 Vienna IV 450, height to lip: 15.5 cm; T.B.L. Webster, *Monuments illustrating Old and Middle Comedy',* *BICS Suppl.* 9, 1960 (2nd ed. *BICS Suppl.* 23, 1969), GV 26c. The vase has carefully rounded ribs. I am grateful to Dr W. Oberleitner for his kindness in giving me every facility to study the Vienna material.

27 Vienna IV 424, height to lip: 16.3 cm. This also has a lid. Taranto 52599 from Taranto, V. Messapia 26.6.1951 (cf. Forti, 90, n. 16). Brindisi 838 from Francavilla Fontana (cf. Forti, 76), who dates it to the beginning of the third century).

28 Berlin inv. 4956, e.g. Pfuhl, *MuZ,* fig. 754; Buschor, *GV* (1940), fig. 280; Forti, pl. 28e. Seemingly very close to this are the fragments of a WS amphora, Athens NM Benachi 1810, from Alexandria.

29 In addition to those mentioned in the last three notes, there are also Vienna IV 502 (Webster, *MMC,* GV 28a) and with it Birmingham 1607.85; Leiden K 95/1.4; Lecce 1785 from Rugge (M. Bernardini, *Vasi dello stile di Gnathia. Vasi a vernice nera,* Bari, n.d., pl. 36, 1–2; Forti, pl. 25c); Lecce 1787 from Rugge (Bernardini, pl. 36, 3–4); Lecce 1786 from Manduria (Bernardini, pl. 36, 5–6); Lecce 4941 from Rocavecchia (Bernardini, pl. 36, 7); Lecce no no. from Rocavecchia (Bernardini, pl. 36, 8); Metaponto from Metaponto, Località Crucinia T 27; Yale from Bari (P.V.C. Baur, *Stoddard Collection,* 1922, 167, fig. 70, no. 271). The last is probably related to Vienna IV 502 and the Birmingham vase.

30 H.A. Thompson's article, 'Two Centuries of Hellenistic Pottery' in *Hesperia* 3, 1934, 311–480, is still fundamental, although Virginia Grace has recently made important modifications to third century chronology: *AM* 89, 1974, 193–200. A useful but mostly unpublished tomb-group in Taranto permits correlation of West Slope and Gnathia. The Attic kantharos is illustrated in *Rivista dell'Istituto Nazionale di Archeologia e Storia dell'Arte* 13–14, 1964–65, 55 fig. 38; the Gnathia probably dates to about 290–280 B.C.

31 Six of the Sicilian examples belong to a single group, the Bonn-Owl Group; Bonn 154 and 155 (*Gnathia Bonn,* pl. 29); Reading 45.vi.31 and 32; Birmingham; Michigan 2639 (*CVA,* pl. 29, 8), the latest. Others include *NSc* 1955, 305, fig. 21, 15; *NSc* 1955, 334, fig. 47, top left; *NSc* 1959, 354 (two); Houston (de Ménil and Hoffmann, *Ten Centuries that Shaped the West,* Mainz and Houston 1970, 435–6); Zürich 2691; Note also the black-glazed example *CVA* Baltimore 3, pl. 37, 5 and *CVA* Copenhagen, 7, pl. 296, 8, both from Agrigento.

32 The fragment is published here by kind permission of Professor L. Bernabò Brea and Dr G. Voza.

33 On the motif, see P. Wolters, 'Die Goldene Ahren', *Festschrift für James Loeb,* Munich 1930, 111–129. He shows that the type generally represented is *triticum compactum.* English terminology is something of a difficulty. My usuage of 'corn' is British; in North American, Australian and sometimes New Zealand English, the word is used more particularly for 'Indian Corn' (*zea mays*), that is maize, sweet corn and the like.

34 Zürich 3330, *CVA,* pl. 51, 17. The vase is illustrated here by kind permission of Professor H. Bloesch.

35 Cf. G. Kopcke, *AM* 79, 1964, 44, nos. 183–190 and pp. 62–63, pl. 33. But one of the pair of lagynos-like jugs from Malta, now in Gotha (*CVA* 2, pl. 94, 4–6), has a motif incorporating traditional ears of corn on the shoulder.

36 *ADelt* 26, 1971, 41 ff. and pl. 11, no. 83.

37 E.g. *AAA* 7, 1974, 57, fig. 19b centre, from Demetrias.

38 F.G. Welcker, *Alte Denkmäler,* Göttingen 1849–64, I, 192 ff.; R. Pagenstecher, *Die calenische Relief-keramik (JdI Erghft 8),* Berlin 1909, 65 and 173–174.

39 Dr G. Voza writes: 'Abbiamo due coppe intere con tale emblema, 1) Inv. 24299 da Licodia Eubea (prov. di Catania) diam. c. 18,4; alt. cm. 6,7, a vernice nera con chiazza arrossata. L'emblema è lievemente sciupato. La figura femminile è caratterizzata come una iside. 2) Altra minore, inv. 43173 da Centuripe, diam. cm. 12,7; alt. cm. 5,00, con vernice interamente arrossata, ricostruita da vari frammenti (con qualche reintegrazione in gesso), in cui la figura femminile è caratterizzata da crescente lunare. Poi vari frammenti di coppe analoghe.' Cf. Pagenstecher (*supra* n. 39), 174, on Welcker. It is probable that at least the majority of Sicilian medallion bowls is Syracusan. Pace's reference (*Arte e civiltà della Sicilia antica*[2], Milan 1958, ii, 485, n. 1) to Orsi in *NSc* 1915, 189–190 (not 580, as Pace), is mistaken in that Orsi was clearly referring to Arretine. Occasional examples appear elsewhere, e.g. *NSc* 1960, 109–110, three from Gela; *NSc* 1941, 293, two from Lilybaeum (note that they have reliefs from impressions of Rhodian coins); *MonAnt* 46, 1960, cols. 309–310, a fragment from Eloro; *MonAnt* 44, 1958, cols. 256–258, one from Butera. The provenience of the bowl in G. Libertini, *Il Museo Biscari,* Milan–Rome 1930, pl. 96, 845, is not stated but one may guess that it was not Syracuse.

40 Pagenstecher's still remains the best overall treatment of medallion bowls. F. Courby, *Les vases grecs à reliefs,* Paris 1922, 220 ff., gives a general survey but makes little attempt to distinguish fabrics. There are useful comments by V. Hadjimichali in *BCH* 95, 1971, 204–208; see also recently Elia, *EAA* III, 325–326 [s.v. emblema (2)].

41 Forti (*supra* n. 3), 84, noting the fine character of the potting, suggests a derivation from metal or glass prototypes and quotes glass examples from Taranto and bronze from Cyprus; see also her p. 93, n. 68. Well-known are the two Egyptian faience bowls from Apulia: M. Mayer, *Apulien,* Leipzig and Berlin 1914, 305. Two of the rare Apulian pottery versions to have reliefs are Amsterdam 2650 and 2661, both said to be from Taranto, *CVA* Scheurleer 1, pl. 2 (46), 4 and 5; compare the metal versions in Wuilleumier, *Trésor de Tarente* (*supra* n. 25), 36 ff. and 103 ff. For Attic, see *AM* 26, 1901, 81, and *Hesperia* 3, 1934, 348, no. C 7, and 372, nos. D 14–15. Occasionally the decoration of the two corresponds as well as the shape. One particular motif shared by the two fabrics is the dolphin shown on the upper wall on the inside. Apulian examples include Amsterdam 2650 (see above), Bonn inv. 164 (*Gnathia Bonn,* pl. 25), and the fragments Athens NM Benachi 1720, from Alexandria. West Slope examples include Forti, pl. 5b. It seems likely that the idea went from Athens to Taranto (a) because this open manner of decoration was unusual by this stage in Gnathia (b) because the dolphin was unknown before this in Gnathia whereas it had a longer tradition in Attica and is very frequent in West Slope (as already Picard, *BCH* 1911, 200), e.g. Forti, pl. 5c, *Hesperia* 3, 1934, 335, 336, 342, *AM* 26, 1901, 70, 71, 80, *Hesperia* 20, 1951, pl. 52a (pyre 7) no. 6. Most of them seem to belong to the earlier side of West Slope. I am unsure of the fabric of the bowl Louvre S 4354 and of the plate Louvre MN 839.

42 For footed bowls in Apulian, see Forti, 85 and *RendNapoli* 45, 1970, 234; in West Slope, e.g. *AM* 26, 1901, 76, *Hesperia* 12, 1943, 359, fig. 60a, *Hesperia* 27, 1958, pl. 13d, but these are mostly later. There is an example from Centuripe, Libertini, *Museo Biscari,* pl. 92, 811; see also Beazley, *EVP,* 241–2.

43 As Adamesteanu, *MonAnt* 44, 1958, 256: 'E vero però che le coppe caleniche non appaiono, almeno a Gela, che nel tardo periodo, dopo il 280 av. Cr.'

ZWEI GRIECHISCHE SCHMUCKSTÜCKE

Adolf Greifenhagen

Tafel 23.

Im Nachlass von Robert Zahn fand ich zwei Photographien eines Kopfgefässes mit dem Vermerk 'Dr. Lederer' (Taf. 23, Abb. 1). Das Kännchen gehörte dem von 1910–38 in Berlin lebenden, hochgeschätzten Numismatiker Dr. Philipp Lederer.[1] 1930 kam es in das Metropolitan Museum und wurde von Gisela Richter veröffentlicht.[2] Beazley hat es in seine 'Class K: The Toronto Class' eingeordnet.[3] Bisher wurde nur die Vorderseite des Gefässes abgebildet. Daher überrascht es, den hübschen Ohrschmuck zu sehen, den der Maler übereinstimmend unter beiden Ohrläppchen hingemalt hat.[4] Die innere Umrandung der Ohrmuschel wird bis an den unteren Rand des Ohrläppchens heruntergezogen. Hier setzt, ohne dass ein Ring oder Haken angegeben wäre, eine Lotosblüte von schön ausschwingendem Umriss an. Zwei Blütenblätter umschliessen ein knospenförmiges Mittelblatt. Mit Gisela Richter datieren wir das Gefäss um 480 v. Chr.

Goldene Ohrringe dieses Typus sind uns, soweit ich sehe, nicht erhalten. Trotzdem dürfte es keinem Zweifel unterliegen, dass dem Vasenmaler in Gold ausgeführter Schmuck vorgeschwebt hat. Ihm kam es vor allem auf die Darstellung des schönen Anhängers an. Auf die Angabe des Hakens oder Ringes konnte er verzichten. In der Zeit der frühen Klassik, wie überhaupt im fünften Jahrhundert, war Goldschmuck selten.[5] Es fehlten die wirtschaftlich-politischen Voraussetzungen für solchen Luxus. Das vorhandene Gold lag vornehmlich in den Tempelschätzen, zu Kunstwerken verarbeitet, als Barren oder in Münzen geprägt.[6]

Immerhin fällt es auf, weder unter dem erhaltenen Goldschmuck noch auf Vasenbildern auch nur ein einziges Paar von Ohrgehängen dieses Typus anzutreffen. Allenfalls lässt sich der Ohrschmuck der Athena (?) auf einem früher in Erbach bewahrten Fragment von einem Glockenkrater des Altamuramalers nennen (Taf. 23, Abb. 2).[7] Doch handelt es sich hier offenbar um eine andere Blumenart. Dagegen gibt es eine phönizische Halskette[8] aus Glasperlen, denen zwei vergleichbare Goldglieder in Gestalt der Lotosblüte eingefügt sind. Die Kette wurde in Tharros auf Sardinien gefunden. Die Typologie ägyptischen Ohrschmuckes bietet keinen Anlass, etwa *hier* nach Vorbildern zu suchen. Die griechische Kunst archaischer Zeit zeigt zur Genüge, wie sehr sie sich die aus der östlichen Kunst übernommenen Elemente anverwandelt. Es besteht keine Notwendigkeit, direkten Einfluss einer fremden, östlichen Schmuckform anzunehmen. An dem Gebälk des Siphnierschatzhauses in Delphi[9] finden wir Lotosblüten, von denen man die grazile, leichtere Spielart unserer goldenen Blüten ableiten könnte. Besser als attische Vasen lässt die rhodische Ornamentik[10] Leitformen der Lotosblüte sehen, welche auch zu der goldenen Blüte dieses Ohrschmucks an dem attischen Kännchen hinführen. So bereichert das Kopfgefäss aufs willkommenste unsere Kenntnis der Typen attischen Ohrschmucks reifarchaisch-frühklassischer Zeit, wobei wir die Möglichkeit eines Einflusses ionischer Vorbilder nicht ausschliessen wollen.

Ein anderes Kopfgefäss, eine der Goldkannen aus dem 1949 entdeckten Fund von Panagjuriště,[11] interessiert hier wegen des Halskettenverschlusses. Besser als die vorhandenen Abbildungen lässt eine von I. Luckert hergestellte Aufnahme (Taf. 23, Abb. 3–4) erkennen, worauf es uns ankommt. Ingrid Blanck beschreibt in ihrer verdienstvollen Dissertation[12] die Halskette an der Kanne von Panagjuriště und erwähnt dabei auch die Besonderheit des Verschlusses 'in Form von drei spitz-ovalen Endgliedern, von denen zwei horizontal gelagert sind und aneinanderstossen, das dritte nach unten hängt.'[13]

Diese am Verschluss herabhängende Bommel hat doppelte Funktion: sie bildet ein Gegengewicht zu der nach vorn herabziehenden Hauptlast der Kette, die durch die Schwere des Anhängers noch gesteigert wird. Zum anderen bietet die Bommel eine Handhabe beim Anlegen oder Abnehmen der Kette, wie auch immer der Verschluss konstruiert war. Ein glücklicher Zufall hat uns auch hier eine Photographie aus dem Nachlass R. Zahns (Taf. 23, Abb. 5)[14] in die Hand gegeben, die eine griechische Kette des vierten Jahrhunderts aus glatten und verzierten Hohlkugeln zeigt mit Stierkopfanhänger und einem Verschluss aus zwei keulenförmigen Gliedern und herabhängender Bommel. Diese setzt sich zusammen aus einer hohlen, doppelkonischen Goldperle zwischen zwei Kugeln, denen sich unten noch eine runde dunklere Perle aus Glas oder Stein anschliesst. Die Kette befand sich einst in Konstantinopel im Kunsthandel und tauchte später noch einmal in einer Auktion in Paris auf. [15] In ihrer Zusammensetzung wirkt sie durchaus überzeugend und vollständig. Damit gewinnen wir ein schönes Beispiel für einen Typus des griechischen Halskettenverschlusses, wie ihn das Kopfgefäss von Panagjurište gleichsam 'in effigie' aufweist.

ANMERKUNGEN

1 Philipp Lederer. Nekrolog von H.A. Cahn in *Schweizerische Numismatische Rundschau* 32, 1946, 69 ff. = H.A. Cahn, *Kleine Schriften,* Basel 1975, 156 ff.

2 Metropolitan Museum 30.11.10. Fletcher Fund, 1930. *BMMA* 25, 1930, 281, Abb. 3 (Richter).

3 *ARV²* 1537, 6.

4 D. von Bothmer danke ich für die Mitteilung, dass die linke Seite des Gefässes den gleichen Ohrring zeigt. Ein Photo des Museums gibt eine Schrägansicht des Gefässes in unverändertem Zustand.

5 R.A. Higgins, *Greek and Roman Jewellery,* London 1961, 118 ff.; C.H.V. Sutherland, *Gold. Macht, Weisheit und Magie,* Wien und München 1970, 81 f. (engl. Originalausgabe: *Gold. Its Beauty, Power and Allure,* London 1959).

6 Inventare der Tempelgeräte (434/3 – 407/6 v. Chr.): *Inscriptiones Graecae,* I², 232 ff. (dazu *Supplementum Epigraphicum Graecum,* X, 184 ff.). Hinweis bei H. Bengtson, *Griechische Geschichte, HAW* III, 4, München 1940, 203. Siehe auch Sutherland a. O (oben Anm. 5).

7 *ARV²* 592, 37. Abb. 7 nach Ch. Lenormant u. J. de Witte, *Élite des monuments céramographiques,* I, Paris 1844, Taf. 29, 1. Siehe auch K. Hadaczek, *Der Ohrschmuck der Griechen und Etrusker,* Wien 1903, 21 Abb. 37.

8 F.H. Marshall, *Catalogue of Jewellery, Greek, Etruscan and Roman in the Dept. of Antiquities, British Museum,* 1911, Nr. 1545, Taf. 24.

9 J. Charbonneaux, R. Martin u. F. Villard, *Grèce archaïque,* Paris 1968, 195, Abb. 234–5.

10 W. Schiering, *Werkstätten orientalisierender Keramik auf Rhodos,* Berlin 1957, Beil. 7. 8 unten.

11 B. Svoboda-D. Končev, *Neue Denkmäler antiker Toreutik,* Prag 1956, 138 ff., Abb. 6 unten, Taf. 14 rechts, 15 unten und oben rechts; der Verschluss: Taf. 15 unten links; E. Simon, *AntK* 3, 1960, 3 ff., Taf. 2, 3; D.E. Strong, *Greek and Roman Gold and Silver Plate,* London 1966, 102.

12 *Studien zum griechischen Halsschmuck der archaischen und klassischen Zeit,* Diss. Mainz, gedr. Köln 1974.

13 *ibid.,* 117. Zu den "conical endings" siehe M.S. Ruxer, Historja Naszyjnika Greckiego (Posen 1938), engl. Resumé 381 (A). Verschlüsse mit abwärts hängender Bommel nennt Ruxer nicht. Der Fund von Panagjurište wurde erst nach Erscheinen ihres Buches bekannt.

14 A. Greifenhagen, *Schmuckarbeiten in Edelmetall,* II, Berlin 1975, Abb. 1, Text zu Taf. 8, 8.

15 *Catalogue de Vente, Hôtel Drouot, Paris, 16/17 mai 1957 (Collection de Madame L. de M.),* Nr. 110, Taf VII.

ATTIC AND TARENTINE RHYTA: ADDENDUM

Herbert Hoffmann

Plates 24, 25, 26.

Dale Trendall first put me on to Tarentine rhyta as a class of objects worth investigating, and encouraged my work on Attic as well. These notes are offered as a small token of my esteem.

In the years since the publication of *Attic Red-figured Rhyta*[1] (henceforth abbreviated as *ARR*) and *Tarentine Rhyta*[2] (henceforth abbreviated as *TR*) a number of interesting specimens of this shape have come to light. Addenda as of mid-1963 were given in *TR* on p. 135. Here are some more that have come to my attention since:

ATTIC RHYTA

EARLY RAM CLASS (*ARR*, 7–8):

Ram-head: ARR No. 2 *bis.* BASEL, Peter Strauss. A fragmentary replica of the Berlin and Naples specimens, likewise stemmed.

MINIATURE CLASS (*ARR*, 16):

Ram-head: ARR No. 25 *ter.* NEW YORK, market (Komor). Here Pl. 24, Fig. 1. Replica of New York 39.11.6, with 'face' glazed black.

LONDON, VICTORIA AND ALBERT MUSEUM C2497–1910:

Campano-Etruscan according to Dietrich von Bothmer, who adds Beugnot No. 94 to the list of dwarf vessels derived from this Class.

BRYGAN CLASS (*cf. ARR*, pp. 10 ff.):

Three more Brygan Class rhyta — a hound-head and two donkey-heads — have come to light. The first two, in and from Aleria (Corsica), were added by the late Sir John Beazley in *Paralipomena*, p. 367 (the donkey-head there numbered doubly by mistake) and are now published by J. and L. Jehasse in *La Nécropole préromaine d'Aléria* (Paris, 1973), cat. nos. 1902 and 1903, pls. 33–34. (The authors' surprising statement, on p. 50, note 27: "on peut douter l'éxistance de moules, contrairement à la thèse d'Hoffmann", appears to be based on a misunderstanding or disregard of the instructions for measuring rhyta given in *ARR* pp. 1f. — "Foundry Painter" is an error for the hound-head; both rhyta are surely by the Brygos Painter). The third rhyton, in and from Melfi, is now illustrated by S. Moscati in *Italia archaeologica* (Novara, 1974), on p. 152.

THE SOTADEAN CLASS (*ARR*, 19–25):

Two statuette-rhyta: one, in the form of a camel accompanied by an Oriental, has now been published by Lilly Kahil:[3] the other, a Pygmy carrying a dead crane, is in a Basel private collection:[4] *ARV²* 1669, No. 2 *bis: Paralipomena*, 415 ('may be by the Sotades Painter himself').

Sotadean proper are also the following:

Ram-head: MOSCOW, Pushkin Museum, 741, from Kerch. *Paralipomena*, 415, 11 *ter.* Fallen Pygmy. Attributed by Beazley to the manner of the Sotades Painter.

Kantharos-rhyton, ram-head: ARR No. 28 *bis.* HAMBURG, Museum für Kunst und Gewerbe, inv. 1977, 220. Here Pl. 24, Figs. 2–4. A, two owls, one perched on an olive twig, an olive twig between them; B, two satyrs, one crouching, holding a stick (to club an owl ?), the other δεφόμενος. Attributed by Herbert Cahn to the Sotades Painter. The only Sotadean kantharos-rhyton known to me.

Ram-head and donkey-head, dimidiated: ARR No. 40 *bis* Swiss Priv.Coll. Here Pls. 25–26, Figs. 5–6, 9–11. B, donkey; A and C, satyr. Manner of the Sotades Painter. For the ornament compare *ARR* No. 42.

Panther-head: ARR p. 22. Two Attic rhyta on the Basel art market (Palladion) are replicas of the lost Sotadean panther-head preserved in Gargiulo's drawing. *Palladion Antike Kunst* (Milano 1976), cat. nos. 39a (Eos and Kephalos) and b (two athletes, stela). Attributed by A. Lezzi to the Group of Class W.

STARA ZAGORA MUSEUM, BULGARIA:

A fragment of a mid-fifth century rhyton decorated with a sphinx.

HEIDELBERG, ARCHÄOLOGISCHES INSTITUT, Inv. 64/7.

Boar-head: R. Hampe and collaborators, *Katalog der Sammlung antiker Kleinkunst des Archäologischen Instituts der Universität Heidelberg* II, *Neuerwerbungen 1957–70,* No. 82, Pls. 58–59 (top). The shape seems to be closer to the boar-heads of the Dresden Class (*cf. ARR* 29, no. 63). The decoration is near the work of the Penthesilea Painter, which would suggest a connection with the Penthesilean Class (*ARR* 33 ff.).

THE VON MERCKLIN CLASS (*ARR,* 49. no. 10).

To this class, for which see *AntK* 4, 1961, 23, n 23 and *TR,* 139, n 33, can be added a fragmentary hound-head rhyton in the Chios Museum.

TARENTINE RHYTA

Some additions to *Tarentine Rhyta* are given in the reviews by Schauenburg and Oliver,[2] others in the fine article by Selma Holo, "Unpublished Apulian Rhyta", in *J. Paul Getty Museum Journal* I, 1974, 85–93, figs. 1–17. To these can be added a set of four rhyta – part of a tomb group from Apulia acquired by the Australian National University at Canberra in 1965:

Cow-horn: Inv. 65.32. *RVAp* II, Chapter 21, number not yet fixed. Seated Eros. For the shape, *cf. TR* No. 42.

Goat-head: Inv. 65.34. *RVAp* II, Chapter 21, number not yet fixed. Fleeing Amazon. *Cf. TR* No. 139.

Goat-head: Inv. 65.35. *RVAp* II, Chapter 21, number not yet fixed. Seated Eros holding a box. Replica of the preceding.

Kantharos-rhyton, bull-head: Inv. 65.33. Maenad on each side. Replica of *TR* No. 42. Bowl of shape I, aligned with the bull-head. Ascribed by Trendall and Cambitoglou to the School of the Iliupersis Painter (*RVAp* 1, p. 202, no. 8/87). The kantharos-rhyton is dated by them near the middle of the fourth century B.C., the three other rhyta around 340–320 B.C.

Other newcomers include the following:

Bull-head: LUCERNE, market (Ars Antiqua). Woman, standing, facing left, leaning on a column and holding a tympanum. To left, a large flower and a quatrefoil. Bowl shape I, aligned with the bull-head. 'Early Group B'.

Bull-head: PARIS, market (Koutoulakis). Woman running to left, carrying a tympanum. Bowl shape I, aligned with the bull-head. 'Early Group A'. Reported to have been found with the following rhyton:

Ram-head: PARIS, market (Koutoulakis). Seated woman to right. Around the bowl, laurel. Carinations of the ram's horns indicated in glaze. Bowl shape I, aligned with the ram-head. Replica of *TR* No. 174, and by the same painter.

Ram-head: THE HAGUE, private. Unglazed. Bowl shape III. 'Main Group'.

Ram-head: COLOGNE, H-U. and J. Bauer. 'Early Group'. Seated youth. Bowl restored. Unseen.

Head of a Laconian hound: ASCONA, market (Casa Serodine). Here Pl. 25, Figs. 7–8. Satyr (?) moving to left, carrying a plate of offerings and a thyrsos. Bowl shape I. Broken and mended, fragments missing from the rim. 'Early Group A'. Reported to have been found with a fish platter and a set of fish plates.

Deer-head: THE HAGUE, private. 'Main Group A'. Missing part of the bowl.

Griffin-head: ZURICH, market (Vollmoeller). *Antiken-Auktion, Galerie am Neumarkt – Galerie Heidi Vollmoeller,* Zurich, Nov. 19, 1970, No. 61 (illustrated). Seated Eros holding a bunch of grapes, a cista, and a wheel on a string. Bowl shape III. 'Main Group H'.

The following was not included in *TR:*

Cow-head: SCHWERIN, Museum. Female head between wings. By the Rhyton Painter. Bowl shape I. 'Main Group A'. Called to my attention by G. von Lücken, who informs me that the piece was acquired in Rome during the seventies of the last century.

Attention is also drawn to a curious sheep-head rhyton of Apulianising form, said to be from Amlash in Iran. The object, mentioned in *TR,* 139–40, n. 44, has now been illustrated:

Antiken-Auktion, Galerie am Neumarkt – Galerie Heidi Vollmoeller, Zurich, Nov. 19, 1970, No. 163.

FAKES

I append a clever 'Attic' fake, apparently of recent date: a Brygan donkey-head rhyton (*cf. ARR* Pl. 3) in a Basel private collection. The bowl is decorated with a running male figure between two standing draped youths.

It may also be of interest that the fake 'Tarentine' rhyton, *TR* Pl. 62, 2, has a replica in the Haifa Municipal Museum; others in Naples, Krakow, and Prague are published by E. Paul in *Klio* 49, 1967, 334 and 346–7, Figs. 10–11. *TR* Pl. 62, 5, the fake silver rhyton formerly in the possession of Ludwig Curtius, may be based on a clay replica in the Naples Museum: *cf.* Ph. Sommer 11180.

NOTES

1 Herbert Hoffmann, *Attic Red-figured Rhyta,* Mainz 1962. Reviews in: *RBPh* 41, 1963, 514–16 (G.M.A. Richter); *JHS* 84, 1964, 226–7 (R.V. Nicholls); *Gnomon* 36, 1964, 311–12 (R.A. Higgins); *AJA* 69, 1965, 77–8 (E. Jastrow); *Erasmus* 17, 1965, 46–7 (K. Schefold); *RBPh* 46, 1968, 203–4 (G.M.A. Richter).

2 Herbert Hoffmann, *Tarentine Rhyta,* Mainz 1966. Reviews in: *Gymnasium* 74, 1967, 561–3 (K. Schauenburg); *RBPh* 45, 1967, 1021–4 (V. Verhoogen); *AC* 36, 1967, 371–3 (C. Delplace); *Neue Zürcher Zeitung* 9.4.1968 (J. Dörig); *Keramos* 40, 1968, 51–3 (R. Lullies); *Erasmus* 19, 1968, 728–732 (A. Oliver); *AJA* 72, 1968, 186–7 (K.M. Phillips); *Gnomon* 41, 1969, 394–9 (M. Schmidt).

3 L. Kahil, 'Un nouveau vase plastique du potier Sotadès au Musée du Louvre', *RA* 1971–2, 271–84, Figs. 1–20.

4 I am beholden to Herbert Cahn for this information.

UNE 'RONDE' SUR UN COL D'AMPHORE EUBEEN

Lilly Kahil

Planche 27.

Une lente danse rituelle, ronde plutôt que danse, exécutée à l'occasion d'une fête: onze femmes conduites par un joueur de double flûte (Pl. 27, Figs. 1 à 3), telle est la scène figurée dont le charme nous paraît bien approprié pour dire nos voeux à celui qui a toujours été un conseiller, un ami.

C'est en 1973 que cette pièce curieuse a été trouvée à Erétrie,[1] dans la region de l'hérôon, non point au cours de la fouille proprement dite, mais au cours de travaux de restauration exécutés dans l'édifice I, au sud-est de la porte ouest de la ville, sous la conduite d'eau dans l'aile nord de r.[2] Le contexte de la trouvaille est à peu près entièrement archaïque; cependant il faut signaler la présence de quelques éléments plus récents, datant des troisième et deuxième siècles, qui s'y trouvent mêlés.

Recollé à partir d'une douzaine de fragments, ce col, dont la hauteur est de 18 cm, le diamètre d'environ 25 cm (Pl. 27, Figs. 1–2), est d'argile orangée, par endroits rouge brunâtre, dure, sans mica et avec très peu d'impuretés. La surface extérieure est recouverte d'un engobe crème, plus ou moins épais; le décor est en vernis noir parfois brunâtre, qui a passé par endroits au vernis brun clair.

La forme du col est celle typique pour les amphores cycladiques et eubéennes de la fin du huitième siècle (Fig. p. 100) assez semblable à celle des amphores béotiennes: elle s'évase légèrement vers le haut, la lèvre soulignée par une moulure qui indique le départ du col proprement dit.[3] Le bas du col est brisé, exactement à l'endroit d'où partait l'épaule, et il a été en quelque sorte égalisé, pour ne pas dire limé: nous verrons plus bas les conclusions que l'on pourrait tirer de ces remarques.

La répartition du vernis noir sur le col est la suivante: au-dessus comme au-dessous de la représentation figurée, cinq filets noirs, puis en haut comme en bas une zone réservée (celle du haut recouvre une partie de la lèvre, celle du bas est en grande partie manquante); sur ces deux zones des groupes de lignes verticales parallèles alternent avec des groupes de lignes brisées ou faux zigzags. La zone du bas, à la naissance de l'épaule, est bordée d'un filet noir, celle du haut d'une bande noire plus large, très usée, qui protégeait l'extrémité de l'embouchure.

Au-dessous de la moulure, sur le col proprement dit, la représentation fait tout le tour sans interruption: c'est une ronde composée de onze femmes conduites par un joueur de double flûte; à l'exception de la première et de la dernière de ces femmes, encadrant le flûtiste, et qui portent chacune une branche verticale dans la main gauche, toutes les autres se tiennent par la main, ou, plus précisément, tiennent deux par deux une couronne dans leurs mains, leurs doigts se touchant. Quant au musicien qui mène la ronde, il tient la double flûte de ses deux mains.

Les personnages sont encore très schématiquement indiqués, le visage est un rond ou un ovale, parfois avec indication très rudimentaire d'un nez ou d'un menton, parfois avec un simple allongement qui ressemble à une sorte de bec. A l'intérieur de cet ovale ou de ce rond noir, un cercle réservé et un point noir central indiquent l'oeil et la pupille. Les cous sont démesurément allongés et ont une forme plus ou moins tronconique; certains cependant, davantage schématisés, sont réduits à une simple bande noire. La chevelure est composée de longues mèches, souvent au nombre de quatre, mais parfois au nombre de trois ou de cinq, qui descendent sur l'épaule en larges ondulations.

Les corps féminins sont composés d'un torse triangulaire quadrillé en losanges, toute la partie au-dessous de la taille, qui n'est que l'extrémité du triangle formant le buste, étant constituée par une jupe quadrillée en losanges elle aussi, évasée à l'arrière et formant une sorte de traîne. Sous la jupe paraît une frange qui dépasse, tandis qu'une ceinture, dont les deux pans à l'avant descendent jusqu'au sol, donne plus d'ampleur à la partie inférieure du personnage. Les pieds et une petite partie des jambes féminines paraissent sous les longues jupes; ils ont déjà une certaine consistance, mais le pied en particulier est parfois réduit à un filet noir. Les bras, eux, sont un peu mieux constitués, mais les mains et les doigts sont réduits à de simples petites barres, le nombre de doigts variant de deux à quatre.

Quant au flûtiste, son torse est semblable à celui des femmes, quadrillé, tandis que le bas du corps, en silhouette noire, a une certaine corporéité — il est relativement lourd et épais. Les bras par contre sont filiformes, surtout les avant-bras, qui ne se distinguent point des mains: les doigts semblent manquer (cela est sûr pour le bras droit, dont la main n'est même pas indiquée). La double flûte, *auloi,* est constituée par deux tubes[4] que l'artiste manie des deux mains; ils sont ici tout-à-fait parallèles, ce qui est relativement rare, car généralement ils sont divergents.[5] On retrouve cependant deux tubes ainsi parallèles sur un fragment de cratère du Musée National d'Athènes (inv. no. 291).[6] Les contours des vêtements, ainsi que le torse du flûtiste, sont cernés d'un filet noir plus ou moins large, souvent assez épais.

Les couronnes des femmes se composent de simples filets ronds, avec des rayons tout autour. Les branches ou rameaux d'arbre tenus par les deux femmes entourant le flûtiste sont figurés comme des arêtes de poisson, avec une tige centrale verticale de laquelle s'échappent de part et d'autre obliquement de petits bâtonnets. Tout le champ est parsemé de lignes brisées, soit simples, soit le plus souvent groupées en zigzag double.

La représentation de la ronde elle-même est exécutée selon un modèle devenu classique du géométrique récent[7] et commun à bien des styles, mais la présence de couronnes dans la main des femmes apparaît comme une originalité, les rameaux d'arbre étant de loin l'élément le plus communément utilisé.[8] Souvent, d'ailleurs, les femmes ne tiennent rien mais se donnent simplement la main. Une des comparaisons les plus proches est avec une amphore attique représentant sur une face des jeunes gens, dansant, et un joueur de double flûte, sur l'autre, des femmes, dont la première tient également une couronne en main.[9]

La pièce est sans aucun doute de fabrication locale érétrienne ou, si l'on préfère, eubéenne, puisqu'il n'a point été possible jusqu'à présent de discerner avec certitude des différences fondamentales entre les diverses fabriques locales de l'Eubée à l'époque géométrique. Elle doit dater de l'extrême fin du siècle, des environs de 700, imitation d'un thème favori en Attique, qui se trouve dès 720 sur des amphores et des hydries du géométrique récent attique.

L'argile, l'engobe, la technique du peintre, tout concorde avec ce que nous connaissons aujourd'hui de la fabrique érétrienne. De plus, nous n'avons, pour cette époque, à Erétrie même, que très peu d'importations étrangères. Parmi les éléments qu'il nous faut souligner, il y a le quadrillage en losanges du torse, qui est très rare en Attique, mais que l'on retrouve sur une hydrie de Markopoulo[10] et qui semble beaucoup plus fréquent sur des pièces eubéennes ou d'imitation eubéenne. Les éléments de remplissage, lignes brisées doubles ou simples, négligemment exécutés, sont eux aussi fréquents dans le géométrique récent local. Au contraire la ceinture à longs pans descendant la plupart du temps jusqu'au bas de la jupe, qu'il s'agisse d'un pan ou de deux ou trois pans, est en fait plus typique de l'Argolide que d'aucune autre fabrique du géométrique grec.[11]

Nos éléments de comparaison sont cependant peu nombreux car nous n'avons jusqu'à présent que peu de représentations de la figure humaine eubéennes de l'époque du géométrique récent. Nous ne pouvons nous fonder que sur les fouilles exécutées en Eubée d'une part (à Erétrie même: fouilles anciennes et récentes du Service archéologique grec, fouilles de la mission suisse, fouilles de l'Ecole britannique à Lefkandi, fouilles du Service archéologique grec à Chalcis),[12] dont la plupart n'ont encore fait l'objet que de rapports préliminaires, et dans les colonies eubéennes d'autre part. Parmi ces dernières, les fouilles de Zagora (Andros) n'ont fourni que peu de materiel géométrique à représentation humaine.[13] Davantage d'éléments de comparaison nous seront certainement apportés par la fouille de Pithekoussai (Ischia), dirigée par le surintendant G. Buchner. Dans les rapports préliminaires,[14] plusieurs pièces figurées ont déjà été publiées. Aucune cependant ne comporte des figures féminines ou masculines exactement semblables aux nôtres: ainsi la pleureuse conservée sur un cratère fragmentaire de Pithekoussai n'est pas exactement du même style que nos danseuses.[15] Il y a cependant des points communs, comme il y en a avec les femmes figurées sur un lécythe en forme le bouteille de la tombe à crémation 984,[16] datée par le fouilleur du troisième quart du huitième siecle. Signalons particu- lièrement la frange qui apparaît sous le vêtement de la pleureuse, le quadrillage en losanges des vêtements des femmes du lécythe. Pour ces pièces, d'ailleurs, notre comparaison ne peut être très étroite, puisqu'elles ne sont point véritablement eubéennes, mais seulement d'imitation eubéenne, d'après les renseignements qu'a bien voulu nous donner le fouilleur lui-même, qui se fonde sur la qualité de l'argile. Une oenochoé géométrique du British Museum,[17] provenant d'Etrurie, a été récemment réétudiée par J.N. Coldstream.[18] D'après ce dernier, elle ne serait point de fabrication étrusque, mais l'oeuvre d'un émigré eubéen travaillant en Italie. Sur son col est figurée une danse où alternent jeunes gens et jeunes filles; si les têtes sont représentées d'une manière assez proche de celles de notre col d'amphore, les corps féminins sont relativement différents. Quant aux torses masculins, ils sont en trapèze plutôt qu'en triangle et comportent l'un un quadrillage normal, l'autre un quadrillage en losanges.

Quoi qu'il en soit, on peut affirmer que, parmi les représentations humaines de la fabrique eubéene du géométrique récent, la trouvaille d'Erétrie presentée ici est d'une qualité excep- tionelle, et je pense que cette impression première ne sera point démentie même lorsque les publications exhaustives nous auront donné davantage d'éléments de comparaison. C'est d'ailleurs alors seulement que, à la suite des études de J. Boardman et J.N. Coldstream, on pourra tenter de constituer une fabrique eubéenne cohérente et d'en établir l'évolution à l'intérieur même du géométrique récent.[19] La ronde érétrienne gardera certainement une place de choix dans cette école locale, dont l'influence a été si considérable en Grande Grèce et en Etrurie méridionale. A Erétrie même, la pièce a dû connaître un grand succès, et peut-être elle a eu un sort particulier. J'ai signalé en effet que le haut de l'embouchure apparaît comme fort usé, avec la bande noire très érodée en cet endroit, et que les cassures au bas du col ont été comme volontairement aplanies. Le contexte archaïque, quoique non entièrement homogène, permet de suggérer que le col a pu être conservé assez longtemps après l'époque à laquelle le vase a été brisé: il a fort bien pu survivre à cause même de son décor pittoresque, et être utilisé comme support, ce qui expliquerait l'usure de l'embouchure. Il n'est pas tellement rare en effet que certains objets aient été conservés à travers les époques: J. Benson a ainsi donné toute une liste d'objets mycén- iens, figurines, vases, fragments, gemmes, retrouvés dans des dépôts ou dans des tombes beaucoup plus récents;[20] de même, pour une autre époque, un cratère à figures rouges du groupe de Polygnotos a été retrouvé à l'agora d'Athènes, avec la partie supérieure brisée à l'embouchure, parfaitement égalisée;[21] lui aussi a pu être réutilisé, et nous pourrions multiplier les exemples de ces sortes de reliques: à Erétrie même, nous avons déjà un précédent, une pointe de lance en bronze retrouvée dans un contexte plus tardif.[22] Si vraiment le col aux danseuses rentrait dans cette catégorie — documents longtemps conservés et réutilisés — ce serait un témoignage supplémentaire de son charme, qui aurait été ressenti par les Anciens, et auquel aujourd'hui encore nous ne sommes pas insensibles.

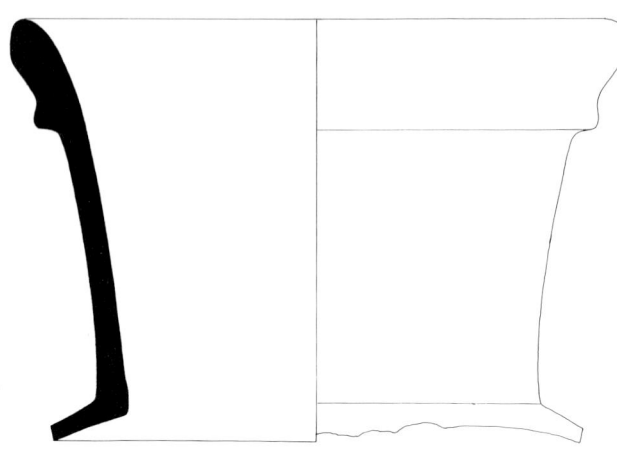

Neck of Euboean geometric amphora.
Eretria Museum (inv. 3275 FK 2786).
Drawing of profile by A. Brenk.

NOTES

1   Inv. 3275, FK 2786. Le professeur J.N. Coldstream et le surintendant-adjoint G. Buchner, directeur des fouilles de Pithekoussai (Ischia), auxquels j'ai communiqué la photographie de la pièce, ont bien voulu me donner de précieux renseignements: qu'ils trouvent ici mes remerciements très sincères.

2   P. Auberson et K. Schefold, *Führer durch Eretria*, Bern 1972, 86, Fig. 15; K. Schefold, *AntK* 17, 1974, 73.

3   Cf. Ch. Dugas. *La céramique des Cyclades*, Paris 1925, 111, 156, 193, 234; John Boardman, 'Pottery from Eretria', *BSA* 47, 1952, 13—16, Fig. 17 Type B; Coldstream, *GGP*, Pl. 41e. Pour le rapport avec les amphores béotiennes, cf. Coldstream, *GGP*, Pl. 45c.

4   Pour les *auloi*, M. Wegner, *Musik und Tanz* (*Archaeologia Homerica* III U), Göttingen 1968, U 19 — U 22.

5   Cf. par exemple, sur une amphore à col de Düsseldorf, Wegner (*supra* n. 4) Pl. U V, b.

6   *Ibidem,* Pl. U IV, c.

7   Les représentations de rondes et de danses ont été étudiées par Wegner (*supra* n. 4), U 40 et ss. Mais les rondes proprement dites ont été surtout rassemblées par T. Tölle, *Frühgriechische Reigentänze*, Waldsassen 1964.

8   Cf. Tölle (*supra* n. 7), Pl. 6, a.

9   Cf. Tölle (*supra* n. 7), Pl. 8: sur cette amphore d'une collection privée, la danse est également conduite par un joueur de double flûte.

10   Cf. Tölle (*supra* n. 7), Pl. 6, b: hydrie d'Athènes, MN 14423.

11   Cf. Paul Courbin, *La céramique géométrique de l'Argolide,* Paris 1966, 435, Pls. 145—147. On retrouve cependant cette ceinture à pans en Attique (cf. une hydrie de la Villa Giulia, 1212, R. Bronson, *AJA* 68, 1964, 176, Pl. 57).

12 Pour une bibliographie commode cf. Auberson et Schefold (*supra* n. 2), en particulier les notes, p. 194–195.

13 Pour Zagora cf. A. Cambitoglou, 'Zagora, Andros, A Settlement of the Geometric Period', *Archaeology* 23, no. 4, Oct. 1970, 302–309; 'Anaskaphè Zagoras Androu 1971', *Praktika tès Archaiologikès Etaireias* 1972, 251–273. Voir cependant A. Cambitoglou, J.J. Coulton, J. Birmingham, J.R. Green, *Zagora I,* Sydney 1971, Figs. 47, 48, 49.

14 Cf. principalement G. Buchner, 'Figürlich bemalte spätgeometrische Vasen aus Pithekussai und Kyme', *RM* 60–61, 1953–54, 37–55; 'Pithekoussai, Oldest Greek Colony in the West', *Expedition* 8, no. 4, 1966, 4–12; 'Recent Work at Pithekoussai', *ArchReps* 1970–71, 63–67. Voir aussi J. Klein, 'A Greek Metalworking Quarter, Eighth Century Excavations on Ischia', *Expedition* 14, no. 2, 1972, 34–39.

15 Je remercie vivement G. Buchner de m'avoir envoyé une photographie de cette pièce encore inédite.

16 *ArchReps* 1970–71, 64, Fig. 3.

17 H 242; *B.M. Catalogue* I, 2, p. 261.

18 J.N. Coldstream, 'A Figured Geometric Oinochoe from Italy', *BICS* 15, 1968, 86–96.

19 Parmi les études les plus récentes sur ce sujet, signalons J.N. Coldstream, 'The Cesnola Painter: A Change of Address' *BICS* 18, 1971, 1–15, et les résultats du Colloque du Centre Jean Bérard, Naples: *Contribution à l'étude de la société et de la colonisation eubéennes,* (Cahiers du Centre Jean Bérard II), 1975.

20 J. Benson, *Horse, Bird and Man,* Amherst 1970, 114–118.

21 P 1855; L. Talcott, *Hesperia* 4, 1935, 497–499; *ARV*^{2} 1057, 101. C'est grâce à H. Thompson que j'ai eu connaissance de cette pièce curieuse: qu'il trouve ici mes remerciements très sincères.

22 Cl. Bérard, 'Le sceptre du prince', *MusHelv* 29, 1972, 219; K. Schefold, *AntK* 17, 1974, 73.

ZWEI UNGEWÖHNLICHE GRIECHISCHE BILDWERKE

Ernst Langlotz

Tafel 28.

Die Interpretation der beiden Bildwerke beschäftigt mich seit vielen Jahren. Die mir wahrscheinlichste Deutung möchte ich diesem Aufsatz zur Kritik vorlegen.

Das rätselhafte Terrakottagebilde in Privatbesitz besteht aus gelblichem tarentiner Ton und dürfte deshalb in Tarent gefunden sein (Taf. 28, Abb. 1—2). Seine grösste Ausdehnung misst 8 cm in Höhe und Breite. Unterhalb des Kopfes ist eine abgebrochene Rundung wie von einem Griff für den haltenden Finger. Auf der Rückseite ist ein Bohrloch von 2 mm Breite. Es diente wohl zum Durchziehens eines Fadens oder schmalen Riemens zum Aufhängen.

Was aber stellt das seltsame Gebilde dar ? Es besteht aus zwei gewölbten sich zu einander senkenden Flächen. Man könnte an eine überreife, aufgeplatzte Feige denken, wären die Flächen nicht leicht gerundet und straff gespannt. In der Mitte ist ein Silenkopf dargestellt, der seinen Kopf ein wenig zur Seite wendet. Sein langer Bart endet in dem Griff. Von seinem Scheitel geht etwas nach oben aus, das wie eine lange Haarsträhne oder wie ein Zopf anmutet. Möglich scheint mir, dies Gebilde als Vulva zu deuten. Der 'Zopf' in seiner betonten Längsrichtung und den schrägen offenbar mit dem Modellierstift nachgezogenen Strichen müsste dann die Vagina sein. Für den Silenkopf an dieser Stelle könnte man an die Personifikation der Clitoris denken, die der Toreut aus Scheu nicht in der veristischen anatomischen Form, sondern in der Personifikation der Libido als Silenskopf, dargestellt hat.

Der Deutungsvorschlag wird gestützt durch die Möglichkeit, dass das Fragment der Griff einer Lampe ist. Denn bisweilen haben Lampengriffe diese eben beschriebene Form zweier sich einander zuwölbender Flächen,[1] wenn auch ohne figürliche Darstellung. Die Bruchstelle unten fände dann ihre Erklärung als Ansatz des verlorenen Lampenbeckens. Die Grösse der sich durch diese Ergänzung ergebenden Lampe könnte die Deutung als Votiv an eine Göttin befürworten.

Die Typologie und Modellierung des Silenkopfes erinnert an die Silenattachen an den Henkeln des Silber-Kantharos in Salerno.[2] Nur ist an der Terrakotta der Bart voller und länger, was sich aus dem anderen Verwendungszweck des Silenkopfes ergibt. Leider fehlt noch ein Corpus der griechischen und römischen Lampen. Nur die in Korinth, Delos, im Kerameikos, auf der Agora gefundenen Lampen sind publiziert.[3] Unter diesen ist nichts Vergleichbares. Die grossgriechischen Lampen sind leider nur zufallsweise publiziert.

Diese Deutung könnte abstrus erscheinen, würde sie nicht durch ein unattisches Schaleninnenbild unterstüzt.[4] Es gehörte zu einer einzigartigen Sammlung griechischer Vasenfragmente, die nach dem Tod des Besitzers leider in mehrere Continente verstreut worden sind. Das Vasenbild kenne ich leider nur durch das Photo des Archäologischen Instituts in Rom (Taf. 28, Abb. 3). Dargestellt sind drei nackte Figuren vor einer Kline, deren kelimartig reich ornamentierte Matratze in Verkürzung gezeichnet ist. Die linke Figur ist ein nacktes Mädchen mit angedeuteter Rima, die in griechischen Zeichnungen aus attischer Aidos meines Wissens nie dargestellt worden ist, im Gegensatz zu italischen, besonders etruskischen Zeichnungen auf Vasen und Spiegeln. Nur auf einem rotfigurigen Fragment im Cabinet des Médailles ist eine Hetäre, offenbar auf Wunsch des etruskischen Käufers mit diesem betonten Geschlechtsmerkmal von dem Dikaiosmaler gezeichnet worden.[5] Rechts sind Arm und Brust einer nackten Figur unbekannten

Geschlechts zu sehen, die sich offenbar auch der Mittelfigur zuwendet und die Hand auf deren Rücken zu legen scheint. Die Figur in der Mitte hat einen eigentümlich unsicheren schlaffen Stand und weichlich-weibliche Körperformen. Die Brustmuskeln sind nicht ganz die eines Mannes, sondern ähneln der eines Mädchen, weil der Busen durch die Zeichnung der sich gabelnden Bögen in der Mitte angedeutet ist. Binnenzeichnung der Muskulatur scheint nach der Photographie zu fehlen, obwohl das Mädchen links eine ausgeprägte *linea alba* hat. Rätselhaft ist vorallem die Wiedergabe des Genitals. Es besteht aus einem penisartigen Gebilde, das aus einer durch zwei gebogenen Linien darüber angedeuteten Höhlung herauskommt. Die Hoden fehlen. Statt ihrer sind zwei Hautlappen angedeutet, die offenbar die Vulva darstellen sollen, wie mein Kollege der Pathologe Prof. Dr H. Hamperl bestätigt: 'Die Mittelfigur ist also ein Pseudo-Hermaphrodit mit einer abnorm grossen penisartigen Clitoris, unter der man noch gut angedeutet den Eingang in die Vagina sieht'. Solche Hypertrophien der Clitoris sind von Pathologen öfter beobachtet worden und waren auch der Antike bekannt.[6] Es soll eine Hetäre gegeben haben, die mit ihrer abnormen Clitoris sogar zu copulieren im Stande war.

Wenn diese Deutung des Vasenbildes zutrifft, so wäre der Terracottagriff einer Lampe die Darstellung des gleichen anatomischen Sachverhalts nur mit dem Unterschied, dass der griechische Koroplast des dritten oder vierten Jahrhunderts eine Scheu hatte, diese anatomische Abnormität realistisch plastisch darzustellen und deshalb in phantasievoller Weise den Kopf eines Silens als menschengleiches Abbild der Libido zur Andeutung der pathologischen Missbildung verwendet hat.

Die interesssante Frage nach dem Sinn der antiken Lampenbilder ist von den mystischen Deutungen Bachofens (Grablampen) abgesehen, nicht weiter verfolgt worden. Sind Lampen mit Bildszenen ins Grab mitgegeben worden, so dürfte die überwiegende Zahl kein Gebrauchsgerät sein, sondern einen rituellen, oder eschatologischen Bezug haben. Die in Häusern gefundenen Lampen haben natürlich dem Gebrauch gedient und sind mit Szenen geschmückt worden, die den Besitzer erfreut haben, vorallem die mit den vielfältigen Symplegmata. Eine andere Gruppe der Lampen mit der Darstellung berühmter Bildwerke könnte zur Gattung der Souvenirs an berührmte Kulturstätten verstanden werden. Die Grösse und auch die ungewöhnliche Darstellung des Lampenhenkels (Taf. 28, Abb. 1–2) könnte an eine Votivlampe denken lassen. Wie meist bei den in den Kunsthandel gefundenen Antiken ist der Fundort beider Bildwerke unbekannt.

ANMERKUNGEN

1 Vgl. Gerald Heres, *Römische Bildlampen der Berliner Antiken-Sammlung*, No. 4, Taf. 2; Wage, *Antiochia III*, Fig. 89, 9; H. Menzel, *Antike Lampen in Römisch-germanischen Zentral Museum zu Mainz*, Mainz 1954, Abb. 25, 11.

2 Direktor Prof. V. Panebianco hatte die grosse Güte mir Photos und Gipsgüsse der Embleme zu senden. Der Kantharos dürfte nach seiner Form und nach der Amazone im Inneren im frühen 4. Jh. enstanden sein. Meines Wissens ist der Kantharos noch nicht veröffentlicht.

3 I. Scheibler hatte die Güte mir brieflich den Hinweis auf die Lampe in Berlin zu geben. Das Corpus der Lampen, das Georg und Siegfried Loeschke vorbereitet haben ist verschollen.

4 Der gegenwärtige Aufbewahrungsort ist leider unbekannt. Dem Deutschen Archäologischen Institut in Rom danke ich für die Publikationserlaubnis des Photos 37.193.

5 Paris, Cab. Méd. 387, *ARV²*, 31, 5.

6 Der Pathologe der Bonner Universität Prof. Dr H. Hamperl hatte die Güte sich meiner anatomischen Beobachtungen anzunehmen und sie zu bestätigen. Er verwies mich auf Spezial-Litteratur wie Claus

Overzier, *Intersexuality,* London and New York 1963, 238, Abb. c und F.K. Netter, *The Ciba Collection of Medical Illustrations vol. 4 (Endocrine System and Selected Metabolic Diseases)* Ciba 1965, 109 f. Ob die auffallende Darstellung einer Hautfalte über dem Glied vorallem an Dionysosstatuen des 2. Jhs. n. Chr. mit einer Degenerationserscheinung dieser Art etwas zu tun hat, könnte nur ein Anatom entscheiden. Sie findet sich besonders ausgeprägt an dem Dionysos in Basel no. 49. Es könnte sein, dass diese Falte, die sich auch an Apollofiguren der Kaiserzeit findet nur auf der Verfettung der Bauchpartie beruht. Es könnte aber auch erwogen werden dass diese Überbetonung nicht nur eine anatomische, sondern auch religiöse Entartung der einst griechischen Götter Dionysos und Apollontypen ist. Zu dem Problem vgl. E. Klimowsky, *Das mann-weibliche Leitbild in der Antike,* München 1972. Vielleicht ist die in Korinth gefundene rotfigurige Schale demselben geistigen Vorstellungskreis zu verdanken (*AJA* 34, 1930, 340 und 339, Abb. 4).

UN VASO APULO CON SCENA FLIACICA*

Felice Gino Lo Porto

Tavola 29.

La ormai cospicua serie dei vasi italioti, specialmente di produzione apula, con soggetti carica-turali e scene teatrali comiche continua ad arricchirsi di nuovi preziosi esemplari, sia in dipen-denza delle esplorazioni archeologiche sia in relazione alla notifica di collezioni appartenenti a privati fin qui rimaste ignote al mondo degli studiosi.[1]

Ci occuperemo in questa sede di un interessante vaso fliacico, sicuramente scoperto in Puglia, di proprietà della signora Renata Maggioni in Malaguzzi Valeri di Bari e facente parte di una ben selezionata raccolta di ceramiche corinzie, attiche ed italiote, notificata con decreto ministeriale ed in corso di pubblicazione da parte dello scrivente.[2]

Si tratta di uno splendido cratere a calice, di discrete dimensioni (alt.m.0,35), ottima fattura e conservazione, perfettamente integro in tutte li sue parti dipinte a figure rosse con largo impiego delle lumeggiature pittoriche in bianco e dei ritocchi a vernice diluita (Tav. 29, Figg. 1−4). Il vaso è collocato da Trendall e Cambitoglou nel "Suckling-Salting Group" e va datato al 365−350 a.C.[3]

Un ramo di lauro corre al disotto del labbro fra due liste risparmiate, un fregio a palmette circoscritte da volute e allineate fra foglioline lanceolate incornicia all'altezza dell'impostazione delle anse il lato principale del vaso, mentre un meandro interrotto da quadri con croci diagonali completa allo stesso modo la decorazione figurata sul lato secondario.

Sul lato nobile del cratere è dipinto un fastoso palcoscenico (λογεῖον, προσκήνιον) costruito con un unico grande asse di legno trattato a vernice nera diluita, anche per rendere realistica-mente i dettagli della sua sezione, e sorretto da quattro colonne ioniche scanalate con capitello e sottostante collarino dipinti in bianco: il primo con le volute descritte a vernice chiara, il secondo adorno di sommario *anthemion.* Una ricca tenda, ornata di svastiche e fiori punteggiati e col bordo a banda nera frangiata, ricade ad ampie curve e vistoso panneggio dagli agganci che l'assicurano in alto all'asse del palco, a cui si accede per una scaletta lignea centrale a sette gradini. Su tale *proskenion* risalta in bianco un'ara ionica con le volute ed un *kymation* disegnati a vernice diluita, mentre dall'alto domina la scena un bucranio in rosso ornato di doppia benda cordonata in bianco con fiocchi terminali.

Davanti all'altare si fronteggiano, saltellando e suonando il doppio flauto dipinto in bianco, due vivaci figure di fliaci con maschera comica dal naso rincagnato, corti baffi e barba aguzza e mobile, chioma nera ed ispida coronata di folta *stephane* di lauro con bacche bianche, e recanti il consueto costume del σωμάτιον a maglia, chitonisco exomide a bordi frangiati e cinto alla vita, mantelletta svolazzante con ricami di stelline e cerchietti e fascia dentellata agli orli, strette brache che inguainano le esili gambe e lasciano scoperti i piedi, *phallos* pendulo visibile nell'attore di destra. Altro fliace a sinistra, canuto a stempiato, col costume analogo ma l'*hima-tion* ripiegato intorno alla vita e raccolto per i capi sul davanti, all'estremità del bastone a cui si appoggia con ambe le braccia piegate, presiede vigile all'azione scenica rivolgendo con gesto autorevole severi moniti agli attori musici. All'estrema destra, quasi all'ombra di un alberello di lauro che emerge gagliardo da sotto il palco, completa la scena l'immagine di un' αὐλητρίς raccolta nella persona e ravvolta nell'ampio mantello che lascia intravvedere la veste ricamata a cerchielli. Essa è intenta a modulare le note che non l'abile giuoco delle mobili dita trae dal dolce strumento, retto dalla φορβειά in bianco che le rinserra la guancia e si allaccia a due corregge trasversali che le cingono la nuca e il capo chiomato ad onda.

Sul lato secondario del cratere è dipinta una calma scena di vita giovanile che fa contrasto con la vivace rappresentazione fliacica del lato principale. Una giovine donna di profilo e vestita di lungo chitone cinto alla vita e ornato di doppia fascia laterale, la gamba destra flessa e la chioma raccolta alla nuca, al centro della composizione figurata è in atto di levare sul capo di un efebo a sinistra una corona dipinta in bianco ora evanido. Il giovane si china lievemente col corpo flessuoso di tre quarti, ammantato e con i calzari ai piedi. Un altro efebo a destra con l'*himation* orlato che gli scopre il petto, assiste all'incoronamento.

Naturalmente è il lato nobile del vaso che più attrae la nostra attenzione per il vigoroso senso umoristico con cui è resa la rappresentazione teatrale. Qui il pittore rivela doti notevoli di artista nella distribuzione delle figure in moto e in quiete che compongono la scena, tocco mirabile del pennello nel marcare i tratti grotteschi degli attori in maschera a cui si sforza di conferire l'espressione che si conviene al ruolo dei personaggi,[4] abilità di ricerca quasi calli-grafica nel trattamento del ricco panneggio dei costumi fliacici e del vistoso drappeggio dell'alto λογεῖον.[5]

Indubbiamente l'alberello di alloro caratterizza il luogo in cui si svolge l'azione scenica che è Delfi;[6] l'altare sormontato dal bucranio[7] ci riporta al santuario di Apollo, sede celeberrima dei giuochi pitici, secondo il mito, istituiti dal dio dopo la sua vittoria sul serpente Pitone.[8]

Piace qui ricordare, per meglio chiarire il senso del soggetto rappresentato, che alla gara musicale, la quale in origine era affidata ai citaredi celebranti con peani le lodi del dio vincitore, gli Anfizioni nel 590 (Ol.XLVII,3) aggiunsero, oltre che i giuochi ginnici e le corse delle bighe, impegnative competizioni di flautisti.[9] Il primo auleta vincitore fu nel 586 a.C. Sokadas d'Argo, che riportò la vittoria nelle due Pitiche successive (582 e 578 a.C.).[10] A partire dal 582 (Ol.XLIX,3) i giuochi pitici subirono un'ulteriore restaurazione, in quanto l'antico ἀγὼν χρηματίτης diveniva ἀγὼν στεφανίτης, cioè d'ora in poi il premio delle gare consisteva in una semplice corona di alloro.[11]

Come è noto, si deve a Sokadas il νόμος πυθικός, vera composizione musicale "a programma", in cui i flautisti avevano modo di esercitare tutto il loro talento e l'abilità virtuosistica. Il testo melodico doveva essere certamente descrittivo ed imitativo, e pertanto veniva accompagnato dall'azione mimica degli artisti che, con il susseguirsi dei diversi ritmi, si sforzavano di rappre-sentare le successive fasi della lotta di Apollo e del serpente.[12]

Il piano dettagliato del nomo con le sue cinque suddivisioni obbligatorie ci è stato trasmesso da Polluce. Nella prima parte (πεῖρα) Apollo ispezionava il terreno preparandosi al combatti-mento; nella seconda (κατακελευσμός) il dio provocava il dragone; la terza (ἰαμβικόν) descriveva la lotta e l'agonia del mostro; la quarta (σπονδεῖον) proclamava Apollo vincitore; nella quinta (καταχόρευσις) il dio celebrava danzando il suo trionfo.[13] Va infine ricordato che i πυθαῦλαι, com'erano chiamati a Delfi i partecipanti a tale gara, indossavano una veste fluttuante ricamata a punti e stelle ed eseguivano il nomo su di un προσκήνιον in legno col capo coronato di alloro.[14]

Alla luce di questa breve digressione sul νόμος πυθικός e per tutte le significative analogie che risaltano al confronto con la scena rappresentata sul cratere della collezione Malaguzzi Valeri in argomento, non pare ci sia dubbio che si tratti qui della parodia in chiave farsesca appunto di questo agone musicale. I due attori auleti, pur nel costume tipico dei fliaci, per quella mantelletta svolazzante al ritmo frenetico della loro danza richiamano immediatamente i πυθαῦλαι saltellanti intorno alla θυμέλη del dio, qui eretta sul palco, e da destra a sinistra personificano rispettivamente Apollo e il dragone in lotta, accompagnando l'azione mimica con i suoni ritmici del doppio flauto.

La figura del vecchio fliace che assiste all'agone ricalca certamente quella dell'ἐπιμελητής che nelle Pitiche riceveva anche la dignità di giudice delle gare.[15] Problematica ci appare invece la presenza dell'*auletria* a destra della scena che, per il sontuoso paludamento e per una certa aria di mistero che spira intorno alla sua persona appartata dietro l'albero sacro, sembrerebbe alludere alla Pizia relegata nel suo ἄδυτον.[16] Essa però non ha la maschera perchè non partecipa all'azione scenica se non come accompagnatrice musicale; e allora, se dovessimo scartare la prima suggestiva interpretazione, non ci resterebbe che riconoscere in lei lo stesso ruolo degli auleti nella tragedia e nel dramma satiresco, dove essi compaiono appunto privi di maschera.[17]

NOTE

*Oltre a quelle accennate all'inizio del volume, in questo articolo si usano particolarmente le seguenti abbreviazioni: Catterucia = L.M. Catteruccia, *Pitture vascolari italiote di soggetto teatrale comico*, Roma 1951; *EncIt* = Enciclopedia Italiana; *LAF* = Lidia Forti, *Letteratura e arte figurata nella Magna Grecia*, Fasano 1966; Lo Porto = F.G. Lo Porto, 'Nuovi vasi fliacici apuli del Museo Nazionale di Taranto', *BdA* 1964; Paribeni = E. Paribeni, *Immagini di vasi apuli*, Bari 1964; *PhV1* e *PhV2* = A.D. Trendall, *Phlyax Vases*, 1.a. ed., *BICS Supplement 8*, 1959, e 2.a ed., *BICS Supplement 19*, 1967.

1 I vasi fliacici che nella prima edizione del catalogo del Trendall (*PhV1*, 15 ss.) comprendevano 165 esemplari, nella seconda edizione (*PhV2*, 19 ss.) assommavano a 202. Per tutta la bibliografia aggiornata sull'argomento si rimanda a M. Gigante, *Rintone e il teatro in Magna Grecia*, Napoli 1971, 13 ss., e a *Ill.Gr. Dr.*, 11 ss.

2 La collezione Malaguzzi Valeri è stata notificata con decreto ministeriale del 17 novembre 1971; un fascicolo del *CVA* illustrerà i vasi che la compongono. Nell'elenco della raccolta il vaso fliacico in esame è indicato col n. 52.

3 *RVAp* I, p. 400, no. 15/28, pl. 140, 5.

4 I tre fliaci portano la maschera del tipo B della classificazione del Trendall (*PhV2*, 12; *Ill.Gr.Dr.*, 13.

5 La forma del palcoscenico con colonne, tendaggio e scaletta di accesso corrisponde al *proskenion* di forma III A della classificazione del Trendall (*PhV1*, 16; *PhV2*, 13; *Ill.Gr.Dr.*, 12. Cfr. L. Massei, 'Note sul λογεῖον fliacico', in *Studi Classici e Orientali* 23, XXIII, 57). I vasi fliacici che più si avvicinano al cratere in esame per la forma del palco sono il cratere a campana apulo di Bari n. 2970 con la visita a Zeus Ammone, databile al secondo quarto del IV secolo a.C. (Catteruccia, n. 4; Bieber, *Hist.²* 132, fig. 483; Paribeni, n. 21; *LAF*, n. 203; *PHV²*, n. 17; *Ill.Gr.Dr.*, IV, 20), il cratere a calice apulo di Napoli n. 118333, della metà circa del IV secolo (Catteruccia, n. 45; Bieber, *Hist.²* 139, fig. 507; *LAF*, n. 195; *PhV2*, n. 83), e il frammento da Taranto in Heidelberg (Catteruccia, n. 62; Bieber, *Hist.²* 142, fig. 518; *PhV2*, n. 30), databile al 380–370 a.C.

6 Pure all'ambiente delfico ci riporta l'albero di lauro sul cratere a campana di Taranto n. 107937 con la parodia dipinta della tragedia *Ion* di Euripide (Lo Porto, 16 ss., figg. 5–6; *LAF*, n. 198, *PhV2*, n. 60). Cfr. inoltre la nota 10.

7 L'ara sormontata dal bucranio, motivo frequente sulla ceramica proto-apula specialmente con soggetti desunti dal dramma tragico (*APS*, 20, n. 1; *Ill.Gr.Dr.*, n. III, 3, 3; *APS*, 22, n. 2, tav. V, 19), si ritrova al centro della scena fliacica con Herakles che porta i Cercopi a Euristeo sul cratere a campana apulo n. 735 di Catania databile al 380–370 a.C. (Catteruccia, n. 6; Bieber, *Hist.²* 133, fig. 486; *LAF*, n. 193; *PhV2*, n. 25). Per i bucrani ornati di bende ved. *PhV2*, nn. 19 e 81.

8 Per i giuochi pitici si rimanda a August Mommsen, *Delphika*, Leipzig 1878, 196 ss; *RE*, s.v. Delphoi (H. Pomtow); Daremberg-Saglio, s.v. Pythia (C. Gaspar); K.J. Beloch, *Griechische Geschichte* I,² Strassburg 1913, 143 ss.; Paul Stengel, *Die griechische Kultusaltertümer*,³ München 1920, 213 ss.; *EncIt*, s.v. Pitiche (G. Gianelli).

9 Paus., X, 7, 4–5; Strab., IX, 3, 10; *Marm. Par.*, I, 53; Schol. Pind., *Argum. Pyth.*, p. 298. Cfr. nota 8.

10 Paus., X, 7, 4; Plut., *De musica,* 8. Cfr. Daremberg-Saglio, s.v. *Pythia,* 790.

11 Paus., X, 7, 8. Cfr. le note precedenti. In tema di agoni pitici, riteniamo non improbabile sul cratere fliacico apulo di Napoli n. 3370 (*PhV*[2], n. 49, tav. IV b), quale esempio di ἀγὼν χρηματίτης, la rappresentazione parodistica della vittoria di un citaredo a Delfi all'ombra del sacro alloro e del conferimento del premio, un tripode, da parte dell'*epimeletes,* giudice della gara (cfr. nota 15). Questo genere di competizione musicale fu perfezionato da Terpandro al quale la tradizione attribuiva quattro vittorie successive a Delfi (Plut., *De Musica,* 4; Daremberg-Saglio, s.v. *Pythia,* 785 ss.).

12 L.B. Lawler, *The Dance in Ancient Greece,* Middletown 1964, 65.

13 Poll., IV, 84. Cfr. Daremberg-Saglio, s.v. *Tibia* (Th. Reinach), 319 e note precedenti.

14 Daremberg-Saglio, s.v. *Tibia,* 322. Un'iscrizione delfica precisa che i partecipanti alle gare musicali si cimentavano su di un *proskenion* appositamente eretto (Homolle, in *BCH* 20, 1899, 565 ss. Cfr. Daremberg-Saglio, s.v. *Pythia,* 792).

15 Plut., *Quaest. symp.,* II, 4, 2; VII, 5, 1; VIII, 4, 1; Mommsen (*supra* nota 8), 167; Daremberg-Saglio, s.v. *Pythia,* 789, 792.

16 *RE,* s.v. *Pythia* (W. Fauth); *EncIt,* s.v. Pizia (G. Gianelli). Suggestiva è apparsa l'interpretazione per quella della Pythia della maschera femminile dominante la scena delfica sul cratere fliacico n. 107937 di Taranto (*PhV*[1], n. 57; *PhV*[2], n. 60; Lo Porto, 16, fig. 5).

17 Ci basti qui ricordare l'auleta nel suo ricco consueto costume del cratere a volute attico de Pronomos (Bieber, *Hist.*[2], 10, figg. 31–33; *Ill.Gr.Dr.,* II, 1). Cfr. A.W. Pickard-Cambridge, *The Dramatic Festivals of Athens,*[2] Oxford 1968, 166 ss.

UN'ANFORETTA NELLO STILE DI KAIRUAN

Paolino Mingazzini

Tavole 30, 31.

La graziosa anforetta che ho il piacere di presentare sulle tavole 30 e 31 – cogliendo l'occasione di fare cosa grata all'attuale proprietario cui mi legano affetto e riconoscenza ed al tempo stesso rendere omaggio al caro collega Arthur Dale Trendall – è giunta a noi in uno stato quasi perfetto di conservazione: le manca infatti solo un'ansa, di cui, a Tav. 31, Fig. 5, sono visibili gli attacchi. L'antiquario che l'ha venduta attesta di averla acquistata a Tunisi; e possiamo ben credergli, dal momento che la grandissima maggioranza dei vasi di questo gruppo proviene dall'antica provincia romana dell'*Africa Proconsularis,* che corrisponde all'incirca alla moderna Tunisia. Di quelle rinvenute in Tunisia, la quasi totalità fu trovata nelle necropoli prossime ai tre centri di El-Djem (che corrisponde alla antica Thysdrus), Sousse (che corrisponde alla antica Hadrumetum), e sopratutto El-Aouja (che non si sa ancora con precisione a quale centro antico corrisponda). Tutti e tre questi centri si trovano nella zona della moderna città di Kairuan, circostanza che ha valso a questa ceramica il nome di ceramica di Kairuan.

Per l'eleganza delle sagome, per il delicato color rosa della superficie e sopratutto per il senso della misura col quale sono distribuite e dimensionate le figure animate e le palmette, questa ceramica si distacca notevolmente dalla ceramica romana posteriore alla sigillata post-gallica; e questo buon gusto è tanto più degno di nota, in quanto nel periodo in cui fu prodotta – il trentennio che va dal 210 al 245 d.C. – era assai più in voga quell' affastellamento di figure incrociantesi ed intersecantesi su tre piani di profondità, il quale rende così disagevole e così poco gradevole la vista della massima parte dei sarcofagi romani del terzo secolo.

Il vasetto misura cm 15,5 di altezza e rientra perciò in limiti che sono normali in questa ceramica. Le figure sono applicate sul fondo, come è la regola in questa classe di vasi. Secondo uno schema quasi del tutto privo di eccezioni sui recipienti di questa classe – ossia sulle anfore e sulle oinochoai – una palmetta (ossia un ramoscello stilizzato, ma nel gergo archeologico sono tutte palmette), ben visibile sulla Tav. 31, Fig. 4, adorna il dorso dell'ansa; due palmette – stavolta due vere foglie di platano – rivvivano sotto l'ansa la superficie rotonda del vaso; altre due foglie (una di esse è ben visibile sulla Tav. 31, Fig. 5) adornano il vaso dal lato opposto, in corrispondenza dell'ansa perduta. Le due figure risultano perciò inquadrate, ognuna, da un paio di belle foglie di platano.

Il lato A (Tav. 30, Fig. 1) non rappresenta un cacciatore qualsiasi, ma uno di quei *venatores* che combattevano contro le bestie nell'arena: la frequenza delle belve su questi recipienti e di uomini che trascinano – quando non le portino addirittura sulle spalle – le fiere uccise, non lascia dubbio su ciò. Questo *venator,* tuttavia, non va ad affrontare una belva, dal momento che è armato unicamente del bastone ricurvo che in latino si chiama *pedum* ed in greco λαγωβολον: un oggetto che è un attributo frequente dei satiri, i quali tanto spesso accompagnano Dioniso. Questo strumento – stando alla etimologia del vocabolo in greco – serviva per cacciare la lepre, se non esclusivamente, certo prevalentemente. Ora, la caccia alla lepre era uno dei numeri del programma dei ludi in onore di Cerere e di Flora, come sappiamo da Ovidio e da Marziale:[1] e poiché la lepre appare spesso sui recipienti di questa ceramica – come è facile riscontrare percorrendo le liste che ho compilato e confinato a guisa di appendice in fondo a questo articolo – non vi è alcuna ragione per dubitare che sia rappresentato un *venator* dei ludi anfiteatrali e non un cacciatore qualsiasi.

Ma perchè mai il *venator* è coperto di quel grandissimo e pesante mantello, legato sotto la gola e gettato indietro, in modo da lasciare libere braccia e gambe ? Per un'azione fulminea come il lancio del bastone su un animale veloce come la lepre, un indumento di quel genere era certamente il meno adatto possibile. Che avesse lo scopo di rendere appunto più difficoltosa l'azione e quindi più acuto l'interesse degli spettatori ? Non mi sembra probabile. Si potrebbe pensare che il cacciatore se ne servisse per spaventare la bestia ed indurla a lasciare il cespuglio (sappiamo che nell'anfiteatro se ne sistemavano artificialmente). Ma questa ipotesi mi sembra più improbabile ancora, giacché è quello un compito dei battitori. Vorrei proporre un'altra soluzione. Poiché l'azione non è ancora cominciata — l'uomo stringe il bastone con la sinistra e non con la destra — si può pensare che sia quello un mantello da parata, ch'egli getterà quando sarà giunto al punto assegnatogli. Per il momento egli volge la testa verso gli spettatori.

Se passiamo al lato opposto (Tav. 30, Fig. 2), neanche qui penso che debba trattarsi di una danzatrice generica: mi sembra più probabile invece che si tratti di una di quelle *mimae*, che si prodigavano sulla scena durante le *Floralia* come sappiamo da Ovidio;[2] all'inizio, sotto una veste più o meno trasparente ed alla fine nude (del resto, dal modo con cui la donna fa svolazzare il leggero velo, è chiaro che questo semi-nudo è più nudo del nudo completo). Avremmo, anche qui, non un soggetto generico, ma un soggetto specifico connesso con i ludi, come la maggior parte degli altri soggetti espressi su questo gruppo di vasi.

Come è facile constatare scorrendo le tre liste di recipienti in fondo all'articolo, una grandissima parte delle figure non è riprodotta, sì che bisogna attenersi, al soggetto, quale è stato definito da chi ha pubblicato il vaso; per conseguenza, è facile sbagliare. Tuttavia mi sia lecito supporre che in molti casi in cui nei cataloghi e nelle prime relazioni è detto che è rappresentato un satiro col *pedum*, si tratti invece di un *venator* anfiteatrale; ed in quei casi in cui si parla di una Baccante o di una Menade, che si tratti invece di una *mima*.[3] Similmente penso che là dove si parla di un oratore, si tratti invece del presidente dei giochi, in atto di proclamare il vincitore; e che là dove si parla di un amorino con gli attributi di Mercurio (caduceo e borsa), si tratti invece di un fanciullino, cui abbiano adattato le alucce dell'amorino e dato l'attributo del caduceo. La borsa non sarebbe, però, una borsa qualsiasi, ma la borsa del premio, che sarebbe consegnata al vincitore in questa maniera, certo più artistica che non se data dalla mano del presidente del ludo.[4]

La ceramica del Kairuan — di cui molti esemplari erano stati via via, quasi anno per anno, resi noti con molta diligenza e con perfetta conoscenza del materiale dagli archeologhi francesi attivi in Tunisia[5] — solo da poco ha ottenuto l'onore di studi riassuntivi. Cominciò il Salomonson che, in un articolo uscito nel 1960, ne trattò in un contesto dedicato ad una questione antiquaria, dando per la prima volta delle riproduzioni fotografiche valide per lo studio.[6] Più importante ancora, perchè la ceramica del Kairuan viene inquadrata nello sviluppo della ceramica di età imperiale in Africa, è un altro articolo del Salomonson, uscito nel 1969 sulla stessa rivista.[7] In esso egli ritorna sull'argomento inquadrando la ceramica africana in tutto lo svolgimento della ceramica romana posteriore alla aretina ed alla sud-gallica.[8] Infine è uscito, nel 1972, un grosso libro di J.W. Hayes, che tratta di tutta la ceramica romana tarda;[9] ed in esso ha luogo, ovviamente, anche la ceramica di Kairuan. Il libro è costituito quasi unicamente di elenchi, senza alcun interesse per i soggetti rappresentati; tuttavia non mi è parso inutile compilare gli elenchi delle tre forme di recipienti (anfore, oinochoai a corpo tronco-conico ed oinochoai a corpo sferico), perchè gli elenchi dello Hayes sono esemplificativi e quindi non sempre completi.

La durata della produzione di questa ceramica è stata fissata in termini abbastanza precisi, mercè cinque elementi di datazione, costituiti da cinque monete, tutte datate in termini abbastanza stretti. Le prime tre furono trovate a Geilsdorf in Renania, non lungi da Bonn, in una tomba intatta, in un sarcofago che esce un poco dallo schema consueto. Due monete portano rispettivamente il profilo di Giulia Domna e di Giulia Mesa, le cui effigi monetali son datate rispettivamente tra il 198 ed il 210 e tra il 218 ed il 222; la terza porta l'immagine di Settimio Severo ed appartiene al principio del suo regno (193–210).[10] Un'altra moneta di Giulia Domna fu trovata, sempre con un esemplare di questa ceramica, in una tomba presso l'antica Hadrumetum.[11] Come si vede, non vi è ragione di scendere molto in giù nel terzo secolo.

Della quinta moneta, che porta il nome di Gordiano III, il quale regnò dal 238 al 244, non abbiamo la moneta vera e propria, ma un calco applicato sul collo di una oinochoe tronco-conica.[12] Che si tratti di un calco di quella moneta (una moneta della città di Tarso: era una soddisfazione puramente formale che Roma concedeva alle città provinciali) è fuor di dubbio; per convincersene, basta confrontare il calco con la moneta stessa[13] (le dimensioni minori derivano dal fatto che l'argilla si contrae per la cottura). Indubbiamente, una moneta può essere stata molto tempo in uso prima di essere calcata, ma il calco è chiaro, segno che la moneta non fu in uso molto tempo. La stessa obiezione del resto, vale per qualunque moneta e per qualunque elemento di datazione, ma, considerando la omogeneità di tutto questo gruppo ceramico, a me sembra che una durata di tre quarti di secolo sia troppo lunga e preferisco racchiuderne la produzione nei limiti di una generazione, all'incirca fra il 210 ed il 245.[14]

Come centro di produzione della ceramica di Kairuan si suole generalmente designare Kairuan stessa, sia perchè da quella zona uscì la massima parte degli esemplari resi noti, sia perchè – come suggerì Salomonson – la zona essendo aridissima e quindi poco adatta ai lavori agricoli, si prestava bene ad una produzione industriale, sopratutto di ceramica. Sono indubbiamenti buoni argomenti, ma non tali da convincere in modo assoluto: la patria della ceramica aretina è Arezzo, ma la zona di Arezzo è tutt'altro che arida e quattro quinti dei vasi attici del periodo fra il 570 e il 450 a.C. sono stati trovati nelle necropoli etrusche (sembra che vi fossero addirittura delle fabbriche, le quali esportavano soltanto in Etruria). A ciò si aggiunga che una buona percentuale delle nostre conoscenze del mondo antico è dovuta a circostanze fortuite, che non possono non deformare un giudizio basato sulla statistica dei trovamenti: non ultima fra esse la predilezione da parte degli studiosi per determinate forme d'arte o d'artigianato e la poca simpatia per altre. A me sembra che una ceramica così fine difficilmente possa essere stata prodotta in un centro interno della Tunisia, e preferisco perciò pensare ad un centro più ricco e più colto, per esempio a Cartagine stessa, e che a Thysdrus – dove era un grande anfiteatro – si inviassero quei vasi, i cui soggetti avessero attinenza con i ludi che si celebravano in quella città.

APPENDICE

Le tre liste che seguono, benché non aggiungano molti numeri alle liste dello Hayes, penso che saranno utili a coloro che s'interessano, oltre che delle sagome dei vasi, anche dei soggetti raffigurati su di essi; inoltre che faticheranno meno per trovare i libri citati. Mi sono limitato a compilare le liste dei soli recipienti, tralasciando le coppe ed i calici, sia per non allungare troppo un lavoro già lungo abbastanza, sia perchè la pertinenza di un vaso alla classe ceramica qui trattata non può basarsi sulle sole forme, ma deve fondarsi principalmente sullo stile delle figure applicate sulla superficie dei vasi. Ora, in quei casi nei quali le figure dei calici e delle coppe sono ben riprodotte, è facile decidere se appartengano o no alla ceramica di Kairuan;[15]

ma in altri casi, non disponendo nè delle figure, nè delle sagome, si resta incerti. Ed anche per questo motivo ho deciso di escludere calici e coppe dalle mie liste.

Abbreviazione: Baur = P.V.C. Baur, *Catalogue of the Rebecca Darlington Stoddard Collection,* Yale 1922; *BullArch = Bulletin Archéologique du Comité des Travaux Historiques;* Foucher = L. Foucher, *Hadrumetum,* Paris 1964; Gauckler = R. de La Blanchère e P. Gauckler, *Catalogue du Musée Alaoui,* Paris 1897; Hayes = J.W. Hayes, *Late Roman Pottery,* London 1972; Merlin-Lantier = A. Merlin e R. Lantier, *deuxième supplément au Musée Alaoui,* Paris 1922; Salomonson, *Mozaïeken* = J.W, Salomonson, *Romeinsche mozaïeken uit Tunesië,* Leiden 1963–64; *SCE = The Swedish Cyprus Expedition,* IV, Stockholm 1956.

A. Lista di anfore

Comune a tutte — o almeno alla massima parte — delle anfore è l'inquadratura degli scomparti figurati mediante quattro ramoscelli (una coppia sotto ogni ansa, oltre uno di un altro tipo sopra la costa di ogni ansa). I ramoscelli — o palmette che dir si voglia — certo non sono identici in tutti gli esemplari; ma dalle descrizioni le differenze non risultano chiaramente e le riproduzioni di questo particolare sono quanto mai rare: mi limito perciò ai soli soggetti figurati. Nelle descrizioni adopero spesso la parola 'festoncino' per designare quello che i colleghi francesi chiamano *guirlande.* Suppongo infatti che i festoni, rovesciati, adornassero le porte sotto le quali entravano nell'arena i *venatores* e forse anche le bestie — feroci e miti — da superare.

Nello schedario dello Hayes, le anfore normali sono elencate sotto la forme 172; quelle col prolungamento tubolare del collo (come il n. 29 dell'elenco che segue) sotto il n. 173; quelle assai snelle sotto la forma elencata al n. 176. Io però, per non complicare troppo le cose, non ho fatto queste distinzioni.

1 Prov: El-Aouja. A, leone in corsa; B, cervo in corsa. *BullArch* 1914, CL, n. 3; Merlin-Lantier, 208, n. 1146.

2 Prov: El-Aouja. A, leone che si avventa contro un *venator;* B, leone che avanza ruggendo. *BullArch* 1914, CL, n. 4; Merlin-Lantier, 309, n. 1150.

3 Prov: El-Aouja. A, cinghiale; B, cinghiale. *BullArch* 1916, CXXVIII, n. 8; Merlin-Lantier, 309, n. 1151.

4 Prov: El-Aouja. A, lepre in corsa; B, lepre in corsa. *BullArch* 1916, CXXVIII, n. 7; Merlin-Lantier, 309, n. 1148.

5 Prov: El-Aouja. A, leone; B, fiore. Merlin-Lantier, 309, n. 1149.

6 Prov: El-Aouja. Ora Louvre Inv. A.O. 6634. A, leone; B, cartellino con l'acclamazione 'Pentasi, nika', *BABesch* 35, 1960, 51, colonna sinistra, nota 158.

7 Prov: El-Aouja. A, cinghiale in corsa verso destra; B, piedestallo con corna, dalle quali si dipartono alcune bende (simbolo profilattico ?); in basso, cartellino con l'acclamazione incompleta 'Tele'; all'anfora manca un'ansa. *BullArch* 1915, CLXXVII, lett. *a;* Merlin-Lantier, 321–322, n. 1228; *BABesch* 35, 1960, 48, figg. 19 *a* (lato A) e 19 *b* (lato B).
   Nota: Salomonson (*BABesch* 35) vede nell'oggetto raffigurato sul lato B un simbolo profilattico, di buon augurio per la fazione venatoria dei Telegenii. Penso anch'io che la scritta sia di buon augurio, ma l'oggetto stesso penso che avesse, nei ludi anfiteatrali, uno scopo essenzialmente pratico: quello di indicare a quale fazione appartenesse il *venator* uscito vincitore dalla lotta con le fiere o con altri animali.

8 Prov: Raqqada (Tunisia). A, felino in atto di avventarsi, benché legato; a destra un kantharos; B, gruppo indefinibile; a destra un vaso. *BABesch* 43, 1968, 111, fig. 26.

9 Prov: El-Aouja. A, *venator,* armato di scudo e spada; B, leone che si avventa contro una maschera barbuta trifronte. *BullArch* 1916, CXXVIII, n. 10, Pl. XXXI (lato A); Merlin-Lantier, 308, n. 1145.

Nota: Benché il lato B non sia riprodotto, penso che la maschera barbuta trifronte contro la quale si avventa la fiera, sia un qualche aggeggio, dietro il quale il *venator* stia nascosto, in attesa della fiera (*cf.* Daremberg-Saglio, alla voce *Cochlea,* nel paragrafo intitolato *Cavea*).

10 Prov: Sousse (Hadrumetum). A, vincitore che agita le mani in segno di vittoria; B, festoncino. Gauckler, 236, n. 207.

11 Prov: Ras Bekeur. A, testa di cavallo, bardata; B, testa di cavallo, bardata. *BullArch* 1905, 115.

12 Prov: El-Djem. A, in alto, un felino in atto di avventarsi; in basso, un *venator* che doma un toro; B, in alto, un rosone; in basso, un amorino. *BullArch* 1914, CLII, n. 1; Merlin-Lantier, 307, n. 1140; la sagoma del vaso è riprodotta in Salomonson, *Mozaïeken,* disegno *m;* le figure A e B, nonché il rosone e la palmetta sono riprodotti in disegni separati, ognuno contrassegnato col n. 56.

13 Prov: El-Djem. A, *venator* che sulle spalle porta il toro ch'egli ha ucciso; B, amorino nelle sembianze di Mercurio (o Mercurio nelle sembianze di un amorino) col caduceo nella sinistra e la borsa nella destra, contenente il premio per il vincitore. *BullArch* 1916, CXXVIII, n. 9; Merlin-Lantier, 308, n. 1143.
Nota: nelle descrizioni del catalogo si parla di Ercole con le spoglie del toro di Creta; ma, dato il carattere della maggior parte dei soggetti di questa ceramica, penso che si tratti più facilmente di un *venator,* che di un Ercole. In quanto all'amorino-Mercurio, penso che possa trattarsi di un fanciullino travestito da Mercurio, che rechi il sudato premio al vincitore.

14 Prov: El-Aouja. A, aquila; B, amorino sotto le spoglie di Mercurio. Merlin-Lantier, 308, n. 1147.

15 Prov: El-Djem. A, leone che assale un cinghiale; B, amorino-Mercurio e menade danzante. Merlin-Lantier, 307, n. !141.

16 Prov: quasi certamente dalla Tunisia. A, *venator* con lo scudo e la spada, ma senza elmo né corazza; B, corona. *BABesch* 35, 1960, 53, riprodotto ivi, 54, fig. 26 *d* (lato A), 26 *b* (lato B).

17 Prov: El-Djem.´A, amorino-Mercurio; B, rosone. Merlin-Lantier, 308, n. 1142.

18 Prov: Bulla Regia. A, Eros fanciullo; B, pesce. Gauckler, 236, n. 208.
Nota: Nel catalogo si specifica che l'amorino è raffigurato come cacciatore; ma penso che l'arco sia semplicemente l'attributo usuale del dio.

19 Prov: Sousse (Hadrumetum). A, pesce; B, corona. Gauckler, 236, n. 206, riprodotto ivi, Pl. XLII.

20 Prov: Geilsdorf (Renania). A, amorino con frutta; B, Dioniso con l'attributo del tirso; accanto a lui, la pantera. *Jahrbuch des rheinischen Vereins* 33–34, 1863, 224–232, Taf. III, figg. 2, 2a; la tomba stessa è riprodotta a Tav. II.
Nota: Nella stessa tomba, ad unica deposizione, fu trovata una moneta di Giulia Maesa (218–222), nonché una di Giulia Domna ed una di Settimio Severo, un poco anteriori, importanti per la datazione assoluta.

21 Prov: El-Aouja. A, donna che danza al suono di un tamburello; B, personificazione di un fiume. Merlin-Lantier, 308, n. 1144.

22 Prov: El-Aouja. Ora Louvre Inv. A.O. 6636. A, Dioniso ritto col tirso; B, due pesci ed un'anguilla, appesi ad un chiodo. *BABesch* 44, 1969, 77, fig. 110 (lato B); Hayes, Pl. IX *a* (lato A).

23 Prov: El-Aouja. Ora Louvre Inv. A.O. 6635. A, aquila; B, protome di cinghiale. Hayes, lista a pag. 196, n. 12.

24 Prov: regione di Kairuan. A, satiro che suona la siringa; B, uomo barbuto, nudo, ritto. *BullArch* 1923, XLI, lett. *a.*

25 Prov: regione di Kairuan. A, maschera tragica; B, kantharos. *BullArch* 1923, XLI, lett. *b.*

26 Prov: regione di Kairuan. Ora Berlino. A, donna e due uomini che danzano attorno ad un altare acceso; B, grifone alato. Neugebauer, *Führer* II, 209, Inv. 31149.

27 Prov: Gargaresch, presso Tripoli. A, felino che si avventa; B, cinghiale. *BABesch* 44, 1969, 76, fig. 109; Hayes, 196, n. 22.

28 Prov: Salonicco. Ora Museo di Salonicco Inv. 357 m. A, pantera che si avventa contro un *venator;* B, amorino con la borsa dei premi. Hayes, 196, n. 24.

29 Prov: Kairuan. Ora Berlino Inv. 31150. A, *venator* in lotta con una pantera; B, gruppo amoroso. Neugebauer, *Führer* II, 209.

30 Prov: El-Djem. A, leone in corsa; B, cane in corsa. Hayes, Pl. IX *b.*
Nota: L'anfora differisce dal tipo consueto per la presenza del prolungamento tubolare del collo. La divisione fra gli scomparti è data da colonnine scanalate.

31 Prov: regione del Sahel. A, gruppo di satiro e menade abbracciati; da ciascun lato, una menade; B, sileno fra due menadi. *BullArch* 1912, CCXIV–CCXV; Merlin-Lantier, 307, n. 1139.

32 Prov: Rodi (a quanto sembra). A, centauro con un amorino in groppa; B, centauro, intento a suonare il flauto, con un amorino in groppa. Baur, n. 546, figg. 109, 110; riprodotto in Hayes, Pl. X *b.*

33 Prov: mercato antiquario di Tunisi. A, *venator* col *pedum;* B, danzatrice col tamburello. È l'anfora che qui si pubblica.

Ci sarebbero infine quattro anfore, che apparterrebero, a quanto sembra, a questa fabbrica, ma che sembra che non abbiano decorazione figurata:

I   Prov: Ras Bekeur (Tunisia). *BullArch* 1905, 113.
II   Prov: Soloi (Cipro). *SCE,* IV pt 3, 81 (accenno), fig. 32, 6 (solo la sagoma).
III Prov: Soloi (Cipro). *SCE,* IV pt 3, fig. 32, 7.
IV   Prov: El-Aouja. Ora nel Museo Alaoui. Hayes, 197, n. 27.

B. Lista di oinochoai a corpo tronco-conico

Le oinochoai a corpo tronco-conico sono frequenti nella ceramica di Kairuan e ne costituiscono una caratteristica particolare. Sullo Hayes questa forma prende il numero 171. Nella enumerazione che segue, non ho tenuto conto della maggiore o minore rastremazione del collo, per non creare troppe suddivisioni ed anche perché, dalla semplice denominazione della sagoma, questo particolare non risulta (la differenza fra le due sagome è assai sensibile nei due pezzi riprodotti in Merlin-Lantier, Pl. XIII, figg. 2 e 5). Vige in questa forma la stessa suddivisione in due scomparti adorni di figure che è normale nelle anfore; ed anche qui si constata che normalmente vi è un paio di palmette sotto l'ansa.

1 Prov: El-Aouja. A, in alto, un *venator* che abbatte un toro; in basso, cinghiale in corsa verso sinistra; B, in alto, *venator* che doma un cinghiale; in basso, cavallo in galoppo verso sinistra. Merlin-Lantier, 313, n. 1174.

2 Prov: El-Aouja. A, cinghiale in corsa verso sinistra; B, cervo in corsa verso sinistra. *BullArch* 1914, CL, n. 2; Merlin-Lantier, 314, n. 1180.

3 Prov: zona di El-Djem. A, *venator* che ha afferrato un cavallo; in alto, il festoncino; B, *venator* in procinto di atterrare un cinghiale; in alto, il festoncino. Come divisione fra i due riquadri, la consueta palmetta è sostituita da tre oggetti che sono, a cominciare dall'alto, una conchiglia, una corona, ed un cartellino ansato con l'acclamazione: 'Sinemati, nika', *BullArch* 1914, CLII, n. 2; Merlin-Lantier, 321, n. 1224; *BABesch* 35, 1960, 50, figg. 21 *a* (tabella iscritta), 21 *b* (lato B).

4 Prov: El-Aouja. A, felino verso destra; B, *venator* che trascina le spoglie di un animale ucciso ed alza la destra in segno di trionfo. In alto il consueto festoncino. Come nel numero precedente, anche qui la bipartizione mediante palmette è sostituita da tre oggetti collocati uno sotto l'altro. Dall'alto in basso, abbiamo: una conchiglia, una corona, ed un cartellino con l'acclamazione: 'Taurisci, nika'. Inoltre, l'ansa, anziché essere affiancata dalle consuete palmette, lo è da due colonnine sormontate da conchiglie. *BullArch* 1915, CLXXVIII, lett. *b;* Merlin-Lantier, 321, n. 1227, Pl. XIX, 5; *BABesch* 35, 1960, 49, figg. 22 *a* (tabella iscritta), 22 *b* (lato B). La sagoma è riprodotta in Salomonson, *Mozaïeken,* fig. i; il

lato A, il lato B, la scritta, la colonnina, la conchiglia e la corona sono riprodotti in disegni separati, ognuno contrassegnato col n. 52.

5 Prov: El-Aouja. A, lepre; in alto, una corona ed il consueto festoncino; B, lepre, in alto, un rosone. *BullArch* 1914, CXLIX, n. 1; Merlin-Lantier, 315, n. 1178. La sagoma è riprodotta in Salomonson, *Mozaïeken,* disegno *h;* le lepri, la corona ed il festoncino, in disegni separati, contrassegnati ognuno col n. 51.

6 Prov: El-Aouja. La forma è meno slanciata del consueto ed anche il sistema decorativo differesce un poco dallo schema usuale. Manca infatti la consueta ripartizione in due scomparti per mezzo di palmette e le figure si susseguono senza interruzione. A–B, da sinistra verso destra: (a) calco di una moneta; (b) lepre con lunghe orecchie, verso destra; (c) maschera barbuta, di faccia; (d) lepre verso sinistra, in atto di spiccare un salto; (e) fiore. *BullArch* 1914, CC, n. 3; Merlin-Lantier, 314, n. 1181, Pl. XIX fig. 3 (lato destro); *BABesch* 35, 1960, 52, figg. 23 (lato sin.) e 24 (ingrandimento del calco della moneta). La sagoma è riprodotta in Salomonson, *Mozaïeken,* alla lettera *j;* la lepre, la maschera, la moneta in disegni separati, contrassegnati ognuno col n. 53.
Nota: La figura indicata con la lettera d, a me sembra, stando alla riproduzione, una lepre; però il catalogo la designa come un cinghiale. La moneta sembra essere un calco di una moneta di Gordiano III (238–244), il che ci fornisce un dato cronologico importante.

7 Prov: Sousse (Hadrumetum). A, *venator* attaccato da un felino; B, aquila. Gauckler, 236, n. 209, riprodotto ivi Pl. XLII.
Nota: Il catalogo interpreta la scena del lato A come Atteone sbranato da un cane, ma mi sembra più consono al carattere generale di questa ceramica vederve una scena di *venatio.*

8 Prov: El-Aouja. A, tre figure, una sotto l'altra: (a) festoncino; (b) leone verso sinistra; (c) leone che si avventa ruggendo. B, tre figure, una sotto l'altra: (a) festoncino; (b) orso (?) (metà della figura è perduta); (c) leone che si avventa ruggendo. *BullArch* 1910, CCX, n. 1; Merlin-Lantier, 312, n. 1169.

9 Prov: rinvenuta, a quanto sembra, nella zona della antica Thapsos, poco lungi da Tunisi. A, due figure, una sotto l'altra: (a) *venator* che doma un orso; (b) *venator* che doma un toro. B, due figure, una sotto l'altra: (a) *venator* che doma un cavallo; (b) *venator* che doma un cinghiale. I due riquadri sono separati, anziché dalla consueta palmetta, da un cartellino ansato, con l'acclamazione: 'Telegeni, nika', sormontato da una corona. *CVA* Kopenhagen 7, Pl. 300, figg. 1a, 1b, 1c. Ivi, la bibliografia anteriore.

10 Prov: El-Aouja. A, lepre sotto il consueto festoncino; B, pantera in atto di slanciarsi; in alto, il festoncino. Merlin-Lantier, 314, n. 1179.

11 Prov: El-Aouja. A, *venator* che alza la destra in segno di vittoria; B, cane verso destra. *BullArch* 1916, CXXVII, n. 5; Merlin-Lantier, 314, n. 1184.

12 Prov: regione del Sahel. A, tre figure, una sotto l'altra: dall'alto in basso: (a) festoncino; (b) Mercurio con la borsa (dei premi ?) nella destra; (c) leone in corsa verso sinistra. B, tre figure dall'alto in basso: (a) festoncino; (b) *venator* rannicchiato dietro un grande scudo rettangolare, verso il quale si avventa un leone; (c) cinghiale. *BullArch* 1913, CCXVII, lett. *c;* Merlin-Lantier, 312, n. 1171.

13 Prov: Sousse (Hadrumetum). A, biga in corsa; B, *cursor.* Gauckler, 236, n. 210, riprodotto ivi Pl. XLII.
Nota: Si può dubitare se si tratti di un atleta in una gara di corsa (più facilmente di resistenza che di velocità), ovvero di un *cursor* in servizio durante una corsa di carri. La seconda ipotesi me sembra preferibile, perchè darebbe un nesso fra le figure dei due lati.

14 Prov: El-Aouja. A, pugile; B, corona. *BullArch* 1916, CXXVI, n. 2; Merlin-Lantier, 313, n. 1175.

15 Prov: El-Aouja. I due scomparti sono separati, anziché dalle consuete palmette, da colonnine ioniche. A, sotto un festoncino, pugile verso destra; B, sotto un festoncino, un uomo che sta per salire su un asino, che si è inginocchiato sulle zampe anteriori per aiutarlo a salire. *BullArch* 1910, CCXI, n. 3; Merlin-Lantier, 312, n. 1168.

16 Prov: Sousse (Hadrumetum). Ora al Louvre. A, sotto un festoncino, *venator* armato di lancia in corsa

verso sinistra; B, figura umana sdraiata sopra un mostro marino. *Comptes-rendus de l'Académie des Inscriptions et Belles-Lettres* 1913, 444—446, 443 fig. 3, (lato A); Hayes, 194, n. 28.

17   Prov: El-Aouja. A, tre figure, una sotto l'altra: (a) festoncino; (b) orso verso sinistra; (c) leone verso sinistra, in atto di avventarsi. B, tre figure, una sotto l'altra: (a) festoncino; (b) figura, in parte perduta, di donna nuda con lo specchio; (c) un kantharos. *BullArch* 1910, CCX, n. 2; Merlin-Lantier, 312, n. 1166.

18   Prov: El-Aouja. A, *venator* che nella sinistra regge una lepre ed alza la destra in segno di vittoria; B, donna nuda con lo specchio, innanzi ad una roccia. *BullArch* 1912, CCXV—CCXVI; benché sia detto che si trova al Musée Alaoui, sul Merlin-Lantier mi sembra che manchi.

19   Prov: El-Aouja. A, sotto il consueto festoncino, struzzo verso destra; B, sotto il consueto festoncino, danzatrice. Merlin-Lantier, 213, n. 1176.

20   Prov: quasi certamente Cipro (fece parte della coll. Cesnola). A, un gallo (?); B, (?). La relazione svedese dà solo la sagoma del vaso, con uno sgorbio che somiglia lontanamente ad un gallo, senza fornire altri particolari. *SCE* IV, pt 3, 71, fig. 32, 3.

21   Prov: El-Aouja. A, sotto il consueto festoncino, donna che danza al suono del tamburello; B, presidente dei giochi, che proclama il vincitore. Merlin-Lantier, 314, n. 1183.
Nota: il catalogo interpreta la figura del lato B come un oratore, ma la mia interpretazione mi sembra più consona al carattere generale dei soggetti di questa ceramica.

22   Prov: El-Aouja. A, donna che danza al suono di un tamburello; B, corona. Merlin-Lantier, 314, n. 1182.

23   Prov: El-Aouja. A, amorino, ritto su un'anfora immaginata che galleggi sull'acqua, con ambo le mani tende una minuscola vela; B, baccante che danza, stringendo un lembo del manto con la destra e reggendo il tirso con la sinistra sollevata. *BullArch* 1916, CXXVII, n. 4, Pl. XXX (lato A); Merlin-Lantier, 311, n. 1164.
Nota: Già a Pompei, nell'atrio della Casa dei Vettii, sono dipinte sulle pareti una serie di figure di amorini che richiamano alla mente l'amorino qui raffigurato (*MonAnt* VIII, 1898, col. 16, fig. 5).

24   Prov: El-Djem. A, baccante che danza al suono di un tamburello; B, tre persone innanzi ad un altare acceso, in atto di fare gesto di adorazione. *BullArch* 1912, CCXVI.

25   Prov: regione del Sahel. A, donna che regge un cesto con dentro un amorino; B, questo lato è perduto. *BullArch* 1913, CCXVIII.
Nota: Se, come è probabile, il lato A rappresenta una venditrice di amorini, il soggetto troverebbe riscontro in una nota pittura pompeiana (anzi, stabiana).

26   Prov: El-Djem. A, amorino con un grappolo d'uva; B, festoncino. Merlin-Lantier, 311, n. 1163.

27   Prov: Ras Bekeur. A, testa femminile; B, soggetto poco chiaro. *BullArch* 1905, 113.

28   Prov: El-Djem. La divisione degli scomparti è sottolineata da colonnine corinzie, assai diverse dal tipo canonico. A, sotto il consueto festoncino, stella entro losanga; B, (?). *BABesch* 44, 1969, testo a p. 69, nota 176. Riprodotto ivi p. 41, fig. 50 (lato A).

29   Prov: Rodi (a quanto sembra). A, Dioniso, ritto, con l'attributo del tirso; B, un gallo, verso destra. Baur, n. 547, figg. 109—110;
Nota: L'esegesi del lato B è dell'A del catalogo. In verità, dalla riproduzione non si ricava nulla di preciso: a destra, sembra di vedere una testa di leone verso sinistra.

30   Prov: El-Aouja. A, *venator* con maschera satiresca, in lotta con una pantera; in alto il consueto festoncino; B, sotto il consueto festoncino, sopra un basso altarino, adorno di un capitello corinzio, sta seduta una scimmia col dorso coperto da una pelliccia. *BullArch* 1916, CXXV, n. 1; Merlin-Lantier, 313, n. 1173; riprodotto in *BABesch* 44, 1969, 68, fig. 90 (lato B).
Nota: Secondo Salomonson (*BABesch* 44, 1969, 66, nota 172) il lato B rappresenterebbe la sfinge di Edipo; ma dalla illustrazione annessa, questa denominazione mi sembra del tutto esclusa, mentre quella ch'io propongo ben si accorda con i *ludi venatori*. Che sia un *venator* camuffato da satiro, come voleva Babelon (*BullArch* 1916, CXXV, n. 1), mi sembra ancor meno probabile.

31 Prov: Sousse (Hadrumetum). Una parte del vaso è perduta. A, sul lato conservato, cartellino ansato con la scritta acclamatoria: 'Pentasi, nika', *BullArch* 1915, CLXXVIII; Merlin-Lantier, 319, n. 1212.

32 Prov: Tunisia. A, tre figure, una sotto l'altra: (a) festoncino; (b) *venator* che doma un orso; (c) *venator* che doma un felino. B, tre figure, una sotto l'altra: (a) festoncino; (b) corona; (c) cartellino ansato con l'acclamazione: 'Pentasi, nika', *BABesch* 35, 1960, 51, nota 156; riprodotto ivi p. 48, fig. 20 *a* (lato A); nonché p. 49, fig. 20 *b* (lato B).

33 Prov: El-Aouja. Ora Louvre Inv. A.O. 6637. A, *venator* in atto di menare un colpo; B, leone in atto di avventarsi. Hayes, 193, n. 18.

34 Prov: El-Aouja. Ora Louvre Inv. A.O. 6638. Divisione degli scomparti effettuata mediante colonnine. A, gruppo di un leone che ha abbattuto un animale; B, capra. Hayes, 193, n. 19.

35 Prov: Sousse (Hadrumetum). A, Ercole; B, Onfale. Hayes, 194, n. 22.

36 Prov: Sousse (Hadrumetum). A, tre figure, una sotto l'altra: (a) festoncino; (b) donna, quasi del tutto nuda, che danza al suono di un tamburello; (c) orso che rode un osso. B, due figure, una sotto l'altra: (a) motivo decorativo (losanga); (b) orso a gola spalancata. *BullArch* 1902, CCIX–CCX, n. 1; Hayes, 194, n. 23.

37 Prov: Sousse (Hadrumetum). A, gruppo di Dioniso appoggiato ad un satiro munito del *pedum;* B, uomo accovacciato che depone offerte entro una coppa. *BullArch* 1902, CCX, n. 2; Hayes, 194, n. 24.

38 Prov: El-Aouja. A, leone verso destra col muso di faccia; B, leone verso sinistra, col muso di faccia. *BullArch* 1916, CXXVI, n. 3; Merlin-Lantier, 313, n. 1177.

39 Prov: El-Djem. A, baccante che danza al suono di un tamburello; B, *venator* che ha catturato una lepre. Merlin-Lantier, 311, 1165.

40 Prov: El-Djem. A, in alto il consueto festoncino; in basso, leone in atto di avventarsi; B, in alto, festoncino; in basso, amorino. Merlin-Lantier, 311, n. 1162.

41 Prov: El-Djem. A, cinghiale; B, (?). *Africa* 2, 1968, Pl. IX, fig. 29 e p. 221, n. 34; Hayes, 194, n. 28. *Nota:* Hayes suppone che questo vaso sia tutt'uno col seguente. La cosa mi sembra improbabile, a causa della diversa provenienza.

42 Prov: Sousse (Hadrumetum). Come divisione fra gli scomparti, colonnine. A, elefante sotto il consueto festoncino; B, (?). Hayes, 194, n. 25.

43 Prov: Sousse (Hadrumetum). A, *venator* con un cinghiale sulle spalle; in alto il consueto festoncino; B, (?). *Africa* 2, 1968, 221, n. 32, Pl. IX, fig. 30; Hayes, 194, n. 26.

44 Prov: Treviri (Germania). A, *venator* armato del *pedum,* in moto verso sinistra; in alto il consueto festoncino. B, losanga; in alto, il festoncino. Hayes, 194, n. 39, Pl. VIII (ambo i lati).

45 Prov: ignota. A, Leda che accarezza il cigno; B, (?). J.J. Bachofen, *Römische Grablampen,* Basel 1890, Taf. XXXV; Hayes, 194, n. 42.

46 Prov: Sousse (Hadrumetum). Si tratta solo di un frammento che Gauckler fu persuaso che provenisse da un vaso di questa forma. A, testa barbata. Gauckler, 236, 211.

47 Prov: ignota (mercato antiquario). Ora nell'Istituto Archeologico di Heidelberg. Festoncino in alto su ambo i lati. A, Dedalo; B, Icaro. *Mélanges Mansel,* Ankara 1974, 25–30, Taf. 18–19.

Lo Hayes cita infine tre esemplari di questa forma, privi di decorazione figurata:

I   Hayes, 195, n. 49; sagoma riprodotta Pl. VII.
II Hayes, 195, n. 50; Louvre Inv. 2806.
III Hayes, 195, n. 51, da Corinto.

C. Lista di oinochoai a corpo sferico

Sullo Hayes questa forma prende il numero 174. Come nelle oinochoai a corpo tronco-conico, anche qui la superficie decorata è divisa in due scomparti mediante palmette o ramoscelli.

Anche in questa forma vi sono alcuni esemplari che presentano un prolungamente tubolare del collo; ma non mi è sembrato opportuno farne un sottogruppo a parte.

1. Prov: El-Aouja. A, *venator* in corsa, armato di spada, contro il quale si avventa un leone; B, *venator,* armato di elmo, scudo e pugnale, in atto di avanzare verso sinistra. Tiene il pugnale nella sinistra e lo scudo nella destra. *BullArch* 1914, CL–CLI, n. 7; Merlin-Lantier, 313, n. 1187; riprodotto in *BABesch* 35, 1960, 55, figg. 27 *a* (lato A) e 27 *b* (lato B). La sagoma è riprodotta in Salomonson, *Mozaïeken,* alla lettera *k;* le figure dei lati A e B, nonché la palmetta sono riprodotti in disegni separati, contrassegnati ognuno col n. 54.

2. Prov: Ras Bekeur. A, cinghiale; B, grifone alato, sotto il solito festoncino. *BullArch* 1905, 113.

3. Prov: El-Aouja. A, *venator* che ha afferrato un toro per le corna; B, presidente dei ludi, in atto di proclamare il vincitore. *BullArch* 1914, CL, n. 6; Merlin-Lantier, 313, n. 1186.

4. Prov: El-Aouja. A, *venator* che alza la destra in segno di vittoria; B, cane verso destra. *BullArch* 1916, CXXVII, n. 5; Merlin-Lantier, 314, n. 1184.

5. Prov: zona fra Sousse e Kairuan. Ora Louvre Inv. A.O. 6563. A, amorino innanzi ad un altarino, con una ghirlanda in mano; B, gruppo per me indefinibile (nonostante l'ottima riproduzione): a me sembra di vedere delle donne danzanti. *Comptes rendus de l'Académie des Inscriptions et Belles-Lettres* 1913, 444–445 e fig. 3, a destra, p. 443 (lato A); *BABesch* 44, 1969, fig. 111 (lato A); Hayes, Pl. X *a* (lato B).

6. Prov: Raqqada (Tunisia). A, animale che termina in coda di pesce; B, gruppo indefinibile (nonostante la riproduzione). *BABesch* 43, 1968, 110, fig. 25 (lati A e B).

7. Prov: El-Aouja. A, cavaliere su cavallo a tutta corsa; B, elefante verso destra. Come avverte il catalogo, il pezzo è incompleto, giacché il frammento è ridotto alla sola pancia, mancando il collo e l'ansa. Poiché il pezzo è enumerato separatamente tanto dalle oinochoai tronco-coniche, quanto dalle sferiche, sorge il dubbio se debba essere classificato fra le prime, o fra le seconde, o addirittura in una terza forma. Giacché si parla di decorazione figurata applicata sul frammento, poiché nelle oinochoai tronco-coniche le figure vengono applicate sul collo e non sulla pancia del vaso, mi sembra più probabile che questo frammento vada elencato fra le oinochoai globulari che fra le tronco-coniche. *BullArch* 1914, CCI, n. 6; Merlin-Lantier, 315–316, n. 1190.

8. Prov: El-Aouja. Su questo vaso non è usata la divisione in scomparti. Abbiamo quindi (da sin, verso destra): (a) satiro con *pedum* nella destra (accanto a lui, kantharos rovesciato); (b) Dioniso, con tirso e kantharos (accanto ai suoi piedi, pantera); (c) satiro con *pedum* nella sinistra; (d) (sotto l'ansa) tre persone innanzi ad un altare. *BullArch* 1914, CC–CCI, n. 4; Merlin-Lantier, 314, n. 1185, Pl. XIX, 4.

9. Prov: Ra Bekeur. A, leone che atterra un asino. B, in alto, festoncino; in basso, corona. *BullArch* 1905, 113. *Nota:* L'espressione 'lion coiffant un âne' penso che vada interpretata come propongo, perché è l'unica interpretazione che si accordi con i *ludi venatori.*

10. Prov: Idalion (Cipro). A, animale non meglio definito; B, animale non meglio definito. *SCE* IV, pt 3, 71 (semplice menzione), fig. 32, 4.

11. Prov: Sousse. A, Dioniso, ritto col tirso; B, leone che assale un cinghiale. *Africa* 2, 1968, Pl. IX, 27; testo a p. 221, n. 35 (Foucher). Hayes, 198, n. 12. Riprodotto in Foucher, *Hadrumetum* Pl. XXXII *c* (lato A). *Nota:* Foucher (*Africa* 2, 221, n. 35) attesta che insieme con questo vaso fu trovata una moneta di Giulia Mammea.

12. Prov: Ras Bekeur. A, testa femminile; B, figura indistinta. *BullArch* 1905, 113.

13. Prov: El-Aouja. A, cinghiale; B, cavallo in gran corsa. Merlin-Lantier, 315, n. 1188.

14. Prov: El-Aouja. A, cinghiale; B, cinghiale che si inalbera. *BullArch* 1914, CL, n. 5; Merlin-Lantier, 315, n. 1189; riprodotto in *BABesch* 44, 1969, 76, fig. 108 (lato B). *Nota:* Secondo il catalogo, il cinghiale s'inalbererebbe sulle zampe posteriori. Ma a me sembra piuttosto un asino, cui un tale movimento sarebbe senza dubbio più facile che ad un cinghiale.

15 Prov: El-Aouja. A, satiro con un cane; B, uomo con berretto frigio che tiene un serpente. Hautecoeur, *Premier Supplément au Musée Alaoui,* Paris 1910, 316, n. 725.
    Nota: È un po' dubbio se la forma sia sferica o tronco-conica.

16 Prov: Hadjeb-El-Aloui. A, persona su letto e cane; B, perduto. Hautecoeur, *Premier Supplément au Musée Alaoui,* 1910, 316, n. 726.

17 Prov: Sousse. La sagoma esatta della oinochoe è dubbia. La divisione degli scomparti è ottenuta mediante colonnine. A, bufalo; B, scudiero accanto ad un cavallo. Hautecoeur, *Premier Supplément au Musée Alaoui,* 1910, 316, n. 723.

18 Prov: Hadjeb-El-Alaoui. A, satiro che suona la siringa; B, biga con auriga. Hautecoeur, *Premier Supplément au Musée Alaoui,* 1910, 316, n. 724; Hayes, 197, n. 7. In Salomonson, *Mosaïeken,* due disegni, uno del lato A ed uno del lato B, contrassegnati ambedue col n. 55.
    Nota: Anche qui si può restare in dubbio se la forma fosse sferica o tronco-conica.

19 Prov: Ibiza (Isole Baleari). A, *venator* in lotta con un leone, sotto il consueto festoncino; B, cinghiale. J. Román y Calvet, *Los nombres y la importancia arqueológica de las Islas Pythiusas,* Barcelona 1906, Tav. LXXVI; Hayes, 198, n. 15 della forma 174.

Le tre oinochoai che seguono sono inedite (ch'io sappia) e provengono dal mercato antiquario romano, né so dove sieno conservate presentemente. La loro conservazione è ottima. Le conosco solo da fotografie.

20 La divisione in scomparti è effettuata mediante colonnine scanalate. A, Edipo; B, pilastrino, cui sta appesa una spada nel suo fodero; sopra ad esso, un oggetto indistinto.
    Nota: La figura di Edipo è una leggera variante dell'Edipo riprodotto in *BABesch* 44, 1969, 68, fig. 91. È certo della stessa mano.

21 Il collo presenta il noto prolungamento tubolare. A, lupa capitolina che allatta i due gemelli; B, testa barbata verso sinistra.

22 Anche questa oinochoe presenta il prolungamento tubolare del collo. A, orso che avanza; B, pantera che si slancia.

Le tre anfore seguenti mi sono note solo da fotografie e son date come esistenti nel commercio antiquario.

23 Fra le figure, colonnine. A, pilastrino al quale è appesa una spada; B, uomo nudo verso sinistra, con un grosso manto sulla spalla.

24 Fra le figure, palmette. A, Cane in corsa verso destra; B, leone verso sinistra. Il collo del vaso presenta il noto prolungamento.

25 Fra le figure, palmette. A, Lupa che allatta i due gemelli; B, testa barbuta verso sinistra. Il collo del vaso presenta il consueto prolungamento.

Vengono infine alcuni pezzi privi di decorazione figurata:

  I Prov: El-Aouja. Alla base del collo si nota un forellino, che deve avere avuto uno scopo che mi sfugge, ma che era certo connesso col culto funebre, o col rito funerario. *BullArch* 1916, CXXVII, n. 6; ivi a fig. 1, la sagoma.

 II Prov: Sousse. *Africa* 2, 1968, Pl. IX, 28; Hayes, 198, n. 17.

III–IV Semplice menzione in Hayes, 198, n. 16 e n. 18; semplice riproduzione della sagoma in *SCE* IV, pt. 3, fig. 32, 4.

NOTE

1 Che la caccia alla lepre facesse parte dei ludi in onore di Cerere, lo sappiamo da Ovidio, *Fasti* V, 571. E che anche nei ludi in onore di Flora, le lepri facessero le spese della festa, risulta da Marziale, *Epigrammata* VIII, 67, 4, dove le miti vittime dell'arena vengono chiamate *ferae floraliciae.*

2   Alle *mimae* che praticavano lo spogliarello allude Ovidio, *Fasti* V, 331—354; con la differenza, tuttavia, dallo spogliarello moderno, che era improvviso e non graduale; anzi, eseguito ad un segnale dato con la tuba militare. Non c'è dubbio che questo numero del programma facesse parte delle *Floralia* e fosse reclamato a gran voce dal pubblico, se tardava ad apparire.

3   I satiri (veri o pretesi) sono elencati così spesso, che mi sembra superfluo enumerarli. Vi è però un caso, in cui mi sembra escluso — stando alla riproduzione — che si tratti di un satiro, come è detto nella descrizione del catalogo. Esso si trova nella mia lesta delle oinochoai a corpo sferico (vedi più giù al n. 9). Infatti non stringe un *pedum* satiresco, ma la palma della vittoria e non si vedono nè orecchie porcine, nè coda equine; inoltre indossa un mantello. Anche le Baccanti (o Menadi) col tamburello sono abbastanza frequenti; e, benchè nemmeno una sia riprodotta, son convinto che sono tratte tutte dal medesimo stampo della nostra. L'unica eccezione è data dal n. 23 del mio elenco delle oinochoai tronco-coniche, dove, nel catalogo, è detto che essa impugna il tirso; io però sospetto che anche in questo caso non si tratti del tirso, ma solo del lembo del manto. Anche ai nn. 17 e 18 dello stesso elenco — dove è detto che una donna nuda stringe uno specchio — sospetto che, invece di uno specchio, regga un tamburello e che quindi non si tratti di Venere, ma appunto di una *mima*.

4   Quello ch'io chiamo il presidente dei ludi si ritrova, nell'elenco delle oinochoai a corpo tronco-conico, al n. 21; nell'elenco delle oinochoai a corpo sferico al n. 3. L'amorino-Mercurio con la borsa dei premi lo troviamo nell'elenco delle oinochoai a corpo tronco-conico al n. 12, nell'elenco delle anfore al n. 28. Non voglio tuttavia tacere che un satiro col *pedum* nella mano sinistra ed una baccante danzante al ritmo di un tamburello da lei stessa percosso, li ritroviamo — ed in pose analoghe — sul mosaico del trionfo di Bacco rinvenuto a Sousse (L. Foucher, *Hadrumetum*, Paris 1964, Pl. XX); ma una coincidenza tipologica non implica necessariamente una identità dei soggetti.

5   I vasi, insieme con altri oggetti, vennero resi noti con molta sollecitudine — tanto più degna di ammirazione, quanto meno comode erano le condizioni ambientali — sulle annate del *Bulletin Archéologique*. Furono poi descritti nei cataloghi del Museo del Bardo a Tunisi: R. de La Blanchère e P. Gauckler, *Catalogue du Musée Alaoui*, Paris 1897; Hautecoeur, *Premier supplément au Musée Alaoui*, Paris 1910; A. Merlin e R. Lantier, *Deuxième supplément au Musée Alaoui*, Paris 1922.

6   J.W. Salomonson, 'The Fancy Dress Banquet', *BABesch* 35, 1960, 25—55; ceramica di Kairuan, pp. 49—55, figg. 19—27 b.

7   'Études sur la céramique romaine d'Afrique', *BABesch* 43, 1968, 80—145; la ceramica di Kairuan (da lui detta 'ceramica di El-Aouja') pp. 109—113 figg. 25—26 e tav. IV; in una tavola doppia sono anche raccolte le varie sagome dei vasi.

8   *BABesch* 44, 1969, 109—111.

9   J.W. Hayes, *Late Roman Pottery*, London 1972. Il libro dello Hayes è purtroppo estremamente sintetico, ed è costituito quasi unicamente da elenchi: su più di 400 pagine, le conclusioni relative all'area di diffusione dei singoli gruppi ne occupano solo pochissime. L'uso — a mio parere eccessivo — di sigle e di abbreviazioni rende assai difficile la consultazione di questo libro per un principiante, il quale è più facile che venga respinto, anzichè attratto da un modo così arido di presentare una materia che fa parte, se non della storia dell'arte, almeno di quella dell'artigianato artistico. Un certo numero di vasi di questa classe furono presentati — sia nelle loro sagome, sia con disegni schematici delle figurine — in un catalogo di oggetti di provenienza tunisina redatto da J.W. Salomonson, intitolato *Romeinsche mozaïeken uit Tunesië*, Leiden, 1963—64; vi sono enumerati ed illustrati anche oggetti di provenienza tunisina di altro tipo. Del catalogo esistono varie traduzioni perchè l'esposizione andò girando per varie città.

10 Insieme con le monete di Giulia Domna, di Giulia Mammea e di Settimio Severo, fu portata alla luce anche l'anfora che nel mio elenco porta il numero 20. Fu questo il primo esemplare di questa classe ad essere illustrato; e lo fu dal grande Otto Jahn, il quale fu il primo che trattò i vasi dal punto di vista della storia della ceramica antica.

11 Questa moneta fu trovata nella stessa tomba, dalla quale usci l'oinochoe a corpo sferico, che nel mio elenco porta il n. 11.

12 Il vaso sul quale fu applicato il calco della moneta di Gordiano III porta, nel mio elenco delle oinochoai a corpo tronco-conico, il n. 6.

13 Il calco è riprodotto in *BABesch* 35, 1960, 52, n. 24; la moneta ivi, al n. 25.

14 Salomonson racchiude la produzione della ceramica di Kairuan fra il 200 ed il 280; il momento culminante della produzione andrebbe fissato fra il 225 ed il 250 (*BABesch* 43, 1968, 112–113), si prolungherebbe sino al 275 e persisterebbe sino alla fine del secolo. In quanto al luogo di produzione, Salomonson ne parla in *Romeinsche mozaïeken* (*supra* n. 9), 46. Hayes tratta la ceramica di Kairuan nel suo libro (*supra* n. 9), 193–199, e si attiene alle date di Salomonson (*ibidem,* 199).

15 Per esempio, l'amorino con la borsa e il caduceo, abbastanza frequente nei vasi dei tre elenchi che ho redatto, si ritrova sulla scodella riprodotta in *BABesch* 44, 1969, 68, fig. 89. L'Edipo del n. 20 dell'elenco delle oinochoai a corpo sferico, si ritrova quasi identico sul calice riprodotto in *BABesch* 44, 1969, 68, fig. 91.

KYLIX INEDITA DA SPINA DEL PITTORE DI ANTIPHON CON *DOKIMASIA*

Giuliana Riccioni

Tavole 32, 33.

Una kylix proveniente dalla tomba 41D della necropoli spinetica di valle Pega e conservata nel Museo archeologico nazionale di Ferrara,[1] merita alcune considerazioni che diano concreta sostanza all'attribuzione del Beazley al Pittore di Antiphon[2] e la confermino, ma soprattutto ne interpretino le rappresentazioni il cui significato, a causa della redazione ad elementi isolati di un più ampio contesto, può facilmente sfuggire.

La kylix é del tipo 'ad occhioni' (Figg. 1, 3–4) ed é quasi gemella di una di Houston (Texas) ugualmente attribuita al Pittore di Antiphon.[3] Hanno, infatti, in comune sia i caratteri stilistici – di cui sarà detto oltre – sia la forma (Figg. 1, 2, p. 126) assai vicina a quella del gruppo 'Dreieck' del Bloesch, prodotte nell'officina del vasaio Euphronios,[4] e sono giustamente incluse dal Beazley in una stessa classe, quella tardo-arcaica delle kylikes 'ad occhioni'.[5]

La tazza esibisce scene della vita quotidiana di Atene; le raffigurazioni del lato esterno A e di quello B (Tav. 33, Figg. 3–4) sono chiaramente connesse fra loro, mentre quella del medaglione, I, (Tav. 32, Fig. 2) è indipendente ed isolata dal contesto narrativo.

Veniamo ora all'analisi delle figure iniziando da quella dell'interno posta in un finissimo ed elegante cerchio a meandro continuo (Tav. 32, Fig. 2). Si tratta di un efebo dal corpo nudo, alto e slanciato, rappresentato dopo una competizione atletica, forse il salto con gli *halteres* (appesi alla parete). É in posizione stante, al centro del medaglione, ha la gamba sinistra tesa e il piede posato a terra, visto di prospetto, quella destra lievemente flessa indietro con la sola punta delle dita del piede che toccano il suolo. Egli ha il torso quasi frontale, la testa un po' reclina é di profilo verso sinistra; ha chioma corta, con contorno a merletti arrotondati, sottilissima frangia e zazzera rese a trattini fittissimi, quasi 'miniaturistici', ininterrotti, espressi a vernice nera diluita. L'occhio ha le palpebre rese con due linee quasi diritte incontrantisi ad angolo acuto dalla parte opposta di dove é la pupilla che é resa con un puntino pieno a vernice nera, posto verso l'angolo interno chiuso. Delle braccia, quello destro é proteso, il palmo della mano tiene un balsamario ariballoide monocromo, a forma di grosso cuore e fornito di minuscolo bocchino; quello sinistro é lievemente flesso in basso, la mano girata indietro, ha il pollice e l'indice che si toccano con la punta delle unghie, mentre le altre tre dita sono tese ed unite.

Dietro la figura dell'efebo, é una *kline,* vista in lontananza, su cui é posato un ampio cuscino (o materasso) a strisce, adorno di fiocchetti; a sinistra, un bastone nodoso, con manico ricurvo, é posto obliquamente nel fondo ed ha la parte inferiore che passa sotto la *kline.* A destra, in alto, sono appesi nel fondo, come a una parete, due *halteres.*

Sui lati esterni A e B,[6] al centro, fra due grandi occhi apotropaici sono rappresentati, rispettivamente, un cavallo e un efebo.

Sul lato A (Tav. 33, Fig. 3) il cavallo, dal corpo asciutto, lunga e folta coda, testa piccola reclinata, corta criniera e ciuffo, sta avanzando verso destra con elegante passo ritmato (zampa destra sollevata). L'animale si trova all'interno di un edificio, probabilmente lo *ammos,*[7] indicato sinteticamente dalla colonna dorica poggiante su largo *plinthos* liscio, posta dietro, nel fondo.

Sul lato B (Tav. 33, Fig. 4) l'efebo, in posizione stante, di riposo, si appoggia a un lungo bastone liscio, posto obliquamente, che passandogli sotto l'ascella sinistra, tiene con la mano, scaricando il peso del corpo sulla gamba destra tesa, vista di prospetto (piede posato saldamente

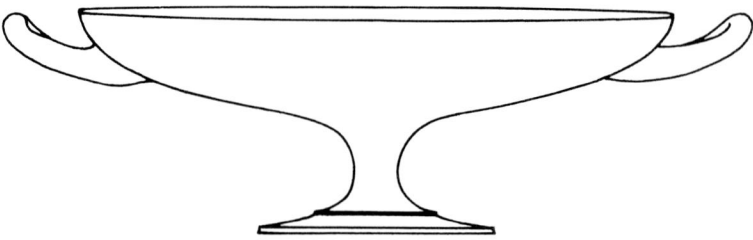

Fig. 1
Attic red-figure eye-cup. Profile drawing.
Ferrara 41.D-V.P.
Drawing by Adriana Cavicchi.

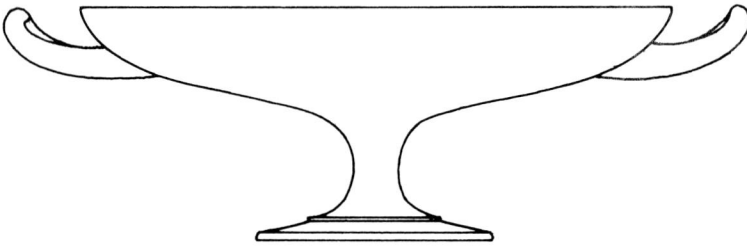

Fig. 2
Attic red-figure eye-cup. Profile drawing.
Houston, Texas; formerly Basel market.

a terra); la gamba sinistra é flessa indietro e il piede sfiora il suolo con la punta delle dita. La mano destra é poggiata al fianco. Il corpo, visto di tre quarti, é nudo ad eccezione dell'*himation* a larghe pieghe che, passandogli dietro sul dorso, gli pende voluminosamente da ambedue le braccia e lungo i fianchi. La testa é assai reclinata verso destra e accompagna armonicamente l'inclinazione del corpo; presenta nel rendimento le stesse caratteristiche di quella dell'atleta raffigurato nel medaglione.

Le ultime due scene esaminate non mostrano difficoltà di esegesi. Come si é già avuto occasione di osservare, entrambi i lati esterni della nostra kylix sono collegati fra loro per il tema trattato, quello della *dokimasia* (Tav. 33, Figg. 3—4). La quale, come ebbi a dire in altra sede, pubblicando la kylix spinetica della tomba 173 C di valle Pega,[8] é una prova a cui dovevano sottoporsi in Atene sia i giovani appartenenti all'aristocrazia che ambivano di essere ammessi nella classe dei cavalieri,[9] sia i loro cavalli. Infatti gli *hippeis* dovevano essere ricchi e robusti e possedere, secondo quanto é tramandato nell'*Athenaion Politeia* di Aristotele (7, 3) e negli *Hippeis* di Aristofane (225), trecento medimmi e due cavalli; anch'essi erano oculatamente ispezionati da una commissione della *boulé* prima di essere ritenuti abili a far parte del corpo equestre.[10]

La nuova kylix spinetica, databile fra il 490 e il 480 a. Chr., come quella di Houston già menzionata,[11] é facilmente attribuibile al Pittore di Antiphon,[12] per i numerosi confronti che si possono addurre soprattutto per le due figure isolate di efebi sui lati B (Tav. 33, Fig. 4) ed I (Tav. 32, Fig. 2), le quali sono 'standardizzate' sia nella loro posizione stante di riposo, con gambe incrociate, sia nel rendimento minuzioso delle teste, sia nella delineazione sommaria dell'anatomia, sia .— infine — nel modellato corposo del panneggio reso, nel nostro caso, con una scorrevole fluidità. I personaggi atletici, longilinei, di stile onesimiano, mostrano talvolta una certa leziosità nei gesti che contrasta in qualche modo con una innegabile sensibilità del nostro pittore per la solida impostazione ponderale e la resa della profondità spaziale, con qualche concessione a virtuosismi prospettici, non sempre felicemente risolti, come nello scorcio dei piedi.

Da quanto si é osservato, risulta evidente che il Pittore di Antiphon risente, nella sua formazione artistica, dell'ultima produzione del ceramografo Onesimos di cui continuò lo stile aggraziato, tendente al manierismo tardo-arcaico.

NOTE

1 Inv. 20508 del registro cronologico di entrata di materiale archeologico del Museo archeologico nazionale di Ferrara. Ricomposta da 20 frammenti, é integrata in una piccola parte dell'orlo e dell'interno del bacino; é di buona conservazione. *Misure:* alt.: cm. 11.4—12; diam. bocca: cm 31; diam. piede: cm 12.5. Il piede esternamente é verniciato in nero ad eccezione del piano di posa, della tromba interna e di una stretta fascia concentrica presso di essa, risparmiati nel colore dell'argilla. Le fotografie sono state eseguite dal Laboratorio Manlio Agodi di Ferrara; i negativi sono conservati nell'archivio fotografico del Museo archeologico nazionale di Ferrara; i disegni sono stati gentilmente eseguiti dalla disegnatrice Adriana Cavicchi di Bologna. Ho il piacere di ringraziare sentitamente il Prof. Nereo Alfieri per avermi gentilmente affidato lo studio di questo vaso e il Prof. Alexander Cambitoglou per avermi onorato di pubblicarlo nella 'Miscellanea' dedicata all'illustre Prof. A.D. Trendall, al quale debbo parte della mia formazione ceramologica. Rivolgo anche un ringraziamento all'amico Prof. Herbert A. Cahn di Basel, per avermi inviato gratuitamente le foto della *kylix* di Houston e per avermi dato alcuni consigli.

2 *ARV*[2] 51, n. 210; 337, n. 30 *bis*.

3 H.A. Cahn, *Münzen und Medaillen, A.G., Auktion 22,* 1961, n. 162; *ARV*[2] 51, n. 210 *bis*; 1573, n. 5; 1596, n. 17; 1622; 1646, n. 85 *bis*. R. Blatter, 'Eine unbekannte Schale des Antiphon-Malers in Berner

Privatbesitz', *AA*, 1968, 646. Fig. 9; H.A. Cahn, *Münzen und Medaillen, A.G., Auktion 40*, 1969, n. 90, figure a p. 36; H. Hoffmann, *Ten Centuries that Shaped the West. Greek and Roman Art in Texas Collections*, Mainz 1970, 388–391, ivi figure, n. 177.

4 H. Bloesch, *Formen attischer Schalen..*, Bern 1940, 73 e segg. (fanno parte del gruppo 'Dreieck' le kylikes di forma B).

5 *ARV²* 51, nn. 210, 210 *bis. Cfr.* anche note 2, 3, *supra*.

6 *La decorazione accessoria* sull'esterno, sotto ciascuna ansa, é risparmiata nel colore dell'argilla; consiste in una palmetta centrale a ventaglio con cinque petali, tre verticali e due orizzontali; da questi ultimi si dipartono due volute, pure orizzontali, con il riccio rivolto in su. Ciascuna palmetta ha cuore centrale e volute di base desinenti in due foglie stilizzate giacenti.

7 *Cfr.* Xenophon, *Mem.* 3, 3, 6. Si trattava di un edificio coperto il cui tetto era sostenuto da colonne doriche.

8 Vedi: *Arte Antica e Moderna* 1958, 18–22, figg. 8 a–b, 9 a, 10 a–b; *ARV²* 407, n. 14. Citata ampiamente da H.A. Cahn, 'Dokimasia', *RA*, 1973, 12–13, e nota 8.

9 Xenophon, *Eq. Mag.* 3, 9. In Atene la cavalleria era infatti un corpo aristocratico (Aristophanes *Eq.*, 225; Andokides, 3, 5).

10 Per ulteriori precisazioni e bibliografia sulla *dokimasia* e altri vasi con la rappresentazione di questo tema, vedi H.A. Cahn, *RA*, 1973, 3 e segg.

11 *Cfr.* nota 3 *supra*.

12 *Cfr.* nota 2 *supra* (kylix tomba 41D, VP). Sul Pittore di Antiphon, *ARV²* 335 e segg., in particolare nn. 1, 13, 14 *bis.* 25; *Paralipomena,* 361; Blatter (*supra* nota 3), 640–652, ivi figg. (non citato dal Beazley nei *Paralipomena*); vedi inoltre nota 3 *supra* (kylix di Houston) per il completamento della bibliografia.

A MUFFLED DANCER AND OTHERS

Martin Robertson

Plates 34, 35.

The curious scene which I publish here is perhaps a not unsuitable offering to one who has done so much for the study of *phlyax* vases, though this is Attic and unconnected with the stage. I cannot explain the subject at all precisely, can only offer a few parallels to some aspects of the picture and leave it to others to take the matter further.

First the vase Pl. 34, Figs. 1−2, acquired a few years ago by the Ashmolean:[1] an *oinochoe* of the form Beazley called Shape 4; round-mouthed, high-handled, and with other consistent characteristics noted in Caskey-Beazley I, where are published four vases of this type by the Chicago Painter.[2] At that time (1931) Beazley knew thirty-four red-figure examples and thirteen black. On a quick count through *ARV²* and *Paralipomena* I find forty-one red-figure examples listed (I may have missed some); and I know of four more (including the Ashmolean vase) not attributed by Beazley and of which he cannot have been aware in 1931.[3] No doubt there are others. His statement that they run from about 460 to the end of the century[4] is borne out by the additions, though there is a similar shape in much earlier black-figure.[5] Of the attributed red-figure pieces, besides the four by the Chicago Painter there are four by the Calliope Painter, twelve by the Shuvalov Painter, and seventeen by various slight painters of the late fifth century, largely represented at Spina, of whom the Bull Painter (with twelve) is the principal. The rest are singletons, ascribed to various painters; one will be mentioned below.[6] They are mostly of about the same size as ours, some a little larger, but a good many are considerably smaller. Many, like ours, have no floral decoration, but others, especially among the later, have elaborate palmette-complexes below the handle. Beazley notes that they regularly have a line below the lip, incised in the clay before the black was laid on. On our vase, exceptionally, this line is incised through the black.

The drawing on our piece clearly puts it among the later though not the latest examples; I suppose in the twenties or possibly the teens of the century. The picture is confined to the front of the vase. This is the regular arrangement on the shape, generally two or three figures; here one might call it two and a half. It is framed above and below by strips of egg-pattern (ubiquitous at this time), which are not continued round the pot. The picture shows two figures, a naked dwarf and a muffled woman, facing each other at a slight distance in a dance. The dwarf is getting an erection, and high between them, at the level of the woman's face and flying towards her, is a phallus-bird, or rather a winged phallus. The phallus-bird proper has the body and legs as well as the wings of a bird; only its long neck ends in a phallus-head. Here, apart from the wings, it is simply a phallus, drawn just like the dwarf's without even the addition of the eye with which phalli are so often endowed.

The drawing of the muffled dancer is so like that of a muffled woman on the Phiale Painter's name-work is Boston[7] that I have no doubt the new picture too is from his hand. It has his vivid quality; his scenes are often uncommon; he likes the dance; and there are other points linking this picture to attributed works, some of which we shall be noticing. It makes an interesting addition to the *oeuvre* of one of the best and most attractive draughtsmen among classical vase-painters. No other picture of a dwarf is ascribed to him but the Dwarf Painter's name-creature is similarly conceived,[8] and the two artists are closely related — must have sat together in the Achilles Painter's workshop. No oinochoe of Shape 4 is attributed to any of these three, but both the Achilles and the Phiale Painter decorated jugs of other types, and one of Shape 4 is given to the Persephone Painter who belongs to the same circle.[9] Our figure's costume is not identical with that of the woman on the phiale. Both have the long chiton, and over it the himation, covering both arms and muffling neck and chin, but on the phiale it does not cover the scarfed hair. Our dancer has pulled it up over the back of her head, and under it she wears a sakkos much like that of the woman on the phiale carrying phialai and a jug.[10]

The dancing dwarf as entertainer was a feature of Athenian life at this period; the muffled female dancer too, though she is perhaps a more familiar figure in the Hellenistic age — one thinks of Tanagras, and in particular of the marvellous bronze from the Baker collection in New York.[11] Most of the Phiale Painter's dancers, children or at least not fully grown, wear the short sleeveless chiton or are naked;[12] but muffled dancers are shown on a two-row calyx-krater in the Astarita Collection, which I know only from the description in *ARV2*.[13] The maenad on a Nolan amphora at Woburn,[14] dancing to a young satyr's pipe, is a woman and wears the long chiton, though hitched up with a deep overfold to leave the feet freer; while her companion on the back of the vase, head thrown back to sing, has the long chiton too and over it the himation, covering both arms and muffling her to the neck. The dancing maenad's legs and body are in almost the same attitude as those of our dancer, though arms and head are quite differently set; and these two figures confirm the attribution. The little dancer on the Boston phiale wears a short dress, but the muffled woman on the same vase is oddly posed and it is possible that she too is about to begin a dance. She is back to back with the dancing-mistress, characterized by her *narthex* (teacher's cane),[15] who directs the child's castanet-dance, while a youth beyond applauds it; on the other side a seated youth turns to speak to or watch the muffled figure. Between the little girl and her admirer is a chair with a bundle on it which is probably her himation; a similar but larger bundle lies on a stool beside the grown girl who pipes to a rapt man, and who likewise wears only a chiton, though a long one, and *kothornoi*. About the eighth figure, the woman with jug and phialai, and the significance of the scene, there will be a word to say later.[16]

In the picture on our jug the flying phallus above must indicate that this is an erotic dance. Dwarfs, like negroes, are sometimes credited (by those of different colour or shape) with great sexual potency, but I cannot find that this was so in antiquity. Another vase on which both a winged phallus and a dwarf appear is a little kotyle in Munich (Pl. 34, Figs. 3–4).[17] One side shows a huge phallus, with small wings at the root and a large eye, set upright on the ground like a pillar, branches on either side, and a table, giving the scale, with a bowl (the all-purpose *lekane*)[18] on it; this is clearly a phallus-shrine. On the other side stands a naked female dwarf with negroid features, a straggling wreath over her scarfed hair, holding a kotyle. A much earlier Attic vase shows a naked woman setting up a monster phallus while a clothed companion dances; one of intermediate date a naked woman running with a monster phallus.[19] The festival in question has been doubtfully identified as the *Haloa*. Whatever it was, the scene on the kotyle too must refer to it; and the fact that the naked woman here is a dwarf need not imply any association of dwarfs with phallicism but may be simply parody or caricature. Some such explanation may equally be the right one for the dancers on our jug.

Another woman, muffled even more closely so that only her eyes can be seen, appears in a still less readily explicable scene on a Nolan amphora in the British Museum (Pl. 35, Figs. 5–6).[20] Though the effect is similar, the garments are different; instead of the chiton with himation over it, the peplos. It is the same contrast as is seen earlier in sculpture between two women with covered head: the Europa (Amelung's goddess) in Ionic chiton and himation; and the Hestia Giustiniani in the Doric chiton or peplos.[21] The garment which the Hestia wears over her hair, however, must be a separate veil, while the woman on the British Museum vase has perhaps rather arranged the upper part of the peplos to cover her arms and head. Beazley knew this vase all his life and never attributed it, and I should not dare rush in; but I should certainly look for the author in the same neighbourhood as our jug, among the companions and followers of the Achilles Painter. The woman reminds me in particular of some of the Phiale Painter's larger figures.[22] The vase is of rather summary make, and the reverse-figure even more summarily drawn, but the strange scene on the front is finely conceived and executed. The woman stands looking down at a monkey, which sits on an ill-defined object, a large block with rounded corners, and looks up at her. It has a fillet round its head, and holds in its left hand a string which is fastened high up round the right thigh. The feet are human, not simian, and the way the hairy pelt ends at ankle, wrist and V-neck might suggest the possibility that this figure is not meant for a true monkey but for a child dressed up; but this is probably to read too much into the draughtsman's inaccuracies.

I do not know what is meant. The muffling here has evidently nothing to do with the dance; suggests rather a wish not to be recognized. Cecil Smith in the British Museum catalogue writes: "Possibly the gesture of the woman has reference to the idea in antiquity of the ape as ill-omened; cf. Lucian *Pseudolog.* 17".[23] Like dwarfs, monkeys are sometimes thought highly sexed. "Goats and monkeys!" cries Lear in such a context; and as though to echo him goats and monkeys are oddly juxtaposed on a cup of the late sixth century: on one side three goats dancing to a satyr's Pan-pipes; on the other five monkeys, or monkey-headed men, playing on a see-saw.[24] However, there is nothing at all to suggest sex in these pictures, and it does not seem that the monkey either had this reputation among the Greeks; indeed the cutler whom Aristophanes in the Birds calls "the monkey" seems from the context to have found his wife too ardent for him.[25] The woman on the vase looks as though she might have come to consult the monkey, as one might consult an oracle or perhaps rather a witch. Possibly the explanation is to be sought in some fable or folk-tale.

The subject-matter of the Boston phiale deserves a further word. Beazley originally described it as "Visit to ladies, with dancing"; later as "Visit to the school of music".[26] The girls must in any case be *hetairai.* Caskey described but did not define the scene,[27] and Beazley added notes in "Narthex":[28] the flute-girl's *kothornoi,* the dancing-mistress's cane. He did not comment on Caskey's account of the woman with the jug and phialai, as "holding them for the men to drink from"; but this is difficult. True, there are three men and three phialai, but the phiale is seldom or never shown in use as an ordinary cup; the context is always religious ritual, commonly libation-pouring, occasionally drinking.[29] The context of a visit to hetairai is odd, but the vessel is itself a phiale — a most unusual form in figured pottery of the classical period — and on the boss in the centre a figure of unquestionably religious character is shown in a clearly ritual context: a winged goddess (presumably Nike)[30] running with a jug and a basket-tray[31] of a kind found exclusively in pictures of religious observance (we saw one crowning the phallus on the kotyle in Munich). I would suppose that the Boston phiale was made for ritual use, perhaps in the worship of Aphrodite, and that the woman in the picture on it is bringing the phialai not merely to drink from but to use in libation or other ritual.

NOTES

1 Oxford, Ashmolean Museum 1971.866; *Sotheby Cat. 1 Dec. 1969*, No. 106, with plate; later in the Bomford Collection. I am most grateful to the Department of Antiquities and in particular to Michael Vickers for opportunity to study the vase and for photographs and permission to publish them. For other acknowledgements see below notes 4, 17 and 20. Height without handle: 18.5 cm; with handle: 22.5 cm. Broken and repaired, the cracks smeared over. Surface rather worn (inner markings on dwarf largely lost). Interior of neck glazed. Relief-contour: dwarf, back of hair, back of right thigh; woman, front of sakkos, upper edge of forward foot and toes; phallus-head. Thinned glaze: phallus-head.

2 Caskey-Beazley, I, 1931, 38—40, Nos. 40—43, Pl. 18. See Caskey quoting Beazley on No. 43.

3 The other three are: *Ars Antiqua A. G., Auktion I, 2 Mai 1959 Luzern*, No. 124, Pl. 59, a late piece; *Münzen und Medaillen A. G. Auktion 26, 5 Oktober 1963 Basel*, No. 147, Pl. 53, another late piece in peculiar style; and *Münzen und Medaillen A. G. Auktion 34, 6 Mai 1967 Basel*, No. 174, Pl. 59. Beazley in *Paralipomena* attributes other vases from the same catalogue but not this fine piece; the catalogue suggests that it is from the following of the Achilles Painter, but it seems to me in a more florid tradition. Since I wrote this another fine example has appeared on the market and been bought by Kiel. It has a most interesting representation of the sacrifice of Iphigenia. Professor Schauenburg, who is to publish it and to whom I am most grateful for permission to mention it, attributes it to the Shuvalov Painter. So far as I can tell from photographs, which show some damage and old restoration, this must be right.

4 Quoted by Caskey (*supra* n. 2). In *VPol*, 32, on Goluchow 113 (a black vase, *CV* Pl. 45, 8), Beazley wrote 'from 470 to 400', but the difference is not significant. I owe this reference to B.A. Sparkes, who also refers me to J.H.C. Kern in *OMLeiden* 34, 1953, 1—12, publishing a black vase from a tomb-group of *c.* 440—20, and to *Sir John and Lady Beazley Gifts 1912—1966*, Ashmolean Museum 1967, 105, No. 392 (Pl. 55: 1966.343), on which Beazley is quoted as writing 'There are a good many black vases of this shape, but I do not remember others with impressed decoration'. Sparkes also notes that the only two fragments from something like this shape found in the Agora at Athens (*Agora* 12, 1970, 65 and 247, Nos. 156—7, Pl. 9) go with the earlier black-figure vases (see *infra* n. 5), and wonders if the fifth-century version was mainly an export-item. The recorded provenances of red-figure examples are mainly Italian, but the piece attributed to the Persephone Painter (*infra* n. 9) is said to be from Athens. There are two late examples in Corinthian red-figure: Athens N.M. 1543 and 1544.

5 Richter-Milne, Figs. 122 f. This piece is *ABV* 442 top, No. 3, and some of the others in the same list are similar.

6 See *infra,* with n. 9.

7 Boston 97.371, from near Sunium; *ARV²* 1023, No. 146, with references. The main publication is by Caskey and Beazley (*supra*, n. 2), 54—6, No. 62, Pl. 29. See further notes 15 and 26—31, *infra*.

8 On pelike, Boston 76.45, from Capua; *ARV²* 1011, No. 13, with references; Caskey-Beazley, I, 52, No. 59, Pl. 27.

9 British Museum E 560, from Athens (*supra* n. 4); *ARV²* 1013, No. 15; three athletes; unpublished.

10 See *infra,* with n. 29.

11 Dancing dwarfs: Lippold in *RM* 52, 1937, 44—7, Pl. 14; Beazley in *JHS* 59, 1939, 11, No. 30 (figured on p. 10). Muffled dancers: in fifth century Athens, *infra* n. 13; Hellenistic, D.B. Thompson in *AJA* 54, 1950, 371—85, Figs. 1—16 (the Baker dancer and comparable terracottas).

12 Some of these charming figures are collected by Beazley in 'Narthex', *AJA* 37, 1933, 400—3, Figs. 1—2 (Boston phiale), 3—4 (lekythoi, Bowdoin 13.11, and Milan, Scala 50; *ARV²* 1021, Nos. 118—119), 5 (Nolan amphora, Brussels, Bibliothèque Royale 13; *ARV²* 1016, No. 37), and 6 (oinochoe, Louvre G 574; *ARV²* 1020, No. 98). Others are on hydriai: *ARV²* 1019 f., Nos. 86 (London E 185; *CVA* Pl. 80, 4), 87 (Palermo, fr.), 88 (Copenhagen Inv. 1942; *CVA* Pls. 154, 3, and 155, 2), 89 (Athens, Agora P 14848, fr.). See also the following notes, *infra*. The girls on *ARV²* Nos. 87—8 and 118—19 are naked; those on Nos. 37, 89 and 98 wear ordinary short chiton girt or cross-girt over the breast — one would

have thought to hold the dress in during the movement of the dance, like a charioteer's cross-girding, but some of the naked girls have the same crossing cords; I do not know what the explanation is. The child on No. 146 (the phiale) has a short chiton, but patterned and fringed, and the two on No. 86 (the London hydria) a garment similarly patterned worn over the ordinary short chiton. On No. 88 a woman sits, and on No. 98 one stands, piping for the dancer. On all the others (except the fragments, where one cannot be sure) the girl is accompanied by the dancing-mistress, who has her narthex; only on No. 86 does the mistress carry another sort of tawse, perhaps the 'kerkos' (bull's pizzle) which is paired with the narthex in Phanias' epigram cited by Beazley (for the epigram see now A.S.F. Gow and D.L. Page, *Hellenistic Epigrams,* Cambridge, 1965, I, 162, lines 2972–7, and commentary in II, 465 ff. On nos. 86, 88 and 146, there is also a man looking on. The dancers on Nos. 37, 98 and 146 have castanets. Very like these is the equally charming girl (in short chiton), the name-figure of the South Italian Painter of the Berlin Dancing Girl: calyx-krater, Berlin 2400; *APS* p. 6, no. 4; *RVAp* I, p. 7, no. 1/8. In his Athenian youth this artist must have known the young Phiale Painter.

13 Vatican, Astarita 42; *ARV²* 1018, No. 68. Another vase with a dancer by the painter which I know only from description is the lekythos, once Agrigento, Giuffrida; *ARV²* 1021, No. 121, 'Pyrrhic (woman dancing and woman). Very much restored.'

14 *ARV²* 1015, No. 19; Beazley, 'A dancing maenad', *BSA* 30, 1928/30, 109–12, Pls. 17–18.

15 See Beazley in 'Narthex' (*supra,* n. 12).

16 See *infra,* notes 26–31. That the bundles on the furniture are the girls' himatia is noted by Caskey (*supra* n. 7). On the oinochoe in the Louvre (*supra* n. 12) a bundle on a stool is surely the dancing-girl's himation; the woman piping for her is wearing hers.

17 Antikensammlungen Inv. 8934; *Münchner Jahrbuch der bildenden Kunst* 18, 1967, 247 f., Fig. 8. I am much indebted to Frau Dr Martha Dumm-Ohly for photographs and permission to publish them and for information. Dr Dumm-Ohly tells me that Hans Diepolder in the last weeks of his life was much interested in this piece, and (noting with amusement the 'tiefen klassischen Blick' of the phallus) ascribed it to the Kleophon Painter; a very attractive idea.

18 On the lekane as all-purpose bowl, see Sparkes and Talcott in *Agora* 12, 1970, 211–16. The one on the kotyle seems to be of the type with handles turned up to the rim, illustrated on Pl. 86, Nos. 1821–34. On the wide range of dates of this type see *ibid.,* 214 f.

19 Both illustrated by L. Deubner, *Attische Feste,* Berlin 1932, Pl. 4: cup, Rome Villa Giulia 50404, *ARV²* 1565, Aristagoras Kalos No. 1 (outside komos); column-krater, Berlin Inv. 3206, *ARV²* 551, Pan Painter No. 10 (other side, youth at Herm); see Beazley in *The Pan Painter,* Mainz 1974, 11, No 10. The phalli are not winged. The branches on the kotyle might be ivy.

20 B.M. E 307, from Capua; not in *ARV²* or elsewhere in Beazley's lists; *CVA,* Pl. 55, 1. See n. 22 *infra.* I am most grateful to D.E.L. Haynes, Keeper of the Dept. of Greek and Roman Antiquities, for the photographs and permission to publish them.

21 E.g. B.S. Ridgway, *The Severe Style in Greek Sculpture,* Princeton 1970, Figs. 103 (Hestia) and 106–8 (Europa).

22 Woman with stamnos, on stamnos Warsaw 142465 (ex Czartoryski 42), *ARV²* 1019, No. 82, Beazley *VPol,* Pl. 23; woman pouring wine on neck-amphora B.M. E 276 (from Capua), *ARV²* 1016, No. 43, *CVA,* Pl. 14, 2; also in some degree the women on the splendid pair of white lekythoi from Oropos, Munich 2797 and 2798, *ARV²* 1022, Nos. 138–9; Beazley, *Attic White Lekythoi,* London 1938, Pls. 1, 2 and 5, Arias-Hirmer, Pls. xli–ii and 189. The stiffly extended arm of the reverse-figure is paralleled on many of the Phiale Painter's more careless reverses, but the harshness of the drawing here rather recalls some reverses by the Dwarf Painter. The woman on the front can also be compared to the Dwarf Painter's beautiful Eriphyle on the hydria Boston 03.798, *ARV²* 1011, No. 16, Caskey-Beazley, I, No. 58, Pl. 27.

23 *B.M. Cat. Vases,* III, 221.

24 Rome, Villa Giulia, from Vulci; *Paralipomena,* 330 near bottom, 'seems to be by an imitator of the Euergides Painter', with further qualifying-remarks; Giuliana Riccioni and M.T. Falconi Amorelli, *La Tomba della Panatenaica di Vulci, (Quaderni di Villa Giulia 3),* Rome 1968, 39–42, with illustrations (the interior has a diskobolos). The figures on the see-saw are wreathed and two of them carry drinking vessels. They have monkey faces and monkey poses, but the naked bodies are hairless and human. Beazley calls them 'youths, revellers, with monkeys' heads', and Riccioni 'comasti, con testa umana coronata da edera e faccia di scimmia',

25 *Birds,* 440 ff. The scholiast says his name was Panaitios. See editors' notes *ad loc.*

26 *Attic Red-figured Vases in American Museums,* Cambridge Mass. 1918, 168, in the list following a delightful appreciation of the picture and the painter. The German text in *Attische Vasenmaler,* Tübingen 1925, 386, no. 74, repeats this description. The new one comes in *ARV* (1924), 658, no. 108, and is repeated in *ARV²*.

27 *Supra,* n. 7.

28 *Supra,* n. 12.

29 See H. Luschey, *Die Phiale,* Bleicherode 1939; Dunbabin in *BSA* 46, 1951, 61–71; E. Simon, *Opfernde Götter,* Berlin 1953. Drinking from a phiale in a clearly religious ritual: fragmentary red-figure cup, Acropolis 396, Graef-Langlotz, Pl. 29; *ARV* (1942), 628, where it is listed with another with the remark 'The general character of these two cups is akin to Penthesilean'. The other cup (London E 74) appears in *ARV²*, 965, No. 1 in list 'Workshop of the Penthesilea Painter: undetermined'; Acropolis 396 appears in the index with a reference to p. 932 (Curtius Painter) where it does not appear and hardly could have. I cannot find it elsewhere, and the index reference is perhaps a false doublet of Acropolis 390, which does appear on that page (No. 21). On the subject see Kardara in *Charisterion eis A.K. Orlandon,* Athens 1965–68, II, 22 ff., Pls. 1 and 2; and *cf.* Martin Robertson, *A History of Greek Art,* Cambridge 1975, 670 (Chapter 5, n. 39).

30 Iris usually has a kerykeion to distinguish her, but one cannot always be sure between her, Eos, and Nike, who is moreover sometimes assimilated to other goddesses.

31 *Supra,* n. 17. Beazley in *Attic Red-Figured Vases in American Museums* (*supra,* n. 26), 168, calls it a cake, but Caskey, surely rightly, a sacrificial basket.

DREI SIANASCHALEN DER BERLINER ANTIKEN-SAMMLUNG

Elisabeth Rohde

Tafeln 36–39.

Seit J.D. Beazley und H.G.G. Payne nach zwei in Siana auf Rhodos gefundenen Schalen[1] eine Gruppe früher attisch schwarzfiguriger Schalen bestimmter Form und Dekoration unter der Bezeichnung "Siana Group"[2] zusammenfassten, sind nunmehr ungefähr 50 Jahre vergangen. Der Begriff der "Sianaschale" hat sich seither in der archäologischen Wissenschaft fest verankert, ihr Typ, in die Formentabelle griechischer Vasen aufgenommen, ist inzwischen in einem immer reicher vorliegenden Material zu verfolgen[3]. Entsprechend dem auf den Aussenseiten der Schalen angewandten Dekorationsschema hat Beazley zwei Grundtypen unterschieden: Schalen mit zweireihiger, in Henkel- und Randzone unterteilter Dekoration "double-decker" und jene mit einreihigem, sich über beide Zonen ausdehnendem Dekor "overlap decoration"[4]. Mit dieser Klassifizierung wurde die grosse Gruppe der Sianaschalen, bei der es sich um die beherrschende attische Schalenform des zweiten Viertels des 6. Jahrhunderts v.Chr. handelt, einer gliedernden Ordnung unterstellt. Formal aus der vorangegangenen Komastenschale[5] entwickelt und stilistisch von der korinthischen Vasenmalerei beeinflusst, bilden die Sianaschalen einen künstlerischen Schwerpunkt in der frühen attischen Gefässkeramik und gleichermassen den Übergang zu den um die Mitte des 6. Jahrhunderts aufkommenden Kleinmeisterschalen[6]. Ein grosser Teil der von Beazley[7] erfassten und stilistisch einer der beiden Künstlergruppen, dem C-Maler[8] und dem Heidelberg-Maler[9] mit ihren Kreisen und Einflussbereichen, zugewiesenen Sianaschalen wurde bisher noch nicht in Abbildungen vorgelegt. Wahrscheinlich bot das in seiner Mehrzahl an bestimmte, sich wiederholende Bildtypen gebundene Schalenmaterial des C-Malers und seiner Gruppe keinen genügenden Anreiz zu besonderen ikonographischen Untersuchungen. Reiterzüge, kämpfende Krieger und vor allem Symposia mit raumfüllendem Beiwerk gehören zu den aus dem Korinthischen übernommenen häufig begegnenden Bilddarstellungen des C-Malers[10], in dessen Werk aber auch wie bereits in den Arbeiten seiner Vorgänger, des Nessos-, Gorgo- und KX-Malers sowie des Sophilos der Mythos eine frühe attische Gestaltung findet[11]. Eine künstlerische Geringschätzung des C-Malers[12] dürfte bei der Breite seines Schaffensradius und der dadurch bedingten Vielschichtigkeit und Unterschiedlichkeit seiner Leistungen nicht in jedem Falle gerechtfertigt sein. Eine Erweiterung der mythologischen Themenkomplexe ist auf den Schalen des Heidelberg-Malers zu beobachten, bei denen die Verbindung mit der archaischen attischen Vasenmalerei[13] stärker spürbar wird als die Einflussnahme aus dem Korinthischen. Zu dem noch wenig bekannten, wenngleich in der Literatur hin und wieder zitierten und von Beazley zugewiesenen Material der Sianagattung gehören drei Schalen des overlap-Typs, die sich in der Berliner Antiken-Sammlung befinden und die hier erstmals abgebildet und untersucht werden sollen.

1. Sianaschale[14] Taf. 36, Abb. 1–3.

Heller orangegelber Ton. Unter A. im Firnis graugrüne Flecke durch Fehlbrand. Aus Bruchstücken zusammengesetzt, an den Brüchen Ausflickungen. Bestossungen an der Fusskante. Verscheuerungen an den beiden rechten Figuren auf B.

Flacher Tellerfuss mit kurzem Stiel, innen hohl. Standfläche und Stielinneres mit Boden tongrundig. Um den inneren Rand der Standfläche Firnislinie, innen auf dem Boden anstelle eines plastischen Dorns[15] Firnisklecks umgeben von Firnisring. Innenfläche des Schalenbeckens gefirnisst mit Ausnahme des Bildmedaillons[16] und eines tongrundigen Streifens unter der Lippe. Tongrundig die Innenseiten der Henkel und ein Streifen aussen um den Schalenboden, darauf vier in verdünntem Firnis aufgetragene Linien. Gefirnisste Lippe, der ein umlaufender Firnisstreifen aussen unter dem Knick der Schalenwandung entspricht, welcher einerseits die Divergenz von Tektonik und Bemalung der overlap-Schalen unterstreicht, während er anderseits die Entscheidung zugunsten eines organisch aufgebauten Schalenkörpers verdeutlicht[17].

Innen: Nackter, nach links laufender Krieger mit korinthischem Helm, hohem Helmbusch, langem Haar, in der Rechten die Lanze, in der Linken den böotischen Schild mit Palmettenverzierung und Tupfenumrandung.

Rot: Helm, Teile des Helmbusches, Palmettenkelche und Palmettenblätter im Wechsel am Schild.

Weiss (Farbe verblasst): Teile des Helmbusches, Palmettenblätter im Wechsel sowie Mittelstreifen und Tupfen am Schild.

Die Bildumrahmung besteht aus einem Zungenkranz (rot-schwarz alternierend, einmal schwarz-schwarz), der von zwei Doppelpunktbändern zwischen Firnislinien eingefasst wird. Die Darstellung greift an drei Stellen in die Rahmenleiste hinein.

Aussen auf umlaufender Bodenlinie: A. Symposion: Drei auf Klinen nach links gelagerte bärtige Männer in langen Mänteln[18], die Schultern und rechten Arm unbedeckt lassen, während sie die Beine, die jeweils mit einem hochgestellten Knie im Steilschema des frühen 6. Jahrhunderts gezeichnet sind, vollständig und faltenlos verhüllen und so dem Unterkörper die Gestalt eines silhouettenhaften Hügels geben. Der Mantel des rechten Symposiasten ist oberhalb des Knies mit einer fein geritzten Schlingensaum-Borte verziert[19]. Das Haar der Gelagerten ist im Nackenschopf eingebunden, um den Kopf ist eine Haarbinde gelegt. Die beiden auf der linken und mittleren Kline gelagerten Männer haben ihre Köpfe nach rechts drei bärtigen, mit langen Chitonen und kurzen bortengesäumten Mänteln bekleideten Männern zugewendet, die von rechts und links an die Kline des mittleren Symposiasten im Gespräch herangetreten sind. Die beiden rechts hintereinander gereihten Figuren haben die rechte Hand erhoben, während die linke Figur in analogem Schema mit erhobener linker Hand dargestellt ist[20]. Alle drei tragen lang herabfallendes Haar und Haarbinden. Die Klinen zeigen den Typ der um die Wende vom 7. zum 6. Jahrhundert erscheinenden ältesten Symposiendarstellungen auf griechischen Vasen[21]. Über ihren oberen Teil ist eine Decke gebreitet, die, mit einer Borte[22] versehen, allseitig herabhängt, so dass von der Klinen-Konstruktion nur die untere Partie der gedrechselten Beine sichtbar ist[23]. Vor jeder Kline steht ein löwenfüssiger Speisetisch mit einem Tablett, auf dem drei in üblicher Weise pyramidal angeordnete spitze Kuchen liegen, daneben je zwei — auf dem rechten Tisch drei — längliche Fleischstücke (?); vor den Tischen je ein Schemel. An der Wand über den Klinen sind drei Trinkhörner und drei Lekanides aufgehängt.

B. Symposion: Vier auf Klinen nach links gelagerte, mit dem Mantel bekleidete bärtige Symposiasten (im gleichen Typ wie auf A.)[24]. Der erste und dritte Symposiast (von links) hat den Kopf nach rückwärts, dem folgenden Gelagerten zugewendet. Vor den Klinen Speisetische mit je drei spitzen Kuchen und zwei Fleischstücken (?), davor Schemel, an der Wand vier Trinkhörner und vier Lekanides entsprechend der Darstellung auf A.

Rot: an Mänteln und Haarbinden.

Weiss: Mäander und Fransen an den Borten der Klinendecken, am Chiton des links stehenden Mannes auf A., an spitzen Kuchen und Lekanides (zum Teil stark verblasst und verrieben). Dass an den Chitonen der beiden rechts Stehenden auf A. ebenfalls einst weiss aufgesetzt war, kann aus dem stumpfen grauschwarz des Grundes erschlossen werden.

2. Sianaschale[25] Taf. 37, Abb. 4–5.

Orangefarbener Ton. Glänzender schwarzer Firnis, feine Ritzzeichnung. Erhalten nur Fuss mit Teilen des Schalenbodens und Innenmedaillons sowie Bruchstücke der Wandung von A. Bruchkanten meist ausgeplatzt und mit Gips ausgefüllt. Bestossung an der Fusskante.

Flacher Tellerfuss mit kurzem Stiel, innen hohl. Standfläche und Stielinneres mit Boden tongrundig. Um den inneren Rand der Standfläche Firnisband, innen auf dem Boden kegelförmiger Dorn mit Firnisresten, umgeben von Firnisring. Innenfläche des Schalenbeckens gefirnisst mit Ausnahme des Bildmedaillons und eines tongrundigen Streifens unter der Lippe. Tongrundiger, mit vier Firnislinien ausgefüllter Streifen aussen um den Schalenboden. Gefirnisste Lippe und Firnisstreifen aussen unter dem Knick der Schalenwandung.

Innen: Bärtiger Triton nach rechts. Der menschliche Oberkörper, mit kurzem engem Chiton bekleidet, ist frontalansichtig, der Kopf ins Profil nach links gewendet. Ein in Windungen angeordneter Fischleib mit Zickzacklinie, Flossen und Delphinschwanz schliesst nach links an den Oberkörper an. Der rechte Unterarm mit Hand und ausgestreckten Fingern ist steil emporgerichtet, die gesenkte linke Hand hält einen Fisch umfasst[26]. Das lange Haar, in zierlichem Nackenschopf aufgenommen, wird von einer Haarbinde gehalten.

Rot: Chiton, Delphinschwanz, Zickzacklinie, Streifen am Nackenschopf. Verblasste weisse (?) Tupfen an der Haarbinde.

Die Bildumrahmung besteht aus einem Zungenkranz (rot-schwarz alternierend), der von zwei Doppelpunktbändern zwischen Firnislinien eingefasst wird.

Aussen auf Bodenlinie: A. Symposion: Drei auf gedrechselten Beinen[27] stehende Klinen, davor je ein löwenfüssiger Speisetisch und ein Schemel. Auf den Klinen, über die Decken mit Fransenborten gebreitet sind, links und in der Mitte je ein nach links gelagerter Symposiast in langem, den Unterkörper verhüllendem Mantel, die Beine im Steilschema hochgestellt[28]. Von der linken Figur sind nur der silhouettenhafte Hügel der Beine und ein Stück des rechten Oberarms erhalten, während das Figürliche auf der rechten Kline verloren ist. Der auf der mittleren Kline gelagerte Bärtige, in Typ und Haltung mit den sich umwendenden Symposiasten der vorigen Schale[29] übereinstimmend, blickt zu einer von rechts an ihn herantretenden männlichen[30] Gestalt in langem Chiton und kurzem bortengesäumtem Mantel, von der Oberkörper und Kopf nicht mehr erhalten sind. Der Mann hat die rechte Hand im Sprechgestus[31] vorgestreckt, der linke Unterarm mit geschlossener Hand war angewinkelt. Eine entsprechende männliche Figur links — gleiche Kleidung, angewinkelter rechter Unterarm, Kopf und Oberkörper ebenfalls verloren — hat sich von der anderen Seite der Kline genähert. Auf dem linken und mittleren Speisetisch je ein Tablett mit drei pyramidal angeordneten spitzen Kuchen, daneben je zwei längliche Fleischstücke (?). Kline und Tisch rechts, zu grossen Teilen nicht mehr erhalten, lassen von den Speisen nur einen der spitzen Kuchen mit dem Rest des Tabletts erkennen. An der Wand über der linken und mittleren Kline je ein Trinkhorn.

Rot: an Mänteln und Haarbinde.

Weiss völlig verblasst, nur noch aus dem stumpfen grauschwarz des Grundes zu erschliessen: Fransen der Klinendecken, Chitone und Kuchen.

3. Sianaschale[32] Taf. 37–39, Abb. 6–12.

Orangefarbener Ton. Guter schwarzer Firnis, feine Ritzzeichnung. Intakt bis auf geringe Bestossungen links auf B. und am anschliessenden Henkel; einige Verscheuerungen.

Flacher Tellerfuss mit kurzem Stiel, innen hohl. Standfläche und Stielinneres mit Boden tongrundig. Am inneren Rande der Standfläche und im Stielinneren je eine umlaufende orangebraune Firnislinie. Auf dem Boden schwacher Dorn. Innenfläche des Schalenbeckens gefirnisst mit Ausnahme des Bildmedaillons und eines tongrundigen Streifens unter der Lippe. Tongrundig die Innenseiten der Henkel und ein Streifen aussen um den Schalenboden, darauf vier in verdünntem Firnis aufgetragene Linien. Gefirnisste Lippe, umlaufender Firnisstreifen aussen unter dem Knick der Schalenwandung.

Innen: Herakles, bärtig, Löwenkappe und über der Brust geknotetes Löwenfell, das, über einem kurzen Chiton in der Taille gegürtet, mit den zwei freien Löwentatzen zu beiden Seiten des linken Oberschenkels herabhängt[33], im Knielauf nach rechts[34]. Mit der Lanze in der Rechten dringt er auf eine nach rechts entfliehende Amazone (Andromache ?)[35] ein, die am linken Arm einen grossen Rundschild und in der rechten Hand ebenfalls eine Lanze hält[36]. Die Amazone hat den Kopf zu dem Verfolger zurückgewendet, der sie mit der linken Hand vermutlich am schildtragenden Arm packt[37]. Sie ist mit einer kurzen, durch Gewandborten eingefassten Tunika bekleidet, trägt Beinschienen und auf dem Kopf den attischen Helm mit hohem Helmbusch. Das Haar fällt in Lockensträhnen herab, als Schmuck dienen Ohrgehänge und Halsband.

Rot: an Löwenkappe, Bart und Chiton des Herakles; an Helm, Schild, Beinschienen, Gewandstreifen, Auge, Halsband und Ohrschmuck der Amazone.

Weiss: Fleischteile der Amazone.

Das Bild wird von einem Zungenkranz (rot-schwarz alternierend, einmal rot-rot) zwischen Firnislinien gerahmt, wobei die Darstellung zum Teil in den Zungenrahmen hineingreift.

Aussen auf umlaufender Bodenlinie: A. Viergespann umgeben von Kampfszenen: Rechts im Bildfeld Bogenschütze[38] (spitze Mütze, kurzes mit geritzten Sternen gemustertes Gewand, umgehängter Köcher) in Kniestellung nach links, mit Pfeil und Bogen auf einen in der gleichen Richtung zu Boden gegangenen Krieger zielend (korinthischer Helm mit hohem Helmbusch, kurzer Chiton), der, bereits vom Pfeil getroffen, hinter einem mit dem linken Arm emporgehaltenen Rundschild Schutz sucht, während er sich mit der rechten Hand, der die Lanze entglitten ist, auf den Boden stützt. Die Gruppe wird von zwei Kriegern überschnitten, von denen der linke (korinthischer Helm mit zwei Ohren[39], kurzer Chiton, Panzer mit Streifen und Zickzack, Beinschienen) vom Wagen eines Viergespannes herabsteigt und mit erhobener Lanze in der Rechten und Rundschild in der Linken nach rechts gegen einen Krieger andringt (korintischer Helm mit Helmbusch, kurzer Chiton, Panzer, Beinschienen), der sich in Gegenüberstellung mit ebenfalls erhobener Lanze und Rundschild zur Wehr setzt. Hinter dem linken Krieger, von diesem stark überschnitten, ein auf dem Wagen nach links stehender Lenker (korinthischer Helm mit Horn und Ohr, langes Gewand), der in der Rechten das Kentron, in der Linken die Zügel hält. Die Kumte der beiden vorderen Pferde sind mit Zickzack verziert. Im Vordergrund, die Pferdekörper zum Teil überschneidend, zwei mit erhobenen Lanzen und Rundschilden nach rechts stürmende Krieger, von denen der linke bärtig ist (korinthische Helme, der linke mit Helmbusch, der rechte mit zwei Ohren, kurze Chitone, Panzer, Beinschienen). Links der Pferde setzt sich die Handlung in Zweikampfgruppen fort. Ein nach links angreifender Krieger (korinthischer Helm mit Ohren, kurzer Chiton mit Wellenborte, Panzer mit Streifen und Zickzack, Beinschienen) mit der Lanze in der Rechten auf einen nach links entweichenden Gegner einstechend, den er mit der Linken am Halse packt. Der Krieger (bärtig, korinthischer Helm mit Helmbusch, kurzer Chiton, Beinschienen) hat in der Linken den schützenden Rundschild, in der gesenkten Rechten die Lanze. Er wendet den Kopf zu dem Verfolger zurück. Die anschliessende Gruppe zeigt einen nach rechts gerichteten Krieger (korinthischer Helm mit hohem Helmbusch, kurzer Chiton, Panzer mit Zickzack und Streifen, Beinschienen), der im Begriff ist, auf einen bereits rückwärts ins Knie gebrochenen Gegner (korinthischer Helm, kurzer Chiton, Beinschienen) mit der Lanze einzustechen, die er in der Rechten hält, während er am linken Arm den in Innenansicht erscheinenden Rundschild trägt. Rundschild und Lanze hat auch der Unterliegende. Ebenfalls nach rechts bewegt ist die folgende Gruppe eines angreifenden und eines entweichenden Kriegers (korinthische Helme, der linke mit hohem, der rechte mit niedrigem Helmbusch, kurze Chitone, der rechte mit Wellenlinienborten, Beinschienen, der linke Krieger mit Panzer, darauf Streifen und Zickzack). Der Angreifer dringt mit der Lanze in der Rechten und Rundschild am linken Arm (feines Zickzackornament am Armbügel) auf seinen ebenfalls mit Lanze und Rundschild ausgerüsteten Gegner ein, während neben ihm ein bereits überwundener Krieger (kurzer Chiton) sterbend rückwärts ins Knie gesunken ist.

Rot: an Helmen, Helmohren und Hörnern, Beinschienen, Chitonen, Pferdemähnen, vorn an Pferdehälsen und Brüsten, an der Schildinnenfläche des letzten Kriegers links, am Armbügel des Siegers der vorletzten Gruppe, Tupfen am Schildrand des Kriegers der drittletzten Gruppe. Reste an den übrigen Schilden.

Weiss: an den Panzern der drei angreifenden Krieger auf der linken Bildhälfte und an den Helmbüschen der entweichenden Krieger der ersten und letzten Gruppe links.

B. Kämpfende Kriegerpaare: Rechts, vom Henkelansatz am rechten Bein überdeckt, Bogenschütze (bärtig, spitze Mütze, geflecktes kurzes Gewand, umgehängter Köcher) nach links pfeilschiessend in den Kampf eingreifend. Neben ihm ein ebenfalls nach links kämpfender Krieger (korinthischer Helm mit zwei Ohren, kurzer Chiton, Panzer, Beinschienen), seinen nach links ins Knie gebrochenen Gegner (korinthischer Helm, kurzer Chiton, Panzer, Beinschienen) mit der Lanze erstechend. Der Unterliegende hält in der Rechten eine Lanze, in der Linken einen Rundschild, hinter dem er vergeblich Schutz sucht. Dicke Blutströme fliessen aus der Wunde des Sterbenden herab. Es folgt links anschliessend ein mit Rundschilden und Lanzen ausgerüstetes Kämpferpaar, bestehend aus einem nach rechts angreifenden Krieger (korinthischer Helm mit Hörnern und Ohren, kurzer Chiton mit Wellenlinienborten, Beinschienen), der seinen nach rechts entweichenden, sich dabei jedoch noch mit der Lanze zur Wehr setzenden Gegner (korinthischer Helm mit Helmbusch, kurzer Chiton, Beinschienen) hart bedrängt, wobei die Schilde der Kämpfenden, von denen der des linken Kriegers die Innenseite mit Armbügel zeigt, sich fast überdecken. Ein vornübergestürzter sterbender Krieger (korinthischer Helm, kurzer Chiton, Panzer mit Zickzack und Streifen, Beinschienen) liegt unter den Kämpfenden blutend am Boden, die Lanze ist seiner rechten Hand entglitten, ein Pfeil sticht in seinen Unterkörper. Ebenfalls nach rechts gerichtet ist die folgende Gruppe. In weitausholendem Schritt dringt ein Krieger (korinthischer Helm mit Ohren, kurzer Chiton mit Zickzackborten, Beinschienen) mit der Lanze auf seinen ins Knie brechenden Gegner ein, den er mit der linken Hand an der Hüfte packt. Der bereits verwundete Krieger (korinthischer Helm mit hohem Helmbusch, kurzer Chiton mit Kreuzborten, Beinschienen) wendet den Kopf zurück, hält in der Rechten die Lanze, während die Linke kraftlos auf der Schulter des Siegers liegt. Sie sollte vermutlich im Gestus des Bittflehens das Kinn des mächtigen Gegners berühren[40], vielleicht aber auch einen verzweifelten Abwehrversuch des Unterliegenden anzeigen, aus dessen Wunde ein breiter Blutstrom zu Boden fliesst. Ein Pfeilschuss von rechts hat den Verwundeten ebenfalls bereits getroffen, ein zweiter Pfeil zielt von oben herab auf seine rechte Schulter. Noch unentschieden ist der Kampf der links anschliessenden Gruppe, bei der es sich um zwei einander gegenüberstehende Krieger mit grossen Rundschilden handelt, die ihre Lanzen gegeneinander erhoben haben (korinthische Helme: der linke mit Helmbusch, der rechte mit Ohren, kurze Chitone, Panzer mit Zickzack und Streifen, Beinschienen, feines Zickzackornament am Armbügel des linken Kriegers). Die letzte Gruppe, bestehend aus zwei nach links gerichteten Kriegern mit Rundschilden, ist durch Beschädigung der Bildfläche nicht in allen Einzelheiten klar erkennbar. Mit erhobener rechter Hand sticht der Angreifende (korinthischer Helm mit Ohren, kurzer Chiton, Panzer, Beinschienen) mit der Lanze (?) auf seinen entweichenden Gegner ein (korinthischer Helm, Beinschienen), der sich mit einer Lanze in der Rechten zur Wehr setzt, von dem am linken Arm getragenen Schild erscheint wiederum die Innenseite.

Rot: an Helmen, Helmohren und Hörnern, Beinschienen und Chitonen der von rechts ersten und vierten Kriegergruppe, der Angreifenden der zweiten, dritten und letzten Kriegergruppe, des Sterbenden unter der zweiten Gruppe, an Bart und Gewandtupfen des Bogenschützen, an den Aussenseiten der Schilde mit Ausnahme desjenigen des rechten Kriegers der vorletzten Gruppe, an den Schildbügeln des vierten und letzten Kriegers, an der Schildinnenseite des linken Kriegers der vorletzten Gruppe, an der Schulter des letzten Kriegers. Rot auch das Blut der Verwundeten.

Weiss: Gewandtupfen des Bogenschützen, Panzer des Sterbenden unter der zweiten Gruppe von rechts, Panzer der beiden Krieger der vierten Gruppe, Chitone der rechten Krieger der zweiten und dritten Gruppe.

Die Gelageszenen der beiden Schalen des C-Malers, deren Bildtypik im Werke dieses Malers keinerlei Sonderstellung einnimmt[41], dürften geeignet sein, an eine in jüngster Zeit wiederholt diskutierte Frage anzuknüpfen. Es ist die Frage nach der Sinndeutung des frühgriechischen Symposionbildes und seiner Beziehung zum späteren Totenmahlrelief, das in seiner ältesten Form allerdings erst im letzten Viertel des 6. Jahrhunderts auftritt[42]. Man wird kaum annehmen, dass es sich bei den Symposien der genannten Sianaschalen um etwas anderes als um Darstellungen irdischer Gelage handelt, denn weder kennzeichnende Beigaben noch Namensbeischriften weisen in eine mythische oder ins Jenseits entrückte Sphäre[43]. Die auf den Speisetischen, den Trapezai, befindlichen spitzen Kuchen, die sogenannten Pyramides, deren Erscheinen beim späteren griechischen Totenmahl die Vorstellung chthonischer Speise aufkommen liess[44], wird man auf den Schalenbildern noch als durchaus irdische Symposionspeise zu deuten haben[45]. Sie mag neben dem Fleisch[46] verzehrt worden sein, bevor der Trank, auf den die an der Wand hängenden Schalen und Trinkhörner[47] hinweisen, den Lagernden gereicht wurde. Dass auf den frühen schwarzfigurigen Gefässbildern diese Reihenfolge von Speise und Trank nicht immer klar zum Ausdruck kommt, liegt an Verständnis und künstlerischer Sorgfalt des Vasenmalers. Auch ein seit geometrischer Zeit vorhandenes, im 6. Jahrhundert dann bereits reifer gewordenes Empfinden für ein ausgewogenes Füllen der Bildfläche wird die Darstellung in ihrer Erscheinungsform bestimmt haben[48], die, als Typ geprägt, weiter übernommen wurde.

Die herrschende Klasse in der altattischen Gesellschaft der ersten Hälfte des 6. Jahrhunderts war der grundbesitzende Adel. Und Angehörige dieser begüterten Oberschicht, der "rosseliebenden vornehmen Grundherren"[49] sind es, die sich zu kostspieligen Gelagen zusammenfanden und die bei Symposion, Reiten und Wagenfahrt auf den Vasenbildern dargestellt wurden[50]. Die sich stets wiederholende nach links laufende Richtung der Gelagerten, ein Bildtypus, der in gleicher Weise in der frühgriechischen Marmor—[51], Bronze—[52] und Terrakottaplastik sowie an den Reliefs etruskischer Aschenkisten zu verfolgen ist, und der seine Fortsetzung in den Darstellungen der attisch rotfigurigen Vasen, der Totenmahl — und Weihreliefs findet, hat man damit erklärt, dass die Bewegungsfreiheit des rechten Armes nicht durch ein Aufstützen behindert sein sollte[53]. Diese Absicht ist für die Symposiondarstellungen, seien sie nun irdischer oder chthonischer Art, wohl denkbar. Wie verhält es sich jedoch bei der Totenaufbahrung, die in der Typik der geometrischen Prothesisdarstellungen das früheste Zeugnis für die in der griechischen Kunst gestaltete Bildform des liegenden Menschen abgibt. Dass die Bilder dieser geometrischen Vasen sowie die nachfolgenden schwarzfigurigen Darstellungen den Toten fast ausnahmslos in der gleichen Richtung gelagert zeigen, wobei der Kopf rechts, die Beine links erscheinen[54], bedarf wahrscheinlich einer anderen Erklärung, da man bei der bestehenden Regelmässigkeit eine Zufälligkeit ausschliessen muss. Der Tote, dessen Oberkörper frontal aufgeklappt in geometrischer Manier als Dreieck in der Fläche erscheint, liegt auf seiner linken Seite[55]. Auch der gelagerte Symposiast hat den Oberkörper frontal gedreht, während Kopf und Beine in Profilansicht dargestellt sind. Darf man nun in der Lagerung beziehungsweise in der schon weit älteren Totenbettung dieses Schemas: Kopf rechts, Beine links im Bildfeld, eine bewusste, aus einer bestimmten Sinngebung erwachsene Ausrichtung erkennen, oder sind es kompositorische Gründe, die innerhalb einer richtungsmässig ausponderierten Flächenaufteilung zu einer vom Künstler vielleicht nur instinktiv vorgenommenen Schwerpunktfixierung führten, aus der man dann eine kunstgeschichtliche Gesetzmässigkeit ableitete. Die von Wölfflin[56] bereits vor etlichen Jahrzehnten an Hand von Gemälden getroffenen Feststellungen, "dass die rechte Bildseite einen anderen Stimmungswert hat als die linke", wobei "es entscheidet über die Stimmung des Bildes, wie es nach rechts ausgeht. Gewissermassen wird dort das letzte Wort gesprochen", dürften schon für die frühgriechische Flächenkunst zutreffend sein. Der Schwerpunkt liegt bei der Totenaufbahrung beim Haupte des Verstorbenen[57], dort, wo einst der wache Geist den Menschen prägte. Die bei Symposion und Totenmahl gelagerte Figur führt in ihrer Bildgestaltung über das frühe Schema der Totenbettung einen grossen Schritt hinaus ohne dass an der erkannten Schwerpunktfixierung: Kopf und Oberkörper des Gelagerten rechts im Bilde, etwas geändert wurde. Im Gegenteil, hier dürfte sich noch eine weitere kompositionelle von Wölfflin herausgestellte Gesetzmässigkeit bewahrheiten und zwar die der steigenden und fallenden Schräglinien: "Was im Sinn der Links-Rechts-Diagonale läuft, wird als steigend, das Entgegengesetzte als fallend empfunden"[58]. Unser Blick wird somit zu Oberkörper und Kopf des Gelagerten nach rechts emporgezogen, der Akzent ist dadurch gesetzt, im Totenmahlrelief als einem in sich geschlossenen Bilde, im Symposion der schwarzfigurigen Vasenbilder als einer Reihung von Einzelbildern, die jeweils für sich die gleiche Gesetzmässigkeit ablesen lassen und nur durch füllende Zwischenfiguren oder Zurückwenden des Kopfes eine gewisse Verbindung untereinander erhalten.

Die Aussenbilder der dritten Schale zeigen eine Folge von Zweiergruppen kämpfender Hopliten, die durch ein Viergespann, zwei Bogenschützen, zwei gefallene Krieger, vor allem jedoch durch einen fein ausponderierten Richtungswechsel in der Bewegung der Kämpfenden kompositorisch und szenisch Abwechslung und zugleich einen natürlichen Zusammenhalt erfahren. Da bekannte Attribute und hinweisende Namensbeischriften fehlen, hat man die Kämpfenden nicht mit bestimmten Gestalten identifizieren können. Die Vermutung, dass der Maler seine Darstellung dem Sagenkreis um den trojanischen Krieg entnahm, liegt nahe. Die grossen Kämpfe der Vorzeit, die sagenumwoben jahrhundertelang mündlich überliefert im Volke gegenwärtig blieben, bis sie in den Gesängen Homers und in den Fassungen des Epischen Kyklos eine dichterische Form erhielten, waren für die griechischen Vasenmaler zum Teil seit frühacharischer Zeit ein beliebtes Bildthema. Wie man erkannt hat, sind gesicherte Iliasmotive in der nordost-peloponnesischen Kunst bereits im letzten Viertel des 7. Jahrhunderts anzutreffen, während sie in der attischen Vasenmalerei, von bestimmten Ausnahmen abgesehen, in grösserer Zahl erst seit der Mitte des 6. Jahrhunderts begegnen, wobei unbestimmte Kampfszenen freilich häufig schon früher auftreten[59]. Zu den letztgenannten könnten die Darstellungen der vorliegenden Sianaschale zählen, aus denen nicht ohne weiteres zu erkennen ist, ob der Vasenmaler bereits auf bestimmte Szenen des Epos Bezug nimmt, die er mit Phantasie und Erzählerfreudigkeit durchwirkt in seinem Werke wiedergibt, oder ob er sich nur einer Aneinanderreihung von Bildschablonen bedient, wie es die Symposien zeigten. Der Maler unterscheidet in den Bildszenen, durch bestimmte Merkmale verdeutlicht, zwei Parteien kämpfender Hopliten. Es ist einmal diejenige der siegreichen Krieger, die überwiegend durch Ohren- oder Hörnerhelme beziehungsweise durch Helme mit hohem Helmbusch charakterisiert sind. Zum anderen ist es die Partei der Unterliegenden, der getöteten, verwundeten und zur Flucht gewandten Krieger, deren Helme zumeist den niedrigen oder auch keinen Helmbusch haben. Aus dieser Beobachtung heraus wird man dort, wo der Kampf noch unentschieden ist, wie bei der Gruppe rechts auf A, den beiden neben dem Gespann anstürmenden Kriegern und bei der vorletzten Gruppe links auf B, den Sieg demjenigen Hopliten voraussagen, der in entsprechender Weise durch seinen Helm gekennzeichnet wurde.

In Buch 7,75 der *Geschichte* des Herodot wird berichtet, dass die asiatischen Thraker eherne Helme und an denselben eherne Ochsenohren und Hörner mit Büschen trugen. Das Vorkommen dieser Art des Helmschmucks[60] wäre damit im 5. Jahrhundert bei den thrakischen Stämmen des nördlichen bis nordwestlichen Kleinasiens und der Propontis zu suchen. Dass die thrakische Pferdezucht seit Homer berühmt war und der Tierreichtum Thrakiens die Jagd zu einer Hauptbeschäftigung seiner Bewohner machte, ist bekannt[61], und so dürfte auch ein Anbringen von Pferde- oder Hirschohren[62] an den Helmen dieses kriegerischen Volkes nicht überraschen. In der Ilias werden die Thraker als Bundesgenossen der Troer genannt[63], wobei man die Thraker am Hellespont, den Stamm der Kikonen und jene Paeoniens unterscheidet. Von letzteren heisst es, dass sie sich als Bogenschützen bewährten. Über die Kikonen[64] wird dann in der Odyssee[65] berichtet, dass ihre Stadt Ismaros von Odysseus und seinen Gefährten zerstört wurde, als diese von Troja kommend an die thrakische Küste getrieben worden waren. Weiter überliefert das Epos[66], dass die Kikonen Vergeltung übten und noch vor Sonnenuntergang den Sieg über die Achäer errangen, die sie in die Flucht schlugen, nachdem sie eine Anzahl der Unglücklichen im Kampf getötet hatten. Der Reichtum der Thraker an landwirtschaftlichen Gütern und Edelmetallen ist durch das Epos sowie durch archäologisches Fundmaterial belegt[67]. Wenn nun, wie angenommen wird, "der 10. Gesang der Ilias wie auch die anderen die Thraker betreffenden Episoden der Odyssee spätere Zusätze zum Homerischen Epos sind, die den Kampf der griechischen Kolonisten mit den thrakischen Stämmen, die im 7.–6. Jahrhunderts v. Chr. an der ägäischen Küste wohnten, wiedergeben"[68], dürfte das für eine Darstellung dieser ins Mythische einbezogenen Thrakerkämpfe auf einem Kunstwerk des 6. Jahrhunderts nichts Negatives aussagen. Überschaut man daraufhin noch einmal die Aussenseiten der vorliegenden Schale, so ist man versucht, aus der Darstellung eine Deutung und damit einen bestimmten Inhalt herauszulesen. Das Geschehen der griechischen Kolonisation mit ihren Kämpfen und Begegnungen mit fremden Völkern und Kulturen hat sich in geistiger und künstlerischer Beziehung auf die griechischen Volksstämme ausgewirkt, wobei sich das aus dem jüngeren Erlebnis gebildete Sagengut mit dem älteren der griechischen Vorzeit verbunden haben mochte. Ist die Kontamination des Thrakererlebnisses mit den Epen Homers ein literarischer Beweis dafür, so könnte die Handlung auf der Schalenfläche den künstlerischen Beweis liefern. Gemeinsam mit den Troern, von denen die Ilias[69] Hektor als den Held mit dem flatternden Helmbusch bezeichnet, kämpfen die thrakischen Bundesgenossen, die sich als Krieger mit Ohren-oder Hörnerhelmen sowie als Bogenschützen zu erkennen geben. Einer der Vornehmsten unter ihnen ist mit dem Pferdegespann in die Schlacht gefahren. Ihr Kampf gilt den achäischen

Eindringlingen, die sie in blutiger Schlacht des Landes verweisen. Auf die Troer wird man die mit hohem Helmbusch ausgestatteten Hopliten beziehen, während man ihre achäischen Gegner in jenen Kriegern sehen möchte, die bis auf zwei Ausnahmen mit niedrigem Helmbusch versehen wurden.

Im Detail seiner Darstellung zeigt der Vasenmaler äusserste Genauigkeit, wie es die fein und sauber durchgeführte Ornamentierung an Panzern, Chitonen, Schildbügeln und Pferdegeschirr beweist und wie es die durchweg korrekte Angabe des gebrochenen Auges der tödlich Verwundeten erkennen lässt, bei welcher der Maler jeweils nur einen schmalen Schlitz einritzt. Nach alledem scheint sich die Annahme zu verdichten, dass hier ein attischer Vasenmaler in seiner Bilderzählung eine Darstellung wählte, die nicht den Ruhm der griechischen Helden preist, sondern die Kraft und den Kampfesmut der kriegerischen Thraker und ihrer kleinasiatischen Bundesgenossen zur Anschauung bringt. Vielleicht war die Schale als Grabbeigabe für einen Toten kleinasiatischer oder thrakischer Abstammung bestimmt gewesen. Dass der Künstler bei der Darstellung seiner Krieger von keiner festen Vorstellung ausgegangen sein sollte und nur rein zufällig den siegreichen Hopliten diese relativ seltene Art des Helmschmucks beigab, dürfte kaum glaubhaft erscheinen. Hier jedoch sind unserem Interpretationsversuch Grenzen gesetzt, und so wird man die Vorlage jener künstlerisch und inhaltlich besonders interessanten Schale nur mit einer offenen Frage abschliessen können.

ANMERKUNGEN

1 London B 380 und B 379 (*ABV* 55, Nr. 91, und 60, Nr. 20).

2 *JHS* 49, 1929, 260. Vgl. zum Schalentyp auch A. Greifenhagen, *Eine attische schwarzfigurige Vasengattung,* Königsberg Pr. 1929, 16 ff., Gattung C und D.

3 Vgl. Beazley, *JHS* 51, 1931, 275–282 (The Heidelberg Group); derselbe, *MetrSt* 5, 1934, 93–106, 108, 110–113; F. Villard, *Revue des Études Anciennes* 48, 1946, 157–159 (Ib); Beazley, *The Development of Attic Black-Figure,* Berkeley 1951, 21–23 und 50–52; *ABV* 51–75; *Paralipomena* 23–29; J.M. Hemelrijk, *BABesch* 46, 1971, 113 f. und 117, Fig. 15; Trendall, *Logie Collection,* Nr. 18/19, Pl. 7–9.

4 *JHS* 51, 1931, 275; *Development* (oben Anm. 3), 21 und 50. Zur Verbindung der beiden Dekorationsweisen: 'double-decker' und 'overlap' auf einer Schale vgl. *JHS* 49, 1929, 260.

5 Payne, *NC,* 194, 197–200, Pl. 51, 1–2 und 4–6, Pl. 52, 1; Beazley, *MetrSt* 5, 1934, 100–102; derselbe, *Hesperia* 13, 1944, 46–50; *Development* (oben Anm. 3), 21; Villard a. O. (oben Anm. 3), 157. Eine Literatur-Zusammenstellung zu den Komasten und Komastenschalen bei K. Schauenburg, *CVA* Heidelberg 1, Text 70 zu Taf. 43, 1–2.

6 Vgl. Beazley, *MetrSt* 5, 1934, 93.

7 Vgl. *ABV* (oben Anm. 3).

8 C = 'Corinthianizing' [Beazley, *MetrSt* 5, 1934, 100; *Development* (oben Anm. 3), 21].

9 Benannt nach zwei in der Heidelberger Universitätssammlung befindlichen Schalen des 'double-decker' Typs Inv. S 61 und S 5 (*CVA* 4, Taf. 149/150 und Taf. 151, 1, 3–4).

10 Dass sich die Arbeiten des C-Malers nicht nur den monotonen Gruppen spätkorinthischer Vasen anschliessen, sondern darüberhinaus auch die feine Miniaturmalerei des Protokorinthischen erkennen lassen, hat Beazley an einer Dreifusspyxis im Louvre [*Development* (oben Anm. 3), Taf. 8, 1 und Taf. 9] aufgezeigt. Zu der den Werken des C-Malers eigenen Farbigkeit vgl. Beazley, *Development,* 21. Einen Hinweis auf das allerdings Nicht-Korinthische spezifisch Attische in Ton, Maltechnik und Schema der Schalendekoration gibt Beazley, *MetrSt* 5, 1934, 100–102.

11 Dazu Beazley, *Development* (oben Anm. 3), 21–25. Vgl. zur Troilos-Schale, New York, auch D. von Bothmer, *BMMA* 31, 1972, Nr. 5. Dass die Anfänge der Sagendarstellungen in der griechischen Kunst

bereits in spätgeometrische Zeit hinaufreichen, wurde von K. Fittschen, *Untersuchungen zum Beginn der Sagendarstellungen bei den Griechen,* Berlin 1969, 199–201, zusammenfassend nachgewiesen.

12 Vgl. H. von Steuben, *Frühe Sagendarstellungen in Korinth und Athen,* Berlin 1968, 77. Anders H. Cahn, *Kunstwerke der Antike* (Katalog Auktion 40 v. 13.12.69), Basel 1969, zu Nr. 58.

13 Zur Verwandtschaft der Werke von Heidelberg-Maler und Amasis-Maler vgl. Beazley, *Development* (oben Anm. 3), 50.

14 Vas. Inv. 4516. Aus Griechenland. H: 14,5 cm; Dm. mit Henkeln: 33,7 cm; ohne Henkel: 25,5 cm; Dm. des Innenmedaillons: 15,9 cm. P. Jacobsthal, *Göttinger Vasen,* Berlin 1912, 39/40, 9b; Neugebauer, *Führer* II, Vasen 66; Beazley, *MetrSt* 5, 1934, 105, Nr. 28; *ABV* 52, Nr. 27; B. Fehr, *Orientalische und griechische Gelage,* Bonn 1971, 143, Nr. 61, IIIB Typus M(3). C-Maler; um 570 v. Chr.

15 Zum Dorn im Fuss der Schalen des C-Malers vgl. *CVA* Mainz 1, Text 44 zu Taf. 41, 3–4. Zum Dorn an attisch schwarzfigurigen Schalen vgl. *CVA* Kassel 1, Text 50 zu Taf. 29, 1 u. 5.

16 Zum Schalen-Innenmedaillon vgl. Beazley, *Development* (oben Anm. 3), 21, Anm. 43.

17 Vgl. Beazley, *Development* (oben Anm. 3), 22.

18 Die Bezeichnungen 'nach links gelagert' oder 'Linksrichtung des Lagerns' bedeuten, dass die Dargestellten mit den Beinen nach links lagern. R. Lullies, *CVA* Kassel 1, Text 50 zu Taf. 30, 1 (Sianaschale T.387) spricht von dunkelroten Decken, mit denen sich die Symposiasten bis zur Brust bedeckt haben. Es handelt sich jedoch auch hier um Mäntel.

19 Zur Darstellungsweise des Unterkörpers der liegenden Figur in der frühgriechischen Flächenkunst vgl. Jacobsthal a.O. (oben Anm. 14), Symposiaka, 36 ff., und neuerdings Fehr a.O. (oben Anm. 14), 27 u. 131 ff. Zum Schlingenband und seiner Verwendung als Textilmuster vgl. A. Kloss, *Mitteilungen des deutschen archäologischen Instituts* 5, 1952, 83, Abb. All. u. S. 88.

20 Zwei der Dargestellten zeigen den Gestus des Grusses und Sprechens, bezeichnet durch erhobene Hand mit vorgestreckten Fingern (vgl. C. Sittl, *Die Gebärden der Griechen und Römer,* 1890, 285, I, 1; G. Neumann, *Gesten und Gebärden,* Berlin 1965, 10 und 41 ff.). Der dem Gelagerten am nächsten Stehende rechts hat drei Finger der Hand geschlossen und scheint in deiktischem Gestus auf seinen Gesprächspartner hinzuweisen (Neumann, a.O. 17 ff.).

21 Zur schriftlichen Ueberlieferung des Sitzens und Liegens beim Mahl in frühgriechischer Zeit sowie zu den ersten griechischen Gelagedarstellungen auf korinthischen Vasen: Typus M(3) und dessen Einfluss-nahme auf den attischen Paralleltypus des zweiten Viertels des 6. Jahrhunderts vgl. Fehr (oben Anm. 14), 26 ff. und 54 ff. Zur Uebernahme der orientalischen Sitte des Liegens beim Mahl und ihrem frühesten Nachweis im Aeolischen vgl. R.N. Thönges-Stringaris, *AM* 80, 1965, 5 ff. Fehr, a.0. 16 ff. und 24, vermutet den Ursprung der Sitte des Lagerns beim Mahl bei den iranischen Reiternomaden, von wo eine Uebernahme durch den assyrischen Hof erfolgte. Zu Sitte und Ikonographie des "banquet couché" in der orientalischen und griechischen Kunst vgl. auch J.M. Dentzer, RA 1971 II, 215 ff.

22 Um eine Fransenborte handelt es sich, soweit an dem verblassten Weiss erkennbar, nur bei der linken Klinendecke. Die beiden anderen Decken werden von einer weissen Mäanderborte gesäumt.

23 Vgl. H. Kyrieleis, *JdI,* 24. *Ergänzungsheft,* 1969, 116 ff., wonach die Klinenbeine der vorliegenden Schale der Gruppe IIIB Möbelbeintypus A (Abb. 22 c) zuzuordnen sind. Zum urartäischen Vorbild für die archaisch-griechischen Möbelbeine des Typus A vgl. Kyrieleis, a.O. 121 f.

24 An der Decke der ersten Kline rechts Mäanderborte, sonst Fransen.

25 F.1755. Aus Griechenland (wahrscheinlich Athen). H.: 13,8 cm; Dm.: 25, 8 cm; Dm. des Innen-medaillons: 17,4 cm. Furtwängler, *Beschreibung der Vasensammlung,* Berlin 1885, XIV und 288 f., Nr. 1755; Pfuhl, *MuZ* I, 277; E. Buschor, 'Meermänner', *Sitzungsberichte München* 1941, 28 (Seinsbild); Beazley, *MetrSt* 5, 1934, 105, Nr. 29; *ABV,* 53, Nr. 32; Kyrieleis (oben Anm. 23), 117, Anm. 481; Fehr (oben Anm. 14), 144, Nr. 67 IIIB Typus M(3). C-Maler; um 570 v. Chr.

26 Selten erscheint Triton als Innenbild der Sianaschalen, vgl. hierzu :die Schalen Rhodos, *ABV,* 52, Nr. 16,

und Hannover, Kestner-Museum 1959.1, *Paralipomena,* 24, Nr. 32 *bis* (*CVA* 1, Taf. 29, 1–2). Buschor (oben Anm. 25), 28 ff. unterscheidet bei den archaischen Tritondarstellungen zwei Hauptbilder: das einfache Seinsbild und das verschlungene Kampfbild. Zu Bildtyp und Sage des Nereus und Triton in der frühgriechischen Vasenmalerei vgl. Steuben (oben Anm. 12), 30 f.

27 Vgl. Anm. 23.

28 Vgl. Anm. 19.

29 Der Versuch, durch Umwenden des Kopfes eines Gelagerten sowie durch das Einfügen stehender Gestalten die Monotonie der in gleicher Richtung gereihten Zecher und Klinen zu unterbrechen, ist offensichtlich; vgl. Fehr (oben Anm. 14), 55.

30 Furtwängler (oben Anm. 25), 289, bezeichnet irrtümlich die beiden Gestalten rechts und links des mittleren Gelagerten als Frauen. Dass eine stehende Frau bei den Symposia der Typen M(3) und M(2) während der ersten Jahrhunderthälfte ungewöhnlich ist, wird von Fehr (oben Anm. 14), 56, vermerkt.

31 Vgl. Anm. 20.

32 Vas.Inv.3402. Aus Griechenland. H.: 14,5 cm; Dm. mit Henkeln: 34,3 cm; ohne Henkel: 25 cm; Dm. des Innenmedaillons: 14,3 cm. W. Wrede, *AM* 41, 1916, 369,4; Neugebauer, *Führer* II, Vasen 65; Beazley, *ABV,* 67 unten; D. von Bothmer, *Amazons in Greek Art,* Oxford 1957, II, 29, S. 9 und 21; F. Brommer, *Vasenlisten zur griechischen Heldensage,* Marburg 1960, (1), 11, 195, (2), 15, 195, (3), 18, 1; Beazley, a.O.: 'related to the Heidelberg Painter: it also recalls the C Painter, whose influence may be seen in several of the Heidelberg Painter's works.' Der von Beazley angegebene Fundort 'Corinth' ist nicht zu belegen. Um 560–550 v. Chr.

33 Zur Anordnung der beiden freiherabhängenden Tatzen des Löwenfells als Ausweis älterer und späterer attisch schwarzfiguriger Typologie vgl. Bothmer (oben Anm. 32), 15 ff.

34 Dass sich der Knielauf des Herakles hier ebenso wie auf der Schale Neapel 2454 [Bothmer (oben Anm. 32), 8, 28] aus der Bildkomposition innerhalb einer festumgrenzten Kreisfläche ergibt, bedarf keiner Erklärung. Dennoch zeigt das Berliner Schalenbild gegenüber der Schale Neapel und vornehmlich gegenüber der Schale New York 12.234.1 (Bothmer a.O. 8, 27 und Pl. 17, 2) eine bereits wesentlich gelöstere Bewegung. In derartigen zweifigurigen Schaleninnenbildern des 6. Jahrhunderts erfolgt die künstlerische Auseinandersetzung mit einer in neuem Rahmen sich entwickelnden Komposition des Handlungsbildes (vgl. dazu auch E. Homann-Wedeking, in *Studies presented to David Moore Robinson,* St. Louis 1953, II, 36 f.).

35 Zur literarischen Ueberlieferung des Herakles-Amazonenabenteuers und der davon abweichenden bildlichen Fassung vgl. F. Brommer, *Herakles,* Münster-Köln 1953, 35 ff., und *Gnomon* 30, 1958, 353.

36 Dass die Lanze die bevorzugte Waffe der Andromache in den schwarzfigurigen Vasendarstellungen ist, kann nicht bezweifelt werden, daneben begegnen jedoch auch Kampfszenen, in denen sie das Schwert führt (Brommer, *Gnomon* 30, 1958, 346).

37 Häufig die Darstellungsweise, bei der Herakles nach dem Helmbusch der Gegnerin greift.

38 Zur Tracht der Bogenschützen und ihrer asiatischen jedoch nicht unbedingt skythischen Herkunft vgl. A. Schaumberg, *Bogen und Bogenschütze bei den Griechen,* Nürnberg 1910, 142 f; M.F. Vos, *Scythian Archers in archaic Attic Vase-painting* (1963).

39 Zu den Tierohren an Helmen vgl. *CVA* New York 2, Text 16 zur Augenschale 44.11.1; dazu die Bauchamphora Hannover, Kestner-Museum 1936, 107 (*CVA* 1, Taf. 7, 3 und Text 20). Zum apotropäischen Charakter des Helmbusches sowie zu den Feder-, Ohren-, und Hörnerhelmen vgl. E. Kukahn, *Der griechische Helm,* 1936, 51. Zum Federschmuck an Helmen vgl. Wrede, *AM* 41, 1916, 369 ff.

40 Neumann (oben Anm. 20), 70.

41 Eine bisher noch unpublizierte Schale dieses Typs befindet sich in Münster, Archäologisches Museum Inv. 579. Ihre Kenntnis verdanke ich der Freundlichkeit von K.P. Stähler.

42 Dazu R.N. Thönges-Stringaris, (wie Anm. 21), 3 ff. A. Effenberger, *Forschungen und Berichte* 14,

1972, 136 ff., wo Darstellungen rein 'irdischer' Zechgelage von solchen unterschieden werden, 'die mythisches oder erhöhtes Sein ausdrücken'.

43 Dass sich auch die Gelageszene des viel zitierten Eurytioskraters (Paris, Louvre E 635, Payne, *NC*, Nr. 780, Taf. 27) in ihrer Bildtypik nicht von den Symposia gewöhnlicher Menschen unterscheidet und ihren mythischen Charakter nur durch die Namensbeischriften erhält, wurde von Fehr (oben Anm. 14), 31 u. 130 mit Recht hervorgehoben.

44 Vgl. Thönges-Stringaris (oben Anm. 21), 19 u. 63; Effenberger, a.O. (oben Anm. 42), 162.

45 Zu den Symposionspeisen auch H. von Fritze, *AM* 21, 1896, 349 ff.

46 Dass es sich bei den länglichen flachen Fladen jeweils links neben den Pyramides um Fleisch handeln dürfte, lehrt die Darstellung auf einem böotisch sf. Schüsseldeckel in Schloss Fasanerie Nr. 120 (F. Brommer, *Antike Kleinkunst,* Marburg 1955, Abb. 11; *CVA* 2, Taf. 63 u. 64, 1–2), wo entsprechende Fleischstücke um Spiesse gewickelt zum Braten hergerichtet werden. Die dazu in Vorschlag gebrachte Deutung auf Obeliaskuchen muss nach Art der dargestellten Szenen zweifellos abgelehnt werden (vgl. Brommer, *CVA* 2, Text 22). Zu Brot und Fleisch auf den Speisetischen rf. Symposiondarstellungen vgl. Beazley, in *Studies presented to David Moore Robinson,* St Louis 1953, II, 78 u. 80.

47 Zum Trinkhorn als barbarischem wohl ursprünglich skythischem Trinkgefäss vgl. Fehr (oben Anm. 14), 30 f.

48 Vgl. Buschor, *GV,* 64.

49 Vgl. W. Jaeger, *Paideia* I, 1936, 190. Zur Darstellung von Pferden und Pferdeköpfen auf den späteren Totenmahlreliefs als Hinweis auf den gehobenen gesellschaftlichen Stand des Verstorbenen vgl. zuletzt Fehr (oben Anm. 14), 234, Anm. 804.

50 So auch Fehr (oben Anm. 14), 129 und Dentzer, a.O. 251–254.

51 Der erste grossplastische Typus der gelagerten Figur, die Gestalt rechts auf der Geneleosbasis, wird von Fehr (oben Anm. 14), 120 ff., auch als das Bild eines Symposiasten gedeutet, nachdem N. Himmelmann-Wildschütz, *Marburger Winckelmann-Programm* 1963, 13 ff., den überzeugenden Nachweis erbrachte, dass es sich hier um eine männliche Figur handelt. Vgl. dazu auch K. Schefold, *Die Griechen und ihre Nachbarn,* Berlin 1967, 168, Nr. 33c.

52 Vgl. die Bronzen des östlichen und westlichen Liegeschemas [Fehr (oben Anm. 14), Nr. 526–540], denen die unpublizierte Bronzestatuette eines gelagerten Mannes aus Samos im östlichen Liegeschema (Berlin Staatl. Museen, Antiken-Sammlung Sa.116) hinzuzufügen wäre.

53 Eine Lagerung in entgegengesetzter Richtung erscheint relativ selten, hierzu: der nach rechts gelagerte Symposiast auf A. der Schale Cambridge 37.19 (ARV^2 135, 13), der Aulosspieler vom Schulterbild der Kalpis Bonn Inv.70 (ARV^2 28, 12 u. 1608), die Schaleninnenbilder London, Brit.Mus. E 37 (ARV^2 72, 17 u. 1623), Baltimore, Robinson Coll. (ARV^2 75, 56 u. 1624), Adria, Museo Civico B.485 (ARV^2 110, 11 u. 1626), Würzburg 472 (ARV^2 137), Heidelberg 147 (ARV^2 916, 178); die nach rechts Lagernden in Rückansicht: Florenz, Mus.Arch. 4221 (ARV^2 119), Oxford 1929.466 (ARV^2 911, 73), Palermo, Museo Nazionale V.662 (ARV^2 812, 57), Mannheim, Reiss-Mus. 62 (ARV^2 866, 2 Cat-and-Dog Painter), Leningrad, Ermitage 661 (*Paralipomena,* 516 Splanchnopt Painter 82), die Fragmente ARV^2 354, 26, sowie der lagernde Hephaistos im Bilde des Kelchkraters Fasanerie 77 (ARV^2 1346, 1 Kekrops Painter) bestätigen darüberhinaus ganz eindeutig, dass man die Vorderansicht eines Gelagerten nur in dem besagten Schema der Linksrichtung wiedergab. Das Redwarefragment im Brit.Mus. B.186 [Jacobsthal (oben Anm. 14), 38, Abb. 64] beweist nichts Gegenteiliges, da sich hier die Rechtsrichtung nur durch die Umkehr beim Ausdrücken aus der Form ergab (vgl. dazu H. Bahlow, *Untersuchungen zur frühgriechischen Flächenkunst,* Liegnitz 1926, 49). Zu den vom Kopfende her gesehenen Klinendarstellungen vgl. Jacobsthal, a.O. 56 ff., und Fehr (oben Anm. 14), 173, Nr. 424–429, denen der zu ebener Erde gelagerte Jüngling Hannover, Kestner-Mus. 1966,99 (*CVA* 1, Taf. 34, 2) und der Symposiast rechts im Bilde des Glockenkraters Syrakus Mus.

Naz. 43927 (*CVA* 1, III I, Taf. 13, 3) anzuschliessen wären. Zum Schwarzfigurigen: die Lekythoi Wien, Sammlung Matsch (*CVA* 1, Taf. 5, 4 — Dionysos) und Palermo, Coll. Mormino 101 (*CVA* 1, III H, Taf. 12, 4 — Aulosspielerin) sowie die etruskisch sf. Amphora Kopenhagen Mus.Nat. 3794 (*CVA* 5, Taf. 217, 4a).

54 Vgl. J.M. Davison, *Yale Classical Studies* 16, 1961, Abb. 1—3, 23, 25—26, 28—29, 35—36, 50, 111a, 139; Sydney, Nicholson Mus. 49.41 (H. Marwitz, 'Das Bahrtuch', *AuA* 10, 1961, Taf. 2, 4). Dazu auch W. Zschietzschmann, *AM* 53, 1928, 19, 22, 24 (mit Ausnahme S. 33, Anm. 5); J. Boardman, *BSA* 50, 1955, 51—66 ('Painted Funerary Plaques'); E. Hinrichs, *Annales Universitatis Saraviensis* 4, 1955, 124—147; M. Andronikos, *Archaeologia Homerica III (Totenkult),* Göttingen 1968, W 45—51. Dass der Leichnam stets mit den Füssen nach der Tür zu aufgebahrt wurde, ist aus der Textstelle bei Homer, *Ilias* XIX, 212, zu erschliessen, so Zschietzschmann a.O., 24, Anm. 3, und R. Hampe, *Die Gleichnisse Homers und die Bildkunst seiner Zeit,* Tübingen 1952, 24. In entgegengesetzter Richtung erscheint der gelagerte Tote in der Ekphora-Szene eines sf. Kyathos Paris, Bibl. Nat. 353 (*CVA* 2, Taf. 71, 9 u. 72, 3). Links- und Rechtslagerung von Toten, allerdings nicht als aufgebahrte sondern als auf dem Schiffsverdeck liegende Leichen, zeigen die Bruchstücke eines geometrischen Kraters Brüssel u. Athen (E. Kunze, in *Festschrift Schweitzer,* Stuttgart 1954, 49 ff. Taf. 4).

55 Zum Verhältnis der Körperteile frühgriechischer Figuren zueinander und zu ihrer Erscheinung in der Fläche vgl. H. Marwitz, 'Das Raumproblem in der frühgriechischen Kunst', in *Festschrift W. Gross,* München 1968, 39 ff. Die abweichende Typik des aufgebahrten, an eine Mumie erinnernden Toten auf dem Kraterfragment Athen NM 812 führte J.L. Benson, *Horse, Bird and Man,* Amherst 1970, 88 ff., zur ikonographischen Herleitung des geometrischen Prothesisschemas aus dem Aegyptischen. Dass ägyptische Darstellungen jedoch nicht an die Einhaltung einer bestimmten Richtung gebunden sind, sondern der Tote auch nach rechts gelagert erscheint (Benson a.O., Taf. 29—4, 30—2, 31—2) darf nicht übersehen werden.

56 H. Wölfflin, *Münchner Jahrbuch der bildenden Kunst* N. F. 5, 1928, 218.

57 Vgl. Zschietzschmann, a.O. (oben Anm. 54), 25.

58 Wölfflin, a.O. (oben Anm. 56), 214.

59 Dazu K. Friis Johansen, *The Iliad in Early Greek Art,* Copenhagen 1967, 46, 191, 223—230. Steuben (oben Anm. 12), 49.

60 Als typisch jonisch bezeichnet von E. Kukahn (oben Anm. 39), 51; anders R.M. Cook, *CVA* Brit. Mus. 8, Text 51 zu den Darstellungen auf klazomenischen Sarkophagen der Albertinum-Gruppe. Als wahrscheinlich pisidischer Brauch gedeutet von A.—B. Follmann, *CVA* Hannover 1 (vgl. oben Anm. 39).

61 Vgl. G. Kazarow, *RE²* XI, 401.

62 Zu Pferde- oder Hirschohren an Helmen vgl. auch Beazley-Magi, *RG,* 26 f. zu Nr. 14.

63 *Ilias* II, 844—849; IV, 519—538; X, 434 ff.

64 Vgl. Kazarow (oben Anm. 61), 406.

65 *Odyssee* IX, 39 f.

66 *Odyssee* IX, 58—61.

67 Vgl. dazu auch D.P. Dimitrov, *Kunstschätze in bulgarischen Museen und Klöstern, Ausstellungskatalog Villa Hügel 1964,* 35 ff., und neuerdings M.I. Venedikov, *Découverte de l'art thrace, Ausstellungskatalog Paris, Petit Palais 1974.*

68 So Dimitrov (oben Anm. 67), 36.

69 *Ilias* II, 816.

DAS MOTIV DER *CHIMAIROPHONOS* IN DER KUNST UNTERITALIENS

K. Schauenburg

Tafeln 40, 41.

Die Oinochoe Kiel, Kunsthalle B 509 konnte 1971 für die Kieler Antikensammlung erworben werden (Taf. 40, Abb. 1, 2).[1] Sie hat die Form III, ist ungebrochen und auch in der Bemalung gut erhalten.

Die Bildzone der Kanne wird oben von einem Kymation, unten von einem Kreuzplatten-mäander begrenzt. Ungewöhnlich ist, dass am linken Ende des oberen Ornamentbandes eine Öse angebracht ist, von der drei überaus dünne Bänder herabhängen. Das Ornament erhält damit eine gegenständliche Bedeutung,[2] ist in die Handlung mit einbezogen. Vor der Bemalung wurden an den Rändern der für den Mäander vorgesehenen Zone und etwa in der halben Höhe der Kanne drei umlaufende Rillen angebracht, die auch noch unter dem Firnis erkennbar sind. Am linken Ende ist der Mäander nicht senkrecht, sondern schräg abgeschnitten.

Zwei hoch aufschiessende Ranken dienen als Rahmen des Bildfrieses, während zwei weitere, die niedriger sind, zwischen die drei Figuren gesetzt sind.[3] Das Bild zeigt den zwischen einem Silen und einer Mänade nach linkshin sitzenden Dionysos. Das felsige Gelände, auf das sich der Gott niedergelassen hat, ist durch zahlreiche kleine Steine angedeutet, wie dies auf italischen Vasen äusserst beliebt ist. Oft dienen demselben Zweck auch einfache Punktlinien.[4] Dionysos trägt die Mitra und hat seinen um den linken Unterarm geschlungenen Mantel über den linken Oberschenkel gelegt. An seiner Schulter lehnt der Thyrsos, der zugleich mit dem unteren Mantelsaum unvermittelt abschliesst und daher sehr kurz ist. In der angehobenen Rechten hält der Gott einer Kranz, über ihm ist eine Tänie ausgebreitet. Rechts von Dionysos hat ein bekränzter Silen, der in der Linken eine herabhängende Tänie trägt, seinen Fuss auf einen Felsen gestellt, während er sich mit dem rechten Ellenbogen auf sein Knie stützt. Er trägt hohe Stiefel mit leicht nach oben gebogener Spitze. Ganz links im Bilde steht, fast frontal wiedergegeben, eine Mänade mit Halskette und einem Kranz im Haar, von dem nur das Stück über der Stirn angegeben ist. Auf ihren kurzen Chiton sind zwei waagrechte schwarze Mäander-borten gesetzt. Dieselbe Färbung weist auch der untere Saum des Gewandes auf. Die Mänade hält auf der Linken ein Hirschkalb vor ihrem Körper und in der Rechten ein nach oben gewandtes Schwert.

Stilistisch wird die Oinochoe dem Leccemaler zugeschrieben.[5] Sie ist somit apulisch und wird um 380 entstanden sein. Besonders nahe steht ihr eine weitere Oinochoe derselben Form, die auch dem Leccemaler zugeschrieben wird. Sie befindet sich in Privatbesitz und kann hier mit freundlicher Erlaubnis des Besitzers veröffentlicht werden (Taf. 40, Abb. 3, 4).[6] Das wieder recht ungenau gemalte Mäanderband ist dem unserer Kanne sehr ähnlich. An die Stelle des Kymations, wie es die Kanne in Kiel zeigt, ist auf der zweiten Vase ein Palmettenornament getreten und an den Seiten ist jeweils eine schmale Leiste mit abwärts gewandten Hakenmuster angebracht.[7]

Auch auf unserer zweiten Kanne sitzt in der Mitte ein nackter Jüngling, der wieder von zwei Gestalten gerahmt ist. Hier handelt es sich aber nicht um eine mythische Szene. Der junge Mann ist bekränzt und hält dem vor ihm stehenden Mädchen eine Phiale mit Früchten entgegen. Er sitzt auf einer 'naturalistisch' wiedergegebenen felsigen Erhöhung, auf der flüchtig gemalte Pflanzen und weisse Punkte zu sehen sind.[8] Das vor ihm stehende Mädchen greift nach einer von der Phiale herabhängenden Tänie, während sie ihre rechte Hand in die Hüfte gestützt hat. Dieser Frau entspricht rechts eine weitere, deren Haar in einen Beutel gefasst ist. Ihre linke Hand ist wieder auf die Hüfte gelegt, während ihre rechte hinter dem Rücken des Jünglings verschwindet. Beide Frauen tragen Ohrringe, Halsketten und Armreifen. Ihre Gürtel sind, wie auch die Schmuckstücke, weiss gefärbt. Auch auf den schwarzen unteren Säumen und einem jeweils senkrecht verlaufenden schwarzen Streifen ihrer langen Chitone sind weisse Punkte aufgesetzt. Hinter der rechten Frau schiesst eine Ranke empor.

Unsere zweite Oinochoe ist durch dreierlei mit der Oinochoe in Kiel verwandt: durch die grossen Köpfe der Gestalten; durch das Dreiviertelprofil des in der Mitte sitzenden Jünglings, das an dasjenige der Mänade erinnert, und durch die Schuhe des rechten Mädchens, die von ähnlicher Form wie die des Silens der Kieler Kanne sind. Besonders zu beachten sind die Füsse und das rechte Bein des sitzenden Jünglings auf der zweite Oinochoe die unförmig und übergross sind.

Ikonographisch bietet die Kanne in Privatbesitz keine Besonderheiten. Dagegen stellt das von dem Maler der Oinochoe in Kiel für die Mänade gewählte Motiv ein Unikum dar. Dies ist umso bemerkenswerter, als Thiasosbilder und Grabszenen die beiden Hauptthemen unteritalischer Vasenmalerei sind. Schwert und Hirschkalb, die die Mänade trägt, gehören zum Typus der sogenannten *Chimairophonos.*[9] Dies Wort bezeichnet an sich die im Orgiasmus eine Ziege tötende Bacchantin.[10] Das mit den Bacchantinnen verbundene Tier ist aber auf attischen Vasen meist ein Hirschkalb, auf italischen vorwiegend ein Hase. Korrekterweise müsste man im ersten Fall von *Nebrophonos* sprechen, wenn das Wort in der antiken Literatur auch vorwiegend für den Adler belegt ist (Aristot., h. a. 9, 32. *Ant. Lib.* 20, 2) und nur bei Nonnos, *Dion.* 44, 198 Dionysos selbst bezeichnet. Für die Mänade mit dem Hasen liesse sich, soweit ich sehe, ein antikes Wort nicht beibringen. Der Beiname *Chimairophonos* ist inzwischen in der Fachsprache aber so eingebürgert, dass man ihn besser beibehalten wird. Die *Chimairophonos* kommt auch in Zusammenhang mit Darstellung der Tötung des Orpheus und des Pentheus vor.[11] Meistens hält die rasende Mänade nur ein halbes Zicklein oder Hirschkalb in der einen, das Schwert in der anderen Hand. Der Typus ist auf attischen Vasen von der spätarchaischen Zeit an nicht selten nachweisbar,[12] durch Nachbildungen aber auch für ein Reliefwerk klassischer Zeit bezeugt.[13] In der römischen Kunst ist es vor allem auf Lampen ausserordentlich verbreitet.[14] Handelt es sich um eine Einzelfigur, kann nicht mit Sicherheit entschieden werden, ob es sich um ein Excerpt aus der Pentheussage oder aus einem Thiasosbild handelt. Letzteres ist mir aber in der Regel wahrscheinlicher, da die Figur als solche nicht den Hauptteil der Sage vom Tod des thebanischen Königs erfasst, für diese also nicht eigentlich kennzeichnend ist. Dagegen ist sie ein voll verständlicher Hinweis auf besonders orgiastischen Dionysoskult. Auf der Pelike Berlin 3223, die um 470 von einem unbekannten Maler bemalt wurde, findet sich die *Chimairophonos* bei einer von der Bühne abgeleiteten Szene, ohne dass dem Vasenbild ein Hinweis auf den Zusammenhang, in dem die Figur auftrat, zu entnehmen wäre.[15] Schliesslich wurde dasselbe Schema auch für Dionysos selbst verwandt.[16]

In Unteritalien findet sich die *Chimairophonos,* abgesehen von der Pentheussage, wieder im Kreis des Dionysos.[17] Fast immer erscheint sie dabei in erregter Bewegung, auch wenn Dionysos selbst sitzend wiedergegeben wird (Taf. 41, Abb. 6).[18] Soweit ich sehe, kommt sie auf italischen Vasen nicht in Verbindung mit einem ebenfalls im Rausch dahinziehenden Dionysos vor. Auf dem apulischen Kelchkrater Bari 6269 folgt die Mänade mit Schwert und Tympanon in erregtem Tanz dem nach links schreitenden Gott. Soweit dieser sonst nicht sitzt, steht er inmitten seines erregten Gefolges. So zeigt ihn etwa der apulische Volutenkrater Genf 5036,[19] auf dem er der

Mänade, die in deutlicher Verzückung ihr Schwert schwingt und zusätzlich einen Thyrsostab hält, eine Glocke entegegenstreckt. Die Glocke oder Schelle ist ein nicht selten mit Dionysos,[20] Silenen[21] oder Mänaden[22] verbundenes Attribut, im dionysischen Bereich somit nicht so selten nachweisbar, wie F. Matz zuletzt meinte.[23] Auf unteritalischen Vasen ist das von den Mänaden gehaltene Tier häufig nicht zerstückelt, sondern noch unversehrt. Vereinzelt wird auch auf attischen und italischen Gefässen gezeigt, wie die Mänaden sich anschicken, das Tier zu Töten beziehungsweise zu zerschneiden.[24] Dasselbe Motiv findet sich auch noch auf römischen Denkmälern, so auf einer Lampe in London.[25] Mehrfach fehlt auf den italischen Vasen auch das Tier ganz, so auf dem Krater in Genf, den wir eben anführten, dem Kelchkrater Bari 6269 und der Gnathiapelike Neapel 82890.[26] Dann weist nur noch die Waffe auf den zugrundeliegenden Gedanken, denn nichts spricht dafür, dass diese etwa auf den Kampf der Mänaden mit Perseus[27] oder die Gigantomachie[28] hinweisen soll. Auf Tarentiner Grabreliefs sind dahinrasende Mänaden mit Schwert und Speer nicht selten.[29] Auch diese Bacchantinnen werden in den hier behandelten Zusammenhang gehören, wenn sie auch, soweit ich sehe, nie mit Tieren verbunden sind.[30] Von besonderer stilistischer Qualität ist eine lukanische Oinochoe in Metapont, auf der die vom Rausch erfasste Mänade in der einen Hand ein Schwert, in der anderen eine Schlange hält (Taf. 41, Abb. 5).[31] Die Schlange dient hier zur Kennzeichnung der wilden Natur der Bacchantin.[32]

Ein wesentlicher Unterschied zwischen attischen und unteritalischen Wiedergaben der *Chimairophonos* besteht, wie schon kurz erwähnt, darin, dass die ersteren die Mänaden vorwiegend mit dem Hirschkalb oder dem Zicklein zeigen, während die Mänaden auf den grossgriechischen Bildern meist mit Hasen versehen sind. Eine Ausnahme bildet die Neapler Lekanis (Taf. 41, Abb. 6).[33] Die römischen Künstler kehren in diesem Punkt zu der attischen Form zurück. Dies dürfte zu einem erheblichen Teil daran liegen, dass vom vorgerückten Hellenismus an das Reliefwerk des Kallimachos, das dies Motiv darstellte, sich besonderer Wertschätzung erfreute und durch die Neuattiker grosse Verbreitung erfuhr.[34] Während die Bedeutung des Bocks für den Thiasos oft behandelt wurde[35] und auch die Beziehungen von Hirsch und Dionysos vor allem in Zusammenhang mit einem Fragment des Alkaios mehrfach untersucht wurden,[36] überrascht der Hase zunächst. Er begegnet uns aber schon in der archaischen Keramik in dionysischen Kreis[37] und ist auf unteritalischen Gefässen nicht selten mit Dionysos und seinem Kreis verbunden.[38] So sehen wir unter dem Panthergespann des Dionysos auf der apulischen Amphora Neapel 1759 einen Hasen, der das Schema der dahinsprengenden Raubtiere imitiert. Man wird allerdings die Tiere, die sich auf italischen Vasen im Thiasos tummeln, nur sehr bedingt mit religiösen Vorstellungen erklären dürfen. Im allgemein sind sie als Hinweis auf die freie Natur zu verstehen.[39] Dagegen hat ihre Verbindung mit den Mänaden, wie sie in Typus der *Chimairophonos* vorliegt, noch eine andere Seite. Einmal weist sie darauf hin, dass die Mänaden auch als Jägerinnen galten,[40] zum anderen klingt dabei die Omophagie an. Die mit diesem Brauch verknüpften Vorstellungen reichen in alte religiöse Schichten zurück, wenn dies den Malern wohl auch nur in begrenztem Umfang bewusst gewesen sein dürfte. Dies gilt insbesondere für die Italiker. Nicht zuletzt deshalb geben sie den Mänaden meistens den Hasen anstelle der Wildziege oder des Hirschkalbs. Dabei ist jedoch nicht zu übersehen, dass die Omophagie als solche im Bereich der dionysischen Mysterien keineswegs in Vergessenheit geraten war.[41] Dasselbe gilt eher noch in stärkeren Umfang für den ekstatischen Rausch an sich, das orgiastische Dahinstürmen.

Zusammenfassend ist festzuhalten, dass die neue Oinochoe in Kiel eine Variante zu den zahllosen italischen Thiasosbildern bringt. Die Mänade ist zwar mit für die *Chimairophonos* typischen Kennzeichen versehen, erscheint selbst aber nicht rauschhaft bewegt und hält Schwert und Hirschkalb gewissemassen demonstrativ wie Attribute vor sich. Dies wird besonders deutlich bei dem nach oben gewandten Schwert. Schwert und Hirschkalb sind hier in gewissem Sinn ähnlich verwandt wie das Rad, das den Myrtilos auf dem campanischen Krater Neapel 3227 kennzeichnet.[42] Auch dort ist keine eigentliche Handlung wiedergegeben, so dass die Deutung auf Pelops und Myrtilos in Zweifel gezogen werden konnte.[43] Unsere Betrachtungen der *Chimairophonos* zogen, soweit sie sich auf Unteritalien beschränkten, ausschliesslich apulische Gefässe zum Vergleich heran. Wie in manchen früheren ikonographischen Untersuchungen zeigt sich somit erneut, dass die einzelnen grossen Fabriken unteritalischer Keramik oft eine eigene Thematik entwickelten.[44]

ANMERKUNGEN

1   H. 22 cm. Die Aufnahmen stammen von Photo Widmer.

2   Vgl. Hierzu Paul Jacobsthal, *Ornamente griechischer Vasen*, Berlin 1927, 29, 87 ff., v.a. 89. Weitere Lit. bei Schauenburg, *RM* 64, 1957, 205 f. Nicht ganz so ausgeprägt ist die Belebung des Ornaments auf Vasen wie der Kanne Schauenburg, *RM* 81, 1974, 313 ff. Taf. 175 u. W. Hornbostel u. Mitarbeiter, *Kunst der Antike*, Katalog Hamburg 1977 Nr. 304, Privatbesitz.

3   Zu derartigen Ranken auf unteritalischen Vasen, Schauenburg, *AA* 1976, 225.

4   Auf attischen Vasen ist diese Art der Geländewiedergabe selten: *CVA* Oxford, 1, III I, zu Taf. 4, 7 f. (Beazley).

5   *RVAp* p. 126, no. 5/230.

6   *RVAp* p. 126, no. 5/231, pl. 41, 3. Die Vermittlung der Aufnahmen verdanke ich H. Humbel, Zürich.

7   Zu diesem Ornament auf italischen Kannen, Schauenburg, *RM* 79, 1972, 319 f.

8   Vgl. den kleinen Fels auf dem Krater, Oxford 1879.211 (V 434) *RVAp* p. 124, no. 5/202.

9   Diese Bezeichnung ist seit langem in der Archäologensprache eingebürgert, antik aber nur selten bezeugt: *Anthologia Palatina* IX, 774; Mänade des Skopas: Picard, *Manuel* III, 1, 734 ff.

10 Zur mythologischen Seite, s.u.a. Roscher, *ML* I, 1, s.v. Dionysos, 1037 ff. (Thraemer); Roscher, *ML* II, 2, 2250 f. (Rapp); Picard, *BCH* 70, 1946, 464 f., Ursprung in Kreta; Martin Nilsson, GGR², I, München 1955, 564 ff. Wichtig als literarische Quelle der Vorstellungen natürlich Euripides, *Bacchen,* v.a. 139, 704 f., 737 f. Vgl. für Dionysos hier Anm. 15.

11 Hubert Philippart, *Iconographie des Bacchantes d'Euripide*, Paris 1930; *Monumentum Chilonense, Festschrift E. Burck,* Amsterdam 1975, 550 f. (Schauenburg).

12 Früh die Makronschale, *ARV²* 478, 312, Louvre. Vgl. weiter u.a.: *ARV²* 649, 42, Lekythos in Syrakus; *ARV²* 987, 2, und *Paralipomena,* 437, 2, Sitzamphora der Bibliothèque Nationale, Paris; *ArchDelt* 19 A, 1964, Taf. 45 ff., Oinochoenfrgte, aus Kavalla; Graef-Langlotz, II, Taf. 54, 717, Oinochoenfrgt.

13 Werner Fuchs, *Die Vorbilder der neuattischen Reliefs*, Berlin 1959, 73 ff., 83 ff., 88 ff. *BCH* 90, 1966, 765, Abb. 25, Relieffrgt. aus Korinth. Jetzt dazu J. Dörig, *Art antique*, Genf – Mainz 1975, zu Nr. 3. Ara im Vatikan, Gall. Lapidaria 2278.

14 G. Heres, *Die römischen Tonlampen der Berliner Antiken-Sammlung*, Berlin 1972, 21, zu Nr. 37. Vgl. auch Philippart a.O. (oben Anm. 11), 43 f. Dazu u.a. noch Lampen in Barcelona, Cambridge (Corpus Christi College), Volterra. *NSc* 1922, 15, Abb. 16 g, Este. Brüssel, Musée du Cinquantenaire 615. Villa Giulia (ex Castellani). Fernand de Cadaillac, *De quelques lampes antiques découvertes dans l'Afrique du nord,* 48, Abb. 51. Worms R 3793. Vgl. auch F. Matz, *Die Antiken Sarkophagreliefs* IV 1, Berlin 1968, 18 f., für attische Sarkophage. 1 Lampe im Louvre, 2 Lampen in Köln, Römisch-Germanisches Zentralmuseum. La Baume, *Gymn.* 78, 1977 Taf. 13, Grabrelief in Köln. Ara in Terracina (3 Mänaden, eine mit Hase). E. Baggio, *Sculture e mosaici del museo di Oderzo* (1976) 131 f., Basis. *ArchDelt* 27, 1972, (77) Taf. 325 unten, Gemmen.

15 *ARV²* 586, 47, Berlin. Erika Simon, *Das Antike Theater,* Heidelberg 1972, Taf. 1.

16 *ARV²* 298, Dörig, *JdI* 80, 1965, 183, Abb. 33, Stamnos in London; *ARV²* 585, 34, Pelike in London; *ARV²* 592, 33, Kraterfrgt. in Amsterdam; *ARV²* 605, 65 bis, Hydriafrgt. in Privatbesitz; *Encyclopédie Photographique de l'Art* III, 41 D, wg. Kyathosfrgt. im Louvre. Zur Bedeutung, A.B. Cook, *Zeus* I, 1914, 654 ff.; Erika Simon, *Opfernde Götter,* Berlin 1953, 52 ff. *CVA* Gela, Slg. Navarra 3, Taf. 34, 4, Lekythos (im *CVA* falsch beschrieben).

17 Amphora Neapel 3220 (Dareiosmaler) Herrmann-Bruckmann, *Denkmäler der Malerei,* München 1906–44, 157, Abb. 46; Glockenkrater Zürich 3585, *APS* 34, no. 14, *RVAp* I, 50, no. 3/34; Kolonettenkrater, Kopenhagen 3633, *APS* 35, no. 22, *RVAp* I, 51, no. 3/41; Glockenkrater Neapel 2013; Glockenkrater, Nocera, Fienga 521 (jetzt Soprintendenza, Salerno), *RVAp* I, 72, no. 4/53, Taf. 25, 1; Volutenkrater Bari 4399, *Ausonia* 3, 1909, 69, Abb. 9, *RVAp* I, 421, no. 16/44. Auffallen diesen Vasen ist das Attributtier der Hase.

18 Lekanisdeckel Neapel 2302, *RVAp* I, 198, no. 8/48, hier nach einer A. de Franciscis verdankten Vorlage. Ebenso auf dem apulischen Volutenkrater in Bari, *Ausonia* 3, 1909, 67 ff. Abb. 7–9.

19 *APS* 35, no. 25, Taf. 12, 53; *RVAp* I, 51, no. 3/43. Waldemar Deonna, *Du miracle grec au miracle chrétien* I, Basel 1945, Taf. 50; ders., *Pro Arte* 1944, 337. Langlotz nennt in *Anthemon, Festschrift C. Anti,* Firenze 1955, 77 Anm. 11, die Vase ohne Hinweis auf Publikation u. Inv.Nr. Zu Dionysos-Glocke jetzt M. Schmidt-A.D. Trendall-A. Cambitoglou, *Eine Gruppe apulischer Grabvasen in Basel,* 1976, 35 f. (Schmidt).

20 z.B.: Sichtermann, *GVU* K41, Volutenkrater Ruvo 1499; *LCS* 74, no. 374, Taf. 35, 5, Kelchkrater Reggio Cal. 5013; apulischer Glockenkrater, Rom, Villa Giulia 43995, *RVAp* I, 97, no. 4/233; Glockenkrater Louvre K 241, *LCS* 206, 44; Glockenkrater Neapel 2074, *LCS* 206, 41. Wie hier hängt die Glocke auf auch der apulischen Amphora München 3300 am Thyrsos, ebenso auf pontischen Münzen: *Sylloge Nummorum Graecorum, Sammlung v. Aulock,* Berlin 1957, I, Taf. 2, 61 (1.Jh.v.Chr.). Vgl. auch Ariadne mit Glocke: Volutenkrater Neapel 3237.

21 z.B.: Langlotz a.O. (oben Anm. 19), 77, Anm. 11, nennt eine Vase in Syrakus ohne Angabe von Form und Inv.Nr. Zu dem dort erwähnten Krater Neapel 1977 hier An. 22; Trendall, *Paestan Pottery,* London 1936, Taf. 14a, Hydria in Wien.

22 Loutrophoros München 3300, Raserei des Lykurgos (selbes Thema auf dem in Anm. 20 erwähnten Krater in Reggio); abgebildet bei A.L. Millin, *Description des Tombeaux de Canosa,* 1816, Taf. 13. Vgl. weiter den Kelchkrater Neapel 1977: hier hängt die Glocke an einem Ast (dazu Stephani, *Compterendu de la Commission impériale archéologique,* St. Pétersbourg 1865, 173 ff.); G. Pesce, *Sarcofagi romani di Sardegna,* Roma 1957, Anm. 5, Abb. 12; Lebes London F. 303; FR Taf. 175, Krater in Neapel; Apulische Schale in Bari, Slg. Lagioia (Mänade mit Glocke u. Tympanon).

23 Matz a.O. (oben Anm. 14), 57 zu Nr. 97. Vgl. weiter: Gotsmich, *Sudeta* 5, 1929, 168 f.; Pesce a.O. (oben Anm. 22); Roes-Vollgraf, *MonPiot* 46, 1952, 50. Vgl. auch H.v. Rohden und H. Winnefeld, *Architektonische römische Tonreliefs der Kaiserzeit,* 1911, Taf. 79, Compiègne.

24 z.B.: Henri Metzger, *Les représentations dans la céramique attique du 4e siècle,* Paris 1951, 56, 38, Taf. 1c, Lekane in Odessa. (Satyr u. Mänade). *ARV²* 1328, 92, Pyxis in London. Vgl. die Silene der Hydria *ARV²* 24, 8, München; apulisch der Glockenkrater, *CVA* Gotha 2, Taf. 82, 1, Berkeleymaler, *RVAp* I, 268, no. 10/54.

25 z.B.: H.B. Walters, *B.M. Catalogue of the Greek and Roman Lamps,* 1914, Nr. 445.

26 *CVA* Napoli 3 IV E, Taf. 66, 1. Dort fehlen die Angabe der Nr. bei Heydemann, *Die Vasensammlung des Museo Nazionale zu Neapel,* 1872, und die von Bulle in *Festschrift J. Loeb,* München 1930, 28 f., mitgeteilte Angabe Mingazzinis, wonach das Schwert der Mänade modern eingeritzt ist (so auch jetzt Mingazzini, *BJb* 173, 1973, 112 f.). Sollte dies zutreffen, wäre für die Haltung der rechten Hand der Mänade eine Erklärung zu suchen. Der Typus der Figur ist in jedem Fall der der *Chimairophonos.*

27 Hierzu Konrad Schauenburg, *Perseus in der Kunst der Altertums,* Bonn 1960, 94 ff.

28 Zu Mänaden in der Gigantomachie, François Vian, *La guerre des géants,* Paris 1952, 87 f., 139 f.

29 H. Klumbach, *Tarentiner Grabkunst,* Reutlingen 1937, 6 f., Nr. 25 ff. Frgte. in Zürich, Galerie Arete (1975). Vgl. auch Gemmen wie *Antike Gemmen in deutschen Sammlungen,* Berlin 384 (Zwierlein-Diehl).

30 H. Klumbach a.O. (oben Anm. 29), Nr. 33, zeigt eine Mänade mit Bock, doch handelt es sich um einen geläufigen Opfertypus.

31 Für die Aufnahme und Abbildungserlaubnis danke ich D. Adamesteanu sehr. A.D. Trendall (brieflich) stellt die Vase in dem Kreis des Pisticcimalers, kennt aber ebenfalls keine Parallele zum Ornament am Hals. Auf der Oberseite des Henkels Palmette. Aus Pisticci. Inv. 20146. Frau Moreno-Cassano, die das Corpus der Vasen in Metapont vorbereitet, hält die Kanne für attisch (Umkreis des Meidiasmalers).

32 Die ersten Schlangen bei Mänaden finden sich gegen 550: Edwards, *JHS* 80, 1960, 80 ff. Vgl. weiter *EAA* iv, s.v. Menadi, 1004 ff. (Simon).

33 Dazu der in Anm. 24 genannte Krater in Gotha. Umgekehrt findet sich auf der sf. Lekythos Athen, Kerameikos 669 u. dem Athener Dinos Beazley, ARV^2 1152, 4 jeweils eine Mänade mit Hase.

34 Hierzu *Helbig⁴,* zu Nr. 1590 (Fuchs).

35 Vgl. auch FR Taf. 175, Krater Neapel 2411 mit Bocksopfer für Dionysos und den Bock auf dem apulischen Krater, *AuA* 10, 1961, Taf. 2, 3, Dresden.

36 Picard, *BCH* 70, 1946, 464 f.; Simon, *AuA* 13, 1967, 105; Schauenburg, *Gymnasium* 64, 1957, 222; *Kleiner Pauly,* II, 80 (Fauth) für die Mänaden. Auf vielen Vasen finden sich Cerviden im Thiasos: Sichtermann a.O. (oben Anm. 20), Taf. 108 f., Krater; *CVA* Schloss Fasanerie II, Taf. 77, Krater; *CVA* Milano, Collezione "H.A.", Taf. 1, 2, Krater; *LCS* 125, 642, Krater Neapel 1989.

37 z.B: *CVA* Heidelberg 3, Taf. 149, 3, Schalenfrgt. Vgl. weiter u.a. den rf. Krater ARV^2 1055, 76, Compiègne; Allgemein zur Grage u.a. Schröder, *BJb* 108/9, 1902, 60; Rodenwaldt, *JdI* 45, 1930, 175 mit Lit.; Kerenyi, *Dioniso* 15, 1950, 7; Diez, *ÖJh* 43, 1958, 37. Vgl. *Anthologia Palatina* VI, 72.

38 z.B.: Glockenkrater Neapel 1541; *RM* 69, 1962, Taf. 14, 2, Krater Neapel 1979; Amphora Neapel 1759.

39 Schauenburg, *JdI* 73, 1958, 76, Anm. 96.

40 *EAA* iv, 1004 (Simon). *Kleiner Pauly,* II, 80 ff. (Fauth). RE^2, IX A 2, s.v. Zagreus, 2241 f. (Fauth). Dort auch für Dionysos selbst. Vgl. oben Anm. 16 zu bildlichen Wiedergaben des Gottes im entsprechenden Typus.

41 Oben Anm. 10 u. 16. *RE* IX A 2, 2247 ff.

42 Schauenburg, *RM* 65, 1958, 61, Taf. 39, 1.

43 *LCS,* 402, 281.

44 Vgl. hierzu auch Verf., *JdI* 89, 1974, 137 ff.

DIE ANDROMEDA DES NIKIAS

Karl Schefold

Dank Ihrem Lebenswerk, lieber Herr Trendall, können wir mehr und mehr die Fülle von erhaltenen Vasen überblicken, mit denen das klassische Grossgriechenland vielfach auf Anregungen
aus dem klassischen Athen antwortet. Die italische Ueberlieferung ist so reich, dass bedeutende
attische Erfindungen, die nur in Kopien überliefert sind, im Schatten der vielen originalen
italischen Werke leicht verkannt werden können.

So hat Phillips[1] das berühmte Gemälde der Befreiung der Andromeda, das am besten in der
Kopie aus dem Dioskurenhaus überliefert ist,[2] in den späten Hellenismus datiert, weil diese
Auffassung der Sage nicht zu der auf den spätklassischen grossgriechischen Vasen passt. Hier ist
Andromeda zumeist an Pfosten oder Säulen, zuweilen an frisch gefällte Bäume oder an den
Felsen selbst gefesselt. Phillips wollte diese dritte Version auf ein tarentinisches Gemälde zurück-
führen, weil Andromeda auf klassischen attischen Bildern nicht an den Felsen gefesselt dargestellt
werde. Der Bildtypus der Befreiung der Andromeda, wie ihn das Gemälde aus dem Dioskurenhaus
überliefert, passe nicht zur klassischen Ikonographie. Ich möchte versuchen, die Gestaltung der
Sage auf diesem bedeutenden Werk doch als klassisch zu erweisen. Dabei wird uns die vortref-
fliche Illustration im Aufsatz Phillips nützlich sein.

Eine wichtige Beobachtung zu dieser Frage verdanken wir Ihnen selbst, lieber Herr Trendall.
In dem gehaltvollen knappen Buch *Illustrations of Greek Drama* (1971),[3] das wir Ihnen und
T.B.L. Webster verdanken, haben sie gegen Phillips die alte Auffassung wieder ins Recht gesetzt,
dass die Andromeda des Berliner Kraters an den Felsen gefesselt zu denken ist, und dass dies
Bild auf die Andromeda des Euripides zurückgeht, deren Rekonstruktion Sie durch neue gross-
griechische Bilder bereichern konnten. Jean-Marc Moret hat in einem gelehrten sorgfältigen Buch
untersucht, inwieweit es möglich ist, Bildvarianten auf verschiedene literarische Vorbilder, bei
unteritalischen Vasen also vor allem auf Werke der grossen Tragiker zurückzuführen.[4] Er hat
mit Recht die Selbständigkeit der bildlichen Ueberlieferung betont, scheint mir aber zu skeptisch
zu sein bei der Zurückführung grossgriechischer Sagenbilder auf berühmte Tragödien, besonders
des Euripides. Die frühhellenistischen Bilderbücher, die sich aus der Reliefkeramik und aus
römischen Sarkophagfriesen erschliessen lassen, zeigen, wie entscheidend und mit welch dauern-
der Wirkung Euripides die Sagen umgestaltet hat.

In der Andromedasage scheint mir die Fesselung an den Felsen die Grundvorstellung zu
sein, die Fesselung an Pfähle aber eine Anpassung an die Bühne. Man braucht dann keinen Berg
anzudeuten. Durchs Binden an die Pfähle war Andromedas Not genug angedeutet. Dafür
brauchte man keine eigene literarische Quelle. Dagegen geht das Bild des Berliner Andromeda-
kraters aus den von Ihnen angeführten Gründen ohne Zweifel auf die kurz zuvor aufgeführte
Andromeda des Euripides zurück. Wenn hier Andromeda an den Felsen gefesselt zu denken ist,
braucht man für die Fesselung an den Felsen auf den römischen Wandbildern keine gross-
griechische Quelle anzunehmen. Damit tritt das Bild aus dem Dioskurenhaus mit seinen Wieder-
holungen in neues Licht. Sein Vorbild, das Gemälde des von B. Neutsch so sorgsam geschilderten
Nikias,[5] lässt sich als klassische Erfüllung dessen verstehen, worum die Meister des fünften
Jahrhunderts gerungen hatten.

Römisch ist zwar die unbestimmte Räumlichkeit der Landschaft, die man sich im Original
so plastisch denken muss wie etwa im treuer kopierten Fries der Kryptoportikus des homerischen
Hauses oder in der Grottenlandschaft von Boscoreale.[6] Der Maler (oder seine Quelle, ein Bilder-

buch) hat manche Details nicht richtig verstanden, so die rechte Hand des Perseus und wie sich der Peplos beim rechten Knie des Perseus am Felsen staut. Sichelschwert und Gorgoneion sind zu klein. Ferner gibt es dies Spiel der Lichter erst in der neronischen Malerei. Aber die plastische Struktur der Figurengruppe ist ebenso rein spätklassisch wie beim Iogemälde, das man mit Recht ebenfalls auf Nikias zurückgeführt hat:[7] wie der Peplos locker um den Körper spielt, gibt es auf keiner Stufe der griechischen Kunst so ähnlich wie in der Zeit des Marsyasmalers.[8] Im späten Hellenismus, an den Phillips dachte, sind immer hellenistische Elemente mit den klassizistischen verbunden, wie es am klarsten das Homerrelief des Archelaos von Priene überliefert.[9]

Ganz anders die Andromeda des Nikias: so kräftiger Bau des weiblichen Körpers ist nach der Alexanderzeit nicht denkbar. Nur diese gross gesehene Fürstin ist künstlerisch und geistig die wahre Entsprechung zur heroischen Gestalt des Perseus. Von besonderem Zauber ist auch, dass sich die beiden nicht anblicken, ergriffen von einem übermächtigen Geschick. Ebenso verhalten ist die Bewegung. Perseus hat Andromeda eben von den Fesseln gelöst. Ihr linkes Handgelenk trägt noch den breiten Reifen, mit dem es angeschmiedet war. In der Haltung des Armes, ja in der ganzen Gestalt glaubt man noch eine Nachwirkung der Not der Andromeda zu spüren. Nun hilft ihr Perseus, vom Felsen herabzusteigen. Dies "Herab", am deutlichsten im linken Bein und rechten Arm, wird durch retardierende Horizontalen zur "Phantasia" eines weiten Weges.[10] Die sparsamen Mittel sind die der Klassik. Die freie Gelassenheit der Haltung atmet den Geist einer in sich beruhigten grossen Zeit.

Auf den klassischen Bildern, die Sie mit Webster auf die Andromeda des Sophokles zurückgeführt haben (III 2, 1–3) wird Andromeda an Pfähle gebunden, trägt orientalische Tracht und wird mit Hochzeitgaben ausgestattet, die ihr gebühren, auch wenn sie unvermählt sterben muss, so auf der Londoner Hydria.[11] Die ahnungsvolle Stimmung zwischen drohendem Tod und ersehntem Glück spiegelt sich in Perseus' Seele, der rechts steht und an seinen Flügelhelm fasst, überwältigt von dem erschütternden Anblick. Nach der Sage erblickt er Andromeda erst, als sie schon ausgesetzt war – es ist eine eindrucksvolle Erfindung eines grossen Malers, ihn zum Zeugen auch der vorausgehenden inneren Not zu machen. Die Vasenbilder dieser Art müssen auf ein grosses Gemälde zurückgehen. Auf dem Krater in Basel[12] blickt Andromeda auf Perseus und weicht unbewusst scheu mit dem Körper etwas aus. Perseus ist eben von seinem weiten Flug durch die Lüfte gekommen, ruht mit aufgestelltem Bein aus und staunt das schöne fremde Wesen an. Der Flügelhut ist so weit in die Stirn gedrückt, dass der Blick etwas Bannendes erhält. Links steht Andromedas weisshaariger Vater und legt in sorgenvollem Sinnen den rechten Arm über die linke Schulter. Wie in der Tragödie tritt das äussere Geschehen zurück; jede Gestalt äussert ihr Schicksal in Wort und Gebärde.

Während auf den italischen Bildern die physische Not der gefesselten Andromeda immer neu ausgemalt wird, geht es den attischen Meistern um ihre innere Bewegung beim Vorgang der Fesselung und der Befreiung. Diese attische Auffassung ist im Gemälde des Nikias zu klassischer Vollendung gereift. Nikias findet eine künstlerische Form, im Vorgang der Lösung von den Fesseln die Ueberwindung der äusseren Not und zugleich die innere Begegnung der Liebenden sichtbar zu machen.

Von der Bedeutung der Erfindung zeugen die Nachwirkungen in der römischen Kunst, zunächst die römischen Repliken des Gemäldes, die es, ihren Bilderbuchvorlagen entsprechend, mit Nebenfiguren ausstatten.[13] Die zauberhaften mythologischen Landschaften dritten Stils allerdings zeigen Andromeda wieder an den Felsen gefesselt.[14] In kontinuierender Erzählung sehen wir in der Art von Bilderbüchern, die als Vorlagen vorauszusetzen sind, wie Perseus herbeifliegt und das Ungeheuer aus der Luft oder im Meer bekämpft und dann bei Kepheus um die

Hand der Tochter bittet. Die Bilderbuchrolle, aus der diese mythologischen Landschaften gleichsam herausgeschnitten sind, wird wie so viele frühhellenistisch gewesen sein. Den Unterschied der kunstvollen motivreichen Bilderzählung der Buchrollen von der monumentalen Verdichtung im Gemälde kann man hier besonders gut beobachten.

Die Berühmtheit des Werkes des Nikias aber zeigt sich darin, dass es nicht nur in der römischen Malerei vielfach nachwirkt, sondern auch in einer plastischen Gruppe, auf Mosaiken und einem der Spadareliefs, das ins Capitolinische Museum gekommen ist.[15] Der Bildhauer des Reliefs hat vom Furchtbaren des Geschehens nur noch den erschlagenen Drachen am Boden übriggelassen. Die zärtliche Begegung des Liebespaares hat er ins Ideale gesteigert, indem er für Andromeda eine neuattische Tänzerin, für Perseus den Hermes von Andros verwendete. Aber das Motiv stammt auch hier vom Gemälde des Nikias. Sucht die griechische Kunst die Wirklichkeit zu verstehen, transzendiert die römische zu Wunschbildern unsterblichen heroischen Daseins. Selbst die schwebende Gruppe im grossen Saal des Vettierhauses in Pompeji ist eine römische Variante nach dem Gemälde des Nikias.[16] Für Andromeda ist eine hellenistische tanzende Mänade verwendet. Die Gruppe ist nicht in griechischer Weise plastisch komponiert, sondern die Figuren sind in der römischen lockeren Räumlichkeit aneinandergeschoben wie die benachbarten Gruppen: es kommt dem Maler der Zeit Neros nur auf die enthusiastische Stimmung an. An die Stelle dieses Illusionismus tritt auf den Spadareliefs feierliche Transparenz. Selten kann man so deutlich wie hier beobachten, wie sich das Motiv einer grossen griechischen Bilderfindung in römischen Schöpfungen verbergen kann, die das Motiv in andere Figurentypen gleichsam verkleiden.

Von den römischen Umbildungen hebt sich die Kopie aus dem Dioskurenhaus durch die spätklassische Art ab, den menschlichen Gehalt zu deuten, das Grosse der Haltung, die Tiefe der Begegnung. Und wenn wir nun zurückblicken auf die attischen Bilder der Befreiung, so fällt uns ein Gemeinsames auf: In Italien wurde die physische Not der gefesselten Andromeda variiert, in Athen ihre innere Bewegung beim Vorgang der Fesselung und der Befreiung. Die Befreiung hat im Gemälde des Nikias ihre klassische Form gefunden. Hier erfüllt sich, worum die Meister des fünften Jahrhunderts gerungen hatten: die Ueberwindung der äusseren Not in der inneren Begegnung der Liebenden.

Wieder einmal erweist sich, dass ein Motiv erst im vierten Jahrhundert seine klassische Form findet, wie es von manchen Göttern, wie Demeter, Asklepios und der Aphrodite längst bekannt ist, und wie auch andere Wesen in ihrer spätklassischen Gestaltung am stärksten auf die Folgezeit gewirkt haben.[17] Galt doch auch die Malerei der Alexanderzeit den Alten als die Vollendung dieser Kunst, was schon im Reichtum der schriftlichen Ueberlieferung zum Ausdruck kommt.[18] Relief und Architektur erhielten durch raumschaffende Formen (korinthisches Kapitell !) klassische Erfüllung.[19] In diesum Zusammenhang tritt Nikias' Gemälde von Perseus und Andromeda in seiner ganzen Bedeutung hervor.

ANMERKUNGEN

1 K.M. Phillips Jr, 'Perseus and Andromeda', *AJA* 72, 1968, 1–23.

2 Neapel, Museo Nazionale 8998 aus Pompeji VI 9, 6–7 (53); Herrmann-Bruckmann, *Denkmäler der Malerei*, München 1906–44, Taf. 129; Pfuhl, *MuZ*, Abb. 647; Phillips, a.O., Taf. 4, 7; K. Schefold, *La peinture pompéienne*, Bruxelles 1972, Taf. 38 mit Lit. Vgl. unten Anm. 7.

3 A.D. Trendall and T.B.L. Webster, *Illustrations of Greek Drama*, London 1971, III 3, 10; Phillips, a.O. (Anm. 1), Abb. 17.

4 Zum Problem zuletzt J-M. Moret, *L'Ilioupersis dans la céramique Italiote. Les mythes et leur expression figurée au 4ᵉ siècle*, Genève 1975.

5 B. Neutsch, *Der Maler Nikias von Athen*, Bern und Leipzig 1939, 36 ff. Weiteres oben Anm. 2.

6 V. Spinazzola, *Pompei*, Rome 1953, 907 ff.; K. Schefold, *Die Griechen und ihre Nachbarn* (*Propyläen-kunstgeschichte* I), Berlin 1967, Abb. 250 a, und Abb. 249.

7 Neapel, Museo Nazionale 9556 aus Pompeji VI 9, 2 (8); Neutsch, a.O. (Anm. 5), 52 ff.; Pfuhl, *MuZ*, Abb. 646; K. Schefold, *Die Wände Pompejis*, Berlin 1957, 111 (Literatur); *Propyläenkunstgeschichte* a.O. (Anm. 6), 123, Abb. 237.

8 ARV^2 1474 f. Besonders Arias-Hirmer-Shefton, Abb. 225–8.

9 K. Schefold, *Die Bildnisse der antiken Dichter, Redner und Denker*, Basel 1943, 148 f.; D. Pinkwart, 'Das Relief des Archelaos von Priene', *Antike Plastik* 4, 1965, 55–65, Taf. 28–35.

10 A. Trendelenburg, *Phantasiai*, 70. *Berliner Winckelsmannsprogramm* 1910.

11 London E 169, ARV^2 1062; FR Taf. 77, 2; *CVA* Taf. 76, 1; Phillips, a.O. (Anm. 1), Taf. 6, Abb. 11–12.

12 Basel BS 403, *Paralipomena*, 456, 15*bis;* E. Berger, *AntK* 11, 1968, 63, Taf. 18, 6.

13 So das schöne Bild vespasianischen dritten Stils aus Is. Occ. 15 in Neapel, Museo Nazionale 8997, Helbig 1187; L. Curtius, *Die Wandmalerei Pompejis*, Leipzig 1929, 256, Abb. 153; A. Maiuri, *La peinture romaine*, Genève 1953, Abb. 79.

14 Phillips, a.O. (Anm. 1), Taf. 1, Abb. 2–3 und Taf. 3–4, Abb. 4–6.

15 Phillips, a.O. (Anm. 1), Taf. 5. Zum Spadareliefs zuletzt P. Zanker, Helbig[4], II, 2000–2007. Das Motiv wurde auf dem Mosaik Albani auf die Hesionesage übertragen; *RM* 60/61, 1953/54, Taf. 53, Helbig[4], IV, 3358 (K. Parlasca).

16 Pompeji VI 15, 1 (q); Schefold, a.O. (Anm. 2), Taf. 33; B. Andreae, *Römische Kunst*, Freiburg i.Br. 1973, Farbtafel 61.

17 K. Schefold, *Klassisches Griechenland*, Baden-Baden 1965, 178 ff.

18 H. Brunn, *Geschichte der griechischen Künstler II,2* Braunschweig 1889, bes. 89 ff.

19 I. Scheibler, *AntK* 17, 1974, 92 ff.; H. Bauer, 'Korinthische Kapitelle des 4. und 3. Jahrhunderts v. Chr.', *AM* 3. Beiheft 1973.

EIN DANAIDENDRAMA (?) UND DER EURIPIDEISCHE ION AUF UNTERITALISCHEN VASENBILDERN

Margot Schmidt

Tafel 42.

Die Tätigkeit der Danaiden ist bekanntlich durch lange Dauer und vielfache Wiederholung gekennzeichnet. Als ich zu Beginn des Jahres 1974 das Danaidenthema in einem Aufsatz zu Ehren unseres grossen Lehrmeisters im Feld der unteritalischen Studien behandelte, hatte ich nicht bedacht, dass ich mit meiner Themenwahl ein schlechtes Omen für die Vollendung und Drucklegung dieser Festschrift heraufbeschwören könnte. In der Tat haben nun auch meine Danaiden in der Zwischenzeit Jahr um Jahr vergeblich Wasser schöpfen müssen, wofür freilich allein verschiedene zusammenwirkende Umstände, keineswegs die Herausgeber verantwortlich zu machen sind. Manches Neue zum Thema erschien, und entsprechend war der Artikel wiederholt zu ergänzen, schliesslich von Grund auf neu zu schreiben. Hätte ich nicht schon hier und da in anderen inzwischen gedruckten Arbeiten auf das baldige Erscheinen meines Danaiden-Beitrags vorausverwiesen,[1] wäre ich nun nicht gehalten, dieses Versprechen einzulösen, sondern dürfte mich auf den vom Fortschreiten der Forschung eigentümlich unberührten Ion beschränken. Doch scheint es mir in jedem Falle noch angebracht zu sein, einiges von dem zusammenzufassen und kritisch zu kommentieren, was heute aus dem Blickwinkel der Archäologie zum Danaidenthema gesagt werden kann. Dabei wird es vor allem um eine kurze Stellungnahme zu einigen der Thesen gehen, die Eva Keuls in ihrem 1974 erschienenen Buch "The Water Carriers in Hades" vorgelegt hat.[2]

In meiner Erstfassung dieses Aufsatzes (1974) war ich von einem wichtigen Neufund ausgegangen, dessen Bedeutung für die Beurteilung des Danaidenmotivs in der Klassik mir damals wie auch heute noch nicht angemessen gewürdigt, ja im allgemeinen nicht erkannt zu sein scheint. Es handelt sich um eine apulische Hydria aus einer Nekropole des 4. Jahrhunderts in Herakleia–Policoro.[3] Die Vase wird noch kurz vor der Mitte des Jahrhunderts zu datieren sein.

Die Hydria trägt zwei Bildzonen, verteilt auf Schulter und Bauch des Gefässes. Im oberen Abschnitt begegnen sich Poseidon und Amymone, gerahmt von Eros und wohl Aphrodite, zuseiten eines Brunnenhauses; in der unteren Bildzone umgeben sechs Danaiden mit ihren Hydrien den berühmten Pithos, den sie vergeblich zu füllen versuchen.

Die Bedeutung dieser Darstellung liegt vor allem darin, dass mit ihrer Hilfe eine wahrscheinliche, aber bisher unbeweisbare Vermutung zur Gewissheit erhoben wird. Vor dem Auftauchen des neuen Bildzeugnisses liess sich nämlich nicht mit Sicherheit entscheiden, ob die Wasserträgerinnen dieses Typus in den bildlichen Quellen des 4. Jahrhunderts schon — wie für uns erst frühestens im Hellenismus schriftlich belegt — als Danaiden, also als mythische Figuren, oder ausschliesslich in allgemeinerer Bedeutung als Uneingeweihte (der Mysterien) aufzufassen sind.[4] Für die neue Hydria kann nun kein Zweifel an der mythologischen Deutung bestehen: Die Benennung der Wasserträgerinnen ergibt sich aus dem Zusammenhang mit der Szene in der Schulterzone, denn die Heroine Amymone zählt in der Sage ebenfalls zu den fünfzig Töchtern des Danaos. Demnach muss das Bussmotiv, die unlösbare Aufgabe, einen durchlöcherten Pithos mit Wasser zu füllen (beziehungsweise, in zerbrochenen Gefässen Wasser zu tragen) schon spätestens in der Entstehungszeit der Vase von Herakleia — und das heisst auch: noch in der Lebenszeit des Platon — mit den mythischen Figuren der Danaiden verknüpft gewesen sein.

E. Keuls bemerkte in einem Addendum ihres Buches[5] merkwürdigerweise nur, dass die neue Darstellung ihre These unterstütze, nach der die Danaiden auf den unteritalischen Denkmälern (als Wassernymphen) mit der Fruchtbarkeit verbunden seien. Den 'springenden Punkt' — eindeutige Darstellung der mythischen Danaiden, nicht anonyme Uneingeweihte — scheint sie dabei zu übersehen.

Die frühere Annahme, das Bussmotiv der Danaiden im Hades sei "eine junge Version......, die Platon noch nicht kennt",[6] hat eine wesentliche Rolle in der Diskussion um die hypothetische Wiederherstellung der verlorenen Teile der äschyleischen Danaidentrilogie gespielt.[7] In die weiteren Ueberlegungen wird man heute auch die neue Hydria von Herakleia—Policoro einbeziehen müssen. Sie wird nämlich, abgesehen von ihrer Bedeutung als bisher ältestes Bildzeugnis für die Danaidenstrafe, im besonderen dadurch zu einem wichtigen Dokument, dass in ihrem Hauptbild in enger Verbindung mit dem Motiv der Wasserträgerinnen die Geschichte der Danaide Amymone geschildert wird, das heisst, gerade das Thema, das Aischylos für das Satyrspiel als Abschluss seiner Danaidentetralogie wählte ! Wir kennen aus den Jahrzehnten bis zur Entstehungszeit der unteritalischen Hydria keine weitere dramatische Gestaltung des Amymonemythos im Zusammenhang mit der Geschichte der übrigen Danaostöchter.[8] Die Wahrscheinlichkeit ist also nicht gering, dass die Darstellungen der Vase von Herakleia — wenn auch vielleicht nur seht indirekt[9] — auf die verlorene äschyleische Tetralogie zurückgehen. Jedenfalls dürfen wir angesichts dieses neuen Zeugnisses nicht mehr mit Sicherheit ausschliessen, dass auch Aischylos schon die Version der Danaiden als Wasserträgerinnen gekannt und verwendet hat.[10]

Eine Schwierigkeit mag man darin sehen, dass zwar Wiederaufführungen der klassischen Bühnenwerke auch im Unteritalien des 4. Jahrhunderts üblich waren, dass es sich aber in der Regel um einzelne Tragödien, nicht um vollständige Tetralogien gehandelt zu haben scheint.[11] Wenn wir einen mehr oder minder engen Zusammenhang der Hydria von Herakleia mit einer solchen unteritalischen Wiederaufführung des Aischylos vermuten wollen, liesse sich erwägen, ob in der Tat nicht die ganze Tetralogie, sondern nut die letzte Tragödie (die auch die Danaidenstrafe oder, vorsichtiger formuliert, das Pithosmotiv enthielt ?) und das Satyrspiel *Amymone* wieder auf die Bühne gebracht wurden.[12] Es ist in diesem Zusammenhang bemerkenswert, dass, soweit wir wissen, gerade diese dritte Tragödie (wie auch die ganze Trilogie?)[13] den Titel *Danaiden* trug, den der untere Bildstreifen der Hydria 'illustriert'.

Wir haben gesehen, dass mit dem neuen Bildzeugnis ein zusätzliches — wenn auch gewiss nur schwaches und mit weiteren Unsicherheiten behaftetes — Argument zugunsten einer der Arbeitshypothesen über den Ausgang der äschyleischen Danaidentrilogie aufgetaucht ist, zugunsten jener Rekonstruktionsvorschläge also, in denen das Pithosmotiv — in welcher Form auch immer — schon für Aischylos vorausgesetzt wird, denn ein wesentliches Gegenargument, der Hinweis auf die erst nachplatonische Entstehung des Danaidenmotivs im engeren Sinne, entfällt offensichtlich. Nun bleibt freilich festzuhalten, dass mit der Annahme, Aischylos habe in der Tat die Unterweltsstrafe der Danaiden geschildert oder angedeutet, eine kaum lösbare Crux ins Spiel kommt, die in den verschiedenen Behandlungen der Rekonstruktionsprobleme durchaus ernstgenommen wird. So bemerkt etwa R.P. Winnington-Ingram in seiner knappen aber vorzüglichen Auseinandersetzung: "Moreover it may well be doubted, whether an Aeschylean trilogy is likely to have come to a conclusion with the eternal punishment of a chorus".[14]

E. Keuls[15] hat die Diskussion mit einem scharfsinnigen neuen Vorschlag belebt: Sie vermutet eine Kombination der beiden Motive, die bisher in der Forschung als einander ausschliessende Alternativen betrachtet wurden. Nach ihr habe die äschyleische Trilogie sowohl das Pithosmotiv wie die schliessliche Versöhnung enthalten. Dies ist anscheinend nur möglich, wenn man mit E. Keuls den 'Pithosritus' als Entsühnungsritus auffasst, der noch auf Erden vollzogen wird, also nicht von vornherein als Unterweltsstrafe. In diesem Falle würde die Verwendung des Pithosmotivs selbstverständlich nicht, wie bisher stets angenommen wurde, den Tod der Danaiden voraussetzen, sondern dürfte auf die noch Lebenden bezogen werden, für die man sich — nach der vollzogenen Entsühnung — durchaus eine von den Göttern sanktionierte Wiederverheiratung, etwa im Sinne der Ueberlieferung bei Pindar[16] oder bei Apollodor[17] vorstellen könnte.[18]

Die Hauptbedenken, die gegen diese zunächst ansprechende Erklärung bestehen bleiben, hat auch E. Keuls nicht ignoriert. Sie räumt selbst ein, dass "no concrete evidence"[19] für die Existenz eines solchen kathartischen Pithos-Ritus in Griechenland auszumachen sei. Schwerer wiegt jedoch ein weiterer Einwand, den die Verfasserin ebenfalls selbst anführt und wie mir scheint nicht befriedigend entkräftet: "Why do we find the Danaids — water carriers in the Greco-Roman literary tradition as symbols of the 'wicked in Hades'?"[20] Die postulierte Vorstellung von den schon zu Lebzeiten durch einen Pithos-Ritus entsühnten Danaiden lässt sich zum Beispiel nicht mehr mit der durchaus in sich kohärenten Schilderung bei Lukian in Einklang bringen, die das Wassertragen eindeutig als Jenseitsstrafe für die Danaiden bezeugt: In einem seiner reizvollen Dialoge der Meeresgötter[21] beschwört Lukian das Liebesabenteuer des Poseidon mit der Danaide Amymone. Nachdem der Gott sein Wunder, die Entstehung einer Quelle, angekündigt hat, verheisst er der von ihm erkorenen Geliebten, dass sie selig sein werde und *nach ihrem Tode* als einzige unter den Danaiden nicht Wasser tragen müsse:

καὶ σὺ εὐδαίμων ἔσῃ καὶ μόνη τῶν ἀδελφῶν οὐχ ὑδροφορήσεις ἀποθανοῦσα.

Amymone wird hier ausgezeichnet, weil sie sich, anders als ihre Schwestern, der Liebe nicht verschliesst. Die Bilder der Hydria von Herakleia machen in ihrer beziehungsreichen Gegenüberstellung den Eindruck, dass auch ihnen schon eine entsprechende Auffassung zugrunde liegt. Der Verstorbenen als einer 'neuen Amymone' wird ein Wassergefäss ins Grab mitgegeben, geschmückt mit den Gegenbildern von Belohnung und Strafe. Sie wird sich im Jenseits nicht mühen, auch keinen Mangel an erquickendem Wasser leiden müssen; ihre Hydria, so mochten es ihr wohl die noch lebenden Angehörigen wünschen, die gerade diese Grabbeigabe auswählten, wird gefüllt bleiben wie die der Amymone im Brunnenhaus, das die betonte Mitte der Darstellung bildet.

Wenn man das Pithosmotiv in der Verbindung mit den mythischen Danaiden weiterhin als Andeutung einer im Jenseits lokalisierten Bestrafung auffasst — und die vorgebrachten Einwände gegen die Hypothese von E. Keuls veranlassen mich, diese Anschauung einstweilen nicht zu verwerfen — ergibt sich aus dieser freilich ebenfalls unbeweisbaren Praemisse eine Begrenzung der weiteren Folgerungen und Annahmen. Hat Aischylos das so definierte Motiv verwendet, so musste er auch den Tod der Danaiden als Voraussetzung einer Unterweltsstrafe einbeziehen. Im Sinne des πρόνοια – Prinzips[22] – der Annahme von vorausverweisenden Andeutungen in der erhaltenen Tragödie, die einige Schlüsse auf die fehlenden Teile nahelegen – lassen sich nun in der Tat in den *Hiketiden* auffällige Aussagen zur Herrschaft des strafenden Hades über die Frevler feststellen, die als Vorverweise auf das künftige Geschick der Danaiden im Rahmen des Ganzen verständlicher scheinen könnten. Ausser den in diesem Zusammenhang schon zitierten Versen 230 ff. und 416[23] wäre besonders noch Vers 790 f. zu beachten, wo die Danaiden ausdrücklich der von ihnen abgelehnten ehelichen Verbindung die Herrschaft des Hades nach ihrem Tode vorziehen.

Im Zusammenhang mit einem postulierten 'bösen Ende' der Danaiden behält das Scholion zur euripideischen *Hekuba* (886) nach wie vor eine nicht geringe Bedeutung, das schon von verschiedenen Autoren für die Rekonstruktion der verlorenen Teile in Anspruch genommen worden ist.[24] In dieser Version werden nämlich die frevlerischen Danaiden von Lynkeus getötet, der allein dem Mordanschlag entgangen war. Eine Reihe von Autoren hat die Auffassung vertreten, im Mittelpunkt der dritten Tragödie habe die Geschichte der schuldlos gebliebenen Hypermestra gestanden.[25] Dieser Rekonstruktionsentwurf liesse sich möglicherweise mit einigen Angaben des genannten Scholion kombinieren, da Lynkeus ja der Gemahl der Hypermestra ist. Im Rahmen der Hypermestrahandlung wäre eine mehr oder weniger ausführliche Erwähnung der Danaidenstrafe möglich, wohl sogar angebracht gewesen.[26] Doch bleibt diese Rekonstruktion des Handlungsfadens wie alle anderen mit verschiedenen Schwierigkeiten verbunden.

Noch ein Wort zu den 'Danaiden' im Zusammenhang der unteritalischen Hadesbilder.[27] Die Hydria von Herakleia–Policoro beweist, wie wir gesehen haben, dass für die Entstehungszeit der Unterweltsvasen des 4. Jahrhunderts schon die Kenntnis auch der mythischen Wasserträgerinnen, der Danaiden, vorausgesetzt werden darf. Dennoch lässt sich nicht mit Sicherheit feststellen, ob die entsprechenden Hydrophoren der Hadesbilder im engeren Sinne 'mythologisch', oder in dem schon für das polygnotische Unterweltsgemälde überlieferten allgemeineren Sinne als 'Uneingeweihte' aufgefasst werden müssen.[28] Wesentlich dürfte das schon von verschiedenen Autoren[29] beobachtete eigentümlich 'schwerelose' Verhalten dieser nicht mehr durchweg als tätige Büsserinnen charakterisierten Gestalten sein. Waren sie einem unterweltlichen Sühneritus unterworfen, so scheint dieser schon seinem Abschluss entgegen zu gehen oder gar überwunden zu sein. Die Hydrienträgerinnen in den apulischen Unterweltsbildern sind allem Anschein nach nicht mehr einer unerbittlich strengen Fron unterworfen, die sich als ὑδρεῖαι ἀτελεῖς,[30] als endloses Wassertragen, zu erkennen gibt, sondern hier wird, wenn nicht alles täuscht, gerade das mögliche Ende, die Ueberwindung der Strafe, angedeutet. Ich habe an anderer Stelle versucht,[31] auszuführen, dass das Motiv der Wasserträgerinnen in der bildlichen Aussage der apulischen Unterweltsdarstellungen möglicherweise gerade jenes Stadium der Existenz nach dem Tode vertritt, in dem menschliche Verfehlungen durch zeitlich begrenzte Sühne aufgehoben werden können, — gleichsam ein Zwischenstadium, das zwischen den Polen des ewigen Büssers (etwa vom Typus des Sisyphos) und des Seligen angesiedelt ist. Wenn diese durch die Bildgestalt der Wasserträgerinnen in den Unterweltsdarstellungen nahegelegte 'versöhnliche' Auffassung der Hydrophoren im Hades zutrifft, wäre zu überlegen, ob auch im mythischen Spiegelbild, in den Gestalten der Danaiden, — etwa aufgrund der besonderen Bedingtheit ihrer durch männliche Hybris herausgeforderten Verfehlung — schon eine entsprechende Versöhnungstendenz angelegt sein konnte. Bestand etwa die glücklichere Verheissung am Ausgang der äschyleischen Trilogie zwar nicht in der schon auf Erden vollzogenen Entsühnung der Danaiden, sondern in dem tröstenden Versprechen, dass ihr Geschick im Jenseits durch Sühne zur endlichen Erlösung befreit werden könne? Diese Hypothese würde freilich voraussetzen, dass die im erhaltenen Text postulierten 'Vorausverweise', die Erwähnungen der unerbittlichen Hadesherrschaft, im letzten Teil gleichsam ergänzt und korrigiert worden wären durch den Ausblick, den wohl nur das Wissen eines Gottes eröffnen konnte: Auch in der anderen Welt kann Erlösung gedacht werden. Doch impliziert diese Ueberlegung so weit gehende Folgerungen zur Religiosität des Aischylos (etwa im Sinne einer Annäherung an gewisse z.B. bei Pindar formulierte Gedanken über abgestufte Sühnemöglichkeiten im Jenseits), dass der Archäologe besser daran tut, sich auf den heimischeren Boden des eigenen Faches zurückzuziehen.

* * * * *

Zu weniger hypothetischen Ueberlegungen veranlasst das zweite unteritalische Bildzeugnis, das hier untersucht werden soll. Denn in diesem Falle handelt es sich um eine Darstellung, die den Stoff eines vollständig erhaltenen attischen Dramas zum Gegenstand hat. Es ist verwunderlich, dass die zweite Seite des seit dem 19. Jahrhundert bekannten schönen Hesperidenkraters des Lykurgosmalers in Ruvo (Taf. 42)[32] nicht längst die Deutung gefunden hat, die doch geradezu 'in die Augen zu springen' scheint, denn wer den auffällig hübschen, langlockigen Jungen mit bindengeschmücktem Zweigbündel neben einem Altar in einem Apollonheiligtum betrachtet, muss sich zwingend an den Ion des Euripides erinnert fühlen,[33] und in der Tat ordnen sich auch die anderen Einzelheiten der Szene überzeugend in diesen dramatischen Zusammenhang ein: Die Frau, die sich von links, begleitet von ihren Dienerinnen (Vertreterinnen des Chores), dem Altar nähert, ist die Mutter des Ion, Kreusa. Am Altar bereitet sich sein Pflegevater Xouthos auf das Stieropfer vor, das er, als βούθυτος ἡδονή in der Freude über den vermeintlich wiedergefundenen Sohn feiern will (650 ff.). Der Greis, der in der Bildmitte in ehrfürchtiger Haltung vor den Apollontempel[34] tritt, ist der πρεσβύτης, hier vielleicht deshalb nicht in der bescheideneren Pädagogentracht, weil er nach dem Ausweis der Verse 725 ff. im Haus der Kreusa Ehren geniesst. Aphrodite, die so oft in apulischen Vasenbildern zugegen ist, hat hier, wo es um die Folgen der Liebe zwischen Apollon und Kreusa geht, mit Recht ihren Platz. Dasselbe gilt für Hermes, der den Prolog der Tragödie zu sprechen hat. Schon diese Aufzählung, die im wesentlichen mit dem Personenverzeichnis des euripideischen Dramas übereinstimmt, macht, wie mir scheint, hinreichend sinnfällig, dass die Deutung auf den *Ion* des Euripides als gesichert betrachtet werden kann. Wir haben damit die bisher einzige noch in den Ausgang der klassischen Zeit gehörende bildliche Darstellung dieser Tragödie gewonnen.[35] Die Vase wird im Jahrzehnt 350/40 v.Chr. enstanden sein.

Von besonderem Interesse ist die sitzende Frau mit phrygischer Mütze links vom Tempel, die ein Gespräch mit Hermes zu führen scheint. Ich möchte in ihr eine Verkörperung 'Asiens' erkennen, also eine Gestalt, die der bekannten, inschriftlich bezeichneten 'Asia' auf der Perservase des Dareiosmalers bis zu einem gewissen Grade entspricht.[36] Wie diese Asia auf dem Krater des Lykurgosmalers aufzufassen ist, geht mit wünschenswerter Deutlichkeit aus dem Wortlaut der euripideischen Tragödie hervor. Im Prolog (74) nennt Hermes Ion den κτίστορ' Ἀσιάδος χθονός, und Athena nimmt zum Schluss in den Versen 1585 ff. diese Verheissung mit grösserem Nachdruck auf: Die Nachkommen des Ion werden als Ionier Europa und Asien besiedeln:

> . . . . . ἀντίπορθμα δ'ἠπείροιν δυοῖν
> πεδία κατοικήσουσιν, Ἀσιάδος τε γῆς
> Εὐρωπίας τε · τοῦδε δ'ὀνόματος χάριν
> Ἴωνες ὀνομασθέντες ἕξουσιν κλέος.

Der hier verwendete Begriff der beiden 'Festländer' Europas und Asiens begegnet wiederholt in den politischen Schriften des Isokrates, also in der Entstehungszeit des Kraters aus Ruvo. Im engeren Sinne geht es dem Redner um das teilweise von Griechen kolonialisierte kleinasiatische Küstengebiet, das er im Panegyrikos (or. 4. 162) umschreibt: ἀπὸ δὲ Κνίδου μέχρι Σινώπης Ἕλληνες τὴν Ἀσίαν παροικοῦσιν. Und eben dieses Gebiet soll Philipp von Makedonien nach dem Willen des Isokrates von den Persern befreien: τὰς πόλεις τὰς τὴν Ἀσίαν κατοικούσας ἐλευθερώσεις. (or. 5, 123)

Die 'Asia' auf dem Krater des Lykurgosmalers wird in diesem Sinne zu verstehen sein. Sie verkörpert die Gebiete Kleinasiens, in denen die Nachkommen des Ion siedelten, also nicht die feindliche Macht des gesamten persischen 'Asiens'. Entsprechend hatte, soweit ich sehe als einziger, L. Curtius auch die Asia auf dem Dareioskrater erklären wollen,[37] obwohl in diesem Falle die der Asia beigegebene Apate die Deutung nicht eben zu stützen scheint.[38] Es ist immerhin bemerkenswert, dass die Asia des Dareiosmalers nicht durch orientalische Tracht als fremdländisches Wesen gekennzeichnet ist, anders als die Frau auf der Ruveser Vase, deren Phrygermütze vielleicht die hier fehlende Inschrift zu ersetzen hat.

Ist man auf die Bedeutung des Begriffspaares der "beiden (von Griechen besiedelten) Festländer" in der politischen Diktion des 4. Jahrhunderts aufmerksam geworden,[39] bietet sich nun auch eine Benennung für die noch ungedeutete Frau am linken Bildrand neben Hermes an. Sie vertritt wahrscheinlich das griechische Stammland, dessen Besitz für die Hellenen unbestritten ist. Deshalb kann Hermes ihr den Rücken zukehren und sich der 'Asia' zuwenden, deren Land den Nachkommen des Ion im euripideischen Drama erst verheissen wird. In den Jahren nach dem 'Königsfrieden', durch den die Griechenstädte Kleinasiens den Persern ausgeliefert worden waren, muss diese Verheissung für die Hellenen aufs neue eine starke politische Bedeutung erhalten haben.[40]

Wenn sich der Blick auf der einen Vasenseite bis zu den Grenzen der hellenischen Welt im Osten weitet, erhält auch die Hesperidendarstellung auf der anderen Seite eine neue Dimension. Denn der Garten der Hesperiden bezeichnet ja den äussersten Westen der bewohnten Welt, der Oikumene.[41] Bemerkenswert ist nun auch, dass der Fuss des Kraters die Darstellungen von Greifen und Arimaspen trägt,[42] die ebenfalls 'topographisch' verstanden werden dürfen: Hier sind wahrscheinlich die nördlichen Randgebiete der griechischen Oikumene gemeint.[43]

Die Bilder des Kraters umgreifen also als Ausdruck eines stolzen aber zugleich bedrohten Selbstgefühls die gesamte griechische Welt, wie sie sich im Zeitalter des Isokrates in der Abgrenzung von den Barbaren verstand. Im Osten hatte einst Herakles nach dem Sieg über Troja "beide Festländer", Europa und Asien, Hellas untertan gemacht, darauf errichtete er im Westen seine Säulen als Zeichen des Sieges über die Barbaren und als Markierung der griechischen Herrschaftsgrenzen: Mit eben diesen Worten und in dieser Gegenüberstellung definiert Isokrates in seinem Brief an Philipp (5, 112) das Hellas, das sich, geführt vom Makedonenkönig, gegen die Barbaren behaupten soll. Die politisch-propagandistische Herakles-Topik gehört als Ergänzung zur programmatischen hellenischen 'Geographie', die in den Bildern der Vase aus Ruvo ihren Niederschlag gefunden zu haben scheint. So ist es wohl kein Zufall, wenn nicht nur der Hesperidengarten den Gedanken an den Heros wachruft, sondern wenn Herakles selbst im Halsbild der Ion-Seite im Schutze Athenas und auch Aphrodites auftritt. In seiner Bezwingung des kretischen Stieres mögen die anderen Siege des Helden mitgedacht sein. Trotz der Anwesenheit der Göttinnen muss er sich sichtlich mühen; die Stirn furcht sich in der Anstrengung. Entsprechend zeigt das dionysische Bild der gegenüberliegenden Halszone, welche Glückseligkeit im Jenseits den erwartet, der sich im Leben bewährte. Die Nike am Thymiaterion im linken Abschnitt spielt vielleicht auf diese Beziehung zwischen irdischer Bewährung und Glück im Jenseits an. Dabei ist daran zu erinnern, dass auch das Hauptbild dieser Vasenseite nicht allein die westliche Grenze der griechischen Welt bezeichnet, sondern dass nach antiker Vorstellung auch jenseitige Glücksvorstellungen mit dem Hesperidengarten verbunden waren.[44] Doch liegt über den wie immer melancholischen Frauengesichtern des Lykurgosmalers noch kein Abglanz solchen Glückes.

ANMERKUNGEN

1   z.B. M. Schmidt, A.D. Trendall, A. Cambitoglou, *Eine Gruppe apulischer Grabvasen in Basel,* Basel – Mainz 1976, 74, Anm. 245 und M. Schmidt, 'Orfeo e Orfismo nella pittura vascolare italiota', *Atti del 14. Convegno di Studi sulla Magna Grecia,* 1978.

2   *The Water Carriers in Hades: A Study of Catharsis through Toil in Classical Antiquity,* Amsterdam 1974. Zum Versuch einer strukturalistischen Untersuchung des Danaidenmotivs vgl. einstweilen den Vorbericht von M. Detienne, École Pratique des Hautes Études, 5. Section, Sciences religieuses, *Annuaire* 84, 1976, 279 f.

3   Policoro 38462. *RVAp* I, p. 407, no. 15/59 und Dinu Adamesteanu 'Hydria apula di Heraclea' in diesem Band.

4   Zur möglichen Datierung und Beurteilung der bisher ältesten schriftlichen Quelle für die Identifizierung der 'uneingeweihten' Wasserträgerinnen mit den mythischen Danaiden, des pseudo-platonischen Dialogs Axiochos, ferner zu den mit dieser Gleichsetzung verbundenen, oft behandelten Fragenkomplexen, vgl. zuletzt Keuls a.O. 44 und passim. Eine ausgezeichnete Uebersicht über die Theorien zum Verhältnis des Danaidenmotivs zu demjenigen der Uneingeweihten gibt A.F. Garvie, *Aeschylus' Supplices. Play and Trilogy,* Cambridge 1969, bes. 234 f. (mit der anschliessenden Bibliographie) und 176 f. Vgl. auch F. Graf, *Eleusis und die orphische Dichtung Athens in vorhellenistischer Zeit,* Berlin 1974, 113 f. mit Anm. 93 sowie hier Anm. 28, unten.

5   a.O. 8.

6   K. v. Fritz, 'Die Danaidentrilogie des Aeschylus', *Philologus* 91, 1936 = idem, Sammelband, *Antike und Moderne Tragödie,* Berlin 1962, 167.

7   Zu den bisher erwogenen Möglichkeiten vor allem Garvie a.O. passim.

8   Der Tragiker Timesitheos, von dem die Suda unter anderem sogar zwei Werke mit dem Titel 'Danaiden' aufzählt, ist für uns nicht zu datieren. Es gibt im übrigen keinen Hinweis darauf, dass er im besonderen auch die Amymone-Handlung einbezog. Von Theodektes, der zeitlich gut zur Hydria von Herakleia passen würde, ist ein Lynkeus überliefert, doch geht aus den Erwähnungen bei Aristoteles (*Poet.* 1452 a 27 und 1455 b 29) hervor, dass die Handlung schon längere Zeit nach dem Danaidenfrevel spielte. Vgl. dazu T.B.L. Webster, 'Fourth Century Tragedy and the Poetics,' *Hermes* 82, 1954, 304 und 302 f.

9   Auf das recht schwierige Problem möglicher Zusammenhänge zwischen Theateraufführungen und unteritalischen Vasenbildern, das ich hier nicht erörtern kann, gehe ich näher ein in meiner Rezension zu J.M. Moret, *L'Ilioupersis dans la céramique Italiote,* Rom-Genf 1975, die demnächst im *Gnomon* erscheint.

10 Die Möglichkeit räumt auch Garvie a.O. 177 ein.

11 Dazu R. Cantarella, 'Aristophanes' Plutos 422–425 e le riprese Eschilee', *Rendiconti Accademia Lincei,* 20, 1965, 363 ff. = idem, *Scritti minori sul teatro Greco,* 1970, 227 ff., bes. 236 ff. Vgl. auch Garvie a.O. 19 ff.

12 Auf besondere Schwierigkeiten im Zusammenhang mit der *Amymone* hat zuerst F. Brommer, 'Amymone', *AM* 63–4, 1938–9, 171 und idem, *Satyrspiele,[1]* Berlin 1944, 21 f. hingewiesen: erst seit etwa 440 v.Chr. treten in Attika Amymonedarstellungen mit Silenen auf, was auf ein nach-äschyleisches Satyrspiel deuten könnte. Vgl. dazu Garvie 13 und 22 (wo statt Bonner Brommer zu lesen ist.) Andrerseits sichert jetzt das vor allem für die Spätdatierung der äschyleischen Danaiden entscheidende Fragment P.Ox. 2256 Nr. 3 (= Oxyrhynchus Papyri 20, 1952) die Zusammengehörigkeit der *Danaiden* und der *Amymone* des Aischylos. Zum Text und zu den Folgerungen Garvie 1 ff. — Zu unteritalischen Amymonedarstellungen, auf die es in unserem Zusammenhang vor allem ankommt, K. Schauenburg, 'Göttergeliebte auf unteritalischen Vasen', *Antike und Abenland* 10, 1961, 84 ff. und zuletzt A.D. Trendall, 'Poseidon and Amymone on an Apulian Pelike' in *Festschrift für F. Brommer* (Mainz 1977) 281 ff., Taf. 75, 3.

13 Dazu Garvie 2 zu Z. 2 des P.Ox. 2256 Nr. 3. Allgemein zum Problem der Titel auch Cantarella, *Scritti minori* a.O. (oben Anm. 11) 234 mit Anm. 17.

14 'The Danaid Trilogy of Aeschylus', *JHS* 81, 1961, 143.

15 *The Water Carriers* a.O. 61 ff. und passim.

16 *Pyth.* 9, 111 ff.

17 *Bibl.* 2, 1, 5.

18 Soweit ich sehe, neigt heute die Mehrzahl der Autoren zur Annahme eines versöhnlichen Endes, das die Entsühnung der Danaiden einschliesst. Vgl. etwa v. Fritz a.O. (oben Anm. 6) oder Winnington-Ingram a.O. (oben Anm. 14), der allerdings auch die Argumente zugunsten der Gegenposition besonders sorgfältig abwägt.

19 a.O. 28.

20 a.O. 57.

21 6. Aus den sehr zahlreichen späteren Quellen greife ich hier als stellvertretend nur den Lukian-Text heraus, weil er mit der Gegenüberstellung von Amymone und Danaiden besonders gut zur doppelten bildlichen Darstellung auf der neuen Hydria passt.

22 Dazu A.J. Podlecki, 'Reconstructing an Aeschylean Trilogy', *BICS* 22, 1975, 3.

23 Etwa bei Winnington-Ingram a.O. (oben Anm. 14) 143.

24 Diskussion bei Garvie 174 mit Anm. 5.

25 Garvie 204 ff. Vgl. auch die Diskussion bei v. Fritz a.O. (oben Anm. 6) 186 ff., der aber die These, die *Danaiden* hätten die Hypermestra-Handlung zum Gegenstand gehabt, verwirft.

26 In diesem Zusammenhang ist noch an Ovid, *Heroides* 14 zu erinnern, wo die eingekerkerte Hypermestra gegenüber Lynkeus erwähnt, dass ihre Schwestern bereits tot sind, was sich eventuell mit dem oben zitierten Scholion zu Euripides, *Hekuba* 886 kombinieren lässt. Garvie 169 beurteilt den Wert dieses Zeugnisses skeptisch.

27 Dazu vor allem jetzt Keuls a.O. bes. 83 ff. sowie Schmidt-Trendall-Cambitoglou a.O. 74 ff.; idem 'Orfeo e Orfismo' a.O. (oben Anm. 1).

28 Zur Literatur vgl. oben Anm. 4. Auch nach der erneuten Diskussion der Frage durch E. Keuls a.O. 52 scheint mir die scharfsinnige Erklärung E. Rohdes, die den Zusammenhang von Uneingeweihten und Unverheirateten, die möglichen Implikationen und Ausweitungen des Begriffs des $\tau \acute{\epsilon} \lambda o \varsigma$, betrifft, nicht zwingend widerlegt zu sein. Gegen die Argumentation von Keuls 54 f. ist unter anderem einzuwenden: Selbst wenn die Danaiden unter Zwang die Ehe mit den später ermordeten Männern noch vollzogen hätten, würde sich dadurch an ihrer grundsätzlichen Fehlbarkeit als Eheverächter nichts geändert haben. Die Danaiden sind — wenigstens im Rahmen ihrer besonderen Situation — intentionelle $\check{\alpha} \gamma \alpha \mu o \iota$. Zu dem von E. Keuls 53 f. in Frage gestellten Zusammenhang der Grablutrophoros mit der im Danaiden-'Ritus' verwendeten Hydria wäre jetzt die interessante Beobachtung von G. Kokula, *Marmorlutrophoren,* Köln 1974, auszuwerten beziehungsweise zu überprüfen, nach der gerade für die Gräber unverheirateter Frauen die 'Lutrophoros-Hydria' (mit drei Henkeln) verwendet wurde. Abschliessend sei noch angefügt, dass mir in dem in literatur- und religionswissenschaftlicher Hinsicht anregenden Buch von E. Keuls die Interpretationen der Bildzeugnisse bedeutend weniger glücklich scheinen, etwa diejenige des Pariser Kraters CA 227, der wohl schon aufgrund des für Danaos wenig glaubhaft wirkenden markanten Tempelschlüssels besser mit der Chryses-Geschichte verbunden bliebe. Eine zusätzliche Hydria auf der Vasenrückseite macht noch keine Danaiden-Darstellung, das Motiv der Wagenräder allein noch keine Unterweltsszenerie (75 f. und 78 f.). Erwägenswert, wenn auch nicht restlos befriedigend, ist jedoch die Deutung der drei Vasen mit den sogenannten 'lokrischen Mädchen' auf den Danaiden-mythos.

29 Vgl. Schmidt-Trendall-Cambitoglou a.O. Anm. 252 und Keuls a.O. 3 und passim.

30 Diesen Ausdruck verwendet der Autor des pseudo-platonischen *Axiochos,* 371 E.

31 'Orfeo e Orfismo' a.O.

*   *   *   *   *

32 Jatta 1097. H. Sichtermann, *GVU* K72, Taf. 120–121 und 119 (Detail); *RVAp* I, p. 417, no. 16/16. Zum Detail der Apollonstatue G. Schneider-Herrmann, 'Kultstatue im Tempel auf italischen Vasenbildern', *BABesch* 47, 1972, 34 f. Dazu hier Anm. 40, unten.

33 Zum Zweigbündel – ein nebensächlicheres, aber schönes Detail – sei daran erinnert, dass dieses Requisit für den euripideischen *Ion* typisch ist. Vgl. die schönen Verse 122 ff. und zuvor 102 ff. Ion reinigt allmorgendlich mit einem jungen Lorbeerzweig den 'Boden des Gottes'. Im Zusammenhang mit den dabei üblichen Lustrationen ist auch das Wasserbecken rechts vom Tempel zu sehen, in das aus einer eigens angegebenen Quelle Wasser fliesst. Vgl. die genannten Verse des *Ion* und überhaupt die zahlreichen Hinweise auf die Quellen in Delphi.

34 Zur Statue im Tempel vgl. hier Anm. 32 und 40.

35 Vgl. die alte Zusammenstellung von Vasenbildern bei J.H. Huddilston (mir zur Zeit nur in der deutschen Ausgabe, Freiburg 1900, verfügbar): *Die griechische Tragödie im Lichte der Vasenmalerei*, 210 f., der sich selbst bereits "nicht von ihrem euripideischen Charakter zu überzeugen vermochte". Auch das ebenfalls von L. Séchan, *Études sur la tragédie grecque dans ses rapports avec la céramique*, Paris 1926, 367 f., behandelte Kasseler Vasenbild muss als zu vieldeutig ausgeschieden werden, zumal weder die zu jugendliche Bedrohte überzeugend an Kreusa, noch der zu wenig jugendliche Angreifer an Ion erinnert: Oinochoe des Shuvalovmalers, *ARV*[2] 1207, 1. Zu dieser Vase auch J. Dörig, 'Kalamis-Studien', *JdI* 80, 1965, 169 ff. mit Abb. 14–15, der die alte Deutung von Panofka auf Orest und Hermione wieder aufnimmt. Ihm folgt A. Lezzi-Hafter, *Der Schuwalow-Maler*, Mainz 1976, 105, S 33, Taf. 100. – Eine Parodie des euripideischen *Ion* liegt wohl in der Phlyakendarstellung des Glockenkraters Taranto 107 937 vor: A.D. Trendall, *Phlyax Vases*[2], BICS Suppl. 19, 1967, Nr. 60, Taf. 1 b; F.G. Lo Porto, 'Nuovi vasi fliacici apuli del Museo Nazionale di Taranto', *BdA* 49, 1964, 16 ff., Abb. 5–6; M. Gigante, *Rintone e il teatro in Magna Grecia*, Neapel 1971, 101. Den Alten am rechten Bildrand möchte ich eher für den πρεσβύτης als für Xouthos halten. Als spätkaiserzeitliches Zeugnis darf nach K. Weitzmanns Deutung wahrscheinlich eine Darstellung auf einem Silbergefäss aus Kustanai in der Ermitage in Leningrad gelten: 'Three "Bactrian" Silver Vessels with Illustrations from Euripides', *The Art Bulletin* 25, 1943, 298 ff., Abb. 7: ders., *Illustrations in Roll and Codex*[2] (Princeton 1970) Taf. 9, Abb. 21 c–e: 'Ion', auch hier mit dem Zweig, tritt von rechts aus dem Tempel auf eine hoheitsvolle Frau (Kreusa?) zu. Hinter dieser eine weitere Frau (Priesterin mit Opfergefäss ?).

36 M. Schmidt, *Der Dareiosmaler und sein Umkreis*, Münster 1960, Taf. 6 b.

37 'Hellas und Asia', *ArchEph* 1937, 493 ff. Dazu H. Metzger, 'A propos des images apuliennes de la bataille d'Alexandre et du conseil de Darius', *Revue des Études Grecques* 80, 1967, 312 f., der für die Asia die allgemeinere Deutung vorzieht. Ebenfalls gegen die Deutung von Curtius T. Hölscher, *Griechische Historienbilder des 5. und 4. Jahrhunderts v.Chr.*, Würzburg 1973, 178.

38 Im Zusammenhang mit der Apate-Darstellung wären die wichtigen Stellen im *Panegyrikos* des Isokrates (or. 4, 133 und 136–7) zu behandeln. Dort wird betont, der Unverstand der griechischen Poleis habe das Unglück in Asien verschuldet, was konkret darauf Bezug nimmt, dass die Griechen wenige Jahre vorher, im Antalkidas-bzw. Königsfrieden von 387/6, die kleinasiatischen Städte dem Perserkönig überlassen hatten. Isokrates gebraucht allerdings nicht den Begriff der Apate, sondern vielmehr den die Griechen als handelnde Subjekte stärker belastenden der ἄνοια (137) oder sogar der μανία (133). Diese Mania treibt nach Isokrates die Griechen dazu, ihr eigenes Land in Armut zu stürzen und zu versäumen, Asien zu "nutzen". Isokrates verwendet für den letzten Begriff das Schlüsselwort τὴν Ἀσίαν καρποῦσθαι, das die wirtschafts-und bevölkerungspolitischen Hintergründe der Asienpropaganda beleuchtet. Ich möchte auf das Apate-Problem an anderer Stelle ausführlicher eingehen und weitere Beobachtungen zum Dareioskrater – als typisches Bildzeugnis des 4. Jahrhunderts – anfügen.

39 Die Gegenüberstellung ist allerdings nicht neu: Vgl. etwa *Herodot* 5, 106.

40 Hier seien noch einige Ueberlegungen zu Einzelheiten der Darstellung auf dem Ion-Krater angefügt, für die eine Vergegenwärtigung des besonderen zeitgeschichtlichen Hintergrunds der Jahre um 350/40 – die Enstehungszeit der Vase – aufschlussreich sein könnte. Da wir als Schauplatz der Szene Delphi ermitteln konnten, wird ein Hinweis von Pausanias interessant, der X, xiii, 5 gerade in Delphi ein Apollonbild im Motiv des auf der Vase dargestellten nennt: "Apollon, der die Hirschkuh anfasst". Es handelt sich um eine makedonische Weihung, genauer: der Makedonen aus Dion im südlichen Makedonien. Der Zeitpunkt der Aufstellung ist nicht bekannt. Angesichts der Bedeutung der Stadt

Dion im 5. Jahrhundert v.Chr. unter Archelaos kommt ein Datum vor der Entstehungszeit der apulischen Vase durchaus in Betracht. G. Schneider-Herrmann (oben Anm. 32) führt die Pausanias-Stelle mit der Bemerkung an, dass sich diese Statue "schwer mit Unteritalien verbinden" lasse. Auf den Hinweis auf Delphi geht sie nicht ein. — Man könnte geradezu behaupten, Isokrates hätte keine treffendere Illustration seiner politischen Propaganda finden können, als sie dieses Vasenbild bietet, in dessen Mittelpunkt als Abschluss wie eine Huldigung an die Makedonen bzw. an Philipp im besonderen ein makedonisches Votivgeschenk erscheint. Doch lässt sich die verführerische Verbindung gerade zu dieser Weihestatue natürlich nicht beweisen. Immerhin ist in unserem Zusammenhang interessant, dass im delphischen Tempel, zum mindesten in älterer Zeit, keine Kultstatue des Gottes existierte (was mit der Vorstellung von der jährilichen Epiphanie des Apollon zusammenhing). Noch Pausanias X, xxiv, 5, spricht in so unbestimmter Form von "einer anderen goldenen Statue des Apollon" im Adyton des Tempels, dass die Unzugänglichkeit auch für seine Zeit vorausgesetzt werden muss. Wer das Innere des delphischen Tempels abgekürzt darstellen wollte, musste vermutlich auf einen anderen, allgemein bekannten Statuentypus zurückgreifen, und dafür mochte sich eine Votivgruppe an der heiligen Strasse durchaus empfehlen. Ein bemerkenswerter Umstand kommt hinzu: Gerade in der Entstehungszeit des Ruveser Vasenbildes war der delphische Tempel als 'Bildvorlage' garnicht verfügbar, da er 373/2 zerstört worden war. Die langjährigen Bemühungen um den Neubau, die sich bis 320 hinzogen, mochten ihn aber erst recht als Darstellungsgegenstand aktuell erscheinen lassen. Eine Verbindung des Makedonenkönigs Philipp mit Delphi, die in den vorangehenden Ueberlegungen zum gedanklichen Hintergrund des Vasenbildes zunächst unbestimmt auftauchte, bestand in der Tat auch in der historischen Realität. Philipp gehörte nämlich-nicht unumstritten gewiss — dem Verband der Amphiktyonen an und erwarb sich in dieser Eigenschaft Verdienste um den Wiederaufbau des Tempels. Seine Aufnahme in die Amphiktyonie erfolgte bald nach der Abfassung des isokratischen *Philippus* (346) und damit im Jahrzehnt, in das auch der Krater aus Ruvo gehört. Zu den Verdiensten der Makedonen um das delphische Heiligtum ist im besonderen Aischines, or. 3, 132 zu vergleichen. — Schliesslich sei noch ein zweifellos zufälliges Zusammentreffen vermerkt, das die bisweilen zu beobachtende, eigentümliche 'poetische Kraft' des Zufalls bewusst macht: Das Vasenbild aus dem mittleren 4. Jahrhundert, das in verschiedener Hinsicht zur Gedankenverbindung mit einer der bedeutendsten politischen Figuren jener Zeit anregte, zeigt in seinem Mittelpunkt die Vorbereitungen für ein festliches Stieropfer. Der Ermordung Philipps beim Hochzeitsfest im Jahre 336 ging nach der Ueberlieferung bei Diodor, xvi, 91, 2 f. und Paus. viii, 7, 6, ein dunkler delphischer Orakelspruch voraus, den Philipp auf einen Sieg über die Perser missdeutet haben soll: Bekränzt ist der Stier; alles ist vollendet, und auch der Opferschlächter ist da: ἔστεπται μὲν ὁ ταῦρος, ἔχει τέλος, ἔστιν ὁ θύσων.

41 So etwa bei Sophokles, *Trach.* 1099 f., wo Herakles den χρυσέων δράκοντα μήλων φύλακ᾿ ἐπ᾿ ἐσχάτοις τόποις zu bezwingen hat. Diese den Baum bewachende Schlange ist auf dem Ruveser Vasenbild das charakteristische Detail, das die Deutung auf den Hesperidenmythos erlaubt. Es muss zwar festgehalten werden, dass der Baum keine Aepfel (mehr ?) trägt. Im Zusammenhang mit der gesamten Typologie der Hesperidendarstellungen wird man jedoch die Deutung nicht in Frage stellen wollen. Ausführliche Behandlung bei F. Brommer, 'Herakles und die Hesperiden auf Vasenbildern', *JdI* 57, 1942, 105 ff; zu den unteritalischen Beispielen 119 f.

42 Sichtermann a.O. (oben Anm. 32) spricht nur von Greifen und Arimaspen. K. Schauenburg, 'Zur Symbolik unteritalischer Rankenmotive *RM* 64, 1957, 215, Anm. 131, führt den Ruveser Krater zweimal an: als Beleg für die Darstellung von Arimaspen und Greifen sowie von Amazonen und Greifen. Es ist mir im Augenblick nicht möglich, nachzuprüfen, ob tatsächlich sowohl Amazonen wie Arimaspen auftreten, (deren Darstellungen ohnehin im 4. Jahrhundert oft schwer zu unterscheiden sind). In unserem Zusammenhang können beide Motive 'topographisch' verstanden werden.

43 Zur Geschichte und Entwicklung des griechischen Weltbildes ist unter anderem jetzt heranzuziehen: H. Schwabl, H. Diller u.a., *Grecs et barbares,* Entretiens sur l'Antiquité Classique 8, Fondation Hardt Genf 1962.

44 H. Metzger, *Les représentations dans la céramique attique du IVe siècle,* Paris 1951, 206 ff.; E.B. Harrison, 'Hesperides and Heroes', *Hesperia* 33, 1964, 76 ff., bes. 79. Weitere Belege bei A. Dieterich, *Nekyia*[2], Leipzig 1913, 21 f.

THE DANCE OF THE AMAZONS

G. Schneider-Herrmann

Plate 43.

Two red-figured Apulian vases, decorated by two different painters, show figures which may be interpreted as dancing Amazons. The first vase, a footed alabastron in the Ashmolean Museum, Oxford (Pl. 43, Figs. 1 and 2), can be dated in the third quarter of the fourth century B.C.[1] The second, a knob-handled dish, in a private collection in Kiel (Pl. 43, Figs. 3 and 4), is somewhat earlier, about the middle of the fourth century.[2]

The Alabastron

Rising above a flower and surrounded by floral tendrils, a female figure moves towards the left in three-quarter view, head in profile, stepping lightly on her toes and apparently performing a dance step (Pl.43, Fig.1). She appears in the Oriental costume of an Amazon, as known from Attic vases of the fifth century B.C.[3] Under a short-sleeved tunic of almost knee length, of patterned material, she wears a close-fitting undergarment decorated with white circles which is visible on her arms and legs; she also wears a white belt, studded straps across her chest, and white shoes. Her head is covered by a white Phrygian cap with flaps falling down over her shoulders; a corkscrew hangs down her cheek. The figure is armed as an Amazon; she brandishes a battle axe in her right hand and holds in her left two spears, partly concealed behind her shield, the typical pelta, which has a white rim and bears a small Medusa head in the centre, flanked by a scroll ornament.

At first sight we visualize wings rising from her back and framing her head, with a rosette in between. However, the undulating or curving lines give the impression of a billowing cloak. At the same time a cloak billowing high up does not seem to go with the conception of the figure's restrained movement. The dance step stirs the folds of the tunic only slightly, causing some inconformity.

The knob-handled Dish

Surrounded by a berried laurel wreath in added white, a female figure, dressed rather similarly to the one on the Oxford alabastron, seems also to perform a dance.[4] She wears a sleeveless, somewhat longer tunic of unpatterned material, which billows out in a wide curve, and a narrow white studded belt from which several ribbons with white beads trail down over her tunic. Her undergarment is decorated with alternating black and white zigzag bands encircling arms and legs; her Phrygian cap has a spiked crest. Large wings in profile, one partly visible behind the other, project from her back.

Whereas the Oxford figure is equipped with the weapons of an Amazon, the other has in her right hand a thymiaterion, held at arm's length, while a tambourine dangles by a ribbon from her left hand. In view of her stance the Oxford figure is likely to perform a war dance, while the other, more relaxed, her hand bent slightly down and her left arm swinging, may be performing a cult dance.

In addition to the archaeological considerations which induce us to suggest the two figures to be Amazons, the literary tradition which connects them with Artemis and Dionysos, also confirms our presumption. In this context the statues of Amazons should be mentioned which Pliny says were made by Pheidias, Polykleitos, Kresilas, Kydon and Phradmon for the temple of Artemis at Ephesos.[5] There is also a literary tradition of legends, some versions of which are here discussed. The oldest is from a lost text by Pindar, mentioned by Pausanias who accuses him of being wrongly informed about the Amazons having established the cult of

Artemis at Ephesos.[6] In fact, according to Pausanias the Amazons had known and worshipped the goddess ever since the time when, pursued by Dionysos, they had sought refuge in her sanctuary.[7] This version is followed by Tacitus who also mentions the surrender of the Amazons to Dionysos and the mercy shown by him to them.[8]

It is interesting to see that the legend of an Amazonomachy near the sanctuary of Artemis survived sporadically in art. A Pompeian wall painting shows the precinct of the goddess whose statue stands high on a pillar, while a Greek is attacking an Amazon on horseback and another Greek lies on the ground.[9] Whereas this reminds us only in a general way of a battle involving Amazons at the sanctuary of Artemis, a relief on a Roman sarcophagus of the second century A.D. in Cortona (well known during the Renaissance), shows Dionysos on a chariot slaying the Amazons in a battle which takes place before a port, presumably the port of Ephesos.[10]

In the third century B.C. Kallimachos described the Amazons' worship of the Goddess at Ephesos in his Hymn to Artemis. The war-loving female tribe is said to have dedicated a statue and a shrine and to have bestowed offers as well as to have performed a war dance, as a chorus circling around the statue:

> "For thee Artemis, too, the Amazons, whose mind is set on war, in Ephesus beside the sea established an image beneath an oak trunk, and Hippo (queen of Amazons, no doubt identical with Hippolyte) performed a holy rite for thee, and they themselves, O Upis queen, around the image danced a war dance first in shields and in armour, and again in a circle arraying a spacious choir. And the loud pipes thereto piped shrill accompaniment, that they might foot the dance together (for not yet did they pierce the fawn, Athena's handiwork, a bane to the deer). And the echo reached unto Sardis and the Berecynthian range. And they with their feet beat loudly and therewith their quivers rattled . . And afterwards around that image was raised a shrine of broad foundations."[11]

It is of course tempting, in the light of this tradition, to interpret the Oxford figure as an Amazon who performs a dance similar to that described by Kallimachos, although her restrained movement does not match the frantic character of the dance in the hymn (Pl. 43, Fig. 1).[12] The winged figure on the dish in a private collection in Kiel may also be linked to the Artemis cult, since the thymiaterion she carries may indicate a cult dance (Pl. 43, Fig. 3). At any rate the two figures could be interpreted as dancing Amazons, possibly inspired by a common origin, a picture or more probably a drama. They could perhaps be imagined as members of a theatrical chorus, since there appears to have been more than one play with a subject relating to Amazons, although their contents are unknown.[13]

There seems to be no literary evidence for the unusual feature of wings worn by an Amazon. One can only point to archaeological evidence which sporadically reveals a close affiliation between representations of Artemis on the one hand, and those of worshipping females on the other.[14] An Artemis figure provided with wings may account for the concept of a winged Amazon. To quote some examples, the Potnia Theron is occasionally represented with wings.[15] One can also mention the winged Artemis shooting arrows on a mid-fifth century black-figured white ground lekythos from the sanctuary of Artemis Brauronia.[16] The closest to our figure for instance is the Artemis on an Etruscan stamnos of the fourth century B.C. which shows a strong Italiote influence.[17] She wears a similar close fitting undergarment.

A head of the Thracian goddess on a Tarentine antefix datable around 400 B.C. is of some interest, as it has small wings between the curls just beneath the lion's scalp on her head.[18]

Wings do not usually belong to the image of this goddess, but there is a connection between Artemis and Bendis, both hunting divinities, in so far as a figure called Artemis-Bendis which blends characteristics of both goddesses, occurs in South Italian art.[19] However, one cannot be sure of the origin of the wings of the Bendis head: they may or may not be derived from an Artemis image. Hence it remains uncertain whether the figure of the Amazon on the dish shows traces of this ambiguous tradition (Fig. 3). It does not seem unlikely that iconographically our figure is influenced directly by a figure of a winged Artemis. Moreover there is no literary evidence for a dance connected with Bendis, whereas dancing is repeatedly mentioned with Artemis and her cult.[20]

Artemis is not the only divinity whose influence can be detected in the two pictures we are discussing. One can also see in them some Dionysiac elements, indicated by the presence of the tambourine on the dish and of the floral ornament surrounding the figure on the alabastron, as a symbol of eternal renewal of life.[21] The literary background to this iconographic mixture may be the legend already mentioned above of the Amazons' surrender and the mercy granted by Dionysos, marking the penetration of the god's cult in Eastern Greece. Our alabastron and our dish show the consequences of the events recorded by Diodorus Siculus: the Amazons came under the spell of Dionysos and became his followers.[22]

Since the power of both Artemis and Dionysos dwells in these figures, one can postulate a merging of the cults of the two divinities, reflecting a syncretism which appears more than once in South Italy in the fourth century B.C.[23] In the case of our two figures the cult of Artemis prevails and Dionysos is recognisable only by his symbols.

In this respect one of the two outside pictures of our dish (Pl. 43, Fig. 4) conveys a more explicit manifestation of Dionysiac influence than does the floral surround on the alabastron (Pl. 43, Fig. 2). The scene with three women and an Eros carrying a bunch of grapes, another symbol of the god, represents one of many variations of this kind occurring on South Italian vases.[24] As on other dishes of this type a correlation between the inside and the outside pictures may be assumed. Finally, not only the winged, but also the armed, Amazon appears as a delegate of both gods.

Further evidence of such a cult syncretism is provided by two other dishes which show an Amazon fully armed driving a quadriga in association with Dionysiac symbols and an Eros scene as well as a satyr.[25]

In one form or another, it would appear that Amazons in contact with divinities belong to an Eastern tradition which seems to have by-passed the Greek mainland but to have found its way to the Western colonies, where it can still be traced on vase painting.

NOTES

1 Inv. 1945.55. Published by courtesy of the Ashmolean Museum, Oxford. *Ashmolean Museum, Department of Antiquities. Summary Guide,* Oxford 1951, Pl. XXXIIIa; K. Schauenburg, 'Unteritalische Alabastra', *JdI* 87, 1972, Figs. 16 and 17; *RVAp* I, p. 429, no. 16/74. For alabastra used by women see T.B.L. Webster, *Potter and Patron in Classical Athens,* Oxford 1972, 102.

2 Published by courtesy of the owner. K. Schauenburg, 'Bendis in Unteritalien?' *JdI* 89, 1974, 177, Fig. 45 (described as a lekane); *RVAp* I, p. 420, no. 16/39.

3 See for instance Arias-Hirmer-Shefton, Pl. 191, and P.E. Arias, *Enciclopedia Classica* III, Vol. XI, V, Pl. CXLVIII.

4 G. Schneider-Herrmann, 'Apulian Red-figured Paterae with Flat or Knob Handles', *BICS* Suppl. 34, 1977, Cat. no. 177.

5 *Nat. Hist.* III, 4, 53; B.S. Ridgway, 'A Story of Five Amazons', *AJA* 78, 1974, 1–17.

6 VII, ii, 6–8. Strabo, XI, 5, 505, and XII, 3, 550, mentions the legends according to which the Amazons had founded Ephesos and other cities.

7 Plutarch, *Quest. Gr.* 56, gives, a different version: the Amazons persecuted by Dionysos fled from Ephesos to Samos, where a great many of them were killed. Further references in L. Preller, *Griechische Mythologie,* Berlin 1860, I, 548, n. 3.

8 *Ann.* III, 61.

9 I am indebted to Professor K. Schefold for this reference; Pompeii IX 2, 16 (e), in K. Schefold, *Vergessenes Pompeji,* Bern 1962, Pl. 58, 3, and p. 76, n. 156; see also K. Schauenburg, 'Neue Darstellungen aus der Bellerophonsage', *AA* 1958, 24, n. 1.

10 Cortona, Museo Diocesano; E. Gerhard, 'Bacchus in Amazonenkampf', *AZ,* June 1845, 82 ff.; A. Neppi Modona, *Cortona Etrusca e Romana,* Florence 1925, Pl. XI; F. Matz, *Die Dionysischen Sarkophage,* III, Berlin 1969, No. 237 (dated around 160 A.D.), pp. 426–28 and Pl. 258.

11 Kallimachos, *Hymn* III (To Artemis), trans. A.W. Mair, London (Loeb) 1921, lines 237–249.

12 For a dancing Amazon, see also *Iliad* II, 814, where the epithet 'polyskarthmos' applied to the Amazon Myrina can be understood as running, jumping or dancing. There is, however, no relation between this Amazon and Artemis.

13 Preller (*supra* n. 7) II, 234, n. 3.

14 See for example the black-figured lekythos Louvre CA2925 in L. Kahil, 'Autour de l'Artémis attique', *AntK* 8, 1965, Pl. 10, Figs. 3–5, on which the dancing figures with chiton and pointed cap are interpreted tentatively as worshippers of Bendis (p. 29); the little girls performing cult rites for Artemis Brauronia in bear costumes (arktoi), *ibidem,* p. 25; M.P. Nilsson, *Geschichte der griechischen Religion*[3], Munich 1967, 485; see also G. Schneider-Herrmann, 'Das Geheimnis der Artemis in Etrurien', *AntK* 13, 1970, Pl. 28, Figs. 1–2, and Pl. 29, Figs. 1–2, for a red-figured Etruscan stamnos with a female worshipper as Artemis herself, wearing tunic, undergarment and Phrygian cap; and Schefold, *Vergessenes Pompeji,* 50, Pl. 34, for a Pompeian wall-painting with Amazons in a short girdled chiton — the well known costume of Artemis — as caryatides.

15 For the Potnia Theron represented with wings, see e.g. the Rhodian gold plaques, dated to the 7th c. B.C., in London (R.A. Higgins, *Greek and Roman Jewellery,* London 1961, Pls. 18 D, 19 D–E, 20) and in Berlin (*EAA,* I, 690, Fig. 886); the Kypselos Chest (W. v. Massow, "Die Kypseloslade", *AM* 1916, Fig. 26; a bronze tripod relief of c.600 B.C. (Schefold *op.cit.,* Fig. 28); the 6th century hydria from Grächwil in Bern (H. Jucker, *AntK Beiheft 9,* 1973, 42 ff.); the terracotta relief from Cimaise in the Louvre, dated around 600 B.C. (*Catalogue Raisonné,* B 344, Pl. XXXVII); the scarab in Hanover, dated to the second quarter of the 6th c. B.C. (*Kestner Mus. Jahrber.,* 1968–70, No. 10); the marble stele from Dorylaion, 550–480 B.C., in the Istanbul Museum (*Hdb.d.Arch.* VI, 2, 1950, 65 f., Pl. 18, Fig. 1 and *EAA* I, Fig. 887).

16 L. Kahil, "Quelques vases du sanctuaire d'Artémis à Brauron" *AntK Beiheft* I, 1963, Pl. 6, Figs. 3–4; Idem. *AntK* 8, 1965, 32. For a winged Artemis see H. Walter, *Griechische Götter,* Munich 1971, Fig. 190. See also Schauenburg, l.c., 179 (*supra* n. 2) and Moret, *Ilioupersis,* Pl. 56, 1 and p. 22. South Italian terracotta figurines (Metaponto): D. Adamasteanu, *La Basilicata Antica,* Cava dei Tirreni 1974 59, Figs. 1, 3, 4 (6th c. B.C.).

17 G. Schneider-Herrmann, *AntK* 13, 1970, Pls. 28, 1–2 and 29, 1–2.

18 P. Wuilleumier, *Tarente,* Paris 1939, 407 f. and 428 f. Pl. XXXIX, Figs. 5, 7; H. Herdejürgen, *"Tarentinische Terracotten der Sammlung Schwitter"* *AntK* 16, 1973, 103, Pl. 20, Fig. 90, suggests the wings may represent the wandering nature of Bendis.

19 For Bendis see C.W. Lunsingh Scheurleer, 'Die Göttin Bendis in Tarent', *AA* 1932, 314–34; *EAA,* II, 49, 'Bendis' (Rocchetti), and K. Schauenburg, 'Bendis in Unteritalien?', *JdI* 89, 1974, 137–186.

20 See, however, Professor Kahil's comments on the dancing female figures with pointed cap and chiton on a Louvre lekythos, (*supra* n. 14).

21 For Dionysiac floral abundance, see *Hom. Hymn* 7, 37–42. For Dionysos Antheios, see H. Jucker, *'Das Bildnis im Blätterkelch'*, Lausanne 1961, I, 201–202. K. Schauenburg, 'Zur Symbolik unteritalischer Rankenmotive', *RM* 64, 1957, 198–220.

22 III, 71, 4.

23 For an association of the Artemis and Dionysos cults see G. Schneider-Herrmann (*supra* n. 14), 59 f., Pl. 30, Fig. 2, and p. 68, Fig. 3.

24 G. Schneider-Herrmann, 'Spuren eines Eroskultes in der italischen Vasenmalerei', *BABesch* 45, 1970, 86–114.

25 Naples 2541/82255 and Bari 5929; G. Schneider-Herrmann (*supra* n. 4) Cat. Nos. 175 and 176, Pl. XVI, Fig. 1. For an Amazon as charioteer, see Strabo XII, 8, 573, referring to Iliad II, 811 ff., where he understood the Amazon Myrina to be an accomplished charioteer. For Amazons on chariots on Attic black-figured vases, see D. von Bothmer, *Amazons in Greek Art*, Oxford 1957, 106 ff., Pl. LXIV, Webster (*supra* n. 1), 107.

UN' ANFORA PANATENAICA DEL PITTORE DI EUPHILETOS

Arturo Stenico

Tavole 44, 45.

Nell'ottobre 1962 potei esaminare a Milano, prima che fosse venduta all'asta, un'anfora panatenaica della quale l'unica documentazione grafica erano le brutte e piccole fotografie di entrambe le facce riprodotte nel catalogo approssimativo dell'asta.[1] Scrissi di questo vaso in una lunga nota a pie' di pagina di un mio studio nel quale trattavo di un altro vaso, etrusco, della stessa asta:[2] ivi, facendo un certo numero di confronti, proponevo l'attribuzione dell'anfora al Pittore di Euphiletos.

Qualche anno dopo l'anfora tornava nuovamente nella Galleria Geri[3] ed in quell'occasione furon fatte delle fotografie nuove, copia delle quali mi fu cortesemente donata dal proprietario della Galleria (Tav. 44, Fig. 1 e Fig. 2).[4] Da quel momento non ho più saputo nulla delle vicende del vaso venduto all'asta.

L'anfora è alta, con il coperchio la cui pertinenza è probabile ma non sicura, cm 67 e ha il massimo diametro di cm 40: è in stato di conservazione buono anche se ricomposta molto bene da grandi frammenti senza lacune. I danni maggiori riguardano la conservazione dei colori sovrapposti, ma anche dove essi sono svaniti è facile, persino in fotografia, riconoscerne la originaria presenza e il loro disegno. Non vi sono ritocchi né aggiunte moderni.

Per la sagoma l'anfora non presenta particolari novità: la bocca e il piede sono ad echino, le anse a bastoncino semplice. Corrente è anche la decorazione accessoria, limitata alla serie di doppie palmette alternate a doppi fiori di loto sul collo e alle baccellature a colori alternati alla fine del corpo sotto il collo. Il recipiente sopra il piede ha una fascia con i consueti raggi.

Lato A: Athena Promachos tra due colonne doriche sormontate da galletti rivolti verso l'interno. Presso la colonna di sinistra, davanti alla figura della dea, l'iscrizione ΤΟΝ ΑΘΕΝΕΘΕΝ ΑΘΛΟΝ in senso verticale, ma che leggermente si discosta dalla colonna in basso. La dea, nel consueto schema, indossa una veste riccamente ornata sia col graffito che col color paonazzo aggiunto e l'egida minutamente descritta; in testa calza l'elmo con alto *lophos*[5] con la minuziosa decorazione a preciso graffito e rosso sovrapposto. Imbraccia uno scudo rotondo col bordo paonazzo e che reca come *episemon* un gallo a sinistra in bianco coi particolari graffiti, identico a quelli posti sopra le colonne. La dea non ha calzari e brandisce l'asta.

Lato B: Entro la 'metopa' tre *hoplitodromoi* a sinistra. Sono rappresentati tutti e tre nel medesimo schema con la gamba destra spinta avanti in una larga falcata e col braccio destro portato piegato all'indietro. Hanno le *knemides* bordate in rosso paonazzo, l'elmo abbassato con ampio cimiero.[6] Il corpo degli atleti è completamente nascosto dai grandi scudi rotondi. Quello del primo corridore, bordato in rosso, ha come *episemon,* in bianco, una coppa peduncolata senz'anse; quello del secondo un delfino inarcato a sinistra il cui bianco è interamente scomparso, mentre tracce del colore rimangono per i puntolini che, spaziati regolarmente, decorano l'orlo. Il terzo corridore ha uno scudo orlato in rosso e come *episemon* tre globuli disposti a triangolo il cui colore bianco e quasi interamente svanito.

Già nella menzione che feci nell'occasione sopra citata proponevo l'attribuzione di quest' anfora al Pittore di Euphiletos.[7] Ed anche ora la confermo.[8] Tipica è l'Athena del lato A che ricompare, con lievi varianti soprattutto nello schema del panneggio, ma sostanzialmente identica sul piano stilistico in tutte le anfore panatenaiche di questo pittore che in questo tipo di vaso risulta specializzato. In particolare ricalca anche nei particolari più minuti la dea del vaso eponimo di Londra, British Museum B 134.[9] Il confronto del particolare della testa dà una perfetta coincidenza anche nei dettagli della decorazione dell'elmo con la dea dell'anfora panatenaica di Milano. Identico lo schema del complicato panneggio del peplo e la descrizione dell'egida squamata e orlata di serpenti. La vicinanza dell'Athena del vaso di Londra e quella dell'anfora Geri è tale che mi induce a ritenerle contemporanee, forse preparate per la medesima tornata dei giochi fra il 530 e il 520 circa a.Chr.

Anche con quella dell'anfora panatenaica di Leida[10] l'Athena ha molte affinità e così pure con quella del pezzo Amsterdam 1897,[11] tanto vicina alla raffinatissima Athena del vaso del Metropolitan,[12] mentre lo stesso stile mostra quella dell'anfora panatenaica di Boston, più malconcia e con diversa soluzione dello schema del panneggio.[13]

Ma, in linea generale, l'Athena del vaso milanese concorda con quella delle anfore panatenaiche che ho potuto riscontrare attribuite al Pittore di Euphiletos anche, pertanto, con quella dell'anfora di Bologna Pal. Univ. 198, il cui lato B poteva suggerire spunti per il controllo stilistico dello stesso lato del nostro vaso, data l'identità di soggetto, tre *hoplitodromoi* a sinistra, che risultava dalle riproduzioni disponibili.[14] Ma anche da esse, pur insufficienti, era evidente la differenza stilistica della pittura del lato B non solo per quanto si riferisce al Pittore di Euphiletos, ma addirittura con la fase della ceramografia a figure nere in cui è collocata la sua produzione.[15] Nuove fotografie (Tavv. 44–45, Figg. 3–6) dell'anfora di Bologna mi furono gentilmente fornite dalla direzione del Museo[16] e attraverso esse risultava confermato il giudizio di differenza stilistica e cronologica fra i due lati e soprattutto veniva messo in evidenza l'ampio lavoro di restauro e ritocco subìto dal vaso. Lo smontaggio dei frammenti eseguito in seguito alla mia segnalazione da parte del Museo rivelò che ben poco dell'anfora era originale e pertinente. A Fig. 5 e Fig. 6 do in un non facilmente realizzabile fotomontaggio la ricostruzione delle parti antiche di quella che era stata l'anfora Pell. 198 PU di Bologna.[17] La direttrice Dott. C. Morigi Govi mi conferma che nessun altro frammento, anche non figurato, è stato ricuperato durante il lavoro di demolizione di quello che nel suo insieme era un vero e pericoloso falso. Mentre trova piena conferma l'attribuzione della metopa con l'Athena al Pittore di Euphiletos, non v'è più dubbio circa l'estraneità del lato con gli *hoplitodromoi.* Non è il caso di mettere in evidenza le differenze stilistiche dei tre corridori con ciò che conosciamo del Pittore di Euphiletos[18] in quanto, anche nei pochi tratti anatomici ora ben esaminabili nelle recenti fotografie, sono discrepanti con quelli del lato B dell'anfora panatenaica milanese.[19]

Ho insistito sull'anfora di Bologna non solo per mettere a punto l'edizione 'critica' di essa[20] quanto per accrescere il valore documentario dell'arte del Pittore di Euphiletos che offre la nuova anfora panatenaica ex Geri. Espungendo infatti dalla produzione del Pittore di Euphiletos il lato B dell'anfora panatenaica di Bologna, la corsa degli *hoplitodromoi* rimaneva esclusa dalla documentazione dei giochi dipinta da questo specialista delle anfore panatenaiche: con l'edizione del vaso ex Geri ora essa torna nel repertorio del maestro. E una composizione calma, ritmata, più una sfilata che una corsa, una marcia che vede nello stesso schema, nello stesso attimo di movimento, staccati, tutti e tre i corridori. Sull'anatomia predomina la 'divisa', i grandi scudi circolari – solo lievemente variati dagli *episema* – coprono interamente il tronco e un braccio, gran parte delle gambe è nascosta dagli scudi o racchiusa nelle *knemides* sottolineate dal rosso contorno. Della testa solo il naso e il grande occhio escono dal compatto elmo pesantemente calzato con le ampie genastere e il coprinuca che giungono al bordo più alto dello scudo. L'aderente *lophos* ha un notevole sviluppo e la sua rigidità è corretta, nel primo e nel terzo *hoplitodromos,* da un tocco veristico, il ripiegamento indietro e verso l'alto della punta anteriore spinta dall'aria mossa dalla corsa: e così (ora poco visibile) si stende obliqua all'indietro la lunga 'coda' del cimiero reso col rosso sovrapposto. Le uniche parti nude sono i piedi, una coscia e il braccio sinistro piegato all'indietro. Sono uguali in tutti e tre i corridori e loro caratteristica è la estrema parsimonia di tratti interni incisi, che peraltro coincidono con quelli di altre figure di atleti o di corridori che i lati B delle anfore panatenaiche del Pittore di Euphiletos offrono in varie pose. In confronto con la varietà e il movimento di questa scena ginnica, il lato B dell'anfora ex Geri può apparire monotono, ma non privo di una marziale monumentalità, arcaicamente e armonicamente scandita.

NOTE

1 *Notiziario della Galleria d'Arte Geri:* No. 119 (stagione 1962–63), ottobre 1962. Nel catalogo il vaso aveva il no. 211.

2 A. Stenico, 'Nuove pitture vascolari del gruppo "Clusium" ', in *Studi in onore di Luisa Banti,* Roma 1965, 298, nota 20.

3 *Notiziario della Galleria d'Arte Geri:* No. 147 (stagione 1965–66), novembre 1965, Suppl. senza numero.

4 Fot. Ripoli Milano: Nn 64–255 A e C.

5 Che interrompe il fregio di baccellature.

6 Lievi differenze di disegno tra i tre elmi.

7 Mi è inaccessibile K. Peters, *Studien zu den panatenäischen Preisamphoren,* Berlino 1942, dove il pittore riceve questa denominazione; J.D. Beazley, *Development of Attic Black-Figure,* Berkeley 1951, 91 seg.; *ABV,* 321 segg., e 694; *EAA* III, 1960, s.v. 'Euphiletos, Pittore di' (E. Paribeni).

8 In *Paralipomena* a p. 143 il Beazley menziona quest'anfora che dichiara di conoscere solo da piccola fotografia, quella del citato *Notiziario Geri* No. 119. Anche per lui l'Athena 'recalls the Euphiletos Painter'. Tuttavia al compianto studioso io avevo spedito l'estratto del mio citato studio della miscellanea Banti con la copia, di formato minore ma chiarissima, della fotografia usata per questo studio che avevo avuto più o meno contemporaneamente agli estratti.

9 *CVA,* British Museum 1, Pl. 2, 2; riprodotta anche con particolare in Beazley, *Development* cit., Pl. 49, 1, 2, 3 (*ABV,* 322, 1).

10 *ABV,* 322, 2; ora ben pubblicata in *CVA* Leiden 1, Pl. 44–45.

11 *ABV,* 322, 8; *CVA,* Musée Scheurleer 1, Pl. 1, 4 e 5.

12 *ABV,* 322, 6; ora ben pubblicata in *CVA,* Metropolitan Museum of Art III, Pl. 39.

13 *ABV,* 322, 7; anche questo pezzo è ora esaurientemente pubblicato in *CVA,* Museum of Fine Arts, Boston 1, Pl. 55.

14 G. Pellegrini, *Catalogo dei vasi antichi dipinti delle Collezioni Palagi e Universitaria,* Bologna 1900, 29; *CVA* Bologna 2, Hg Pl. 1, 1–3.

15 Sulla scorta anche del Beazley (*ABV,* 322, 5), non mancai di sottolineare ciò nella già citata menzione che feci del vaso di Milano.

16 Neg. No. 1052/E.9 e neg. No. 1886/E.10. Con commossa gratitudine ricordo la compianta direttrice del Museo Dott.ssa R. Pincelli che a suo tempo mi procurò queste fotografie e quelle citate più avanti, autorizzandomi alla loro utilizzazione a stampa.

17 Ottenuto riaccostando le immagini dei singoli frammenti riprodotti nelle fotografie del Museo Civico Archeologico di Bologna Neg. No. 3428/E.133 e Neg. No. 3429/E.134. Una completa panoramica dei frammenti antichi è pure nella fotografia Neg. No. 3430 recentemente fornitami molto cortesemente dalla Dott.ssa Morigi Govi alla quale va l'espressione della mia gratitudine per aver voluto controllare le caratteristiche tecniche e metriche dei due gruppi di frammenti.

18 Oltre che il disegno dei profili e degli elmi, il modellato delle braccia con la precisa descrizione a graffito della mano destra in avanti dell'ultimo corridore è nettamente diverso da quello delle figure del Pittore di Euphiletos che stilizzano le lunghe mani aperte con la descrizione isolata e tutta pittorica delle dita tese.

19 Anche al di là del confronto stilistico tutto un insieme di dati tecnici porta ad escludere l'appartenenza dei frammenti con gli *hoplitodromoi* all'anfora da cui deriva l'Athena: diverso il colore e l'aspetto dell'argilla, diverso lo spessore a uguale altezza dal presunto piede delle pareti, diversa la curvatura dei due lacerti (e le tracce del lavoro di lima sono ben riconoscibili nei frammenti laterali dei due complessi di frammenti).

20 Che precedenti editori avevano trascurato completamente.

SOME TERRACOTTA DEDICATIONS

T.B.L. Webster

In *Potter and Patron in Classical Athens,* I suggested that the picture of Dionysos between eyes on the small lekythos dedicated by Phanyllis to Hera at her shrine in Delos was irrelevant: 'The goddess was expected to accept it for the perfume, not the picture'.[1] Since examining the terracottas dedicated at a number of shrines, however, I have wondered whether this was not a hasty judgement.

It remains true in general that a vase, whether filled with perfume or not, is a beautiful object in which a goddess may find pleasure (just as Apollo is expected to find pleasure in boxing, dancing, and singing performed in his honour at Delos)[2] and that the dedicator can make the vase relevant by having it inscribed before or after firing. Although dedicatory inscriptions are common on vases from sanctuaries, they are extremely rare on terracottas. Indeed I know only three such inscriptions, one of which is doubtful: the first is an early fifth century Attic terracotta of a seated goddess dedicated by Aigon to Hekate,[3] the second a late sixth century protome dedicated by Mnelaris to Hera in Delos,[4] and the third a seventh century Cretan plaque representing a naked woman on which the inscription may or may not be a dedication.[5]

The number of votive terracottas is enormous and since most of them bear no inscription, we must assume that the deity honoured was expected by the dedicator to accept them as a relevant gift: she could not use them as she could have been expected to use vases and they must have had some other relevance. The purpose of these notes is to point out the existence of a pattern which may be relevant in terracotta dedications to Hera, Demeter and Persephone, Athena and Artemis.

The terracottas to be considered are, for Hera, those from Perachora (seventh to third century B.C.)[6] and Samos (ninth to seventh century).[7] For Demeter and Persephone, those from Acrocorinth (seventh to third century),[8] from the Gypsades at Knossos (eighth to second century),[9] from the sanctuary of Demeter Malophoros at Selinous (seventh to sixth century),[10] from the Thesmophoreion at Gela (seventh to fifth century,)[11] from the temple of Persephone at Locri (sixth to fifth century),[12] from Medma, probably dedicated to Persephone (sixth to fourth century),[13] from Troy, probably dedicated to Demeter and Persephone (Hellenistic),[14] and from Halikarnassos, probably dedicated to Demeter and Persephone (fifth to fourth century).[15] For Athena, the terracottas are those from Lindos (seventh to fourth century),[16] the Acropolis sanctuary at Gortyn, probably dedicated to Athena (Sub-Mycenaean to Hellenistic),[17] and from Emporio, Chios.[18] For Artemis, the terracottas are those from the Artemision at Thasos (sixth to second century),[19] and the Artemision at Paros (seventh to fourth century).[20]

One comes to these goddesses with certain preconceptions based on literature, but the terracottas do not always fit the preconceptions. Although some represent male figures, the majority are of women, standing or seated, as would be expected. Within these major categories, some individual figures need interpretation and can be assigned to sub-categories, the variety of which is in some instance surprising. If we consider the terracottas from all the shrines listed above we find that a pattern seems to appear in which three groups are of interest: a first group of figures representing Dionysos or characters connected with him, a second group of other gods or heroes, and a third group of female figures which seems to need some special explanation.

The first group is the easiest to identify. The fat males of Ptah-type belong to the same general family as the padded dancers, hairy satyrs, satyrs, and comic actors; the fat men of Ptah-type carrying a child may be regarded as the ancestors of the classical statuettes of Papposilenos carrying the infant Dionysos; the figure of the kneeling man has a twin in a kneeling satyr, as Higgins points out.[21] These types of male figurines appear in all the sanctuaries mentioned, except Halikarnassos, where, however, Dionysos himself is represented, and the temple of Persephone at Locri, where Dionysos is shown visiting Persephone on one of the relief plaques. We have therefore to assume that these male 'givers of life', or whatever they should be called, were felt as relevant to the goddesses to whom they were dedicated. In this context it is very interesting that the lower row of pectorals on one of the female votive terracottas from Agrigento includes satyr heads (the middle row has disks, the top row bulls' heads).[22] This element of the pattern suggests that Phanyllis' dedication to Hera of a lekythos with a picture of Dionysos was not irrelevant.

Similarly in the second group there is no need to argue the relevance of the figures of Zeus and Herakles given to Athena at her sanctuary at Lindos, or of Apollo given to Artemis at Thasos, or of Triptolemos given to Persephone and Demeter at Locri. However, offerings of statuettes of Herakles to Demeter and Persephone and of Hermes to Artemis, Demeter, and Persephone, are less obviously relevant and merit some discussion. Perhaps the dedicators thought of Herakles primarily as a strong male, and as such akin to the 'Dionysiac' offerings; perhaps also his ultimate arrival at Olympus was felt to be relevant, particularly in cults of Demeter and Persephone. As to the presence of votive figurines of Hermes, one might suggest the following explanations: firstly as the god of herds and flocks he is relevant to Artemis in her aspect of Artemis Eileithyia at Thasos and Paros,[23] secondly as the devine guide who leads Aphrodite to Persephone's wedding and guarantees Persephone's own return,[24] he is relevant to Persephone at Locri.

In the third group, as already mentioned, some of the votive female figurines need explanation. These are single figures of goddesses who have power to give life, such as Aphrodite or Kybele, groups of female figures with children, and twin women, seated or standing, sometimes united by a single himation round their shoulders. It would appear that a figure of a life-giving goddess was considered an appropriate gift to any female deity, since we find statuettes of Kybele offered to Artemis at Thasos, to Athena at Chios and Lindos, and to Demeter at Selinous, Gela, Troy and Knossos, and statuettes of Aphrodite offered to Artemis at Thasos, to Demeter at Selinous, and to Demeter or Persephone at Medma. Aphrodite is also represented on plaques dedicated to Persephone at Locri.[25] If one accepts that a figurine of a life-giving goddess is an appropriate gift to any female deity, there is no difficulty in accepting as relevant the dedication of women with children even to 'virgin' goddesses like Athena or Artemis, or to goddesses like Demeter and Persephone, whose worship is not obviously connected with children. As for the pairs of female figures, it is worth remembering that such twins have a long ancestry, going back through the Mycenaean period to the Early Bronze Age.[26] Twins, as a symbol of fertility and life-giving, might be appropriate to Artemis at Thasos, or Athena at Lindos, or Demeter at Knossos.[27]

Among the female figures discussed so far I have included the protomes found at Perachora, Samos, Selinous, Gela, Locri, Medma, Troy, Halikarnassos, Lindos, Thasos, Paros, Chios and Knossos. These protomes should, however, be more fully discussed here: they vary from a simple head[28] to a full bust. The arms hang straight down the sides in some;[29] in others the hands are curved around the breasts,[30] or hold a flower.[31] A feature common to all these figurines is that they are sharply cut off, which may suggest that they represent a goddess rising from the ground, an *anodos,* and that the flower held in the hands, or decorating a crown, may be a symbol of fertility and creation. One could perhaps relate these figures to Pandora, Aphrodite, or Persephone, who often appear in *anodos* scenes in the iconography of Attic vase-painting.[32]

Finally in the third group are the naked figures, standing at Gortyn, seated at Paros, Locri, and Troy, standing dolls at Acrocorinth, Knossos, Lindos and Chios, and a bust at Thasos. A possible clue to understanding is that for all these types a corresponding draped type is known. The Astarte plaques, from which the standing naked figure derives, have a draped version, and a derivative draped version is also known from Greek sites.[33] A standing doll with painted drapery actually occurs in the sanctuary of Athena at Lindos. The draped version of the seated figures is well known from Troy and elsewhere.[34] Draped busts have been dealt with in the last paragraph. It is possible (though this does not apply to the Thasos bust or to the Astarte plaques) that the naked figures could be given and perhaps were given drapery of real fabric. However, one should remember here the ceremonies in which the goddess was bathed and dressed,[35] and that the Bears apparently raced naked at Brauron,[36] and consider that the figures were intended to be naked. It is possible then that the naked figures are intended to show the goddess at the moment before she appears robed and crowned in the splendour of the new year's fertility.

If this interpretation of the pattern is right, these figurines may carry on a tradition going back to such representations of a goddess as the one on a Late Geometric Boeotian amphora,[37] or even on the faience figurines of Middle Minoan Knossos, or the Early Bronze Age 'frying pans' of the Keros culture.[38] In this connection one should bear in mind that in all probability the figurines in question were dedications made primarily by women, who, it would seem, preserved consciously, or unconsciously, very old memories of the goddess who gave all kinds of life.

NOTES

1 T.B.L. Webster, *Potter and Patron in Classical Athens,* London 1972, 286; lekythos in C.H.E. Haspels, *Attic Black-Figured Lekythoi,* Paris 1936, 199, No. 1.

2 *Homeric Hymn,* III, 149.

3 R.A. Higgins, *Greek Terracottas,* London 1967, 72.

4 L.H. Jeffery, *Local Scripts of Archaic Greece,* Oxford 1961, Pl. 57, No. 43a.

5 *Ibidem,* Pl. 60, No. 18.

6 Humfry Payne, *Perachora* I, Oxford 1940; Higgins (*supra* n. 3), 47f., 104.

7 *AM* 74, 1959, 26–49; *AM* 76, 1961, 68–183; *AA* 1964, 506–522; Higgins (*supra* n. 3), 18, 37.

8 R.S. Stroud, *Hesperia* 34, 1965, 1–25; *Hesperia* 37, 1968, 299–330.

9 J.N. Coldstream, *BSA* Suppl. Vol. 8, 1973.

10 Ettore Gabrici, *MonAnt* 32, 1927; Higgins (*supra* n. 3), 52–53, 86–88, 124; Günther Zuntz, *Persephone,* Oxford 1971, 93 ff.; Ernst Langlotz, *Die Kunst der Westgriechen,* Munich 1963, Pls. 34, 35, 68.

11 *ArchReps* 1966–67, 42; P. Orlandini, *Kokalos* 12, 1966, 8–35; Zuntz (*supra* n. 10), 93 ff.

12 Zuntz (*supra* n. 10), 93 ff., 160 ff; Orsi *NSc* 1913, Supplement, 5–54; Helmut Prückner, *Die Lokrischen Tonreliefs,* Mainz 1968 (and review by Zuntz, *Gnomon* 43, 1971, 490–501); Langlotz (*supra* n. 10) Pls. 6, 18, 58–59, 71–75.

13 Orsi (*supra* n. 12), 55–144; Langlotz (*supra* n. 10), Pls. 22, 56, 57, 60, 67, 94, 96, 97.

14 D.B. Thompson, *Troy, Supplementary Monograph 3,* Princeton 1968, from Contexts V and VI, pp. 8–10 and 58–60.

15 Higgins (*supra* n. 3), 65–68, 110, and *Terracottas in the British Museum* I, London 1954, 102.

16 Christian Blinkenberg, *Lindos, I, Les petits objets,* Copenhagen 1931; Higgins (*supra* n. 3), 29, 61–64, 109.

17 G. Rizza and V. Santa Maria Scrinari, *Il Santuario sull'Acropoli di Gortina,* I, Rome 1968.

18 J. Boardman, *BSA* Suppl. Vol. 6, 1967.

19 Inscriptions of the 1st century B.C. give her the titles Polo and Eileithyia: F. Salviat and N. Weill, *BCH* 82, 1958, 808–814; *BCH* 83, 1959, 775–780; *BCH* 85, 1961, 919–930; *Archaeology* 13, 1960, 97 ff.; Higgins (*supra* n. 3), 41, 85, 106. See also P. Bernard and F. Salviat, *BCH* 86, 1962, p. 594, n. 2.

20 Otto Rubensohn, *Das Delion von Paros,* Wiesbaden 1962.

21 Higgins, *Terracottas in the British Museum,* p. 55, Nos. 82–84.

22 Agrigento, from the so-called Temple of the Dioskouroi; Langlotz (*supra* n. 10), Pl. 20 right. At Agrigento and Gela (Zuntz, *supra* n. 10, Pls. 15a, 16b), she is Athena, but her aegis looks like a special addition. On her identity see Zuntz, 116 ff.

23 For Artemis Eileithyia, see Salviat and Weill, *Archaeology* 13, 1960, 104. The Kriophoroi at Gortyn, Knossos and Medma probably also represent Hermes.

24 *Cf.* the Attic red-figured bell-krater New York 28.57.23 (Persephone Painter); ARV^2 1012, 1, and Pfuhl, *MuZ* fig. 556. The youth with a boy on his shoulder at Medma may be Hermes with the infant Dionysos, and so belong to the 'Dionysiac' element in the pattern.

25 On an Attic black-figured olpe Demeter and Persephone are accompanied by a lion: Henri Metzger, *Recherches sur l'imagerie Athénienne,* Paris 1965, 25, comments that popular belief tended to confuse the Eleusinian and the Phrygian goddesses.

26 Colin Renfrew, *AJA* 73, 1969, 19, Pl. 9b. For a discussion of the type, see T. Hadzisteliou-Price, *JHS* 91, 1971, 48–69.

27 For twin fertility goddesses in Arnhem Land, see Phyllis Kaberry, *BICS* 4, 1957, 50. For the 'Two Queens' at Mycenaean Pylos, see Pylos tablets Fr. 1222, etc. (wrongly doubted by M. Gérard-Rousseau, *Incunabula Graeca* 29, 240 f.).

28 E.g. Selinous; Gabrici (*supra* n. 10), Pls. 40–66.

29 E.g. Halikarnassos and Thasos, *BCH* 85, 1961, p. 921, Fig. 5.

30 E.g. Lindos; Blinkenberg (*supra* n. 16), Pl. 120; Thasos, *BCH* 85, 1961, 921, Fig. 4; Higgins (*supra* n. 3), 64, Fig. 17.

31 E.g. Locri; Orsi (*supra* n. 12), Fig. 81.

32 For Pandora, Aphrodite and Persephone see ARV^2 1720 ff. and *Ill.Gr.Dr.,* 151 ff.; for Persephone see Nilsson, *GGR,* Pl. 39, 1; for Demeter Thesmophoros at Thebes see Pausanias, lx, 16, 5; for *anodoi* see Claude Bérard, *Anodoi,* Institut Suisse de Rome 1974.

33 *Cf.* P.J. Riis, *Berytus* 9, 1949, 69 ff., Pl. 16, and the Greek draped version from Perachora, *ibid.,* Pl. 19, 1.

34 Thompson (*supra* n. 14) Nos. 58 and 64.

35 C. Kardara, *AM* 76, 1961, 81, interprets the front of the Ludovisi throne as such a ritual bathing, and this interpretation might also be true of the Locri plaque with the birth of Aphrodite.

36 C. Sourvinou, *Classical Quarterly* 21, 1971, 339–342, on Aristophanes' *Lysistrata* 641–647, and L. Kahil, *AntK* 8, 1965, 20 ff.

37 Athens Nat. Mus. 5893, Coldstream, *GGP,* Pl. 45d.

38 See for the Keros culture, Christian Zervos, *L'Art des Cyclades,* Paris 1957, Fig. 223, and Colin Renfrew, *Emergence of Civilisation,* London 1972, p. 421 and Pl. 29, 1 (cutting off the female pudenda).

STESICHOROS' FABLE

Nikolaos Yalouris

Plates 46, 47.

Among the numerous myths about horses constantly referred to in ancient texts, there is one which has scarcely been examined by modern research. It is the fable of the horse and the stag, first mentioned in connection with Stesichoros. According to Aristotle the poet related this fable in order to oppose Phalaris, before the latter became tyrant of Akragas.

As Aristotle tells it, when Phalaris, who was already proclaimed military dictator of the Himeraeans, asked to be given a body-guard, as Peisistratos was later to do in Athens, Stesichoros tried to warn his compatriots about the real intentions of Phalaris. To stress the fact that civil liberties were imperilled he supported his advice with the following fable:

'. . . For Stesichoros, when the people of Himera had chosen Phalaris dictator and were on the point of giving him a body-guard, after many arguments related a fable to them: "A horse was in sole occupation of a meadow. A stag having come and done much damage to the pasture, the horse, wishing to avenge himself on the stag, asked a man whether he could help him to punish the stag. The man consented, on condition that the horse submitted to the bit and allowed him to mount him javelins in hand. The horse agreed to the terms and the man mounted him, but instead of obtaining vengeance on the stag, the horse from that time became the man's slave. So then," said he "do you take care lest, in your desire to avenge yourselves on the enemy, you be treated like the horse. You already have the bit, since you have chosen a dictator; if you give him a body-guard and allow him to mount you, you will at once be the slaves of Phalaris." '[1]

This fable, here evidently adapted to the poet's aim of political admonition, in all probability belongs to the cycle of mythical narrative formed in the course of the second millennium B.C. The radical changes and upheavals of this period in the Eastern Mediterranean were to a great extent due to the introduction and widespread use of the horse, both for peace and war, one millennium after its domestication.[2] This precious animal, 'das Geschichte machendes Haustier', as Hančar calls it,[3] at first yoked to chariots and later ridden, took the place of stags, wild goats and other related animals which were up to then the only means of transport.

Stesichoros' fable may reflect these two different phases of civilisation. In the first phase, the stag was the animal mainly used for peaceful tasks and transport, a practice common to the Greek world and its neighbouring areas throughout the prehistoric period, as demonstrated by several representations of stags and wild goats drawing chariots on Creto-Mycenaean and Anatolian seals.[4] Memories of this use survived into the historic age when gods were portrayed on chariots drawn by stags.[5] In the second phase, the horse replaced the stag; being an animal of incomparably greater strength and endurance, it proved to be of greater service to man during the extensive migrations of the second millennium and in the battles waged in their course.

The close relationship between the two rival animals is also evidenced in the Geometric period by the production of a great number of bronze figurines representing horses and stags. The two were quite often shown together, particularly on vases. A good example of this practice can be seen on an Attic Geometric neck-amphora in Munich which shows on one side a male figure, the 'Master of the Animals', taming two stags and on the other two harnessed horses (Pl. 46, Figs. 1—2).[6]

An even more plausible allusion to the second-millennium use of the two animals referred to in Stesichoros' fable might be detected on the fragment of a bichrome painted larnax in the Ashmolean Museum; its provenance is unknown but it is regarded as not being Greek but rather Anatolian, more specifically a Phrygian work of the sixth century B.C. (Pl. 46, Fig. 3).[7] On this fragment is depicted a horseman in silhouette who is attacking a stag (in outline, spotted with black dots); the rider has managed to wound the stag with a spear and brandishes another spear in his right hand. The drawing is schematic and naïve: the man is riding side-saddle, and is barely seated on the horse's back, as if he were suspended in mid-air. Nevertheless the correlation of this picture with Stesichoros' story about the man proposing to help the horse if the latter 'submitted to the bit and allowed him to mount him javelins in hand' is obvious;[8] the very bit that the horse 'submitted to' is here emphasised and drawn as a straight metallic rod with button-like bulges at the ends. It is fitted between the animal's jaws and held in position with leather straps, while the rider holds the reins. The fact that this is not a Greek but a Phrygian work suggests that stories similar to that told by Stesichoros were perhaps widely spread in Anatolia, reflecting parallel events in the Eastern Mediterranean.

An unusual version of the story is represented on a mid-sixth century black-figured Attic amphora in the Vatican (Pl. 47, Figs. 4—5).[9] A male figure (wearing oriental costume, according to Albizzati), riding a winged horse, is chasing a stag. He has already thrust a spear into the animal's back and is about to attack it again with another one. The horse-bit, of the type which had been developed at Corinth a century earlier and had then spread all over Greece,[10] is again clearly drawn on the horse's jaws. It is probable that, in drawing this horseman, the painter had in mind Bellerophon, the sole rider of the divine winged horse, which he had tamed near the Peirene fountain with the golden harness — the gift of Athena.[11]

Therefore the story of the horse and the stag, known to Stesichoros and preserved by Aristotle, may have survived also in Attic vase-painting of the sixth century, in representations of the myth of Pegasus. Whereas in Stesichoros' rationalised version the horse-tamer was 'a man', in the Corinthian story Bellerophon is named specifically as the 'πρῶτος εὑρετής' the first inventor of horsemanship.

Both Stesichoros' fable and the legend of Bellerophon deal with the subject of taming and riding the horse and may reflect this event which occurred in the times between the Late Mycenaean period and the eighth century B.C. The fable of the horse and stag and the legend of Bellerophon and Pegasus may well have been created during that period.[12]

NOTES

1 *Rhetoric* II, 20, 5, trans. J.H. Freese, Loeb Classical Library, London 1967.

2 Joseph Wiesner, *Fahren und Reiten* (Archaeologia Homerica), Göttingen 1968, *passim; Fahren und Reiten in Alteuropa und im Alten Orient[2]*, Hildesheim—New York 1971, *passim;* Franz Hančar, *Das Pferd in prähistorischer und früher historischer Zeit,* Wien—München 1955, 536 and *passim.*

3 Hančar, *ibid,* p. 536.

4 V.E. Kenna, *Cretan Seals,* Oxford 1960, p. 64, Fig. 138, and Pl. 12, No. 308, Pl. 18, No. 21P. J.P. Nauert, 'The Hagia Triada Sarcophagus', *AntK* 8, 1965, p. 92, Fig. 1 and Pls. 25, 1—4.

5 See Nauert's important comments on the 'κάνναθρον', the ceremonial chariot drawn by wild goats at the Hyakinthia festival in Sparta (*supra* n. 4, 93); also Xenophon, *Agesilaus,* 8, 7, and Plutarch, *Agesilaus*

19, 5. For these last two references I am deeply indebted to my colleague Dr I. Sakellarakis. See also Hedwig Kenner, *Der Fries des Tempels von Bassai-Phigalia*, Vienna 1946, Pl. 4; *CVA* Louvre 17, Pl. 42 (CA 1795, Boeotian red-figured krater with female figure on a chariot drawn by two stags); *APS*, 48, No. 21; *RVAp* p. 212, no. 8/154 (Madrid 11050, Apulian calyx-krater with Dionysos and maenad in a chariot drawn by deer); Sichtermann, *GVU*, Pl. 126, Ruvo Museo Jatta 424 (Apulian volute-krater by the Baltimore Painter).

6   Munich, Staatl. Antikensammlung, Inv. No. 8748; Coldstream *GGP* pl. 8, d.

7   Inv. No. 19291. Width: 18.5 cm; Height: 22.8 cm. Bought at Sotheby's, London, 23rd November 1921, from the collection of Mr L. Rosenberg of Paris. I owe this information to the generous help of Professor John Boardman and Mr P.R.S. Moorey of the Ashmolean Museum; the latter was also kind enough to advise me about the following parallel works which make certain the attribution of the larnax to a Phrygian workshop: Tahsin and Nimet Ozgüc, *Ausgrabungen in Karahöyük . . . 1947*, Ankara 1949, Pl. XII; H.H. von der Osten, *The Alishar Hüyük Seasons of 1930–32*, (O. I. P. 30), Chicago 1937, Pt III, 46–47, Figs. 55–56; E.F. Schmidt, *The Alishar Hüyük Seasons of 1928–29*, (O. I. P. 20), Chicago 1933, Pt II, frontispiece; see Pls. V and VI, *ibidem*, for the ware-type.

8   The connection between this scene and Stesichoros' fable first occurred to me during a visit to the Ashmolean Museum in 1958. Sir John Beazley accepted my view and urged me to publish it.

9   Albizzati, *Vasi antichi dipinti del Vaticano*, No. 310, p. 107 and Pl. 32; *ABV* 91, 5, Painter of Louvre E 826.

10 Nikolaos Yalouris, 'Athena als Herrin der Pferde', *Mus. Helveticum* 7, 1950, 19–102.

11 Pindar, *Ol.* XIII; N. Yalouris, *ibidem*, and *Pegasus, The Art of the Legend*, London 1975.

12 Wiesner, *Alteurope* (*supra* n. 2); N. Yalouris, *Athena* (*supra* n. 10), 46 ff. and *Pegasus* (*supra* n. 11), XV ff.

THE PLATES

Plate 1

1

3

2

Figs. 1–3   Apulian red-figure hydria from Herakleia.
             Policoro 38462.
             Photos: courtesy author.

Plate 2

Figs.   1—4   Etrusco-Corinthian olpe.
Los Angeles. Collection of Mrs. Aaron Dechter.
Photos: Dietrich Widmer; courtesy Dr. Herbert Cahn.

Plate 3

5

6

7

Figs. 5—7   Etrusco-Corinthian olpe.
              Munich, Staatliche Antikensammlungen S.H.641.
              Photos: Staatliche Antikensammlungen; courtesy Dr. F.W. Hamdorf.

Plate 4

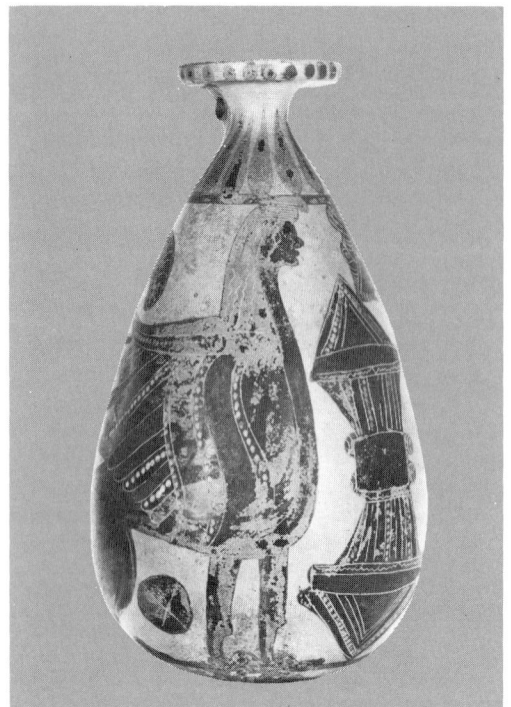

8

9

10

Figs. 8—10   Etrusco-Corinthian alabastron.
Cambridge, Museum of Classical Archaeology No. 137.
Photos: Museum of Classical Archaeology; courtesy Professor R.M. Cook.

Plate 5

1

2

3

4

Figs. 1—4   Hydria decorated with relief panels.
Bassano del Grappa. Chini Collection R.7.29-1-72.
Photos: Sopr. alle antichità Taranto; courtesy Professor F.G. Lo Porto.

Plate 6

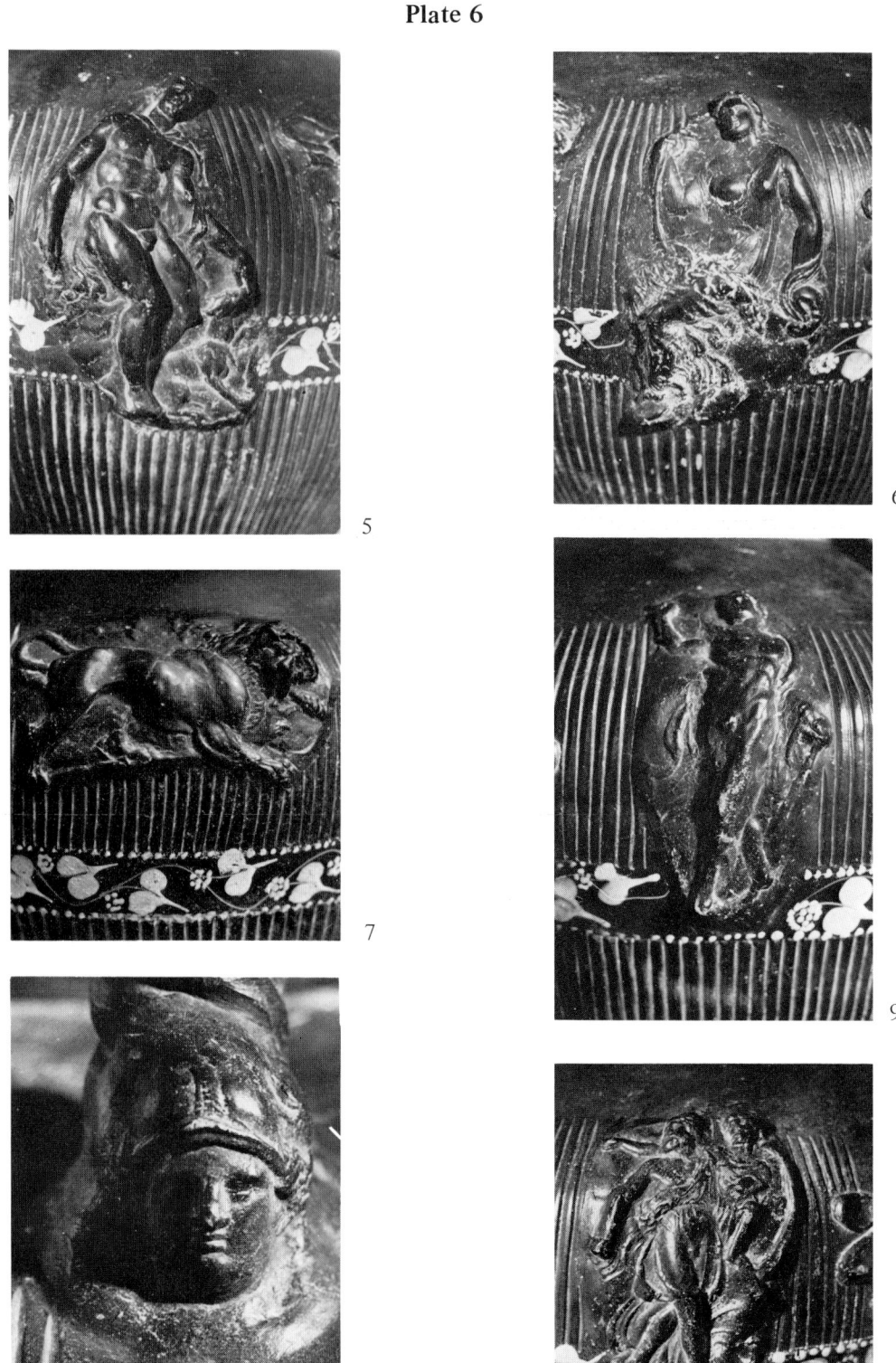

5

6

7

9

8

10

Figs. 5–10   Details of vase illustrated on Pl. 5.
Photos: author.

Plate 7

Figs. 1—3   Corinthian aryballos.
Basel, Antikenmuseum Kh.97 (Borowski Loan).
Photos: Antikenmuseum; courtesy owner and Dr. Margot Schmidt.

Fig. 4   Corinthian aryballos.
Laon, Musée 37.727.
Photos: courtesy Musée de Laon.

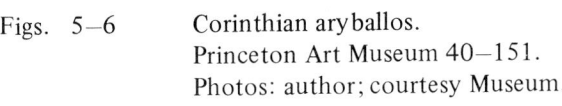

Figs. 5—6   Corinthian aryballos.
Princeton Art Museum 40—151.
Photos: author; courtesy Museum.

Plate 8

Figs.   1—3   Attic red-figure cup.
                Aberdeen, Marischal College No. 748.
                Photos: author; courtesy of the College.

Plate 9

4

5

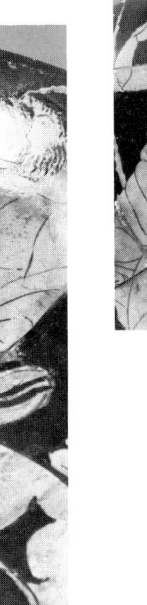

6

7

Figs. 4—7   Details of the cup illustrated on Pl. 8.
Photos: author; courtesy of the College.

Plate 10

Figs. 1–2   East Greek skyphos.
             Private Collection.
             Photos: courtesy of the owner.

Plate 11

Fig. 1   Fragment of an Apulian red-figure calyx-krater.
Sydney, Nicholson Museum No. 51.47.
Photo: Mr. R.K. Harding.

Plate 12

Figs. 2–3   Two fragments of an Apulian red-figure amphora.
Sydney, Nicholson Museum No. 51.48 (Fig. 2) and 53.12 (Fig. 3).
Photos: Mr. R.K. Harding.

Plate 13

Figs. 4—5   Apulian red-figure amphora.
             Naples, Museo Nazionale 2147 (inv. 82138).
             Photos: Museo Nazionale, courtesy Museo Nazionale.

Plate 14

Figs. 1—2   Etruscan fish plate.
Cerveteri, Museo Nazionale Cerite.
Photo: courtesy Dr. Mario Moretti.

Plate 15

1

3

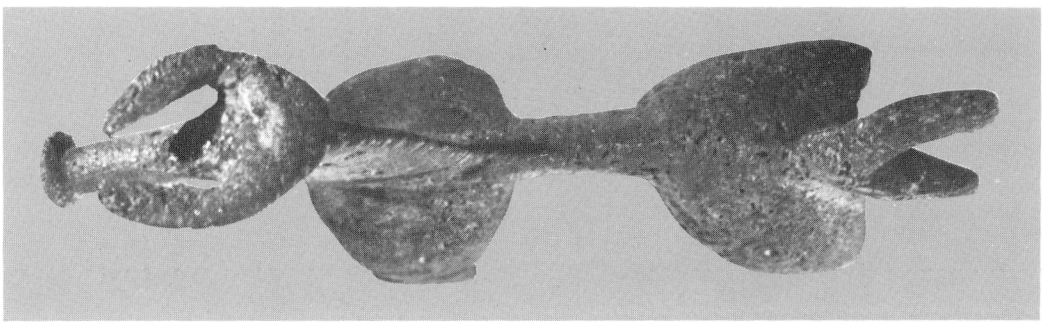

4

Figs. 1, 3–4   Geometric bronze horse.
                 Melbourne, University of Melbourne Inv. Mus.15.

Fig.   2   Geometric group of two horses back-to-back on long stand.
                 Copenhagen, Ny Carlsberg Glyptotek.
                 Photo: courtesy Ny Carlsberg Glyptotek.

Plate 16

Fig. 1   Corinthian cup (reverse).
Cambridge, Museum of Classical Archaeology CE1.
Photo: courtesy Mus. of Class. Arch.

Fig. 2   Italo-Corinthian amphora.
Cambridge, Museum of Classical Archaeology CE2.
Photo: courtesy Mus. of Class. Arch.

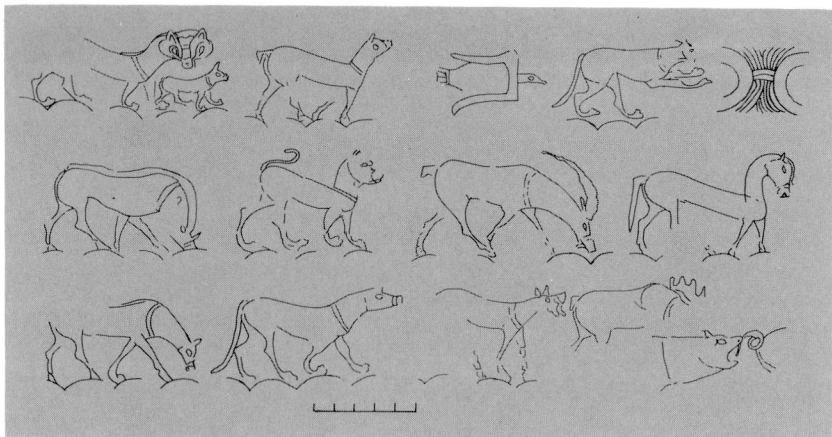

Fig. 3   Details of vase illustrated in Fig. 2.
Drawing by Mr. B.D. Thompson.

Plate 17

Fig.   4   Bucchero jug.
Cambridge, Museum of Classical Archaeology CE3.
Photo: courtesy Mus. of Class. Arch.

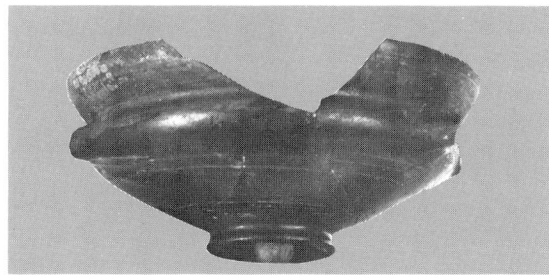

Fig.   5   Bucchero cup.
Cambridge, Museum of Classical Archaeology CE4.
Photo: courtesy Mus. of Class. Arch.

Fig.   6   Bucchero kantharos.
Cambridge, Museum of Classical Archaeology CE5.
Photo: courtesy Mus. of Class. Arch.

Plate 18

Figs. 1—2   Lucanian red-figure chous.
                Malibu, J. Paul Getty Museum inv. 71.AA.445.
                Photos: J. Paul Getty Museum.

Plate 19

Figs. 1—2   Mouth of Attic red-figure lekythos on modern stem stuck on to ancient foot.
             Paris, Louvre inv. G.614 (Campana 3218).
             Photos: author, courtesy Musée du Louvre.

Plate 20

Figs. 1–2   Gnathia epichysis (parts missing).
                   Corinth Museum C-32-64.
                   Photos: Corinth Museum; courtesy Professor Charles K. Williams.

Fig. 3   Gnathia round-bodied epichysis.
                   Corinth Museum C-69-138.
                   Photo: Corinth Museum; courtesy Professor Charles K. Williams.

Fig. 4   Gnathia deep bowl (fragment).
                   Athens, Agora Museum P12748.
                   Photo: Agora Museum; courtesy Professor H.A. Thompson.

Plate 21

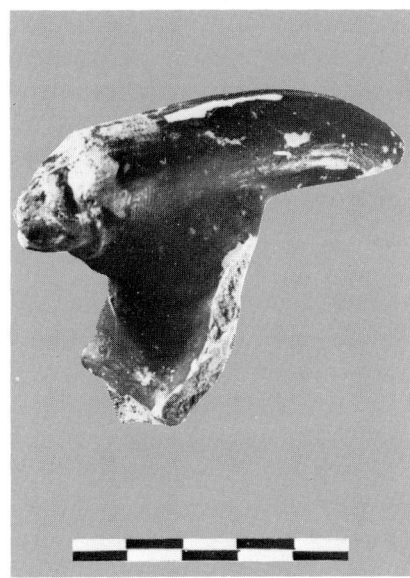

Fig. 5   Gnathia handle of oinochoe.
Athens, Agora Museum P18336.
Photo: Agora Museum; courtesy Professor H.A. Thompson.

Fig. 6   Gnathia pelike.
Athens, National Museum 2162.
Photo: author; courtesy National Museum.

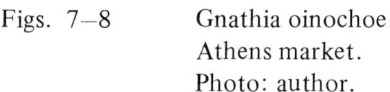

Figs. 7—8   Gnathia oinochoe.
Athens market.
Photo: author.

Plate 22

Fig. 9   Gnathia amphora, West Slope type.
Vienna, Kunsthistorisches Museum IV 450.
Photo: author; courtesy Kunsthistorisches Museum.

Fig. 10   Gnathia amphora, West Slope type.
Detail of vase illustrated in Fig. 9.
Photo: author; courtesy Kunsthistorisches Museum.

Fig. 11   Bowl fragment, Gnathia technique.
Syracuse, Museo Archeologico Nazionale.
Photo: author; courtesy Professor L. Bernabò Brea and Dr. G. Voza.

Fig. 12   Round mouthed jug, Gnathia technique.
Zurich, Archäologisches Institut der Universität inv. 3330.
Photo: Professor H. Bloesch; courtesy Professor H. Bloesch.

Plate 23

1

2

Fig. 1   Attic head-vase (oinochoe).
              New York, Metropolitan Museum 30.11.10.
              Photo: archives of the the late R. Zahn.

Fig. 2   Fragment of bell-krater.
              Once Erbach.
              After *Élite céramographique* I, pl. 29.

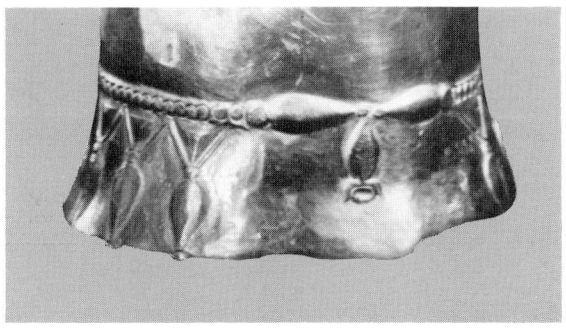

3

4

Fig. 3   Gold head-vase (detail).
              Plovdiv.
              Photo: I. Luckert.

Fig. 4   Gold head-vase (same as Fig. 3) (detail).
              Plovdiv.
              Photo: I. Luckert.

Fig. 5   Necklace.
              Once Constantinople market.
              Photo: archives of the late R. Zahn.

5

Plate 24

Fig. 1   Attic rhyton.
New York market (Mathias Komor).
Photo: courtesy of the owner.

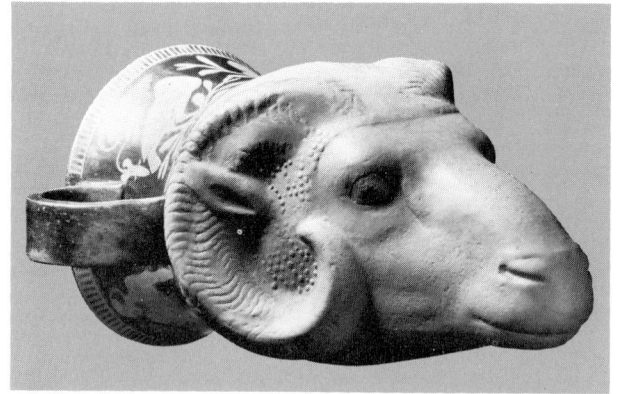

2

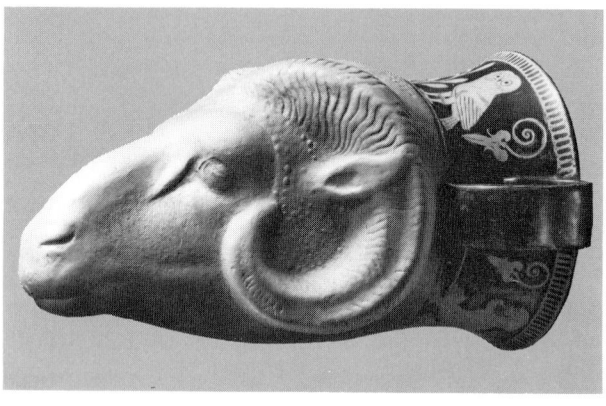

3

4

Figs. 2–4   Attic red-figure kantharos-rhyton (ram-head).
Hamburg, Museum für Kunst und Gewerbe.
Photo: Dietrich Widmer; courtesy Mus. für Kunst und Gewerbe.

Plate 25

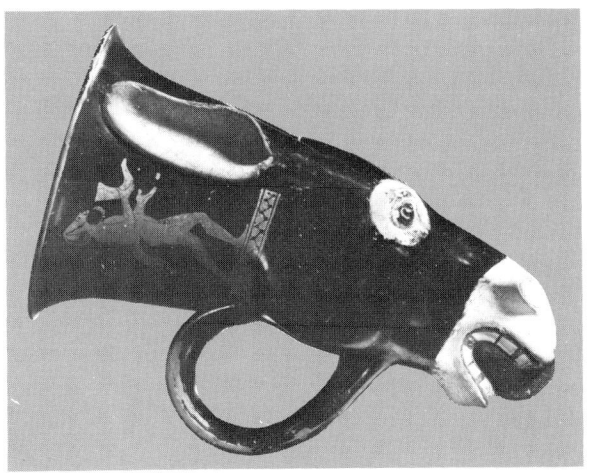 

Figs. 5–6   Attic red-figure rhyton: ram-head and donkey-head (dimidiated).
Swiss private collection.
Photos: courtesy of the owner.

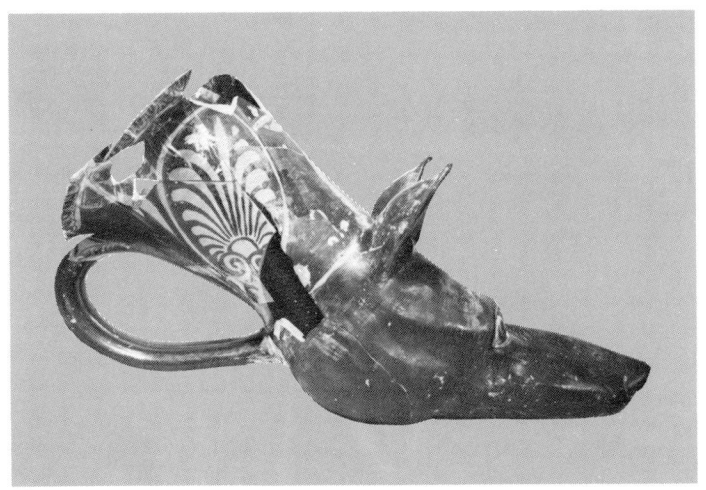 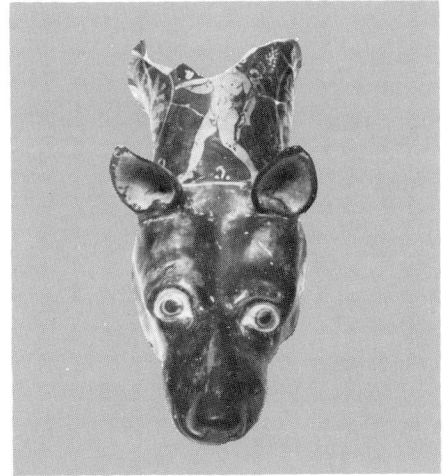

Figs. 7–8   Apulian red-figure rhyton (head of Laconian hound).
Ascona market (Casa Serodine).
Photos: courtesy Casa Serodine.

Plate 26

9

11

10

Figs. 9—11   Details of the red-figure rhyton illustrated on Pl. 25, Figs. 5—6 (satyr with drinking
    horn, ithyphallic donkey, satyr).
    Photos: courtesy of the owner.

Plate 27

Figs. 1–2   Neck of Euboean geometric amphora.
Eretria Museum inv. 3275, FK 2786.
Photos: courtesy Eretria Museum.

Fig.   3   Five of the dancers decorating the neck of the Euboean geometric amphora illustrated
in Figs. 1–2.
Drawing by A. Brenk.

Plate 28

 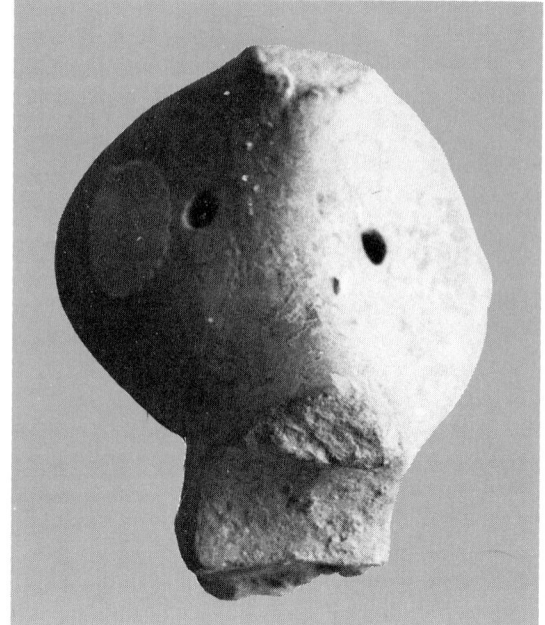

Fig. 1   Handle of a terracotta lamp (top).
               Private collection.
               Photo: author; courtesy of the owner.

Fig. 2   Underside of the object illustrated in Fig. 1.
               Photo: author; courtesy of the owner.

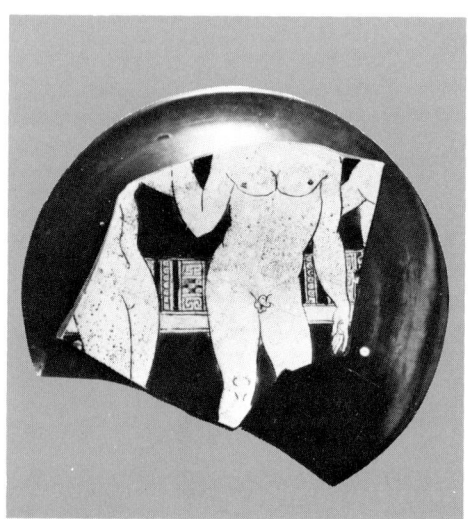

Fig. 3   Tondo of fragmentary red-figure cup.
               Lost.
               Photo: I.G. 37193; courtesy of the German Archaeological Institute, Rome.

Plate 29

Figs. 1–3   Apulian calyx-krater (details of the obverse).
             Bari, Malaguzzi-Valeri Collection No. 52.
             Photo: Museo Archeologico; courtesy of the owner.

Fig. 4   Reverse of vase illustrated in Figs. 1–3.
          Photo: Museo Archeologico; courtesy of the owner.

Figs. 1–3   Small amphora in the Kairuan style.
Private collection.
Photos: courtesy of the owner.

Plate 31

Figs. 4—5   Two other views of the vase illustrated on Pl. 30.
Photos: courtesy of the owner.

Plate 32

Fig. 1   Attic red-figure eye-cup (B).
              Ferrara 41D-V.P.
              Photo: Laboratorio Manlio Agodi; courtesy Museo Archeologico Nazionale di Ferrara.

Fig. 2   Attic red-figure eye-cup (I); same as Fig. 1.
              Ferrara 41D-V.P.
              Photo: Laboratorio Manlio Agodi; courtesy Museo Archeologico Nazionale di Ferrara.

Plate 33

Fig. 3   Attic red-figure eye-cup (A); same as Figs. 1—2.
Ferrara 41D-V.P.
Photo: Laboratorio Manlio Agodi; courtesy Museo Archeologico Nazionale di Ferrara.

Fig. 4   Attic red-figure eye-cup (B); same as Figs. 1—3.
Ferrara 41D-V.P.
Photo: Laboratorio Manlio Agodi; courtesy Museo Archeologico Nazionale di Ferrara.

Plate 34

Figs. 1—2   Attic red-figure oinochoe (side and front views).
                Oxford 1971.866.
                Photos: Ashmolean Museum; courtesy Mr. Michael Vickers.

Figs. 3—4   Attic red-figure kotyle (A and B).
                Munich, Antikensammlungen inv. 8934.
                Photo: C.H. Krüger-Moessner; courtesy Antikensammlungen.

Plate 35

Figs.   5—6   Attic red-figure Nolan amphora (A and B).
                   London E 307.
                   Photos: British Museum; courtesy Trustees of the British Museum.

Plate 36

1

2

3

Figs. 1–3   Siana cup.
Berlin, Staatliche Museen, Antikensammlungen Vas. Inv. 4516.
Photos: Staatliche Museen zu Berlin.

Plate 37

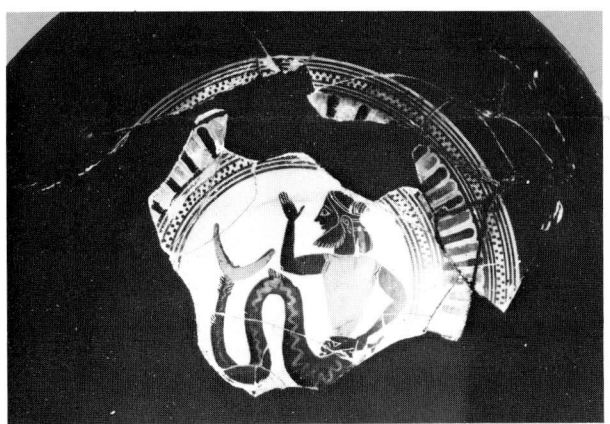

Figs. 4—5   Siana cup.
              Berlin Staatliche Museen, Antikensammlungen F.1755.
              Photos: Staatliche Museen zu Berlin.

Fig.   6   Siana cup (I).
              Berlin Staatliche Museen, Antikensammlungen Vas. Inv. 3402.
              Photo: Staatliche Museen zu Berlin.

Plate 38

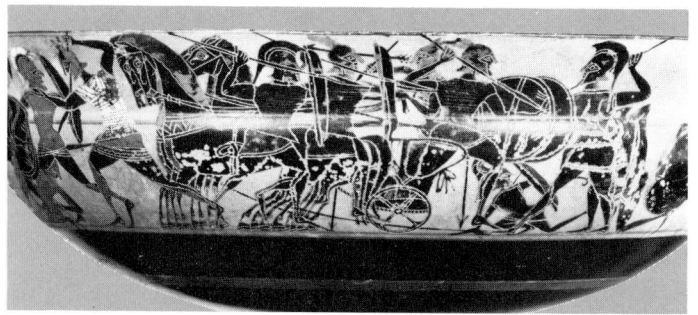

Figs. 7–9   Siana cup (A and B); same as Fig. 6.
Berlin, Staatliche Museen, Antikensammlungen Vas. Inv. 3402.
Photos: Staatliche Museen zu Berlin.

Plate 39

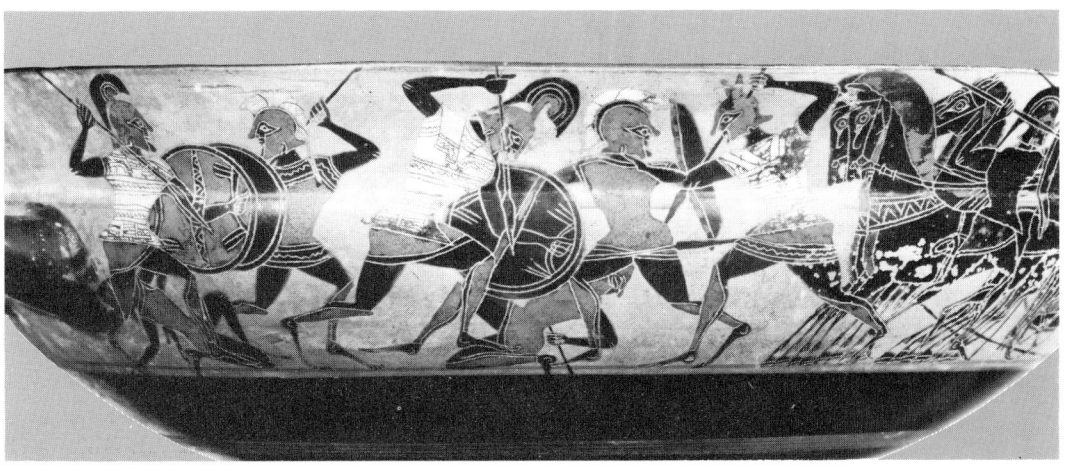

Figs. 10—12   Siana cup (A and B); same as Figs. 6—9;
                 Berlin Staatliche Museen, Antikensammlungen Vas. Inv. 3402.
                 Photos: Staatliche Museen zu Berlin.

Plate 40

Figs.   1—2   Apulian oinoche (shape 3: chous).
                   Kiel, Kunsthalle B509.
                   Photos: Dietrich Widmer; courtesy Kunsthalle.

Figs.   3—4   Apulian oinochoe (shape 3: chous).
                   Private collection, formerly Zurich market.
                   Photos: courtesy Mr. H. Humbel.

Plate 41

Fig. 5   Lucanian oinochoe (shape 3: chous).
Metaponto inv. 20146.
Photo: courtesy Professor D. Adamesteanu.

Fig. 6   Apulian lekanis-lid.
Naples, Museo Nazionale 2302 (inv. 82198).
Photo: Museo Nazionale; courtesy Professor A. de Franciscis.

Plate 42

Apulian volute-krater.
Ruvo, Museo Jatta 1097.
Photo: courtesy German Archaeological Institute, Rome.

Plate 43

Figs. 1—2   Apulian alabastron.
             Oxford 1945.55.
             Photos:Ashmolean Museum; courtesy Department of Antiquities, Ashmolean Museum.

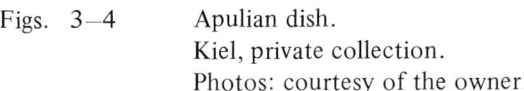

Figs. 3—4   Apulian dish.
             Kiel, private collection.
             Photos: courtesy of the owner.

Plate 44

Figs. 1–2   Panathenaic amphora.
Once, Milan market.
Photos: courtesy Galleria d'Arte Geri.

Fig.   3   Panathenaic amphora (A) (before removal of modern restorations).
Bologna, Museo Civico PU198.
Photo: Museo Civico; courtesy Dr. R. Pincelli.

Plate 45

Fig. 4   Panathenaic amphora (B) (before removal of modern restorations).
Bologna. Museo Civico PU198.
Photo: Museo Civico; courtesy Dr. R. Pincelli.

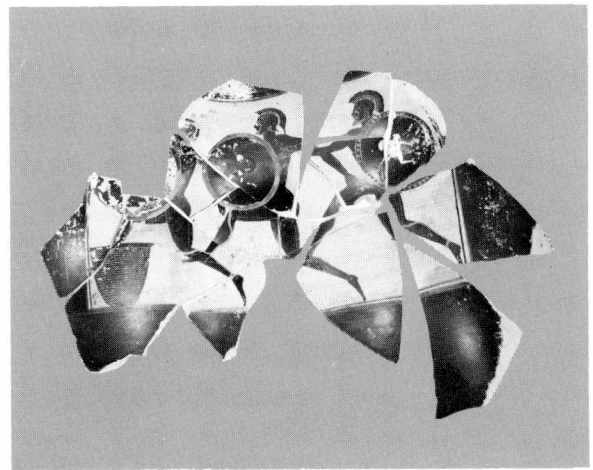

Figs. 5—6   The panathenaic amphora illustrated in Figs. 3 and 4: authentic parts after removal
of modern restorations (A and B).
Photos: Museo Civico, Bologna; photo-montage: Dr. Morigi Govi.

Plate 46

Figs. 1—2   Attic Geometric neck-amphora (A and B of neck).
Munich, Staatliche Antikensammlungen Inv. No. 8748.
Photos: Staatliche Antikensammlungen.

Fig. 3   Fragment of bichrome painted larnax.
Oxford Inv. No. 19291.
Photo: Department of Antiquities, Ashmolean Museum.

Plate 47

Figs. 4—5   Attic black-figure neck-amphora.
                    Vatican 310.
                    Photos: Museo Vaticano.